# CANADA AT THE OLYMPIC WINTER GAMES

The Official Sports History and Record Book

# The Official Sports History and Record Book

# CANADA AT THE OLYMPIC WINTER GAMES

*See you at the Games Roger!*

## WENDY BRYDEN

*Wendy Bryden*

*3 December 1987*

*all the best*
*Barbara Bourler*

*Best Wishes*
*Cathy Priestner*

Hurtig Publishers   Edmonton

Hurtig Publishers Ltd.
10560 - 105 Street
Edmonton, Alberta
Canada T5H 2W7

Canadian Cataloguing in Publication Data

Bryden, Wendy.
    Canada at the Olympic Winter Games

    Bibliography: p.
    ISBN 0-88830-324-6 (bound). — ISBN
0-88830-308-4 (pbk.)

    1. Winter Olympic Games (15th : 1988 :
Calgary, Alta.).  2. Winter Olympic Games -
History.  3. Winter Olympic Games - Records.
I. Title.
GV842 1988.B79 1987    796.9′8    C87-091321-2

Design: FIRST EDITION BOOK CREATIONS/Doug Frank
BOOKENDS DESIGNWORKS/Bob Young
Typeset in Garth Graphic Condensed by Pièce de Résistance
Printed and bound in Canada

Every reasonable effort has been made to contact holders of
photograph copyrights. The author and publisher would be
pleased to have any errors or omissions brought to their
attention.

Cover photographs: (l. to r. from back cover) Mario
Gosselin, Lloyd Langlois, Pierre Harvey (photo by Alec
Pytlowany), the Canadian Bobsleigh Team, Brian Orser,
Gaetan Boucher, Kathy Kreiner (Deutsche Presse-Agentur
GmbH), all courtesy the Athlete Information Bureau/Cana-
dian Olympic Association, except where otherwise credited

# Contents

# Acknowledgements

The author is grateful to her very supportive family and for the kind assistance of those who helped achieve *Canada at the Olympic Winter Games*.

Special recognition is due to Father David Bauer, Dave King, Ken Read, Victor Emery, Shirley and Sharon Firth, Bjorger Pettersen, Doug Hansen, Pierre Harvey, Horst Bulau, Fred Morris, Brian Orser, and Gaetan Boucher.

A note of thanks to secretary Gerry Dyer, a very dedicated OCO'88 volunteer.

Participation by an athlete in the Olympic Games often represents the input of two people whose love and encouragement are as necessary as the devotion of the athletes themselves.

These people are called parents, and it is to them that I dedicate this book.

All royalties realized from the sale of this book have been gifted by the author to the Olympic Trust of the Canadian Olympic Association for the encouragement and support of amateur sports in Canada.

# Foreword

This is a book that is a must-read for all Canadians interested in sport. For the first time it pulls together untold stories of the colourful history of winter sports in Canada.

This Olympic reference book was conceived and produced by a talented Albertan. Wendy Bryden of Calgary came up with the unique and useful concept of putting together a comprehensive and affordable sports guide book of *Canada at the Olympic Winter Games* as a prelude to our holding for the first time in Canada the Olympic Winter Games in Calgary in 1988.

Then Wendy took the initiative to see the idea become a reality. She contacted each Canadian athlete who has contributed an introduction to an Olympic sport in the book. Each agreed without hesitation to volunteer the time and effort to make the history and background of each winter sport an accurate portrayal for fellow Canadians.

When I asked the author which colleagues had played a significant role in the development of her book, she singled out two people—Mr. Frank King, Chairman of the Board of Directors of the XV Olympic Winter Games Organizing Committee, for his guidance through the difficult early stages of her project, and her publisher, Mel Hurtig, for his confidence in her. From the very beginning this book was intended as a volunteer contribution to the Olympic Winter Games in Calgary and it took three full years of research and planning to produce it.

But it is to the athletes and their coaches that the author gives the principal credit for the high technical and historical quality of this book.

This book will help to educate Canadians, young and old, on the many obstacles that Canadian winter sport athletes had to overcome, whether in finding a place to train for the bobsleigh or speed skating, or arranging in other sports for the opportunity to compete with top athletes from other parts of Canada. I am sure this book will help encourage the young athletes in all the winter sports who participated in the trials and test events leading up to the Games and to citizens from all parts of Canada who watch the Games in 1988.

I sincerely hope *Canada at the Olympic Winter Games* will provide an important contribution to your understanding of the Olympic movement and your pride in Canada's winter athletes.


The Honourable Peter Lougheed
*Honorary Chairman*
*XV Olympic Winter Games Organizing Committee*

# Introduction

Hosting an Olympic Games characterizes the purest form of a nation's aspirations, representing the culmination of a collective effort and symbolizing the spirit and vitality of its people.

When I was asked to make a contribution to the introduction of this book I thought of the remarkable performances of Nancy Greene-Raine, of the Canadian hockey teams, of Gaetan Boucher and of the countless other memorable performances and events which have come to epitomize these games. Canadian athletes have had a long and distinguished record of accomplishment at Olympic Winter Games.

*Canada at the Olympic Winter Games* will no doubt be an indispensable resource book for those who wish to follow the history and background of each winter sport and for those future Olympians who are searching for a gainful insight into the determination and self-sacrifice of these remarkable athletes. Wendy Bryden has chronicled not only the various histories of the events, but she has captured the indefatigable spirit of the Canadian athletes.

What is most remarkable about this book is that it is a volunteer effort with Wendy Bryden donating her royalties to the Olympic Trust of the Canadian Olympic Association in support of amateur sport in Canada, as well as those individual contributions submitted by the athletes. It is truly an Olympian effort, characteristic of the countless volunteers who have donated their time and energies to make the XV Olympic Winter Games in Calgary the **Best-Ever**.

In 1988 the world will look to Calgary for inspiration; for the fact that so many people have come together in the spirit of friendly competition is both invigorating and heartening.

On behalf of the Government and people of Canada, I am pleased to support this worthwhile endeavour and I am looking forward to seeing you in Calgary in 1988.

The Right Honourable Brian Mulroney
*Prime Minister of Canada*
OTTAWA
1987

# Welcome!

Few events are remembered in history — the Olympics are one of them.

Why do millions of young people around the world dream of becoming Olympic champions? Why do people in 165 countries volunteer their time, energy, and money to help the Olympic Movement? Why do cities compete, often over several decades, to host the Olympic Games? The answers to these questions can be found on the pages of this book. The basic reason is that people everywhere love sports.

In 1981, when Calgary was selected by the IOC to host the XV Olympic Winter Games, it signalled a special role for Canada. Montreal held the 1976 Olympic Games. Now Calgary has made Canada only the third non-European nation in history to celebrate both the summer and winter versions of "the world's most inspiring athletic event."

I have often had the opportunity to speak to Canadian audiences about Olympic Winter Sports. On many occasions I asked the audience how many of those present have ever practised skating, skiing, or tobogganing. The answer is always the same — everyone! Skating, skiing, and tobogganing are the only sports activities in the Olympic Winter Games. That is why Winter Games have a very special significance to all Canadians.

*Mathieson, Calgary*

Each Olympic host city makes its own special contribution to the Olympic legend. Calgary is no exception. The willingness to overcome obstacles and to take risks to achieve success are part of the Calgary story. Like the Olympic athletes for whom the Games exist, Calgarians wanted a chance to be the best that they could be. The Olympic Games offer a chance for a city and a country to be part of something that is simply the best in the world.

Quite often historians recall the success of Olympic Games mainly in financial terms or in terms of the legacy of new sports facilities built by the host. This book places the focus where it should be — on the athletes and on the people who make the Olympics a special triumph among all sporting events.

The Olympics combine the magic of youth, sport, excellence, and universality. The Olympic Games are made of pure joyful emotion for individuals, for cities, and for countries. The great feelings of pride and accomplishment may never be matched for those lucky enough to be involved. Readers of *Canada at the Olympic Winter Games* will realize that Canada's role in the Winter Olympics is a story too special not to be shared by all.

Welcome to Calgary! Welcome to the XV Olympic Winter Games!


Frank W. King
*Chairman*
*XV Olympic Winter Games Organizing Committee*

# The Modern Olympic Games

The most important thing in the Olympic Games is not to win but to take part, just as the most important thing in life is not the triumph but the struggle. The essential thing is not to have conquered but to have fought well.

This statement originated with Baron Pierre de Coubertin and has been written on the scoreboard at the opening ceremonies for the Olympic Games since 1908. The motto pays tribute to Baron de Coubertin and exemplifies the philosophy and the creative imagination of the founder of the modern Olympic Games.

The original Olympic Games began in 776 B.C. at Olympia in ancient Greece and were held every four years in the summer to honour the god Zeus. The Games reached their height of fame during the fourth century. However, as warlike people began to invade Greece, the youth of the country became less and less content with peaceful athletic contests. In A.D. 394, during the reign of Emperor Theodosius I, Olympic athleticism had declined to barbarism, and a decree was issued that prohibited the celebration of the Games of Olympia.

The revival of the modern Olympic Games did not take place until 1894 in Paris when a dream was realized by a diminutive Frenchman who devoted more than thirty years of his life to the restoration of the Games.

Born in Paris in 1863, Baron de Coubertin was an accomplished young man and an avid sportsman. Educated at the famous military academy of St. Cyr, he enjoyed the individual sports of fencing, boxing, and rowing. Throughout his education in France, de Coubertin had come to admire the British school system which combined sports discipline with education.

The Franco-Prussian War of 1871 led Baron de Coubertin to consider the restoration of the Olympic Games. The War had filled de Coubertin with bitterness for the humiliation of his beloved country. He decided to try to convince his countrymen of the merits of nations competing against each other athletically, rather than militarily. He identified three ideals, education reform, the essence of sports, and access for the underprivileged to cultural participation, as his lifework. The restoration of the Olympic Games would be the vehicle for reaching his objective.

Baron de Coubertin had long been inspired by the history of the ancient city of Olympia in Greece. He respected the original purpose of the ancient Games, which was to increase the understanding and harmony among nations.

Although France remained indifferent to Baron de Coubertin's ideas, he continued trying to persuade other countries and governments to incorporate the Olympic concept. In 1890 de Coubertin was chosen as secretary-general of the Union of French Athletic Associations. Attending international conferences that researched the principles of sports and amateurism, he used every opportunity to add the restoration of the Olympic Games to the agenda. Using his own funds for travelling to various countries in hopes of urging them to accept his proposals, de Coubertin visited supporters and Olympic devotees in the United States and England and conferred with representatives from New Zealand, Jamaica, and Sweden.

Baron de Coubertin. *International Olympic Committee Archives, Lausanne, Switzerland*

Finally, in June of 1894 the International Games Congress met at the Sorbonne in Paris. Thirteen countries represented by seventy-nine delegates and forty-nine sports associations voted by acclamation to restore the Olympic Games. Proposing to hold the first Games of modern history in Athens, Greece, in 1896, the representatives paid homage to the country that had originated the Olympic ideal.

At the meeting at the Sorbonne, a motion was made to form the International Olympic Committee which would have supreme authoritative and governing powers. The original Olympic Charter was also drawn up at that time. Two years later the international Olympic Committee and structure of the Olympic movement were established.

Baron de Coubertin served as President of the IOC from 1896 until 1925. Having made a thorough study of the ancient Olympic Games, de Coubertin designed many of the ceremonial aspects of the modern Olympic Games today. Although it took time for the designs to be incorporated in the Olympics, de Coubertin is credited with the Olympic Flag with five interlocking rings intended to signify the five major continental groups of the world: Europe, Asia, Africa, Australia, and both North and South America. The flight of doves, as the symbol of peace to accompany the opening ceremonies of the Games, was also one of Baron de Coubertin's suggestions, as was the Athlete's Oath and the Olympic Torch. The inclusion of national Fine Arts exhibitions held concurrently with the Olympic Games was initiated by him as well.

As Baron Pierre de Coubertin was in favour of helping the underprivileged Olympic competitor with financial assistance, the controversial issue of professionalism versus amateurism was of great concern to him, as it is in the Olympic Games today.

The fact that Baron de Coubertin wanted the Olympic Games to be separate from any other exhibitions and fairs raised such a controversy that he actually refused to attend the Games of the Third Olympiad at St. Louis, Missouri, in 1904. Disillusioned by the total misunderstanding of the Olympic spirit by the general public, the roots of de Coubertin's concerns stemmed back to the early chapters in the history of the restored Games. To his credit, the Olympic Games of today may not be staged at the same times, or in association with, commercial exhibitions of any kind.

After the First World War, the Games of the eighth Olympiad were held in France as a gesture to de Coubertin who had announced his retirement as President of the IOC at the age of sixty-one.

Although he experienced financial difficulties and his con-

At the 1896 Games: (l. to r.) seated, Baron Pierre de Coubertin, Demetrius Vikelas (Greece), General A. de Butovski (Soviet Union); standing, Dr. Wilhelm Gebhardt (Germany), Jiri Guth-Jarkovsky (Czechoslovakia), Fr. Franz Kemeny (Hungary), General Victor Balck (Sweden). *International Olympic Committee Archives, Lausanne, Switzerland*

tribution was forgotten upon his retirement to Lausanne, Switzerland, de Coubertin nevertheless retained his faith in youth and the Olympic ideal. A short time before his death, Baron Pierre de Coubertin wrote, "Effort is the supreme joy. Success is not a goal, but a means to aim still higher." While walking in the Lagrange Park in Geneva on September 2, 1937, Baron de Coubertin died of a massive heart attack.

The heart of the founder of the modern Olympic Games rests in Olympia, Greece, in a memorial erected to honour the French visionary.

Today, the headquarters of the International Olympic Committee are in the Château de Vidy in Lausanne, Switzerland. The President of the International Olympic Committee is Dr. Juan Antonio Samaranch. Born in Barcelona in 1920, Dr. Samaranch is a former Spanish Ambassador to Moscow. He was Vice-President of the Spanish Olympic Committee from 1955 to 1970 and entered the IOC in 1966. He succeeded Lord Killanin as President in 1980.

# The Olympic Winter Games

Before the first Olympic Winter Games were held in Chamonix, France, in 1924, the winter sports of men's and women's figure skating were included in the Olympic Summer Games. The skating competitions were held in conjunction with the Olympic Games in London in 1908 and did not capture much interest or draw particularly large crowds. The event was dropped from the Olympic Games at Stockholm in 1912.

World War I preempted the Olympic Games in 1916, and it was not until the Games of the seventh Olympiad at Antwerp in 1920 that figure skating was reintroduced to the program. At the same time, a new and exciting game was introduced to the Olympic format. Ice hockey was won by Canada, represented by a club team, the Winnipeg Falcons.

Following the Olympic Games at Antwerp, bobsleigh and skiing enthusiasts began a campaign to have their sports included in the Olympic Games under the patronage of the IOC. After intensive debate, the International Olympic Committee opted for the idea of a separate Olympic Winter Games celebration to take place in the same year as the Summer Games. The proposed charter read:

> The International Olympic Committee will carry out a special cycle of the Olympic Winter Games, which have to take place in the same years as the Summer Games. They will be called the first, second, third Winter Games, etc., and are subject to all the rules of the Olympic protocol. The prizes, medals and diplomas must be different from those of the Olympic Summer Games, and the term "Olympiad" shall not be used in this connection. The International Olympic Committee will select the place for the Olympic Winter Games and will reserve priority to the country arranging the Summer Games of that particular Olympiad provided that the latter can furnish sufficient guarantee of its ability to organize the Winter Games in their entirety.

This proposal was accepted in Lisbon, in May of 1926 by the IOC. Due to the fact that a year earlier the "Chamonix International Winter Sports Week" had taken place, the first Olympic Winter Games at Chamonix, France, in 1924 were accorded their status retroactively.

Mathias Zdarsky of Austria first attempted to adapt cross-country skiing to the Alps in 1896 using only one pole for balance. *Canadian Ski Museum*

Skiing in Rockcliffe Park, Ottawa, Ontario, 1887. *Public Archives of Canada*

# A Retrospective

## I  Chamonix 1924

The original countries that pioneered Olympic Winter Games were: Austria, Belgium, Canada, Finland, Czechoslovakia, France, Great Britain, Hungary, Italy, Latvia, Norway, Poland, Sweden, Switzerland, the United States, and Yugoslavia.

The 294 competitors took part in fourteen events at Chamonix, in five categories of sport: figure skating, speed skating, Nordic skiing, bobsleighing, and ice hockey.

The Canadian Olympic Team for the first formal Olympic Winter Games was composed of the ice hockey team, two figure skaters, and a speed skater.

Canada holds the distinction of winning the first official Olympic Winter Games gold medal for ice hockey at Chamonix, France, in 1924. Canada's team knocked off Sweden 20 to 0, Czechoslovakia 30 to 0, Switzerland 33 to 0, and Great Britain 19 to 2. None of the European teams were a match for the Canadian team from the Granite Club of Toronto, coached by William Haddock. The Canadians won the final game in the medal round 6 to 1 against the United States. Combined total score for the Canadians was 110 goals. Combined total score for other ice hockey teams was 3 goals.

*The Weather:* Snow the week before the Games, 1.10 m.

Sonja Henie of Norway made her debut at the 1924 Games. *Courtesy Oslo Skøytekleibb, Norway*

The Winnipeg Falcons of 1920. (l. to r.) G. Sigurjonson, H. Axford, W. Byron, S. Halderson, F. Fredrickson, W.A. Hewitt, K. Johansson, M. Goodman, A. Woodman, F. Fridinnson. *Hockey Hall of Fame*

## II St. Moritz 1928

The second Olympic Winter Games established the fact that winter sports had come of age in the 1920s. Twenty-five countries took part and there were 363 competitors in the Olympic events.

In hockey, Canada was represented by the University of Toronto Graduates team with W. A. Hewitt accompanying the team as Honorary Manager. Three speed skaters, four figure skaters, and four skiers made up the rest of the Olympic contingent.

During the pre-Olympic practices, the Grads played so brilliantly and were so obviously superior to any of the European teams that a plan was suggested that was unheard of in Olympic competition. The Swiss Olympic Committee proposed that the ten other countries would play in an elimination series of three pools. After the elimination round, each winner would play against the Grads on three successive days. The Canadian hockey players watched and waited. In the three final games, Canada made it three Olympic gold medals in a row (1920, 1924, 1928) with scores of 11 to 0 Sweden, 3 to 0 Switzerland, and 14 to 0 Great Britain.

The history of the second Olympic Winter Games would be incomplete without mention of a tiny fifteen-year-old Norwegian girl from Oslo, Sonja Henie. Before her twelfth birthday, Sonja had won the Norwegian Championship in 1924 and had gone on to compete in the Olympic Winter Games at Chamonix, France. Finishing in last place, she returned to Oslo to train and study ballet, incorporating dance into her freestyle skating program.

At the Olympic Winter Games at St. Moritz, Henie revolutionized women's figure skating with the invention of incredible new manoeuvres performed flawlessly and with extraordinary speed. Points ahead of her nearest competitor, Sonja Henie won the first of her three Olympic gold medals (1928, 1932, and 1936). She turned professional after 1936, became the princess of the skating world by demonstrating her superb talent and popularized figure skating in Europe and North America. Becoming a star in the motion picture industry in California, Sonja made eleven films between 1938 and 1960. During her ice skating career, she won three gold medals in Olympic competition, ten World titles, and six European titles.

The International Skiing Federation (FIS) was persuaded to include downhill and slalom events experimentally in international competition in 1928. The future of Alpine skiing was assured; however, eight years were to elapse before the first Alpine skiing events were held in the Olympic Winter Games.

The Nordic skiing events at the second Olympic Winter Games were dominated by the Scandinavian countries.

*The Weather*: Blizzard at opening ceremonies. Uncertain ice-rink and snow conditions throughout the Games due to warm winds from the south, disrupting events.

The Canadian Olympic team at the Opening Ceremonies in 1928. *The Tourist Information Bureau, St. Moritz, Switzerland*

## III  Lake Placid 1932

The third Olympic Winter Games were held in 1932 at Lake Placid, New York, a new resort near the Canadian border.

The proximity proved beneficial as truckloads of snow from Canada had to be hauled in to restore the snowless cross-country runs. Fourteen events were held in 1932, twelve for men, one for women, and one for skating pairs. The athletes numbered 278, representing seventeen countries, and were watched by twenty thousand spectators.

Turnout from the Alpine and Scandinavian countries was low, however. This was due in part to the cost of the transatlantic crossing and the world depression at the time of the Games.

Figure skating was held in an indoor arena for the first time in Olympic competition, and Canada's Montgomery Wilson won a bronze medal in the men's division.

Speed skating became one of the major controversies of these Games. The speed skating event was the first Olympic competition to be held off the European continent, and the Americans voted to conduct the race under man-to-man rules. European skaters had always started their races in pairs, racing against the clock, with the fastest time determining the winner. Under the American rules, pace and strategy became major factors, as head-to-head competition was required of participants. The racers would then advance in the trial heats until only two skaters were left to race in the final event. The times for the speed skaters were relatively insignificant.

The Europeans protested vehemently, but to no avail, and the speed-skating events took place introducing free-for-all massed starts. Cheered on by spectators, the Canadians and Americans surprised everyone by winning ten of the available medals. Canadian women speed skaters Jean Wilson and Hattie Donaldson won one gold and two silver medals between them for demonstration events in the three races. The 500, 1,000, and 1,500 metre events were included for the first time for women.

At the 1932 Games: (l. to r.) Willy Logan of St. John, New Brunswick; William E. Oughton, president of the Canadian Association; and Alex Hurd, of Sudbury, Ontario. *Courtesy John Hurdis*

Canada's speed skating trio of Alex Hurd, William Logan, and Frank Stack finished in the third, fourth, and fifth positions in the 500 metre event and were second, third, and fourth in the 1,500 metres. Logan then captured a bronze medal in the 5,000 metre race and Stack a bronze in the 10,000 metre final. A vintage year for the Canadians in speed skating.

The lack of representatives from Europe in the speed-skating competition at Lake Placid contributed to the protests against the mass-starts becoming adamant. Proving their point, the Europeans saw that the traditional starts in pairs were restored for the fourth Olympic Winter Games at Garmisch-Partenkirchen in 1936. Never again would spectators see a rollicking free-for-all race start in Olympic competition like the one seen at Lake Placid in 1932.

The introduction of the two-man bobsleigh event, and the Canadians' winning a fourth gold medal in ice hockey added to the immensely exciting Olympic experience in 1932. For Canada, the total medal count of seven was the highest number awarded to Canadians at the Olympic Winter Games since 1924.

*The Weather:* Changeable snow conditions. Soaking-wet ski jumpers treated to an involuntary baptism in the pool of melted snow at the bottom of the outrun.

## IV  Garmisch-Partenkirchen 1936

The fourth Olympic Winter Games were awarded to the Bavarian twin cities of Garmisch and Partenkirchen near Munich, Germany.

When Adolf Hitler became the Nazi Führer in 1933 in Germany, Henri de Baillet-Latour of Belgium was the fourth President of the International Olympic Committee. Baillet-Latour insisted on a guarantee from Hitler that the rules of the Olympic Charter would be observed during the Games, one of the fundamental principles being that no discrimination be allowed against any country or person on grounds of race, religion, or politics.

The Olympic Winter Games of 1936 were the first winter celebrations with a genuinely mass following. The introduction of Alpine skiing was of primary interest to the half million spectators who came to watch over seven hundred athletes from twenty-eight countries compete.

The Alpine medals were awarded on the basis of the combined positions in the men's and women's events. There were no medals awarded for the individual races in the slalom and downhill events; however, all events proved to be a great success, with the Alpine nations dominating the races.

The European speed skaters made amends for their disappointments at Lake Placid by winning numerous medals. Sonja Henie was appearing in her fourth and last Olympics and performed superbly, winning her third gold medal.

For the first time in the history of the Olympic Winter Games, the Canadian ice hockey team was unseated. The competition began with official squabbling directed toward the hockey team from Great Britain. Canada charged that a number of Canadian players had moved to Great Britain for the

The British ice hockey team that unseated the Canadians to win the gold medal in 1936. *Deutsche Presse-Agentur GmbH*

sole purpose of playing hockey without seeking official releases from the Canadian Amateur Hockey Association. The British Olympic ice hockey team did, in fact, consist largely of English-born Canadians including the best goalie in the amateur ranks, Jimmy Foster. Although the Canadians filed a protest with the Olympic officials, the objection was finally withdrawn and the tournament proceeded. In the most controversial event of the Games, Britain won the gold medal and Canada lost the Olympic hockey title that once had belonged to the Falcons, Granites, and Grads. It was apparent that there were now three powerful and competent teams in Olympic ice hockey and future tournaments were to become extremely competitive in the Olympic Winter Games.

Sapporo, Japan, was adopted by the IOC at Berlin in 1936 as the official site of the Olympic Winter Games for 1940. However, due to the outbreak of the Sino-Japanese War, Games would not be held on the most northerly Japanese island of Hokkaido until the winter of 1972.

With war clouds gathering in Europe, and the Olympic site options eliminated, Garmisch-Partenkirchen approached the IOC with an offer to stage the Games again in 1940. In spite of the advent of the war in September 1939, preparations for the Olympic Winter Games continued in Germany until November 1939, at which time the Games were cancelled for the duration of World War II.

An entire generation of young prospective Olympic athletes had come and gone by the time the Olympic Winter Games were to resume at St. Moritz in 1948.

*The Weather*: Favourable. Snowfall on the eve of the Games ensured good conditions for all competitions.

## V  St. Moritz 1948

Since the Olympic Winter Games of 1936 had been staged at Garmisch-Partenkirchen, the intervening years of war had taken their toll. The revival of peaceful competition was happily anticipated by sports enthusiasts, although Germany and Japan were not admitted to the fifth Olympic Winter Games at St. Moritz in 1948. Twenty-eight countries competed at the Olympic Winter Games with 878 competitors taking part in the events.

The Summer and Winter Games were separated into two organizational entities at St. Moritz. The concept of pairing the Summer and Winter Games, as done in the United States in 1932 and Germany in 1936, could not endure due to problems of cost. No single country has been able to hold both events in the same year since 1936.

The revival of Olympic ice hockey was a stormy one and the United States, with a civil war of its own, dominated the controversy. The Americans sent two hockey teams to the Olympic competition, and with officials unable to decide which of the two was the legitimate Olympic entry, the IOC declared both teams ineligible.

The Canadian hockey players, used to playing on indoor ice, found the open air ice rink exposed to variable weather conditions. Warm winds, named the "Föhn," set in and the soft slush on the rink defied the hockey players to even carry the puck. The only way to make any progress in the game at all was to hit the puck forward like a golf ball, and power plow up the ice chasing it.

Despite the problems, the Canadian Olympic ice hockey team from the Royal Canadian Air Force was awarded the gold medal, recapturing Olympic ice hockey supremacy. The gold medal was awarded to the Canadians on a better goal average compared with the Czechoslovakians, who had tied them in the final game. The remarkable showing by the Czechs indicated the approach of eastern European world hockey supremacy and a turning point for the Canadians.

In North America hockey was evolving into an extremely hard-hitting physical sport where brawls on the ice were not only accepted, but often keenly anticipated. However, many of the European countries were not following this pattern and it was becoming apparent that European and North American hockey were developing along different lines.

Alpine skiing made its official Olympic debut in international

Maria and Otto Jelinek, Prague, Czechoslovakia, 1948, shortly before escaping across the border, and moving to Canada. *Courtesy Henry Jelinek*

ski competition at St. Moritz in 1948. Gold medals were awarded for six Alpine events which included the downhill, slalom, and a two-part competition composed of equal portions of downhill and slalom racing. There were three events for women and three events for men.

Canadian figure skaters Suzanne Morrow and Wallace Deistelmeyer competed against thirteen other skating pairs, and won a bronze medal. Another sensational skater was part of the Canadian team at St. Moritz, Barbara Ann Scott. A young Ottawa girl, she was to become the toast of skaters and spectators at the fifth Olympic Winter Games, winning Canada's gold medal in women's figure skating. Blessed with natural talent and dedication to her sport, Barbara Ann Scott would train six days a week, all day, in the Shumacher Arena in Ottawa.

She left Canada in January 1948 to compete at Prague, Czechoslovakia, and won the women's European title. Three weeks later at St. Moritz she won her gold medal in the Olympic Winter Games. A week later, at Davos, Switzerland, Scott, who was in a class apart from all her contemporaries, won the World title. She was the national heroine of Canada, triumphant with the triple crown in women's figure skating.

*The Weather*: Variable conditions due to the Föhn. Excellent weather for the opening ceremonies.

## VI  Oslo 1952

A record number of thirty nations and 732 athletes competed in the sixth Olympic Winter Games at Oslo and were watched by 561,400 spectators. At last, the country whose national identity was personified by winter sports, and a country that would provide highly knowledgeable spectators, was host of the Olympic Winter Games in 1952.

Sondre Norheim (1825-97), the father of modern skiing, was honoured at the Oslo Games at the opening ceremonies. From the hearth of the home where Norheim had been born in southern Norway, the Olympic flame was lit. Carried not from Greece, but from the humble cottage, the flame was lit in Bislet Stadium.

The outstanding individual Canadian athlete at Oslo was speed skater Gordon Audley, who won a bronze medal in the 500 metre event, Canada's first medal in speed skating since the Olympic Winter Games at Lake Placid, New York, in 1932.

Norway, Sweden, and Finland provided virtually all the medalists in the Nordic events of cross-country skiing and ski jumping. The first women's cross-country skiing event was also held at the Games and covered a 10 kilometre course.

Predictably, the Nordic countries were less than enthusiastic when the Alpine ski events were officially introduced into the Olympic Winter Games format. Ironically, this changed overnight when a young Norwegian downhill skier named Stein Eriksen won the gold medal in the giant slalom event and became a national Norwegian hero. Stein Eriksen was to become one of the best known skiers in the history of Alpine skiing, and holds the distinction of winning the first gold medal ever presented for the giant slalom event.

Eigil Nansen carries the Olympic flame into the Bislet Stadium in 1952. His grandfather, Fridtjof Nansen, wrote *The Crossing of Greenland*, which gave modern skiing its impetus. *Norsk Telegrambyra, Oslo, Norway*

In ice hockey, Canada was represented by the Edmonton Mercuries, who played eight games, winning seven of them and tying one. Canada now had six gold medals in seven tries, on the basis of game points, and an unbeaten Olympic record.

Dick Button, who won a gold medal in 1948 at St. Moritz, delighted spectators at Oslo with the first triple rotation jump in Olympic Winter Games history. Again winning the men's figure skating event, Dick eventually established himself as a television sports broadcaster, and will be covering the Olympic Winter Games in Calgary in 1988 for ABC Sports.

The International Bobsleigh Federation was forced to introduce weight restrictions in the four-man and two-man bobsleigh events. The German teams had stretched the principle that weight equals speed just a little too far during the sixth Olympic Winter Games. The weighty members won both the two-man and four-man events. The well-nourished sledders looked more like Sumo wrestlers than athletes, and since 1952, maximum weight limitations have been imposed for the bobsleigh events.

*The Weather*: Excellent.

## VII  Cortina d'Ampezzo 1956

The staging of the Olympic Winter Games at Cortina d'Ampezzo, Italy, introduced a new era of professionalism and commercialism to the Games with the first televised coverage of the various events. Although black and white television did not fully do the Games justice, throughout the world people were given the opportunity to view the pageantry of the Olympic Winter Games for the first time. The 923 competitors represented thirty-two nations.

The Games were dominated by an exceedingly handsome twenty year old from Kitzbuhel, Austria, who raced with such perfect timing, skill, and speed that he won international accolades as the best skier in the world. Skiing on slick, unpredictable ski slopes that were virtually sheets of solid ice, Anton (Toni) Sailer gained the first Alpine triple crown in Olympic history.

Winning the downhill, the slalom, and the giant slalom by extraordinary margins, Sailer skied with such daring that none of the contestants came within ten ski lengths of him in any of the three events. He was the fifth Olympic Winter Games Olympian to have captured three gold medals at the Winter Games, joining esteemed Scandinavian athletes Thorleif Haug, Clas Thunberg, Ivar Ballangrud, and Hjalmar Andersen. The incalculable benefit that the ski holiday industry gained from "Toni Sailer's Games" is beyond compare.

The Canadian Alpine skiers who had taken part in the Olympic Winter Games to date had never won an Olympic medal and had had very few opportunities to race in European competition. In 1956, the Canadians travelled to Europe two weeks prior to the Olympics and trained extensively in Austria, participating in several prestigious international ski meets. Lucile Wheeler of St. Jovite, Quebec, proved to the ski racing elite that she qualified for membership in such esteemed company. The young Canadian girl finished just two-tenths of a second

Canada's Lucile Wheeler races to a bronze medal at the 1956 Games, the first for her country in Alpine skiing. *Canada Sports Hall of Fame/AP*

behind the girl who won the downhill event, and also delighted her team-mates with a second-place finish in the combined events in one of the races on the European circuit. When Olympic competition began at Cortina, the Canadian skiers were well prepared.

Finishing less than a second behind the silver medalist in the women's giant slalom, Lucile Wheeler gained a sixth-place finish in a field of fifty entrants. In the women's downhill event, she completed her run with a third-place finish to win a bronze medal and Canada's first Olympic medal for skiing.

In the figure skating pairs event at Cortina, Canadian skaters Frances Dafoe and Norris Bowden won the silver medal. Having won the Worlds championship in 1954 and again in 1955 at Vienna, Austria, plus an Olympic silver medal in 1956, they were elected to Canada's Amateur Athletic Hall of Fame.

The U.S.S.R. competed in the Olympic Winter Games for the first time in 1956, and had its first Olympic hockey team at Cortina d'Ampezzo. With Soviet representation in hockey, the Canadian hockey dynasty came to an end and the start of a long period of Russian domination began. In 1946, the Czechs, with their scientific approach to conditioning and play strategy, had begun to coach the Russians. In their maiden Olympic try ten years later in 1956 at Cortina d'Ampezzo, the Russians were unpredictably victorious, winning five straight games in the six-team final round. Excelling in skating, they shut out both Canada and the United States to win the gold medal. The Canadians finished a disconsolate third, as the Americans took revenge for the Games in 1952 by knocking off their Canadian opponents by a score of 4 to 1.

*The Weather*: Variable. Good snow conditions for Nordic events; hardpacked and icy ski slopes for the Alpine events.

## VIII  Squaw Valley 1960

The Olympic Winter Games were once again held in the United States in 1960 after an absence of twenty-eight years and 648 athletes came from thirty countries to participate.

When Squaw Valley, California, was awarded the Games by the International Olympic Committee, it was the result of the excellent entrepreneurial expertise of American Alexander Cushing. He envisioned a "village" Olympic site at Squaw Valley that would create an atmosphere of a close-knit family for the competitors. However, at the time Squaw Valley was chosen by the IOC, all that existed there was a small tourist hostel.

The construction of the first all-purpose Olympic centre began amidst the predictable controversy that often precedes large-scale athletic events. The Scandinavians complained that the altitude of 1,900 metres was dangerously high for their cross-country skiers. Some FIS rules had to be adjusted in order to add artificial obstacles to the downhill course to make it more challenging. With only nine countries interested in competing in the bobsleigh event, the Olympic organizers decided against construction of a bob run.

In spite of all the problems that had to be dealt with, Squaw Valley proved to be the most popular Olympic venue ever constructed for the Olympic Winter Games. Transportation and communication difficulties were virtually eliminated and the athletes were able to keep in close touch with each other throughout the games.

The biathlon event was reinstated at the Olympic Winter Games in 1960 after being dropped from the Games in 1948 by Avery Brundage, who felt that the Olympics were no place for the military.

Women's speed skating races for 500, 1,000, 1,500, and 3,000 metres were inaugurated at the eighth Olympic Winter Games at Squaw Valley in 1960.

Canadian figure skaters Barbara Wagner and Robert Paul had trained diligently during the three years after their sixth-place finish at Cortina d'Ampezzo in 1956. Their Canadian, North American, and World championships proved they were in contention for a medal at Squaw Valley. The gold medal that the skating duo won was the first gold medal for Canada in pairs skating. Oshawa's Donald Jackson won the bronze medal in the men's figure skating competition, and would go on from the eighth Olympic Winter Games to become a World champion.

It was the Alpine skiing at Squaw Valley that provided Canadians with their favourite performer in 1960. Anne Heggtveit was a young Ottawa girl whose twenty-second-place finish at Cortina d'Ampezzo had provided the inspiration she needed to dedicate herself to her sport for the next four years.

Proving that a Canadian skier was able to match the best in international competition, Anne won a gold medal in the women's slalom event at the Olympic Winter Games in 1960. Canada rejoiced for Anne's victory, as did her young roommate in Olympic village, a wide-eyed and wondering new member of the Canadian National Ski Team, experiencing her first Olympic Winter Games. Sixteen-year-old Nancy Greene from Rossland,

Alpine gold medal winner Anne Heggtveit at the 1960 Games. *Deutsche Presse-Agentur GmbH*

British Columbia, stood at the threshold of a skiing career that would bring her international fame.

The Canadian Olympic ice hockey team was represented by a Kitchener-Waterloo team which defeated teams from Sweden, Russia, Czechoslovakia, Japan, and Germany. However, the Canadians were, surprisingly, beaten by the United States. Playing on "home ice," the Americans astounded the world by winning the first Olympic gold medal in ice hockey for their country. Canada finished in second place with a silver medal.

*The Weather:* Excellent.

## IX  Innsbruck 1964

The village concept of Squaw Valley contrasted with the first big-city Olympic Winter Games at Innsbruck, Austria, in 1964. Olympic events were held at satellite locations up to 25 kilometres away from the Innsbruck city centre.

Spectators were transported to Axamer-Lizum to see the slalom and giant slalom events, and to Seefeld to attend the cross-country events. Igls, near Innsbruck, was the site of the bobsleigh track.

Innsbruck welcomed a record number of over one thousand Olympic competitors and nearly one million spectators to the ninth Olympic Winter Games. A record thirty-six nations were represented by 933 winter athletes.

The Innsbruck Games also set a precedent by being the

first Olympics to be fully computerized. Event results were compiled in seconds by electronic machines.

Radio and newspaper reporters outnumbered the competitors. Thirty-four television networks were in attendance and the commercial aspects of the Games came under fire from IOC President Avery Brundage. Brundage particularly objected to the Alpine skiers displaying their brand-name skis in full view of television cameras and newspaper photographers.

Canada dispatched its largest-ever Olympic team to Innsbruck in 1964. However, the ice hockey team wasn't even in contention for the bronze medal and Sweden's better goal average relegated the Canadians to a fourth-place finish.

Canada's Alpine ski team gained experience and Nancy Greene showed promise with a seventh-place finish in the women's downhill event.

The speed skaters were commended for their sportsmanship, but were outclassed by the Russians and Scandinavians. Twenty-four-year-old Russian school teacher, Lidija Skoblikova, won four gold medals in speed skating and became the first competitor to win that many medals in one Olympic Winter Games.

Canadian figure skaters were medalists in two events at Innsbruck in 1964. Petra Burka won a bronze medal for her third-place finish in the women's singles event. Debbi Wilkes and Guy Revelle were silver medalists in the figure skating pairs events. Canada's figure skaters had proved themselves dependable in international competition and provided two of the three medals won at the ninth Olympic Winter Games.

The third medal Canada was awarded at Innsbruck in 1964 was a gold, won by the four-man bobsleigh team which competed in an event for which no Canadian training facilities even existed. The Canadian team, tagged the "intellectual sled," included a Montreal aircraft engineer, Victor Emery; his brother John, a plastic surgeon; geologist Peter Kirby; and Douglas Anakin, a teacher. The crew pulled off one of the biggest upsets in Olympic bobsleigh racing history. The team won the gold riding to victory on a bobsleigh designed by an Italian, Edwaldo d'Andrea, who was a master of sled technology. Finishing in fourth place in the two-man bob competition, and nearly winning a bronze medal, Vic Emery and Peter Kirby proved that the four-man bobsleigh victory was not a fluke. Setting a track

Vic Emery, Doug Anakin, John Emery, and Peter Kirby go for the gold in the 1964 Games. *Deutsche Presse-Agentur GmbH*

record on the first day of competition, the Canadian crew held onto their lead in the next three runs, and won gold on the fourth and final run—Canada's first medal in bobsleighing.

*The Weather*: Clear skies, no snow. Nordic and Alpine ski trails inadequately covered.

## X  Grenoble 1968

As in Innsbruck, the tenth Olympic Winter Games were held in a large thriving city, Grenoble. The French government allotted over $200 million to Olympic organizers to prepare Grenoble for the Games.

For the 1,293 competitors from thirty-seven nations, and the media represented by 1,000 newspaper, radio, and television personnel, Grenoble suffered a host of transportation inadequacies.

Satellite sites up to 40 kilometres away from the Olympic Village proved unsatisfactory for the bobsleigh competitors, who were forced to live in Alpe d'Huez in mountainside hotels. The bobsleigh events were held in early pre-dawn hours, due to the unrefrigerated run not being shaded from the sun. The skiers were billeted at their own mini-Olympic village at Chamrousse near the ski courses, but miles away from the main activity.

Canada had entries in figure skating, bobsleighing, ice hockey, speed skating, luge, and alpine skiing in these Olympic Winter Games.

During the Games, the amateur-professional conflict was beginning to take on larger proportions because many of the national ski teams had become reliant on the ski equipment manufacturers to sponsor them. As the Winter Games were now being televised, the International Olympic Committee took exception to the advertising of trade names on skis and other equipment used by racers. IOC President Avery Brundage considered this advertising practice to be nothing less than commercial exploitation of the Olympic Winter Games. The IOC tried to curb this trend by placing a ban on such support, only to be met by threats of revolt against the ruling by the skiers. The controversy was finally settled with a compromise being reached prohibiting skiers from being photographed or televised until they had removed their equipment.

As the Olympic Winter Games were held in France, it seemed appropriate that a dashing twenty-four-year-old Frenchman named Jean-Claude Killy should win all three men's Alpine gold medals. It was a tremendous personal accomplishment for "le superman" who became the first skier since 1956 to win the Alpine grand slam.

If Jean-Claude Killy was the hero at Grenoble, twenty-five-year-old Nancy Greene of Canada was the female skiing star of the Games. Nancy had achieved an unprecedented string of international victories at ski meets in Canada, the United States, and Europe during the 1967 and 1968 racing seasons. The thrill of winning the World Cup in 1967 had been her proudest moment. When she was named Canada's Athlete of the Year in 1967, Nancy told Prime Minister Lester Pearson that she wanted to repay the honour by winning an Olympic gold medal.

Gold medalist Nancy Greene, Canada's top female athlete of 1968.
*Deutsche Presse-Agentur GmbH*

Starting ninth down the 1,610 metre giant slalom course, Nancy turned in a fantastic run to win the gold medal by a margin of 2.64 seconds, one of the widest margins in the history of a major skiing event. After Nancy's victory at Grenoble, she became a vital and integral member of the Canadian skiing community by promoting, developing, and sponsoring highly successful junior ski programs for young Canadian skiers across Canada.

In Olympic ice hockey, the Canadian national team was beaten by both the U.S.S.R. and Finland. The Bauer National Team concept (players training and living together while attending school) led the Canadians to a bronze medal at Grenoble, and proved that the youth plan developed Olympic calibre players. The Canadian professionals never fully accepted, or supported the idea of assembling a group of promising hockey players into the same university to develop together. Whether out of self-interest or not, the professional players contributed to the continued failure of the national team program to become established after 1968. As a result, Canada withdrew from the Olympic ice hockey scene until its re-entry at Lake Placid, New York, for the thirteenth Olympic Winter Games in 1980.

Canada's best standings in figure skating were seventh in both the men's and women's events. For sheer poetry on ice, the Russian husband-and-wife figure skating pairs champions, Ludmilla Belousova and Oleg Protopopov, treated their audience to the ultimate Olympic performance. Winning their second gold medal, the Protopopovs communicated through their magical skating to Olympic spectators their feelings for each other, for skating, and for their audience.

*The Weather*: Variable. Some events postponed due to bad weather.

## XI  Sapporo 1972

Sapporo, Japan, situated on the northerly island of Hokkaido, provided a gracious welcome to the eleventh Olympic Winter Games.

With three thousand press, television, and radio personnel in attendance, the competitors, representing 35 countries, were outnumbered two to one. The media facilities for the Games were a phenomenon of the Japanese electronics industry.

The smallest margin of victory in Olympic history was recorded on sophisticated timing equipment, and indicated a gold medal finish for American Barbara Ann Chochran in the Alpine special slalom. The event was won by two-hundreths of a second and was an example of the tremendous advances made in the manufacturing of electronic timing devices for the Olympics. The data-processing centre and the broadcasting facilities enabled numerous programs, with over sixty commentaries, to be sent out simultaneously. The centre established a communications achievement record for the Olympic Winter Games.

Sapporo, while establishing itself as a financial and leisure centre for sports enthusiasts during the Games, was also to highlight many of the difficulties of the modern Olympic Games. The ideal of Olympic amateur purity, held in such high regard by IOC President Avery Brundage, was to come under intense and hostile criticism in Sapporo, ending with the expulsion from the Games of the great Austrian ski racer Karl Schranz.

The Nordic events demonstrated the increasing geographical diversification of winter sports, by providing Spain with its first gold medal in special slalom. The U.S.S.R. won eight medals in cross-country events, and Norway seven. The surprising upset of the Sapporo Games was the Japanese ski jumping team that won four Olympic medals. Nothing could compare with the spectator frenzy as crowds watched the 70 metre jump at the Miyanomori hill. The joy of a home victory was hoped for by the Japanese, to retain the Olympic tradition of the host country always winning at least one medal at the Games. Yuko Kasaya, Akitsugu Konno, and Seiji Aochi did not disappoint their countrymen. They won the gold, silver, and bronze, the first Asians to ever win medals in the Olympic Winter Games.

The first skater to take three titles in men's speed skating since 1952 was Ard Schenk of the Netherlands who was known as the "Flying Dutchman." He captured gold medals in the 1,500, 5,000, and 10,000 metre events and became the hero of Sapporo. Canadian speed skater Sylvia Burka of Winnipeg made her Olympic debut at Sapporo. Her best finish was a respectable eighth in the 1,000 metre event. In 1973, Sylvia went on to win the unofficial junior world championship in the Netherlands and would also set a world record for the 500 metres of 175.050 points. Sylvia Burka also set world records twice in the 100 metre event at Davos, Switzerland, in 1973.

Austria's Trixi Schuba, well ahead of the rest of the women's figure skating field in the compulsory figures, finished with a cautious freestyle display to win the gold medal. Runner-up Karen Magnussen of Canada skated with such enthusiasm and excitement that her performance won her a silver medal.

Vancouver's Karen Magnussen, winner of Canada's only medal at the 1972 Games in Sapporo, Japan. *Canada Sports Hall of Fame*

The Russian gold medalists in the pairs competition were accorded the most attention. Olympic spectators were very intrigued by a romantic liaison between gold medalist Aleksei Ulanov and the beautiful Ludmila Smirnova. Smirnova, partnered by Andrei Suraikin, had been awarded the silver medal in the pairs competition. Ulanov's skating partner was the volatile and talented Irina Rodnina, who appeared petulant and resentful at the prospect of losing her handsome skating companion. Russian skating officials denied that the romance was of any significance, but Ulanov and Smirnova were later to marry.

The U.S.S.R. took its third consecutive gold medal in Olympic ice hockey. Canada was noted for its absence at the Olympic ice hockey scene in 1972.

Overlooking the Sea of Japan, Sapporo's "sayonara" or goodbye, ended the closing ceremonies of the eleventh Olympic Winter Games that had been held in the very memorable setting on the island of Hokkaido.

However, an Olympic Games tragedy would take place during the summer months of the 1972 that would overshadow the triumphs of the athletes at Sapporo, and the site of the Olympic Summer Games at Munich, Germany. On the eleventh day of the 1972 Olympic Summer Games, world television audiences would watch in disbelief as a group of Palestinian terrorists took over the Olympic village. Demanding that the government of Israel release two hundred imprisoned Palestinian guerrillas, they also demanded transportation out of West Germany. The terrorists then proceeded to kill two Israeli athletes, take nine hostages, and

escape by helicopter to an airfield where negotiations with German officials were held.

By the following day, all nine of the hostages had been killed, along with five of the terrorists and a German police officer. The civilized world condemned the barbaric intrusion of terrorists into international Olympic celebrations being held to further the cause of peace.

*The Weather:* With the juxtaposition of the Siberian high and the Pacific low-pressure weather systems, Sapporo was subject to violent changes of weather during the Games.

## XII  Innsbruck 1976

The twelfth Olympic Winter Games were originally to be held in Denver, Colorado. However, after two years of preparation, disagreement and financial controversies led to the withdrawal of Denver as the Olympic site. The International Olympic Committee accepted the invitation from Innsbruck, Austria, to host the celebrations of the Games of the twelfth Winter Games.

The relatively peaceful Games at Innsbruck resulted from a deliberate attempt by Austrians to underplay the Olympics. Austria spent only $148 million providing Olympic venues. These were the Games with the "Tyrolean Touch" and a low-key approach. The athletes numbered more than twelve hundred and represented thirty-seven nations as they competed in the seven disciplines of the Olympic Winter Games.

The first athlete to take the spotlight in the Games was, fittingly, a twenty-two-year-old Austrian, the world's best downhiller, Franz Klammer. Although drawing the last starting position on the day of the finals, Klammer captured the first gold medal of the XII Olympic Winter Games in the men's downhill event.

A twenty-five-year-old veteran racer with ten years' experience in international ski competitions was to emerge as the star of women's Alpine skiing. Nicknamed "Omi" (the German name for Granny), West German Rosi Mittermaier had never been victorious in a major downhill race, and had accustomed herself to always being a runner-up on the racing circuit.

Racing down the Olympic courses in perfect control, Rosi won both the downhill and the slalom, beating the favourites. But it was Canadian National Ski Team member, youthful Kathy Kreiner, who pushed Rosi Mittermaier into a second-place finish in the giant slalom event, and obliterated the West German's dream of an Alpine grand slam.

Speed skater Sheila Young accumulated six speed skating medals for the United States during the first eight days of the Games at Innsbruck. The sentimental Canadian favourite in the women's speed skating was twenty-five-year-old Sylvia Burka of Winnipeg, a veteran Olympic participant and World Champion competitor. However, it was Cathy Priestner of Calgary who won the silver medal in the 500 metres event at Innsbruck. Cathy Priestner became the first Canadian woman to win an Olympic medal in speed skating.

Kathy Kreiner's and Cathy Priestner's triumphs were not

the only victories for Canada at Innsbruck. One of the glamour events of the Games, men's figure skating, provided Canada with another medalist. Toller Cranston's performances in the disciplined school figures, compulsory short program, and his brilliant skating in the freestyle competition earned him the bronze medal.

As a flu epidemic raged through the Olympic village, the IOC Medical Commission kept busy testing various participants who were accused of taking controversial antibiotics. Prestigious cross-country skier Galina Koulakova of the Soviet Union, who had eight Olympic medals to her credit, was disqualified for using nasal spray for her cold before the 5 kilometre race. Reinstated for the 10 kilometre and 4 x 5 kilometre relay race, Galina won a bronze and gold medal respectively for the U.S.S.R.

The Czechoslovakian ice hockey team had several of its members ruled out of the finals by the Medical Commission as the team doctor had not informed the IOC that he had administered codeine to the Czech skaters. Threatening to boycott the final game against the U.S.S.R. if several of their players were not reinstated, the IOC relented and the Czechs finished up in the final round with a silver medal.

As the two Olympic flames were extinguished at Innsbruck, it was apparent that the trend of the host city to erect structures and produce a grander spectacle than its predecessors had been rejected at these Games. The XII Olympic Games ended with a relatively low expenditure and demonstrated to the world that a small country could host a successful and peaceful Olympic Winter Games at reasonable cost.

*The Weather*: Unseasonably warm. Poor snow conditions. No events cancelled, or postponed.

## XIII  Lake Placid 1980

Canadians joined their neighbour to the south to celebrate the thirteenth Olympic Winter Games at Lake Placid, New York, in 1980.

Thirty-seven nations were included among the entries and the 1,283 athletes were housed in an Olympic village that was to be converted into a minimum security prison after the Games.

A standing ovation for Canada by the crowd of twenty-three thousand spectators during the opening ceremonies provided a warm welcome to the fifty member Canadian Olympic team. The ovation was also directed toward the Canadian Ambassador to Iran, Ken Taylor from Calgary, Alberta. Taylor had become a national hero in Canada and the United States just a few weeks before the thirteenth Olympic Winter Games had begun. The Canadian Embassy staff in Iran had made world headlines, when six American diplomats had been hidden in the Canadian Embassy compound, and eventually returned safely to the United States. Unfortunately, fifty of their American colleagues were to remain in Tehran as hostages for some time.

Canada had fared well at the third Olympic Winter Games at Lake Placid in 1932, winning a total of seven medals. The Canadian team of 1980 hoped to win at least four medals and

have several of their team-mates finish in the top ten of many of the events.

Before the Canadian team left for the Games, the Canadian Olympic Association became involved in a controversy with the Canadian Figure Skating Association over a decision to change the Olympic selection standards for skaters. To meet the COA criteria, the skaters would have to prove their ability be placing in the top half of their field in any national or international championship. The COA felt there was little to be gained by sending skaters with no medal potential to be outclassed by world champion skaters at the Olympic Winter Games. This decision was protested by the skating association and the Olympic association eventually relented. However, when the Games ended, Canada was out of the medal standings in all the figure skating events. The best-place finishes were a sixth in pairs figure skating and a twelfth in men's singles by Brian Pockar of Calgary.

The superhero of the speed skating events at Lake Placid was United States skater Eric Heiden. His five gold medals at one Olympic Winter Games set a precedent in men's speed skating. Twenty-one-year-old Gaeten Boucher from Ste. Foy, Quebec, finished in second place in the 1,000 metre event.

Twenty-nine-year-old Sylvia Burka of Winnipeg was the sentimental favourite as Canadians watched the women's speed skating events. Rated in the top three in the world before the Games, Burka was denied a medal with her best finish seventh place in the 1,000 metres event.

By 1980, the "Crazy Canucks" ski team had established

The Canadian Olympic Team marches into the Stadium for the Opening Ceremonies at the 1980 Games at Lake Placid, New York. *Robert Riger/ABC Sports*

its credibility in speed and agility on the international and national downhill racing circuit. Ken Read of Calgary, was the Canadian medal favourite for the downhill event at the Games. Read came into the thirteenth Olympic Winter Games in second place in the men's World Cup series. He also held the distinction of being the first North American male to ever take a World Cup downhill race in the 1975-76 season at Val d'Isere, France.

Canadians, hoping for gold, watched as Read started his descent of Whiteface Mountain in the prestigious downhill event but he fell at the top of the course. With Ken Read out of medal contention, Canadians pinned their hopes on Steve Podborski, another "Crazy Canuck" from Toronto. Cheered on by his teammates, the cherubic twenty-three-year-old hurtled down the men's downhill course to win a bronze medal for Canada.

Canadian men were not represented on the cross-country ski-team in 1980; however, a five-woman team participated in the Nordic events at Lake Placid. Like the Olympic bobsleigh team representing Canada, none of the Nordic participants broke into the top ten of their field. But a best-ever performance by a North American was recorded with the eleventh-place finish in the luge competition by Bruce Smith of Mississauga, Ontario. Another Canadian best-ever finish was the women's luge event. Carol Keyes of Woodstock, Ontario, came eighteenth in her Olympic debut at Lake Placid in the singles luge race.

The Canadian Olympic ice hockey team re-entered the Olympic Winter Games hockey competition at Lake Placid in 1980. Father David Bauer was back where he started in 1964, working with a group of young, talented amateurs. This time around, the Olympic ice hockey team was based permanently in Calgary, Alberta, and managed by Father Bauer and three coaches.

Father Bauer was cautious about medal prospects as the Canadian National ice hockey team left for Lake Placid in 1980. The 1968 team that won the bronze medal at Grenoble, France, had been together for several years. The National team of 1980 had been assembled in the summer of 1978 and was short on skills and experience and ended up in sixth place.

The American team was composed of a group of amateur college hockey players who had developed an esprit de corps similar to the Canadians. Proving that the youth plan concept worked, the United States beat the Russians 4 to 3 in their final game and won the gold medal.

At the time the Olympic Winter Games had ended at Lake Placid in New York, CODA had been successful in gaining the endorsement by the Canadian Olympic Association for Calgary's bid to host the XV Olympic Winter Games in 1988.

*The Weather*: Poor snow conditions.

The Olympic Flame enters the stadium at the Opening Ceremonies for the 1984 Games at Sarajevo, Yugoslavia. *Deutsche Presse-Agentur GmbH*

## XIV  Sarajevo 1984

An all-time record of forty-nine flags of national Olympic Committees were raised when the XIV Olympic Winter Games began at Sarajevo, Yugoslavia. Competing under those flags were 1,490 athletes who, over the thirteen-day festival, would be watched by over two billion television viewers on five continents.

On January 29, 1984, at the stadium of ancient Olympia in Greece, the rays of sun were tamed to kindle the symbol of peace and friendship, the Olympic flame. A flame bearer started the Olympic torch on its way to Athens airport where it was put into a lantern and carried by plane to its first stop at the ancient city of Dubrovnik in Yugoslavia. The flame was welcomed and ignited by the President of the Organizing Committee of the XIV Winter Games, Branko Mikulić. The Olympic torch would pass through 197 places in Yugoslavia on its journey to Kosevo Stadium at Sarajevo. Finally, Yugoslavia's best ice skater, Sandra Dubravcic, carried the torch up the grand pedestal in the Stadium and ignited the Olympic flame that would burn for the duration of the Games.

During the opening ceremonies, the parade of delegations of the participating countries welcomed the handicapped athletes participating in the Olympic Games for the first time. The disabled athletes were given a standing ovation by all forty-five thousand spectators who filled Kosevo Stadium.

Weather forecasters predicted snow, fog, and wind for the Games, and the heaviest snowfall in ten years at Sarajevo caused postponements and delays in several of the Olympic events.

Jure Franko, a gracious Yugoslavian, epitomised the Olympic ideal at the 1984 Games. *International Olympic Committee Archives*

IOC President Samaranch with the amputee skiers who took part in the demonstration events at Sarajevo in 1984. *International Olympic Committee Archives, Lausanne, Switzerland*

No one faced a longer wait for their event than the men's downhill skiers. The weather-plagued event was postponed daily as organizers had no other choice than to surrender to the unending winter storm over Sarajevo. The waiting game continued and when the bad weather finally lifted, organizers had to combine two days of slalom events into one to open a space for the men's and women's downhill events.

Twenty-one-year-old Jure Franko, a sports student from Ljubljana, Yugoslavia, won the first Olympic Winter Games medal for his country. And, much to the amusement of the television audiences around the world, the young Yugoslav celebrated his silver medal win by honouring a bet made before the Games, by giving his coach a haircut on national television.

The starting gate of the downhill event at Sarajevo was in a restaurant on top of the summit. The course was extended in such an unusual way to increase the 800 metre vertical drop required for the men's downhill. Fast-talking American downhiller Billy Johnson said: "This course was designed for me, and everyone else is here to fight for second place." He was right, and from the outset of the event, the race was Johnson's. The American finished in a gold medal time of 1:45.59, Peter Müeller of Switzerland won the silver medal in 1:45.86, and Anton Steiner won Austria's only medal in the entire Games with his bronze medal finish. The Games at Sarajevo marked the last time the veteran Canadian downhiller Steve Podborski would compete on the Olympic ski team. The last of the original Crazy Canucks, Podborski announced that he would retire at the end of the season.

The most successful athlete at Sarajevo was cross-country skier Lisa Haemaelainen from Finland who won three gold medals and one bronze medal. With her first appearance in the Olympic Winter Games, the twenty-nine-year-old Haemaelainen established herself as the Queen of Veliko Polje, the cross-country venue. "I am so happy," said Lisa, "and what I received at Sarajevo is the result of my many years of hard work."

Television audiences around the world and spectators at the Zetra Ice Hall could only watch in awe at the ice dancing perfection of British team Jayne Torvill and Christopher Dean as they performed to the music of Ravel's Bolero. From the moment they skated onto the ice, the artistic impression and flawless technique the two effused was almost beyond belief, and earned them an unprecedented perfect score from all nine judges. Canadians were treated to a silver medal performance by skater Brian Orser.

Bad weather did not seriously disturb the luge events on the 1,532-metre-long combined bobsleigh and luge run at Trebević. The women's singles event was a clean sweep for robust East German sledders Steffi Martin, Bettino Schmidt, and Ute Weiss. Thirty-one-year-old Paul Hildgartner competed in the men's singles event for his fourth Olympic Winter Games and won the gold medal for Italy.

Ice hockey was the most represented sport at the Games at Sarajevo with thirty-six ice hockey games in total, and twelve teams. The superiority of the Soviet players was best illustrated by the fact that their team won every single game, only let in five goals in the entire tournament, and beat the bronze medalist Swedish team by a goal difference of nine. The Czechoslovakian team, always a bridesmaid and never a bride, won the silver medal. Team Canada had become hotshots-not-longshots in the tournament and had battled the United States, Austria, Finland, and Norway until the Olympic ice hockey event boiled down to a four-team race for three medals. Having fought so hard to get to the match with Sweden, under tremendous pressure, and fighting alien officiating, the young Canucks simply ran out of gas in the bronze-medal match. Nevertheless, Team Canada's performance was more than creditable against such formidable opponents.

The exhibition of disabled skiing was very well received at Sarajevo, and along with a cross-country race for the totally blind, will again be included as an exhibition at the XV Olympic Winter Games at Calgary in 1988.

*The Weather:* The heaviest snowfall in ten years.

# The Olympic Venues

*Mathieson, Calgary*

There are few dates that stand out as clearly in my mind as September 30, 1981. Sitting in the grand old casino in Baden Baden, West Germany, after almost three years of preparation and anticipation, we anxiously awaited the announcement we had come halfway around the world to hear. IOC President His Excellency Juan Antonio Samaranch stepped onto the stage, and in a few brief words proclaimed—"La ville de Calgary." For a short moment the world stopped. Then the pent-up energy and emotion of three years burst forth. The dream had come true!

That was six years ago. And now, as I cast my eyes over the Calgary skyline and to the Rocky Mountains beyond, I find it hard to believe what the dream has become. There is a tremendous feeling of pride in this grand accomplishment, and a tremendous feeling of gratitude to the thousands of people whose spirit and effort made it happen. In just a short time our city has been transformed, and now with its magnificent new sport facilities, it patiently awaits the arrival of the first Olympic athletes in 1988.

For me personally, the Olympic venues and facilities hold a special meaning. Very early in the bid we looked at the task ahead and divided the responsibilities among the few of us then involved. I took on the Games facilities. With the generous support of a Calgary engineering firm, Underwood McLellan, we set about the task of designing the very unique sport facilities required for the Games, the kind most of us had seen only in books, or on television. It was a fascinating experience, and one that took us around the world several times, introducing us to the many fine people who make up the family of international sport. It was on their advice that we created the facilities that won us the Games in Baden Baden.

The facilities that now surround us are a product of the imagination of hundreds of people. By drawing on a vast resource of international sport planners, engineers, and creative minds, the facilities designed and constructed for the Games are the most technically advanced and challenging in the world. They are unique by Olympic standards and are a positive expression of the modern world of sport which, while building on the ideals of friendly competition and personal development, recognize the reality of technology, transportation, and communication as an integral part of the evolution of sport.

All the major facilities for the Games were funded and built through the kind generosity of our three levels of government. The Government of Canada funded and built Canada Olympic Park, the venue for ski-jumping, bobsleigh and luge, and home of Canada's new Olympic Sports Hall of Fame. They further funded the Olympic Oval, the venue for speed skating, and the Father David Bauer Olympic Arena, the venue for short track speed skating, and home to Canada's National Hockey Team. The Province of Alberta funded and developed the Nakiska Ski Area at Mt. Allan, the venue for the alpine events, and now a popular recreational ski resort. They also funded and built the Canmore Nordic Centre, the venue for cross-country skiing and biathlon.

The City of Calgary, in support of its overall commitment to the Games, funded and built many aesthetic and infrastructure elements to the Games. A major City of Calgary project is the Olympic Plaza, located directly opposite City Hall. It also helped fund and build the Father David Bauer Olympic Arena at the University of Calgary. In addition to those projects undertaken by the three governments, the University of Calgary has made a major contribution as a Project Manager for the Games, building both the Olympic Oval and the Olympic Village. For their tremendous commitment to the project, and for their enthusiastic support and cooperation along the way, we are deeply indebted to our four Olympic partners.

For a small group of Calgary sportsmen these facilities, and this dream, have been a long time coming. Thirty years ago they had a vision that one day Canada might have the honour of hosting the Olympic Winter Games. They saw this great event as an opportunity to introduce Calgary to the world as a new and exciting winter sport centre, and more importantly, to create an opportunity for the development of young athletes from across this country and around the world. Now with the coming of the XV Olympic Winter Games, and the legacy of sport facilities and programs they will leave behind, their vision has been realized and Calgary will finally take its place among the leading winter sport nations of the world. The Games are just the beginning!

Robert D. Niven
*Vice-Chairman, OCO'88*

# Canada Olympic Park
## A Special Tribute

When the world's best Olympic bobsleigh, luge, and ski jumping athletes compete in their various disciplines at Canada Olympic Park in 1988, among the spectators will be the former owners of the area.

The partnership has shared a unique success story of true pioneering spirit in ski area development.

Canada Olympic Park owes its origin to the Bowness Golf and Country Club and the construction of the Trans-Canada Highway. In order to construct the new highway, several golf holes on the course were offered for sale by the city. However, a condition was attached to the sale contract. As the original use of the land had been recreational, it would remain so, to be enjoyed by the citizens of Calgary.

The property was sold to Calgary oilmen Fred Cummer and Bob Elias, dentist Gord Minty, and realtor Elmer Berg. The ski area opened with a rope tow Fred Cummer had constructed out of old junk from used oil field equipment. An old CPR dining car was moved onto the bottom of the 1,200 metre hill and was used as a day lodge. Homemade snow guns were installed and water was trucked in daily to keep the snow-making machinery working. As there were several telephone poles on the property when it was sold, the partnership decided to make use of them. Mercury lights were placed on top of the poles and the new ski area advertized that their hill operated from 10 A.M. to 10 P.M. The recreational park was named Paskapoo, an Indian word meaning "fault in rock" as the small hill was part of a sandstone quarry.

Failing to fire the enthusiasm of local skiers, Paskapoo received little more than bemused smiles and lofty glances as people drove by on the way to the ski slopes of the famous Rocky Mountains.

For the first few years of operation, Paskapoo remained a small and humble ski community managed by the optimistic partnership. Bob Elias left the partnership in 1969 and Calgarians Joe Couillard and Al Brooker were hired to operate the area and the ski shop. At that time the area employed one maintenance man, one lift operator, and one cafeteria cook. Joe ran the ski school and Al ran the ski shop.

The City of Calgary.

The Day Lodge at Canmore Nordic Centre.

During the 1970s each year opened at Paskapoo with new goals stimulated by the growing demand and competition in the ski industry.

In 1970, Joe Couillard approached the Calgary Board of Education to get a learn-to-ski program started for children during school hours. From the outset of the school children's program until the time of purchase by the Federal Government in 1984, nearly one hundred thousand children had learned to ski at Paskapoo.

By 1973, Joe Couillard had been invited to join the partnership and Al Brooker expanded the ski shop. At the time Joe joined the Calgary ski area developers, a major expansion was taking place. Extra land was purchased to increase the ski slope area, a bigger day lodge was constructed, a double chair and new rope tow were added, and the parking lot was improved.

In 1973, McMahon Stadium was expanding on the east side of the stands and sold the old light towers to Paskapoo for scrap weight. The towers replaced the old original mercury lights on the telephone poles.

At the time the bid by the Calgary Olympic Development Association (CODA) to host the 1988 Olympic Winter Games was accepted by the IOC in 1981, Paskapoo had an impressive record of accomplishments.

- Alberta's largest ski school.

- Fully serviced by Western Canada's most extensive snow-making system.

- 1,500 sets of rental skis, boots, poles—downhill and cross-country.

- Over 40,000 people taught in the GLM (graduated ski length method) ski school classes.

- Lift capacity of 6,200 people/hour serviced by a triple and double chair, two T-bars, and two free beginner rope tows.

- Considered one of the most financially successful ski hill operations in Canada.

The base lodge buildings at Nakiska.

McMahon Stadium.

The University of Calgary, site of the Olympic Village and the Olympic Speed Skating Oval.

The Olympic Saddledome.

The XV Olympic Winter Games Organizing Committee approached the owners with an offer to purchase the area in 1982. The Committee proposed to turn the site into an international class Olympic park and training centre for Canada's luge, bobsleigh, and ski jumping athletes. The existing ski operations would not be affected by the addition of the new facilities.

OCO'88 handled the purchase negotiations for the area and a price of $16.2 million was accepted as of April 1, 1984.

The International Olympic Committee endorsed the site decision by OCO'88 and the Federal Government offered to construct the new recreation centre with a budget set at $60.4 million (1982/83 dollars).

The combined bobsleigh/luge track on the west side of the ski runs is the first one in Canada. The only existing bobsleigh and luge run in North America is located at Lake Placid, New York. The 70 metre and 90 metre ski jumps are on the ski hill to the east of the triple chairlift. The only existing Olympic standard ski jumps in Canada are at Thunder Bay, Ontario.

Dreams have been known to take on dimensions. However, it is unlikely that the owners who saw Paskapoo's rope tow and old CPR diner beginning ever envisaged the area as Canada's first all-round winter recreation and training centre.

The Canada Olympic Park site—before (left) and after (right).

# Alpine Skiing

Nakiska
February 14, 15, 16, 18, 19, 20, 21, 22, 24, 25, 26, 27

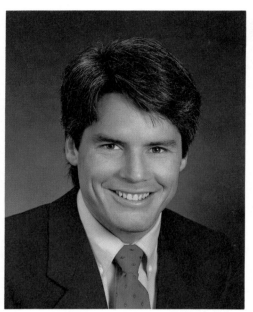

*Mathieson, Calgary*

Alpine skiing is consistently the most colourful and exciting sport of the Olympic Winter Games. From the brash daring of downhill, the smooth rhythm of giant slalom, to the speed and gymnastics of slalom, no other sport enjoys such diversity.

The crown jewel of the Games is downhill. No other sport so rivets the attention of both competitor and spectator. The challenge of man against the mountain—plummeting down icy slopes in what appears to be a free fall, at speeds exceeding 130 kph, seemingly without protection.

There is nothing quite like downhill racing. Imagine—a meticulously prepared race course snaking over 3,000 metres down the side of a mountain with a vertical drop almost twice the height of the CN tower (900 metres). Safety nets and willy bags, filled with straw or foam, are strategically placed for protection, and course control has cleared the slope of errant skiers.

The downhill lies in wait for the ski racer—designed to challenge, with jumps that catapult the athlete over 30 metres down the slope, sidehills, and rough terrain to test their confidence, and tough turns to measure their technical proficiency. It's a test of physical limits.

Downhill racing is also a challenge of mental toughness. The athletes must find the limits of their ability, and then push them further—*but* also know when to take that extra risk which is the margin of victory.

I had the privilege of representing Canada in international competition for ten years, including the Olympic Games of Innsbruck and Lake Placid. I'll never forget competing in the Olympic downhill at Innsbruck—the race course lined with a crowd of over seventy thousand spectators as the greats of downhill racing careened down the Patscherkofl in an attempt to dethrone the ''Kaiser'', Franz Klammer.

In the years since the Innsbruck Olympics, the sport has undergone some dramatic changes. At the time we were only scratching the surface with technological advances in downhill suits, waxes, and skis. Today the racer has the advantage of video analysis of the training run, extensive wax and ski base development, aerodynamic ski suit design, and sophisticated training programs that last year round. The result is a better trained athlete as well as a highly competitive tour with as many as twenty nations able to field world class competitors.

Through this period, our men's team left a permanent imprint on the skiing world. The "Crazy Canucks" transformed the art of ski racing into a highly specialized and thrilling spectacle. It can be said without reservation that Canadians became world leaders not only on the result sheet, but also in the technical advancement of the sport.

But it has been our "Golden Girls" who have won Olympic medals for Canada in the past, and as we look forward to 1988 some of our best medal chances rest again with our women's team. With World Cup winner Laurie Graham leading the way, we have a team with talent and depth.

On the men's side, there is much anticipation of the developing talent of a new generation of ski racers to carry the fortunes of Canada into the Olympics. Look for the names Boyd, Stemmle, Read, and Villiard.

We in Canada have much to be proud of through our contribution to the sport of alpine skiing. We have always had challengers for world supremacy. We make an annual contribution through staging World Cup events, which are considered to be some of the best-staged events on the tour. Now, with the Olympic Games, we can display our greatest talent—challenging race venues for truly exciting ski racing. This is what will make the Calgary Olympic Winter Games the "best ever."

Ken Read
*Winner of 5 World Cup Downhill Races*
*Member—Canada's Sports Hall of Fame*

# The History

Ottawa, Ontario, was the first city in Canada to host an official demonstration of Alpine skiing.

Lord Frederick Hamilton, an aide-de-camp of Governor General Lord Lansdowne, skied down the slopes of Rockcliffe Park in January of 1887. His efforts met with jeers and laughter from the spectators gathered near the vice-regal residence of Rideau Hall.

All things considered, downhill skiing at that time was an awkward piece of business. Skiers used one long pole for balance and braking, and never considered turning or traversing.

On the other side of Canada, a Scandinavian immigrant named Olaus Jeldness introduced the sport of skiing to the citizens of a little mining community in British Columbia in 1892.

Twenty-two-year-old Jeldness, a native of Norway, first saw Red Mountain while travelling the Dewdney Trail into the boom town of Rossland, British Columbia, in the late 1800s. During the Gold Rush, he staked his first claims and hit pay dirt. Being an influential mining promoter in Rossland gave him the time to pursue his boyhood passion of skiing. In February of 1898, Jeldness organized Canada's first ski jumping and ski racing championships and he won both events on a pair of 275 cm (nine-foot) long skis.

Alpine skiing, an adaptation of cross-country skiing to downhill, was first attempted in 1896 by an indomitable character from Austria named Mathias Zdarsky. He was the first man to develop an entirely new approach to skiing in the mountains, instead of on the flat terrain of Scandinavia. Zdarsky persevered at his downhill technique despite avalanches, broken legs, dislocated shoulders, and universal derision from his countrymen. He is known as the father of downhill skiing. With plenty of sport to be had in skating and tobogganing, downhill skiing remained something of a curiosity in the Alps for some time to come. Spending an entire morning climbing up a mountain for a five-second run down didn't appeal to many winter sport vacationers.

In the early 1900s a sports club was formed in Switzerland for wealthy vacationers from England. The Public Schools Alpine Sports Club was founded by Henry Lunn, an English Methodist missionary turned travel agent. Lunn booked hotels with the best addresses at the winter resorts of Klosters, Crans-Montana, Wengen, and Mürren. With the influx of a young, sporty clientele, the interest in downhill skiing increased.

Henry Lunn established an annual ski competition for the Englishmen at Crans-Montana in 1911. Lord Roberts of Kandahar named the three-mile race and ten men took part in the inaugural event. After an arduous seven-mile hike up the course, the men slept overnight in a mountain hut, and started the race the following morning.

Cecil Hopkinson was the winner. He skied the course in sixty-one minutes, with time off for a drink and a crack-up at Shambles Corner. Because no one knew how to turn around the ninety-degree corner, the midway wipe-out was an accepted part of the race.

The Kandahar is the oldest recorded downhill race in the world and is still held every year in Europe.

After World War I, Henry Lunn's son Arnold decided that the downhill needed a technical counterpart, so he invented the slalom race in 1922. In the slalom, racers skied through a series of double poles, or "gates," spaced along the mountainside. The times for two runs were added together and the fastest time determined the winner. This event tested the skier's technique rather than the sheer speed of the downhill. The first world championships for slalom were held at Wengen, Switzerland.

The person who really put skiing on the map was Swiss engineer Gerhard Müller. Müller used motorcycle parts and a rope to invent a ski tow that pulled people up the slopes near Davos. The invention was a simple one but it revolutionized the ski business, even across the Atlantic.

The first tow rope in Canada was installed at Big Hill in Shawbridge, Quebec, in 1932. Alex Foster owned the operation, and would crank the tow up to 40 kph, full speed, for skiers who paid 25¢ a day.

The first ski school in Canada was founded in 1932 at St. Jovite, north of Montreal, by a German expatriate named Billy Pauly. Pauly skied in a low crouch position with a lot of daylight between his legs. His "Berlin squat" technique suited the Laurentian terrain and he passed on his expertise to the newly formed Red Birds Ski Club of McGill University.

By 1933 the Red Birds were ready for international competition, and travelled to Mürren to race in the Kandahar. Canadian George Jost won the trophy and so impressed Arnold Lunn that he challenged the Canadians to a rematch. One month later, the inaugural Quebec-Kandahar race was held at Canada's first big ski resort, Mont Tremblant. The competition was a straight schuss to the bottom and Jost won again.

The Quebec-Kandahar is held every year at Mont Tremblant, and the most famous Canadian winner was legendary skier Ernie McCulloch, who later became the ski school director at Tremblant. Canada's first chairlift and T-bar were installed at Mont Tremblant in 1937.

The downhill and slalom events gained Olympic status at the Winter Games in Garmisch-Partenkirchen, Germany, in 1936.

The only Olympic medal presented for Alpine skiing was the Alpine Combined. The event consisted of two slalom and two downhill runs, for both men and women.

Canada's Diana Gordon-Lennox raced in both events with one of her arms in a cast and skiing with one pole. She placed twenty-ninth, and actually wore a glass monocle to improve her eyesight while doing so. The monocle is now displayed at the Canadian Ski Museum in Ottawa. Norwegian Birger Ruud placed second in the downhill race and first in the 90 metre ski jump, an accomplishment that would be unheard of today in Olympic competition.

The Alpine Combined event was again held at the 1948 Olympics at St. Moritz, Switzerland, after World War II. Medals were also awarded to both men and women for the slalom event and the downhill event.

America's first mark in international ski racing was made by Gretchen Fraser, a Vancouver, Washington, housewife who surprisingly finished in second place behind Trude Jochum-

Alex Foster's rope tow at Shawbridge, Quebec, was the first in North America. *Canadian Ski Museum*

Beiser of Austria. Fraser jolted the Europeans again with a gold medal win in the slalom and Hedy Schlunegger of Switzerland won the downhill event. Henri Oreiller of France won both the men's Alpine Combined and the downhill. Edi Reinalter of Switzerland won the men's slalom.

The Alpine Combined event was discontinued at the 1952 Olympic Winter Games at Oslo, Norway. In its place, a new race—the giant slalom—was added to the Alpine events. The giant slalom was again a two-part affair but combined downhill and slalom skiing in a single race. And another American housewife, Andrea Meade Lawrence, from Rutland, Vermont, won the giant slalom and the slalom events.

One of the Alpine officials at the 1952 Olympics was slalom referee Sir Arnold Lunn. To referee a sport at the Olympics that he had invented was a significant achievement for Lunn, who had campaigned so long for Olympic recognition of the Alpine events.

The real superstar of the 1952 Olympics was Oslo's first Alpine gold medalist, Stein Eriksen. Eriksen won the least Nordic of skiing events, the Alpine giant slalom.

Eriksen left Norway for the United States in 1957, and directed ski schools in California, Colorado, Vermont, and Utah. Over the span of his skiing career, the ruggedly handsome Norwegian glamorized the life of a ski instructor. The idol of a thousand women, Eriksen's formula for success seemed simple enough. All a man needed was wealth, an Olympic gold medal, his own ski school, and the looks of a Viking.

Anton (Toni) Sailer, a handsome twenty-year-old from Kitzbuhel, Austria, captured the first Alpine triple crown win in Olympic history at the 1956 Winter Games at Cortina d'Ampezzo, Italy. After winning both the giant slalom and slalom events, nothing could stop Sailer, who careened downhill on a course so icy that eight competitors ended up in hospital.

Sailer's Games were the first televised in history and established a landmark ski boom in the industry. After his Olympic success, Sailer had a brief career as a movie star. Eventually he ended up in the ski clothing business, marketing one of the industry's most tightly appreciated inventions, the stretch pant. Involved with coaching the Austrian team during the 1970s,

Triple gold medal winner Toni Sailer in the starting gate at the 1956 Games. *Keystone Press AG, Switzerland*

and the ski school operations, Toni Sailer still resides in Kitz-buhel today.

Madeleine Berthod and Renée Colliard won golds in down-hill and slalom for Switzerland, and Ossi Reichert of Germany won the giant slalom.

By the time the 1956 Winter Games were staged, Canada had sent Alpine Olympic teams to three Olympics, but no skier had ever won a medal. Austrian master coach Pepi Salvenmoser changed all that with a young Canadian protégé he'd been train-ing in Kitzbuhel.

Lucile Wheeler's parents ran the famous resort hotel, the Gray Rocks Inn, in the Laurentians near St. Jovite, Quebec. Lucile started skiing at two years of age and by the time she was twelve, Ernie McCulloch had coached her all the way to the junior Canadian championship.

Lucile was the first Canadian skier to realize the benefits of European training, and went to Europe before the Games to train with Salvenmoser.

In her pre-Olympic season, the seventeen-year-old had worn out eight pairs of skis by training five hours a day. But at the Games, she was disqualified in her first slalom run. Neverthe-less, in the giant slalom event she placed a creditable sixth out of fifty entrants. Buoyed by her success, she went on to win a bronze medal in the downhill event. Wheeler's medal was the first Olympic medal ever won by a Canadian skier.

Two years later, Lucile won the downhill and giant slalom in the 1958 Worlds, Canada's first world championship titles.

Being at the right place at the right time was never one of Anderl Molterer's strengths. In 1952 he had shown downhill potential, but was considered too young to make the Austrian Olympic team.

After the 1952 Olympic Winter Games, Molterer won Europe's big three, the Lauberhorn, the Arlberg-Kandahar, and the Hahnenkamm. But, at the 1956 Olympics he had Toni Sailer to contend with, and placed second behind him in the giant slalom and third behind him in the downhill. He still hadn't won his Olympic gold medal. At the 1960 Olympics at Squaw Valley, California, he had been named to the Austrian down-hill and giant slalom team, but was dropped from the slalom team.

The downhill event was won by Jean Vuarnet of France, the first gold medalist to wear metal skis. Anderl Molterer placed a disconsolate nineteenth. Swiss skier Roger Staub was the surprise winner of the giant slalom and Molterer finished in twelfth place.

Molterer was invited to forerun the slalom as he wasn't a member of the Austrian slalom team. A fore-runner precedes the race and skis the course at racing speed. The times must not be published. His fore-run time in the slalom was one of the best of the day, although not many people knew about it.

Ernie McCulloch, considered one of the best all-round Alpine skiers in Canadian racing, could not compete in the Olympics as a professional, though he defeated the greats of his time. *Courtesy Ernie McCulloch.*

Anderl Molterer was probably Squaw Valley's most disappointed Olympian.

Ottawa's Anne Heggtveit didn't disappoint Canadians in her slalom event, even though she had missed the top ten in the downhill and giant slalom races.

Heggtveit had come a long way from the days when her father used to ski at Camp Fortune, in the Gatineau Hills, with his baby daughter strapped on his back. For years Anne Heggtveit had skied with Lucile Wheeler, and under Ernie McCulloch's coaching experienced her first international race in 1956. At fifteen years of age, she brought home Canada's first giant slalom win from Oppdal, Norway. In half a century of competition, Anne Heggtveit was the youngest person to win an event at the prestigious Holmenkollen.

Anne accompanied the Canadian ski team to the 1956 Olympics at Cortina, though not fully recovered from a broken leg she had sustained in 1955 at Mont Tremblant. After the Olympics, she followed Lucile Wheeler's example, and began to train with Pepi Salvenmoser. Pepi's training paid off when Heggtveit won the famous Arlberg-Kandahar race at Garmisch-Partenkirchen, West Germany in 1959. She was the first non-European to win the event.

Anne Heggtveit brought nineteen years of ski experience with her to the 1960 Olympic Winter Games, and was undoubtedly Canada's feature performer. Racing against a field of forty-one competitors, she skied superbly and won the gold medal. In a sport that defines winners and losers by hundredths of

seconds, Heggtveit's 3.3 second victory margin was remarkable.

In fact, Anne Heggtveit won three major skiing titles in 1960. She won a gold medal at Squaw Valley, the world championship Alpine combined title, and the world championship slalom title. And, realizing it would be pretty tough to top those accomplishments, she retired at age twenty-one.

Two sisters from France dominated the women's Alpine events at the 1964 Olympic Winter Games at Innsbruck, Austria. Nineteen-year-old Christine Goitschel won the slalom, and her eighteen-year-old sister Marielle won the giant slalom.

The sisters had contrasting personalities. Christine, the shyer of the two, was embarrassed by all the attention the media gave her after her gold medal win. Marielle, a veteran competitor with two world championships to her credit, loved to tease the press. Surrounded by a horde of media and photographers after her gold medal victory, she added to the pandemonium by announcing she was engaged to be married to the handsome star of the French Olympic team, Jean-Claude Killy. When journalists and reporters finally caught up with Killy at the Olympic Village, Jean-Claude said that his impending marriage was all news to him.

Austria's Egon Zimmerman won the gold medal for the host country in the downhill, but the event had been overshadowed by the death of a downhiller. Ross Milne, an Australian, was killed when he crashed into a tree on a practice run just before the Games opened. It was the first time in Olympic history that a skier had been killed.

United States skiers finally cracked the Olympic winners' circle with the second and third-place finishes of Billy Kidd and Jimmy Heuga in the men's slalom, behind gold medalist Josef "Pepi" Stiegler of Austria. The Olympic silver and bronze medals were the first won by the United States at the Winter Games.

Anne Heggtveit's gold medal victory at the 1960 Games was a Canadian first for an alpine skier. *Canada Sports Hall of Fame*

Nancy Greene placed seventh in the women's downhill event. It was won by sturdy Austrian Christl Hass, who won her gold medal on an almost snowless course. In fact, the one missing ingredient at the Innsbruck Games was snow, and there were no snowmaking machines at the sites. Olympic organizers had the Austrian army haul in almost 20,000 cubic metres of snow from the surrounding mountain passes during the games.

In 1966, the Grand Prix of the ski racing circuit, the World Cup, was inaugurated. The idea was inspired by ski writer Serge Lang, a sports journalist for *L'Equipe* newspaper.

For people who never got closer to a ski race than their television set, the World Cup point system seemed complicated, but the racers thrived on the competition. Throughout the season, competitive skiers raced for a system of points at pre-selected races in Europe and the United States. The best race results counted and the racer who amassed the most points in the downhill, slalom, and giant slalom won the Cup.

The objective of the World Cup competition was to declare the world's best skier every year instead of every four years at the Olympics. The Alpine skiing community was the first sports federation to initiate a World Cup event, a format that has been copied by many other winter sport governing bodies today. The World Cup series brings together the top athletes in the world to compete at an international level.

The first winner of the World Cup in 1967 was Jean-Claude Killy of France. He won all three disciplines, a record that still stands. The first winner of the women's World Cup was Nancy Greene from Rossland, British Columbia.

Nancy Greene was born into a skiing family and all six Greene children skied the slopes of Red Mountain every winter. Nancy and her older sister, Elizabeth, were members of the B.C. junior team, and both were intensely competitive, especially with each other. At the 1958 Canadian junior championships at Rossland, fourteen-year-old Nancy finished second in the downhill, just seconds behind Elizabeth. From that day on, Nancy's greatest ambition was to beat her sister in any competition open to them.

Within two years the sisters were named as members of the Canadian ski team that competed at the 1960 Olympic Winter Games at Squaw Valley, California. Nancy's roommate at the Olympic Village was Anne Heggtveit, and as she watched her receive her gold medal on the victory podium, Nancy Greene made herself a promise. Greene vowed that one day she would have the same experience, and from that day forward her quest for an Olympic gold medal became her own personal crusade.

Nancy knew that Canada's two Olympic medalists had both raced and trained in Europe. She could no more afford that than could her coach and fellow Rosslander, Verne Anderson. But Lucile Wheeler and Anne Heggtveit hadn't grown up in a ski crazy town like Rossland, B.C. When hometown fans found out about the situation they launched a door-knocking campaign in 1961 that raised $3,500. Nancy Greene and Verne Anderson headed overseas at Christmas with the Canadian National Ski Team.

From then on, Nancy embarked on a decade of winter training in Europe and summer training on the glaciers of Canada

Nancy "Tiger" Greene demonstrates the determination that made her an Olympic silver and gold medalist at the 1968 Games in Grenoble, France. *Canadian Sports Hall of Fame*

and South America. No stranger to broken legs, sprained ankles, dislocated shoulders, and DNFs (Did Not Finish), Nancy was nicknamed "Tiger" by her racing buddies.

The last World Cup race of the 1967 season at Jackson Hole, Wyoming, was a showdown between Nancy and her two archrivals, Marielle Goitschel and Florence Steurer of France.

In the middle of the season, Nancy had lost her first place World Cup standing when she returned to Canada with the National Team to fund-raise and promote Canada's first international ski meet, the du Maurier.

In her absence, the two French skiers had amassed more points than Greene, and the only way she could keep Goitschel and Steurer from winning the World Cup was to win all three races herself. It was the kind of situation Nancy Greene thrived on. The final World Cup totals: Nancy Greene 176, Marielle Goitschel 172. Canada had its first World Cup champion.

The skiers to beat in the Alpine events at the 1968 Olympic Winter Games at Grenoble, France, were Nancy Greene and Jean-Claude Killy. Although they were both the best skiers in the world, they had very different characters. Nancy was a healthy outdoors type who resembled everyone's favourite kid-sister. Killy, on the other hand, was a fun-loving French playboy who not only was the best skier in the world, but also a keen Formula 1 auto racer. Throughout his skiing career, Killy had proved himself as an exceptionally talented and technically

Jean-Claude Killy on his way to winning the gold medal for France in the giant slalom race in 1968. *Deutsche Presse-Agentur GmbH*

innovative racer. One of his biggest contributions to racing technique was his kickstart manoeuvre that propelled him out of the start gate. The technique, still in use today, was necessitated by the updated electronic timing and Killy taught racers throughout the world how to get enough of a lead out of the start gate to win races.

It was common knowledge that several racers on the circuit were sponsored by ski manufacturers who wanted the racers to endorse their equipment on television. International Olympic Committee President Avery Brundage was not impressed. He put a ban on all trademarks and trade names on skis at the Games, and insisted that no racer could hold up skis to be photographed at the finish line.

Nevertheless, when Jean-Claude Killy flashed across the finish line in a gold medal time in the downhill, television cameras zoomed in for close-up shots of his gloves and jackets emblazoned with manufacturers' trademarks. The commercialization of Alpine skiing at the Winter Games had begun, much to Brundage's chagrin.

Killy's only easy win was the giant slalom. He seemed to luxuriate in controversy and he had more than his share of it in the slalom race. Most of it centred around Austria's Karl Schranz.

Killy won the first run of the race, and Schranz came third. A thick fog rolled in on Schranz's second run and he stopped at Gate 21 after missing Gates 18 and 19. He claimed that he

had been distracted by a course policeman who had walked across the course above Gate 21. The start referee consented to give Schranz a provisional re-run, but cautioned him that the decision would be subject to a final judgement by race officials after the event.

Schranz's re-run put him in first place for the gold and Killy finished in second place. Then the French lodged a protest.

How, claimed the French, could Schranz have been so distracted to miss Gates 18 and 19 by someone on the course further down at Gate 21? The fact remained, the French insisted, that Schranz had missed two gates and he should be disqualified. The jury voted to accept the protest. It was amid bitter controversy that Jean-Claude Killy won his third gold medal. He joined Toni Sailer in an elite club of two racers to have won all three Olympic gold medals in the Alpine ski events.

Nancy Greene had two objectives in 1968. One was to win the World Cup again, and the other was to win a gold medal at the Olympics. But her medal seemed a long way away after her tenth-place finish in the downhill, leaving the gold to Olga Pall of Austria. Nancy had used the wrong wax, and the disappointment was terrible. The slalom was next and her pessimism vanished when she found herself close to the top after the first run. On her second run, she came from behind to win the silver medal. It was the proudest moment of her skiing career.

Yet, she still wanted her gold medal and decided matter-of-factly that she was going to win one in her final event. And when Nancy whipped across the finish line in the giant slalom she knew she had done it. Later she said that once it had finally happened, she could hardly believe it. "I feel great," she said. "It is the best race I've ever skied."

Nancy was at the peak of her skiing career, and after the Games won four World Cup races. By the end of March, Nancy had an unbeatable lead in her World Cup points. The end of her storybook year came on the slopes of Red Mountain in Rossland in her last race of the 1968 season. Her hometown fans cheered her on to victory and her second consecutive World Cup. The 1968 World Cup was her last skiing victory and for the second year in a row, Nancy Greene was voted Canada's top female athlete.

In 1969 Nancy married Al Raine of Vancouver, the coach of the National Ski Team. Compared to Nancy's meagre 1960 Olympic team budget, head coach Al Raine had an annual budget of $600,000 for coaches, racers, scholarships, and summer training.

The National Ski team was definitely in the ski business full-tilt, and so was Calgary's "Jungle" Jim Hunter. A farm boy from Shaunavon, Saskatchewan, eleven-year-old Jim Hunter first tried skiing while being towed around the farm by a rope attached to a horse. When he grew tired of that, his father pulled him behind the half-ton truck speeding along the country roads. Jim would ski in the deep snow in the ditches, holding onto a forty-foot rope attached to the rear bumper of the pickup.

The Hunter family moved to Calgary when Jim was twelve and spent summers on the farm in Shaunavon. Training in Calgary with the Skimeisters, Jim worked his way up through the junior ranks and tried out for the Alberta team in 1968. He didn't make it. "Not good enough," the coaches said.

Hunter decided to skip the provincial team and wrote a letter to Al Raine. After skiing with Raine for a day, sixteen-year-old Jim Hunter was invited to train with the National Team at Lake Louise, Alberta. "I go as fast as I can every day, every time, and take as many chances as I can," said Hunter. The gung-ho Hunter quickly earned the nickname "Jungle Jim" from his team-mates.

In previous years, the men's Canadian National Ski Team hadn't picked up anything at the Olympics except experience. As the Canadian ski coaches looked ahead to the 1972 Olympics at Sapporo, Japan, a decision was made to develop a core of young racers who had strong technical backgrounds in slalom, giant slalom, and especially downhill.

"Jungle" Jim Hunter's hell-bent-for-leather style may have started in the roadside ditches of Saskatchewan, but it suited the new philosophy of the National Ski team perfectly. By 1971 Hunter had earned his points on the World Cup circuit with a ninth-place finish in the giant slalom at Heavenly Valley, California. He topped off his season by winning the Can-Am championships at Whistler, British Columbia.

Back at work on the farm at Shaunavon for the summer, Jim Hunter prepared for the 1972 Olympics. The prairie flatlands were a good place to practise balancing in his racing tuck position at seventy miles an hour. All he needed was his father's

half-ton. He nailed an old pair of skis onto a raised platform he had built at the back of the truck. When he stepped into the skis and got into his racing crouch, he was just higher than the top of the cab. As his father raced the truck along the back country roads around Shaunavon, "Jungle" Jim Hunter practised handling wind resistance, the Saskatchewan way.

The first Olympic Winter Games to be held outside Europe or America took place at Sapporo, Japan, in 1972 and the Games opened in an explosive atmosphere.

Eighty-four-year-old Avery Brundage, then the President of the International Olympic Committee, had announced he would retire after the 1972 Olympiad. That was too late as far as Austrian ski hero Karl Schranz was concerned. Schranz had been racing on the ski circuit for fifteen years and had won everything in Alpine skiing except an Olympic gold medal. Granted, he had won a gold in the 1968 Olympics, but had to give it back to Jean-Claude Killy when he'd been disqualified.

Karl Schranz was the son of a poor railway worker from St. Anton and was a self-made man. He had acknowledged publicly that he was paid almost $50,000 a year for ski equipment endorsements, a blatant violation of the rules of amateurism.

Just before the Games, Schranz had criticized Avery Brundage in a newspaper article by calling him a millionaire with no understanding of penniless amateur athletes. He demanded that the IOC change its attitude toward professionalism or the Olympics would end up being Games only for the very rich. By going public with a statement like that, Karl Schranz lost the support of many members of the Alpine ski community, and he succeeded in singling himself out as someone who had gone just a little too far.

Brundage was infuriated by the statement made by Schranz, and called a meeting of the IOC members. Three days before the Games were to begin, Karl Schranz was banned from the Olympics.

The much anticipated showdown of world champion Bernhard Russi of Switzerland and Karl Schranz was destined never to take place, and Russi was presented with his gold medal for winning the downhill.

Gustav Thoeni won Italy's first medal since 1952 in the men's giant slalom but the big surprise was Francisco Fernandez Ochoa's gold medal win in the slalom, the first ever won by Spain in the Winter Olympics. At a press conference following his medal presentation Ochoa was so overwhelmed by emotion that he was unable to speak.

Switzerland's Marie-Thérèse Nadig won both the women's giant slalom and the downhill. The downhill provided one of the biggest upsets at the Games. Prior to the Olympics, Nadig's best finish had been a fifth in international competition and the big favourite to win the gold had been an Austrian racer. Austria's Annemarie Moser-Pröll's defeat was one of the most devastating of her career. America's Barbara Cochran's two hundredths of a second victory in the slalom made Olympic history. It was the narrowest win ever recorded for a gold.

"Jungle" Jim Hunter was disappointed. In his first Olympics he had finished in nineteenth place in the slalom, twen-

Young Jim Hunter is pulled by his brother behind his horse on the family farm at Shaunavon, Saskatchewan. *Courtesy Jim Hunter*

tieth in the downhill, and eleventh in the giant slalom. But, he was in for a pleasant surprise.

The Alpine Combined had been awarded as an official Olympic medal for the last time at the 1948 Winter Games. The medal was still presented by the International Ski Federation at the closing ceremonies, and the winner was determined by the FIS points earned in each of the three Alpine events. It was an International Ski Federation medal, and although not an Olympic medal, eighteen-year-old Jim Hunter was awarded the world championship Alpine Combined bronze for his third-place finish.

At the first race of the 1972-73 season, Hunter broke into the top five with his fourth-place finish in the World Cup race at Val d'Isère, France. It was the best finish ever for a Canadian male racer.

The 1973 ski season also marked the introduction of four new recruits onto the National team. For more than a decade, they would keep pretty fast company. Ken Read, Dave Irwin, Dave Murray, and Steve Podborski were destined to become Canada's new force in the most prestigious of all Alpine events—the downhill.

Relaxed and friendly Dave Murray of Abbotsford, British Columbia, was the late bloomer of the new rookies. He had begun racing at the relatively late age of fifteen, and by 1973 was a member of the World Cup Team.

Calgarian Ken Read started skiing when he was three years old, and at eight had started racing. Read worked his way up in the Pontiac Cup, a ski series for young Canadians. At seventeen, he was racing internationally in the Europa Cup, a type of farm league to the World Cup circuit.

Steve Podborski of Don Mills, Ontario, started to ski before he started kindergarten. At sixteen, he was on the National ski team, and had won both the North American and Canadian Junior Downhills by the time he was eighteen.

Injury-prone Dave Irwin from Thunder Bay, Ontario, was destined as a wonder of human survival, and for nine years would be a devoted member of Canada's daring kamikazes, the Crazy Canucks.

In the early 1970s, downhill skiing was dominated by the Austrians and their great racer, Franz Klammer, who pioneered a new era of the ski racing specialist. Instead of competing in all three events, he opted to concentrate his efforts on downhill.

Franz Klammer had a record of eight straight downhill wins in the 1974-75 season. In comparison, the Canadian World Cup downhill results had been less than impressive. Prior to the 1974-75 season, the Canadians had only one single top-ten finish by Jim Hunter.

Canada's National Team head coach was intrigued with Klammer's downhill performance. Scott Henderson was an old downhiller himself, and had competed in the 1964 Olympics at Innsbruck, Austria.

When the National Team started summer training on the glaciers of South America and Europe, coach Henderson initiated an all-out assault on downhill. His five young racers had enthusiasm and competitiveness. Henderson used both qualities to generate the best possible results individually, and as a team. The success of one team member was viewed as a success for all. The tightly knit group was held together by a common goal to beat the Europeans, and they had nowhere to go but downhill.

As a rule, the racers who win are seeded in the top group of the first fifteen, and have the advantage of racing when the course conditions are good. It takes years of racing and dedicated hard work to break into the prestigious top racing group.

A jubilant Canadian ski team is all smiles after placing five racers in the top ten at a World Cup race at Val D'Isère, France in 1980. Left to right are: Dave Murray (7th place finish), Ken Read (a close second), Steve Podborski (in 3rd spot), Dave Irwin (5th place finish), and Chris Kent (4th place finish). *Courtesy of Serge Lang/Walter Keller*

"Jungle" Jim Hunter was the first Crazy Canuck to make it into the top group in 1973. Ken Read was the second to make it in 1975.

A competitor's starting place is decided by the coach who draws the numbers of the team on the morning of the event. Number-one spot is not a favourite, as generally times for the first racer are slower than for the competitors who race later. Not only must the first racer ski through new snow, he must also establish a line for the rest of the field.

The 1975 World Cup season kicked off at Val d'Isère, France. As coach Scott Henderson left for the race draw Read said: "I'll bet you draw number one for me." When his coach returned with the race numbers, Henderson handed Ken Read's to him and said: "Looks like you got the number you wanted."

It was number one. On December 7, 1975, Ken Read chalked up a few firsts. Wearing number one, Ken Read started from the first seed, for the first time, in the first race of the Men's World Cup Downhill, and placed first. "They are absolutely flabbergasted," beamed an ecstatic Ken Read as he was mobbed by racing fans and reporters at the finish line.

What the Austrians and the Swiss were flabbergasted about was Ken Read. At twenty years of age, the handsome Calgarian became the first North American to win a men's World Cup Downhill. Not only had Ken Read beaten the invincible Franz Klammer, but Hunter, Irwin, and Podborski all placed in the top ten. It was the first ever victory for Canada.

Sports reporter Serge Lang was in awe. In all his years of covering the World Cup, he'd never seen such a wild and aggressive group of skiers race a downhill. Lang wrote a feature article in the newspaper *L'Equipe* about the race with an accompanying photo of an airborne Ken Read showing his breakneck

style at 102 kph. The newspaper story was entitled the "Kamikaze Kanadians." The Canadian press picked up the news story and changed the name to the Crazy Canucks.

Those who knew skiing in Canada knew what the Crazy Canucks had achieved. Two weeks later, Dave Irwin proved to the ski crazy Austrians that the Crazy Canucks had a "new" way to race the downhill when he won another World Cup race at Schladming, Austria.

In 1975, the average Canadian wasn't too interested in hurtling down ski slopes in pursuit of fractions of seconds. It was different in Europe. With thousands of aspirants to choose from each year, the competition for national team selection was vicious.

The Canadian squad was small and the Europeans were both impressed and envious of the spirit of camaraderie the Canadians shared. The Canucks would study the downhill course as a group, and were one of the first racing teams in history to use two-way radio communication. The first down to the bottom in the race would report via radio to his or her mates at the top.

The Austrian and the Swiss racers found it incredible that the Canadians co-operated with each other. Not only were the members of the European teams not inclined to help each other, the rivalry between the Swiss and Austrians was intense and deep-seated.

The team spirit of the Canadians worked well for everyone, with one exception. As far as Betsy Clifford was concerned, skiing was an individual sport. As a member of the national team, she found it difficult to accept the team-person psychology. "Nobody coaches me," she once said. "I have to do it myself."

Apparently she did that very well. At ten, Betsy was rac-

Betsy Clifford discovered it wasn't easy to follow in Nancy Greene's footsteps. *Canada Sports Hall of Fame*

Jim Hunter and Kathy Kreiner celebrate Kathy's gold medal win at the 1976 Games. *Canada Sports Hall of Fame*

ing for the world's largest ski club, Camp Fortune, near Ottawa. At fourteen she was the youngest skier in Olympic history to compete at the 1968 Olympic Winter Games. At sixteen, she won the giant slalom at Val Gardena, Italy, and became the youngest-ever World champion.

But the eighteen-year-old's dream of competing in the 1972 Olympics came to a tragic end when she broke both her heels while training in Switzerland.

Betsy returned to the racing circuit after the Olympics and won the 1972-73 Can-Am overall title on North America's top

circuit. At the 1974 World Championships at St. Moritz, she won the silver medal in the downhill.

Despite her success, Betsy Clifford's problems began to mount as the 1976 Olympic Winter Games approached. Conflicts with her coaches and expectations that she was the gold medal successor to Nancy Greene were compounded by the fact she was tired and fed-up with life on the racing circuit. An unsympathetic Canadian press and a public who perhaps should have known better contributed to her disappointing 1976 Olympic results. She finished in twenty-second place in both giant slalom and downhill, with a DNF in the slalom. At the end of the 1976 ski season, Betsy Clifford announced her retirement.

Everyone loves a winner and West German Rosi Mittermaier looked like the big one at the 1976 Olympic Winter Games at Innsbruck, Austria. Her chances increased for the first women's Olympic grand slam with wins in the downhill and slalom events. All she had left to win was the giant slalom.

With all the media attention being lavished on Mittermaier, eighteen-year-old Kathy Kreiner had been virtually unnoticed at the Games. A native of Timmins, Ontario, twelve-year-old Kathy skied out of obscurity in 1968 as the youngest racer to win the Taschereau downhill at Mont Tremblant, Quebec. Since the age of fourteen, she had skied on Canada's National Team with her older sister Laurie. She and Laurie were both members of the 1972 Olympic Team at Sapporo, Japan. During the 1974 season, Kathy won her first World Cup gold medal in the giant slalom at Pfronten, West Germany.

On the day of the Olympic giant slalom at Innsbruck, Kathy Kreiner drew number one. "What a bad number," she said to Jim Hunter at breakfast time. But the day before, Jim Hunter had watched Ernst Good of Switzerland race down the giant slalom course first. The Swiss skiing ace won his first run. Hunter noticed the course had deteriorated after the first few skiers and the men who had gone down first had recorded the best times. "Kathy," he said, "you've got the best number on the hill." And, with a victory margin of 0.33 seconds over Rosi Mittermaier, Kathy Kreiner proved Jim Hunter was right.

When the race was over, Hunter leaped over the fence into the finish area and lifted Kathy up on his shoulders. As a participant in his last Olympic Games, "Jungle" Jim shared Kathy Kreiner's moment of victory.

Twenty-two-year-old Franz Klammer was a man under pressure. The Austrian was the favourite to win the downhill and had clocked some of the best times in the training runs.

It was not unusual for the great Franz Klammer to win all of his training runs during practice, and then win the official race. But at Innsbruck, the training runs had turned into one long horserace with Klammer winning one, Russi winning the next one, Anton Steiner taking the following one, and Ken Read winning another one.

Read's strategy between the first and second timing intervals had paid off when he posted the fastest times on the Bareneck section of the course. By developing a direct line through the sweeping turns leading into the drop off, he could ski closer to the edge and take some spectacular air time off the bump instead of keeping his skis on the snow like the rest of the racers. Although the manoeuvre carried more speed, it was also more of a risk, and on race day Ken Read decided to ski a more conservative line and finish in one piece.

The course at the 1976 Winter Games was one of the best downhills ever designed for the Olympics. Switzerland's Bernhard Russi set the pace with the best time, Anton Steiner fell, and Ken Read finished with a time good enough to put him into the top four. Then Klammer, skiing in fifteenth place, took off from the starting gate.

Racing in fifteenth position was less than ideal for the Austrian. The course, lined with seventy thousand fans, had deteriorated after the first few racers and, to make matters worse, Klammer made a major error at the top when he skidded out of a turn, losing valuable seconds. Franz Klammer knew he had to ski the race of his life, and to make up for lost time, he took Ken Read's line through the Bareneck. Even the Crazy Canucks had never seen anything like Klammer's hair-raiser of a finish that seemed beyond the limits of human achievement. And, it was Ken Read's line between the first and second timing intervals, and his own performance on the last 1,000 metres of the downhill, that won Franz Klammer his coveted gold medal.

Ken Read stood at the finish line unaware that Franz Klammer had used his own abandoned strategy to take top honours. Serge Lang walked over to Read and asked him: "Why didn't you take the line you took during all your training runs?" When Ken Read told him, Lang replied, "Franz Klammer just skied your run." Ken Read finished fifth, Bernhard Russi won the silver, and Italian Herbert Plank took the bronze.

Franz Klammer won the 1976 Olympic downhill by only a 0.33 second margin. The gold medal marked Klammer's last Olympic performance and his downhill results suffered a decline after the Games due to equipment problems and injuries.

Injuries seem to be written into the script of some racers, and for Dave Irwin to experience his first serious injury just one month before the 1976 Olympics was the cruelest twist of fate.

The 1975-76 season was proving to be Irwin's best. His World Cup victory at Schladming, Austria, had put him in contention for the number-one world ranking with Franz Klammer. But as he exploded out of the start gate at Wengen, Switzerland, his Olympic dream would be sabotaged. Just seconds into his run, Irwin hurtled out of control on the same bump Ken Read had fallen on moments before. He bounced down the course at 120 kph and slammed into the protective netting and hay bales along the side.

Read, first to arrive at the scene of Irwin's spectacular crash, relayed the ominous news to the coaches via two-way radio. "Irwin's skis and equipment destroyed," said Read, "blood-filled goggles." Within fifteen minutes of his terrifying crash, Irwin was in a rescue helicopter en route to hospital. His smashed eye glasses caused multiple facial lacerations, and he had two broken ribs and an eight-day concussion.

Three weeks later Irwin was back on his skis at the Olympic Games. With tape wrapped around his broken ribs, Dave Irwin astonished his team-mates with an eighth-place finish in the downhill. Jim Hunter finished tenth, but Ken Read, the original Kamikaze Kid, rocketed into Olympic history by cracking the Austro-Swiss monopoly in the downhill. His fifth-place time of 1:46.83 was the best ever for a North American male skier.

Steve Podborski passed up the 1976 Olympics in favour of a plaster cast. Just weeks before the Olympics, Steve suffered a high speed fall at 85 kph on the Hahnenkamm at Kitzbuhel. The hard-luck Canuck flew home to Canada for his first of two knee operations he would have during his decade of racing.

Nevertheless, with three Canadians in the top ten at the Olympics, the Crazy Canucks were looking not-so-crazy.

The only victories for the Crazy Canucks during the 1976-77 season were two wins by Ken Read. A Canadian first was recorded with his fastest downhill ever, averaging a speed of 117 kph at Cortina d'Ampezzo in Italy. Another first-place finish at Sugarloaf in America kept him in the first group.

The downhill style of the Crazy Canucks was aggressive, not reckless, and many argued that the team's nickname was a misnomer. It wasn't for Dave Irwin. Irwin skied at full throttle all the time, and was the most physically powerful of all the Canucks.

Irwin started the 1976-77 season with his second serious injury. The Crazy Canucks had been training at Cortina d'Ampezzo, Italy, for the first race of the season, the FIS downhill in December. The day of the race, the course was glare ice from top to bottom and much slicker than it had been for the training runs. The fenced-off finish area was poorly planned by officials who had underestimated the distance it would take racers to stop.

As Dave Irwin tucked through the last set of control gates, he was unable to stop in the short confines of the finish area and slammed into the barricades. He crumpled onto the snow in a heap of hay bales, skis, and fencing. With his second major concussion in less than a year, Dave Irwin was advised by coaches to return home to Thunder Bay to fully recover.

Irwin returned to the National Team in 1977 and started his fall training on the Hintertux Glacier in Austria with a renewed enthusiasm. On one of his first training runs of the 1977 season, Irwin leaned into a turn as he cruised around a blind corner. He looked up just in time to see a shadow moving across the course. At the apex of his turn, Irwin collided with coach Heinz Kappeler at 90 kph.

Passing over the back of Kappeler's skis, Irwin hit him in the back with his left thigh, and knocked him flying. After spinning around, Dave Irwin cart-wheeled head-first down a five metre embankment. Back in hospital at Thunder Bay, doctors diagnosed two compression fractures in Irwin's back. He was unable to bend his left leg due to calcium deposits in his swollen left thigh.

Physicians advised surgery; Irwin declined. Instead he worked his way back to health with his own exercise regimen. At Christmas he was skiing at Thunder Bay, and by March he was back with the National Team.

In spite of the Olympic victories of the year before and

The great Franz Klammer skis the race of his life and wins gold in the 1976 men's Olympic downhill event. *Deutsche Presse-Agentur GmbH*

Ken Read's two top placings in the 1976-77 season, the team spirit hit an all-time low. Technical problems related to finances, racing suits, ski waxes, and coaching resulted in an unsuccessful year. "Jungle" Jim Hunter announced he would leave the amateur ranks at the end of the year to try his hand at professional racing. In October of 1977, just weeks before the beginning of the 1977-78 season, coach Scott Henderson was fired.

Two new coaches, Heinz Kappeler and John Ritchie, took over the Crazy Canucks, and top-ten results came immediately. After a winless year and a half, Ken Read ended the drought with his second World Cup victory at Chamonix, France, in 1978. Team-mate Dave Murray finished up in second place for a one, two Canadian finish.

The Canucks' assault on the World Cup races continued at Schladming, Austria, for the new season of 1978. Ken Read and Dave Murray placed first and second respectively. Dave Irwin finished seventh and Steve Podborski ninth.

After an absence of two years with injuries, Irwin's seventh-place finish at Schladming was remarkable. Racing thirty-ninth, he finished only sixty-hundredths of a second behind winner Ken Read. It looked like the cards were finally stacked in his favour.

The best starting positions for downhillers are in the top fifteen, not the higher numbers. By the time half the field of competitors has raced the course, conditions can be rough and snow sparse. The week after his success at Schladming, Dave Irwin had again drawn a high start number at the downhill event at Val Garděna, Italy. By the time Irwin pushed out of the start gate, bare spots had started to show through at the intermediate section of the course. He looked smooth and fast on the upper section of the course as he approached the three big rollers known as the Camel Bumps.

On the last of the three bumps, Irwin passed over an exposed flat rock and his skis ground to a halt. He was catapulted five metres forward into space and bounced like a rag-doll down the course. Those who saw the splatter thought it was the end of Dave Irwin. A major concussion, a temporary paralysis of the left side, facial lacerations, and a fractured knee cap would have left most racers senseless. Not Dave Irwin. After three weeks of recuperation in Canada, he was back in Europe racing on the Europa Cup circuit.

Marzine-Avoriaz, a little ski resort on the Franco-Swiss border, played host to one of the biggest World Cup upsets in history in January 1979. Steve Podborski was first out on the downhill course and posted the best time until number fourteen came down. It was Ken Read, and his run was spectacular. He beat Podborski's time by forty one-hundredths of a second. But the elation for their one, two victory was short-lived. The Italians lodged a protest and the controversy centred around Ken Read's new racing suit.

The Italians had introduced one-piece plastic racing suits in 1970. The skin-tight suits cut down on wind resistance and improved race results. Unfortunately, when the Italians fell in a race, they couldn't stop. At Val d'Isère in 1975, one racer skidded down the course like a greased pig and landed up in the trees after a chilling 182 metre fall. Shortly after the incident, the FIS officially banned the plastic racing suits and to ensure safety requirements were met, imposed arbitrary permeability standards on all racing suits manufactured after 1978.

When Read's racing suit was tested after the race, the minimum requirements were not met, and he was disqualified. It was the first and only race that he had ever had taken away from him.

Steve Podborski moved up to first place, and his victory was his first on the World Cup circuit. The 1978-79 ski season was Podborski's best, and he finished among the top ten in all but one of his World Cup downhills. Ken Read was runner-up to the World Cup downhill title.

The year prior to the 1980 Olympic Winter Games, Dave Murray and Ken Read were less than a ski length of beating each other at races, and both in pursuit of Olympic gold.

In preparation for the Winter Games, it is compulsory that each Olympic site host pre-Olympic trials the year before the Games are staged. The trials are a final check for the technicians, officials, and volunteers who run the competition. Generally, the winners of the official Olympic events are predetermined by the winners of the pre-Olympics.

At Lake Placid, New York, the winners of the 1979 pre-Olympic downhill were Peter Wirnsberger of Austria, Peter Müeller of Switzerland, and David Murray of Canada. They placed first, second, and third. Murray's third-place finish at Lake Placid indicated he was a strong contender for the 1980 Olympic Winter Games.

Ken Read's 1979-80 season was one of triumph and tragedy. He opened his season with a fall in the downhill at Val d'Isère in France and used the wrong wax at Val Gardena, Italy, and finished in seventh place. At Pra Loup in France he placed fourteenth. Then he turned on the jets and won two consecutive World Cup downhills.

Read won Kitzbuhel's storied Hahnenkamm and David Irwin placed fifth. Steve Podborski had skied superbly in his training runs, but fell at the top of the course and badly bruised his ankle. The next race on the circuit was at Wengen, Switzerland, and Ken Read won it. Steve Podborski skied on a severely swollen ankle, and placed eighth.

Read and Podborski then finished in second and third place in the following race in Switzerland. Read lost to Peter Müeller by only two hundredths of a second. The third-place finish for Podborski was his best of the season.

All eyes were on the Crazy Canucks as they headed into the Olympic Games at Lake Placid. But, the Austrians had the ultimate weapon in Leonhard Stock, an alternate team member.

Compared to the record of the Crazy Canucks, Leonhard Stock's downhill career had been less than memorable. In fact, he had never won a major race in World Cup downhill before he arrived at the 1980 Olympics.

Based on Austria's famous downhills at Kitzbuhel and Schladming, the downhill course at Lake Placid's Whiteface Mountain was different. The 3,028 metre-long slope was shorter and it had a cover of man-made snow. Most Europeans had to adapt skis, base waxes, and racing technique to the man-made conditions, but not Leonhard Stock. He found Whiteface Mountain to his liking, and proved it by recording the fastest times on the first two training runs.

Austrian Alpine officials, anxious to repeat the 1976 Olympic medal of Franz Klammer, faced a dilemma. Stock was promoted to a starter along with Harti Weirather. The remaining three members had one run to determine who would be dropped from the four-member team. World champion Josef Walcher lost. The fact that the Olympic gold medalist Franz Klammer and the world champion were not on the team indicated the depth of talent the Austrians had to choose from.

For millions of Canadians who watched the 1980 downhill event on television, Ken Read's Olympic performance may remain in their memories for all the wrong reasons. The two-way release of the ski binding eliminates injury at high speeds and is of primary importance to the competitor. Conversely, the premature release of a binding at 100 kph is nothing but dangerous. To avoid such a situation, a racing binding is designed with a heavy spring in the heel with only releases when incredibly strong forces are applied to it.

Ken Read's 1980 Olympics lasted fifteen seconds. He had skied through three gates at the top of Hurricane Alley when his binding released prematurely, and he stepped out of his left

Ken Read crashes at the 1980 Games at Lake Placid, New York, as his left ski binding releases prematurely. *Robert Riger, ABC Sports*

ski. Assistant coach Heinz Kappeler watched from the sidelines in disbelief. Read somersaulted twice and ended up vertical, just in time to see Steve Podborski race by. The entire episode had taken less than one minute. "This one's going to be hard to forget," said Read.

Steve Podborski was irate. He realized how painful the loss was for his friend Ken Read, and, to add insult to injury, Austria's Leonhard Stock had come out of nowhere to post the best time of the day.

Podborski was also fed up with the North American press. Overseas, he and the Crazy Canucks were the toast of European ski connoisseurs and projected a diplomatic vision of Canada. The handsome trilingual Canadians breezed through press conferences and had been the subject of several television documentaries in ski-mad Europe.

But in their own backyard at Lake Placid, the media asked the Canucks at what age they had learned to ski, and why they had holes in the tips of their downhill skis.

Because the press hadn't done its homework, Podborski figured a Crazy Canuck demonstration might draw them a picture. His downhill performance was the season's quintessential sampling of Canadian talent at its finest, and Steve Podborski walked off with the bronze medal.

Stephen Gregory Podborski was the first North American male to ever win an Olympic medal for downhill skiing. In spite of the bronze medal win, Steve Podborski exhibited an amazing post-race composure after his illustrious Olympic achievement. To an astonished North American press, he indicated that it was just a typical day of downhill racing for him.

From 1975 to 1983, Sweden's Ingemar Stenmark won the World Cup for giant slalom seven times and the slalom eight times. His record still stands. But, when he entered the 1980 Olympics at Lake Placid, he had never won an Olympic medal. If only he could win one, he said, then he would be happy.

Stenmark, the Silent Swede, was known for his slow starts in both slalom and giant slalom. A man of few words, he said he skied better when he was angry. In the slalom event, Phil Mahre of White Pass, Washington, beat Stenmark by half a second in the first run. Mahre's run was one of courage. He had suffered a severe ankle break at the 1979 pre-Olympics at Lake Placid, and his doctor had designed a plate with three screws in it to hold the bones of his ankle together. He skied four slalom runs and one downhill with the metal plate during the 1980 Olympics. But Mahre's second slalom was not as good as his first, and Stenmark picked up his speed in his second run and won the gold medal. He ran true to form in the giant slalom, finishing fourth in his first run and winning the second, for a double-gold victory.

Giant slalom silver medalist Andreas Wenzel was half of a brother-and-sister team from the tiny country of Liechtenstein. Hanni Wenzel had never won an Olympic medal before entering the Lake Placid Games. By the time the closing ceremonies were held, she had won the gold in the giant slalom and slalom, and silver in the downhill. Her Olympic medal wins matched the accomplishments of Rosi Mittermaier at the 1976

Olympics. After the Games, the remarkable brother-and-sister duo won the men's and women's overall World Cup. The feat was impressive considering the population of Liechtenstein was only twenty-five thousand.

Austria's Annemarie Moser-Pröll's victory in the women's downhill was a well-deserved gold medal. Granted, she had retired for the 1975-76 season and did not participate in the 1976 Olympics, but she had won two silver medals in the 1972 Olympic Winter Games at Sapporo, Japan. From there, she had gone on to win the overall World Cup title six times, the downhill World Cup seven times, and the giant slalom World Cup three times. Her world championships included two bronze and two gold medals.

With credentials like that, she was the Olympic favourite and raced the downhill in near-perfect form, winning by 0.7 seconds.

Ken Read hoped to rebound from his Olympic disappointment at the first World Cup championships ever held at Lake Louise. He had accumulated seventy World Cup points during the racing season and was in contention for the World Cup, if he could beat Switzerland's Peter Müeller.

But, the bad-luck demon followed him to the championships. The showdown at Lake Louise was not won by either Read or Müeller, but by an Italian named Herbert Plank. Müeller finished in fourteenth place, and Read's eighth-place finish did not give the required World Cup points to the disappointed Crazy Canuck. Read lost the World Cup title to Peter Müeller by two points.

Read had never lost a race before on his home hill at Lake Louise, but nevertheless he had come closer to winning the men's World Cup than any other North American downhiller. As runner-up to the World Cup for the second year in a row, Read established himself as the first non-European to challenge the title of world supremacy in downhill. It set the stage for a Canadian assault on the last European bastion of ski racing. Read gave much of the credit for his success to Heinz Kappeler, his coach since 1977.

Late in May on the Hintertux Glacier in Austria, Steve Podborski capped off his most successful season ever by tearing all the ligaments in his right knee during a routine equipment testing run. After surgery Podborski spent his summer undergoing thirty hours a week of therapy to strengthen his knee. By October he was able to catch up with the team in Europe.

The 1980-81 downhill season opened at Val D'Isère, France, with a Canadian sweep. Uli Spiess of Austria won the race, followed in succession by Ken Read, Steve Podborski, Chris Kent, and Dave Irwin. Dave Murray finished seventh. Nineteen-year-old Kent from Calgary was the 1978-79 Canadian junior downhill champion. "To have this many guys in the top ten is unbelievable," Ken Read said triumphantly, as the Crazy Canucks soaked up the praise.

The second World Cup downhill of the season at Val Gardena, Italy, was won by Peter Müeller. Steve Podborski picked up a third-place bronze and Ken Read finished eleventh. Chris Kent, the teenage prodigy whose goal was to break into the top twenty during the season, rocketed out of control in the three enormous Camel Bumps, and injured his right knee. He was out for the season.

Next stop for the Canucks on the World Cup circuit was St. Moritz, Switzerland. The racers questioned if the Swiss had declared open season on the downhillers.

The training runs, held on a course that was far too fast, were marred by several injuries, including a spectacular fall by Uli Speiss, leader of the World Cup at that point. Speiss tore all the ligaments in his knee and the frightening fall had a devastating effect on his ski racing career. Equipment and ski technology was advancing rapidly, and the outdated course safety was not keeping pace with the changes. There had been twenty-six casualties during the first five races of the season. At St. Moritz, sixteen of the seventy-five racers decided to withdraw from the competition.

It had been seven months since Steve Podborski had torn all the ligaments in his right knee. At the time of his accident, Podborski had been written off by the experts as a doubtful starter for the next World Cup season. Instead, during his return season, he had finished in the top ten in all his downhill races.

Steve Podborski won the downhill. His remarkable victory, despite knee surgery the previous summer, moved him to the forefront of the Crazy Canucks. He led the World Cup downhill standings with sixty-one points.

Ken Read welcomed the New Year in with a stupendous header on January 10, 1981, at Garmisch-Partenkirchen, West Germany. He had posted the fastest times in the last two training runs, but as he came into his final turn 50 metres above the finish line on race day, he caught an edge in some soft snow, hit face first, broke his nose, and slashed open his forehead. His left ski binding did not release, and he tore two of the four major ligaments in his knee.

Knees do not give when a skier bounces and somersaults down a race course at 100 kph with his skis on. But, if your name is Ken Read, it's one way to make the acquaintance of an orthopedic surgeon who specializes in knee surgery. Read's bid to capture the World Cup had eluded him for the past two years, and the spill at Garmisch-Partenkirchen ended his season. In January of 1981, Ken Read passed on the legacy of the Crazy Canucks to Steve Podborski, just as "Jungle" Jim Hunter had passed it on to him in 1977.

Packing up his room-mate's blood-soaked racing helmet and stained racing suit for his flight back to Canada wasn't exactly how Steve Podborski had planned to celebrate his second World Cup victory with Ken Read. But, with his ski buddy gone, Podborski had his work cut out for him. The following week he picked up his hat-trick with a victory on the tough Hahnenkamm course at Kitzbuhel. The three-in-a-row victories had not been equalled since the great Franz Klammer had won all three in 1977.

The twenty-three-year-old Torontonian needed only one more victory to win the World Cup, but by the end of the season, his World Cup points were topped by Austria's Harti Weirather. It was another near-miss for the Canadians and Steve Podbor-

ski was the runner-up to the World Cup title. At the end of the season, Steve Podborski was ranked as the world's top downhiller of 1980-81 by the International Ski Federation.

The Crazy Canucks took in a new recruit for the 1982 season. Tall and powerful, six-foot Todd Brooker of Paris, Ontario, towered over his new team-mates. From the outset, he was Ken Read's protégé and at the end of his first season, Brooker was ranked seventh in the world.

Steve Podborski entered the 1982 World Cup season with the intention of winning the title and proceeded to chalk up his points. He opened his season with a fourth at Val D'Isère, France, and another fourth at Crans-Montana, Switzerland. At Kitzbuhel he placed second and first in two consecutive races. Then he crossed the Atlantic and followed the white circuit to Whistler Mountain, British Columbia. There he took a second-place finish before heading south to Aspen, Colorado, for the last two races on the circuit.

At that point, the World Cup championship was a three-way race between Steve Podborski and Austria's Harti Weirather and Peter Müeller. Weirather needed two wins to catch Podborski, but Müeller won both races. The World Cup circuit ended in a tie for first place between Podborski and Müeller with 115 points each.

Peter Müeller was the arch rival of the Crazy Canucks, and insiders knew it. He had won the World Cup for two years in a row, and had robbed Ken Read of his coveted championship by just .02 seconds in the previous season. But in January Steve Podborski had beaten Müeller in the prestigious Hahnenkamm at Kitzbuhel and Müeller finished a lowly sixth. Podborski had amassed the most victories in the World Cup races and his total points broke the tie.

Steve Podborski, the Crazy Canucks' most winning racer, reached another milestone in his distinguished career as he took his place on the victory podium at Aspen. He was the first North American to win the World Cup downhill title.

Gerry Sorensen, a twenty-four-year-old native of Kimberley, British Columbia, led a strong women's team into the World Cup circuit in 1982 with back-to-back downhill victories in Europe. By the end of the season she had three World Cup wins and a gold medal from the world championships to her credit. Gerry Sorensen's victories heralded the first time in twelve years that a Canadian woman had achieved a World Cup title.

The summer of 1982 marked the end of the original group of five. David Irwin and David Murray both announced their retirement from the Crazy Canucks. Dave Irwin finished his career off as a top competitor with an upbeat third-place finish in Canada at the 1982 World Cup in Whistler, British Columbia.

Steve Podborski and Ken Read began their tenth year with the National Team for the 1982-83 season. Neither one of the veterans won a race that year, but they had good results. Podborski's best finishes were two second-place spots at Kitzbuhel and Sarajevo, Yugoslavia. Read's best finishes were a second at Val d'Isère, France, and a third at Kitzbuhel.

The dynamo of the new generation of Canadian racers was Todd Brooker. An exciting skier to watch, Brooker had ended his 1982 season with an upbeat second-place finish in the last race of the World Cup circuit at Aspen, Colorado. His 1983 season proved to be his best ever with two first-place finishes at Kitzbuhel and Aspen. He was ranked number one in the world in downhill by the International Ski Federation.

Brooker, Read, and Podborski all ended their 1983 season with wipe-outs. Read had announced he would retire after the last race of his career at Lake Louise in March. Brooker, the heir apparent to the World Cup, had to beat Austria's Franz Klammer and Helmut Hoeflehner for the title at the same race.

Ken Read's grand finale ended in a dramatic fall at the top of the course in front of ten thousand hometown fans. Brooker was next on the course and skied a superb run until he hit Double Trouble, the most difficult section of the downhill. He had risked holding his racing tuck position through the bumps to gain time, but the gambit backfired and he fell. Helmut Hoeflehner won the race, but Klammer, in an amazing comeback, had accumulated the most points overall during the season. He won the World Cup for an unprecedented fifth time.

Apart from his Olympic bronze medal and his World Cup title, Steve Podborski will also be remembered for his brutal determination to recover from knee damage. His third major knee injury was a result of a high-speed crash at the March 1983 World Cup downhill at Aspen, Colorado. Podborski spent his summer in rehabilitation, but promised he'd be back to compete at the 1984 Olympic Winter Games at Sarajevo, Yugoslavia.

Two things symbolized the passage of time in Alpine skiing at the XIV Olympic Winter Games. The first was marked by the absence of two Olympic gold medalists from the 1980 Winter Games.

Gerry Sorensen from Canada laughs for joy after learning she won the gold medal for the women's downhill event at the World Cup in 1982. *Canapress Photo Service*

When a "B" card classification is issued by the FIS, the skier is given a professional classification. Both Hanni Wenzel of Liechtenstein and Ingemar Stenmark of Sweden held "B" classifications. They were informed by the FIS that in order to take part in the 1984 Olympics, they would be required to disclose their earnings prior to the Games. Wenzel complied, but Stenmark, who was estimated to be earning more than $1 million a year, refused the request stating that he would be forced to pay an excessive tax in Sweden. The eligibility commission of the IOC supported the request by the Ski Federation that both cases be treated in the same manner, and the pair were declared ineligible for participation at Sarajevo.

Austrian-born Marc Girardelli, who races for Luxembourg, was also noted by his absence at Sarajevo. Unfortunately, Girardelli didn't hold a Luxembourg passport, and was not permitted to race at the Olympics.

Second, a generation of newcomers began to emerge at the 1984 Winter Games, and the television public had never seen anything like their racing suits before.

In the late 1970s, the feisty Crazy Canucks surprised the ski world by appearing in fluorescent yellow racing suits. By comparison, it looked like a pajama party at Sarajevo with rainbows of psychedelic colour snaking up the legs and arms of the racers' skin-tight suits, and spiralling down the back in hot pinks, yellows, tangerine orange, and black.

The Americans were dressed for success in their eye-popping suits and raced better than ever before. The Alpine ski team won three gold medals and two silvers.

No one was more surprised to win a gold medal for giant slalom than twenty-year-old Debbie Armstrong from Seattle, Washington. She had joined the United States team only three months before the Games. Team-mate Christin Cooper was right on her heels for the silver medal, and Perrine Pelen of France won the bronze.

The women's slalom event was held in thick fog and several competitors fell or missed gates. The surprise winner of the gold was another newcomer, nineteen-year-old Paoletta Magoni from Italy.

America's Phil and Steve Mahre broke through their season-long slump to pick up the gold and silver in the men's slalom event. It was their final Olympic performance, and a fitting last hurrah for the twenty-six-year-old identical twins.

But the Alpine event that provided the most sentimental moment of the Games was the men's giant slalom.

Throughout the history of the Olympic Winter Games, each country that had hosted the Games had won at least one medal. For the past sixty years during fourteen Winter Games, Yugoslavia had yet to claim an Olympic medal. Yugoslav sports student Jure Franko was well aware of that fact as he pushed out of the start gate on his second run of the giant slalom. After his first run, he was in fourth place and a long way away from leader Max Julen of Switzerland.

To the chant of "Jure, Jure" by the seven thousand Yugoslavs lining the course at Bjelasnica, Jure Franko had the run of his life and sent the crowd into a frenzy as he crossed the

Ingemar Stenmark, the greatest skier of all time in slalom. *Robert Riger/ABC Sports*

finish line. His combined time of 2:41.41 put him in second place for the silver medal, just 0.23 of a second behind Max Julen.

Thousands of jubilant flag-waving Yugoslavs cheered for their nation's newest hero as Jure Franko received his medal on the victory podium. When asked what it felt like to receive his Olympic medal on the platform, Franko replied, ''I just can't describe it,'' and put his hand on his heart. ''It's in here.''

The men's and women's downhills were repeatedly postponed due to fog, snow, and high winds at Sarajevo. A blessing in disguise was the delay and eventual cancellation of the women's downhill event.

Gerry Sorensen's three World Cup victories and world championship gold medal proved that she was Canada's most winning female downhiller, and a major medal contender at the Olympics.

A thick fog rolled in on the upper section of Mount Jahorina as Gerry Sorensen pushed off out of the start gate for her Olympic downhill run. Just thirty seconds into her run, she hit a deep hole in the course at Gate 5 and her right ski binding kicked out. Ken Read, covering the Games as a television commentator, saw his 1980 newspaper headlines from Lake Placid flash before his eyes, as he watched Sorensen's binding release. Remaining upright on her one ski, Sorensen skied off to the side of the course and collapsed on the snow in a flood of tears. The sounds of her sobs drifted up through the mist and fog as television cameras zoomed in for a close-up view of Gerry Sorensen.

However, her agony was short-lived. One more skier ran the course after Sorensen before the fog bank increased, and visibility was reduced to almost zero. Race officials ordered a one-day postponement and a rerun of the entire event.

Gerry Sorensen didn't win her Olympic medal when the women's downhill was eventually held, but her Olympic second chance has been experienced by very few athletes in the history of the Games. Michela Figini, another new face from Switzerland, won the gold in the downhill.

Anyone at Sarajevo could have predicted who would win the men's downhill if they listened to Billy Johnson. The twenty-three-year-old Californian repeatedly told everyone he would, and he did. There was nothing bashful about Johnson, but as ninth-place finisher Todd Brooker said, ''You've got to give credit where credit is due. It's one thing to be sure of yourself, but another to be one hundred percent right about it.''

The 1984 Winter Games marked the first time that a non-European had won the gold medal in Olympic men's downhill. Nearly a decade had passed since Ken Read burst into the Austro-Swiss downhill monopoly with his World Cup victory at Val d'Isère, France, in 1975. The increasing frequency of success of the Crazy Canucks at Schladming, Austria, and Chamonix and Morzine, France, were the first challenges by the Canadians to the European stronghold on world-class downhill. The fact that Ken Read was twice runner-up to the World Cup and Steve Podborski achieved success by winning the 1982 World Cup title, was a triumph of team-work in a given sport.

As the 1984 season ended, the last of the original Crazy Canucks announced he would hang up his racing skis. His decade with the National Ski Team distinguished Steve Podborski as the most decorated ski racer in Canadian history.

In 1985, the XV Olympic Winter Games Organizing Committee announced that ''Jungle'' Jim Hunter had been hired to manage the Olympic Torch Relay across Canada for the 1988 Olympic Winter Games. The torch relay will provide Canadians in all ten provinces and two territories with an opportunity to participate in the spirit of the Olympics. In the three months leading up to the opening ceremonies on February 13, 1988, the torch will be flown from Olympia, Greece, to St. John's, Newfoundland, where it will be carried by uniquely Canadian

Todd Brooker, in the men's downhill event in 1984 at Sarajevo. *Canapress Photo Services*

methods throughout the country—a distance of approximately 18,000 km (11,185 miles).

The Torch Relay program will bring together Canadian Olympians throughout the country, including former Crazy Canucks Dave Murray, Whistler, British Columbia, Dave Irwin, Sunshine Village, Alberta, Ken Read, Calgary, and Steve Podborski, Toronto, Ontario.

## The Venue

Overlooking Alberta's spectacular Kananaskis Valley, Nakiska at Mount Allan awaits the 1988 Olympic Alpine events.

Nakiska, a North American Cree Indian name meaning "meeting place," was constructed by the Alberta Government at a cost of $27.1 million.

The new recreational ski resort is located approximately 90 kilometres southwest of Calgary, Alberta, on the northern edge of Kananaskis Country, a major provincial year-round recreation area. Mount Allan is on the eastern slopes of the Rocky Mountains.

Competitors will have access to all Olympic events via the Gold, Silver, Bronze, and Olympic chairlifts. The temporary Olympic Platter Lift will carry the competitors up to the start of the men's downhill and will be dismantled after the Games to protect wildlife.

The Silver and Olympic chairlifts represent a revolutionary milestone in chairlift design and capacity. The chairlifts come off the main cable as they enter the loading platform, and go onto another track for loading spectators and skiers. From there, the chairlifts are attached back onto the main cable and whisk people up the mountain in record time. The Silver chairlift has a capacity of 2,400 people per hour and each chair is halfway up the mountain in six minutes.

Although all chairlifts at Mount Allan have been designed by Dopplemeyer Lifts of Austria, over 55 per cent of each lift was manufactured in Canada in the province of Quebec.

The major ski trails are confined to a total of 103 hectares. The ridge line that extends southeastward near the summit divides the ski area and the habitat for bighorn sheep and elk. To minimize contact with the wildlife in the area, the start for the women's downhill (2,160 metres in length) was lowered by 100 metres to below the treeline.

Men will reach the Olympic downhill course via the Silver Chairlift, the Gold Chairlift, and the Olympic Platter Lift. The men's downhill begins near the unloading station of the Olympic Platter Lift and is the longest Alpine course at 3,097 metres, with a vertical drop of 854 metres.

Both the women's and men's super giant slalom events cross under the Silver Chair as they descend into the finish area. The men's Super Giant Slalom begins 177 metres from the women's downhill start and the women's Super-G begins 365 metres from the women's downhill start.

Vertical drop for the 1,175 metre men's giant slalom run is 372 metres and 326 metres for the women's giant slalom. The length of the women's course is 849 metres and the run has been designed with several pitches and benches (hollows and bumps to the uninitiated), with the last pitch steepening into the finish area.

Slalom skiers will cross the finish line 300 metres below Nakiska's Mid-Mountain Lodge. The day-use facility features a lounge and eating area for skiers and spectators. Slalom runs will be serviced via the Gold Chairlift, which has a capacity of 2,160 people per hour.

All events will be monitored by Swiss timing and split times will be taken at several intervals along the courses. Television cameras will be mounted at various locations along each course and will cover races from top to bottom. The electronic score boards will be located near the base of Mid-Mountain Lodge and at the finish area near the base lodge.

The layout of Nakiska has made possible the design and construction of a competitive training run, a facility that is generally not available at a recreational ski resort. The training run is separate and allows racers to train and compete without interfering with the skiing public.

Approximately 76 per cent of the total trail system at Nakiska will be served by snowmaking. The average snow conditions at Mount Allan mid-season are 85 cm of natural dry powder. The snow conditions can be supplemented by snow-making hydrants which line the entire length of most courses.

Nakiska at Mount Allan is the second recreational ski resort designed and constructed for the Olympic Winter Games in North America. The first area was built at Squaw Valley, California, for the 1960 Olympic Winter Games.

Whistler Mountain's Paul Matthews, of Ecosign Mountain Recreation Planners Limited, the company that designed Mount Allan, remarks: "I have designed over 150 ski areas, and Mount Allan is one of the best at matching the needs of the public skiing market, with the requirements of the competitive racer."

## The Technique

### Downhill

When the Crazy Canucks joined the National Team, they all had a good technical foundation in the three Alpine disciplines. As highly accomplished racers, they honed their slalom and giant slalom technique into the fine art of downhill racing.

The essence of the downhill event is speed. It is the most highly regarded of all the Alpine events, and also the most dangerous. The discipline involves endurance, split-second timing, instant reflexes, and, most of all, courage.

Prior to the race, the downhiller memorizes the course and calmly determines the fastest "line" down it. A minimum of three training runs are required to learn the course.

At the final beep of the timer, the racer pushes back on his poles and propels his upper body up and out of the start gate. As he pulls his legs forward, his knees trip the timing wand. After one or two powerful skating steps the racer will assume "the tuck" body position.

After considerable experimentation with wind resistance, the racing tuck position was developed from one of the simplest aerodynamic shapes in the world, the egg. "Egging it"

Swiss gold medalist Michela Figini demonstrates a perfect tuck position in the women's downhill event. *Deutsche Presse-Agentur GmbH*

reduces wind resistance and has proven to be the fastest position on skis. The downhill racer is on the course for approximately two minutes, and is constantly thrown out of the tuck position by the bumpy terrain of the hill. But, it is essential for the racer to "tuck it out" as much as possible. Elbows and arms flung out like windmills only decrease speed. The hands are kept close together within the line of vision. Elbows touching the knees and shoulders forward in a near perfect tuck position produce maximum speed. Poles are tucked under the arms and close to the body.

A limited number of control gates are strategically placed on the course to mark the racer's path. The cardinal rule is to keep the weight on the downhill ski when turning through the control panels. Through years of specialized training, a downhiller develops a "feel" for the ski edges, and applies just enough pressure to carve the perfect arc as if it were drawn by a compass.

Traditionally, the large bumps on a downhill course pose the greatest challenge, and the key to success is precise timing, concentration, and judgement. The best way to keep off the casualty list is to take off perfectly, hold the tuck, and land perfectly. Good air time is one of the ultimate joys to the downhiller.

Maintaining and gaining speed on the flats has a lot to do with ski wax, and many races have been lost with the choice of the wrong one.

When possible, the pre-race plan of the Crazy Canucks was to hold the tuck through the pitches, no matter how steep or mean they were. It was the Canucks' passion for "tucking out" on the pitches and flats at Val d'Isère, France, that earned them the nickname the "Kamikaze Kids" in 1975.

### Slalom

The slalom event is a test of the skier's technique, balance, manoeuvrability, and speed. It is run in two separate races, and the lowest total time determines the winner.

Slalom is skied in a more upright position than the downhill, and the racer attempts to keep his upper body facing down toward the finish line.

The legs of a racer appear to swing back and forth like a pendulum of a clock, as he skirts down the course boobytrapped with numerous combinations of poles. The slalom poles, placed alternately down the course, are aptly named "gates" as the ski tips of the racer must pass between each matching pair.

The slalom racer uses his ski poles for quick sharp turns through the gates. The closer his skis come to the flag poles, the faster his run. The essential trick is not to hook a ski tip on a slalom pole and spin out of the course, or lose a ski.

To the untrained eye, it would appear that the arms and shoulders of the slalom skier would be black and blue after knocking down the bewildering sequence of flag poles. However, the plastic rapid gates (spring-loaded at the base) do not hurt the competitors as they weave through the gates.

There are two types of slalom gates: open and closed. Open gates are set perpendicular to the course line and closed gates are set parallel to the course line. Each pair of gates must be 10 feet (3.05 metres) wide, and a minimum of 2.5 feet (.76 metres) from the next set.

The slalom course-setter designs various combinations and patterns of gates. Some of the more notable ones are named flushes, which are three or four vertical gates, and hairpins, which are two vertical gates.

Despite the fact the slalom course is set the day before the Olympic event, the racers are allowed access to it only one hour prior to the start.

The competitors and their coaches slowly climb up the side of the course, carefully analyzing each gate pattern and memorizing the terrain of the hill. Occasionally a competitor will stop during the inspection, close his eyes, and weave his hand back and forth through the air.

The slalom event is the ultimate obstacle course.

## Giant Slalom

The giant slalom is a large scale slalom. Poles are further apart on the course and with 8 metres between each set, the patterns are open and wide.

There will be at least thirty slalom gates in the Olympic giant slalom event and valuable seconds will be eliminated if the racer holds the upper body in a quiet, calm, and efficient position while the legs absorb the contours of the hill.

The resulting speed from the steep schusses of the rolling terrain must be combined with a skier's ability to change weight from one ski to the other quickly and precisely through the poles.

Compared to the often confusing maze of poles in the slalom event, the giant slalom is one of the easiest events for the spectator to follow. It is longer and faster paced than the slalom event, and the vertical drops of 372 metres on the men's course and 326 metres on the women's course promise a spectacular Olympic giant slalom event at Nakiska.

The giant slalom was Nancy Greene's favourite kind of race, long and smooth. It suited her technique so well that she won a gold medal in the event at the 1968 Olympic Winter Games.

## Super Giant Slalom

The super giant slalom could be described as a hybrid between the downhill and the giant slalom.

Whereas the giant slalom event relates more to slalom, the super giant slalom relates more to downhill. Super giant slalom courses resemble downhill courses to the extent that large bumps and drop-offs are designed into the contours of the terrain. But, from a racer's perspective, that is where the similarity ends.

The lowest and most aerodynamic body position for a downhiller is nicknamed the "bullet tuck." For the super giant slalom racer, the tuck position required is a higher, more stable stance. This is achieved by extension of the legs, although the shoulders and arms are still kept in a forward position like the "bullet tuck" to cut down on wind resistance.

The more stretched-out tuck position is necessary for the super giant slalom skier who is concerned not only with aerodynamics, but also with the ability to initiate a series of turns through the slalom poles on the course.

As the racer approaches one of the gates on the race course, the skier angles the body into the radius of the turn. While skiing through the gate combinations, a racer will have some contact with the slalom poles. This would be unheard of in the downhill event. Once the sequence of turns is completed, the racer snaps back into the high stable tuck position to increase speed out of the last gate.

While downhillers prefer to take the corners in the tuck, the slalom racers make short quick turns in their event. By comparison, the super giant slalom racers carve big, high-speed floaters.

Once the technique of the super giant slalom is mastered, it must feel like taking a corner at Le Mans on two wheels in a Formula 1.

## Alpine Combined

The Alpine combined was first introduced at the 1985 World Ski Championships and will be featured for the first time in Olympic competition at Calgary in 1988.

The purpose of the combined is to encourage more racers to ski the slalom and downhill events and may herald a move away from the specialist in one Alpine discipline. Consisting of a downhill event held on one day, and a special slalom held on another, the combined is independent from the Olympic downhill and slalom events and is open to both men and women.

Held one day prior to the Olympic event, the combined downhill is raced on the same course but with a lower start, and as a separate event.

The combined slalom is held on a different day from the downhill, and is set with less technical difficulty than the other Olympic slaloms. With more open gates, it gives competitors the advantage of finishing the race and qualifying for the combined medal.

A DNF (Did Not Finish) in either the slalom or the downhill disqualifies a competitor from the medals. But, if both downhill and slalom are successfully completed, the lowest aggregate time determines the winner.

# The Rules

The International Ski Federation (FIS), the world governing body of skiing, has devised a world ranking system to determine the top racers in all five Alpine disciplines. Most Olympic medalists come from the top group.

Throughout the season, racers are awarded points for their top five finishes, and to be promoted to the top fifteen in any discipline brings with it a great honour. Theoretically, the competitors seeded one through fifteen have the optimum course conditions. The start order in the first fifteen is determined by drawing lots on race day.

## Downhill

The downhill event consists of one official run.

There are no slalom gates on the course per se, but a limited number of control gates mark the racer's path and offer a safety feature by checking excessive speed. The direction gates are marked with red flags for the men's event, and red and blue flags for the women's event. All racers must cross the line between the inner poles of the gates with both feet.

The minimum vertical drop required is 800 metres to 1,000 metres for men, and between 500 metres and 700 metres for women.

One quarter of a million dollars was spent on protective fencing at the 1980 Olympic Winter Games. The entire downhill course at Nakiska will be enclosed with protective netting and willy bags (plastic-wrapped hay bales) required at dangerous sections of the run. Narrow sections through wooded terrain have a wide, cleared safety zone of 20 metres on each side.

The downhill course is set several days before the Olympics and must be available to competitors for a minimum of three official timed training runs before the event is held. All racers must participate in the training runs. All competitors must wear FIS approved crash helmets for training and official runs.

The racers will start at equal intervals of approximately 120 seconds for the Olympic downhill event at Nakiska.

## Slalom

The winner of the slalom is determined by two runs held one after another on two different courses.

The slalom course is set the day before the race and the slope remains closed. The course is opened for inspection one hour before the race begins and competitors are permitted to climb up the course and through gates. The rules forbid a racer to ski down through the gates during inspection of the course.

Slalom gates should be set on snow that is as hard as possible, and number fifty-five gates minimum and seventy-five maximum for men, and forty-five gates minimum and sixty maximum for women.

Consecutive slalom gates alternate in colours of red and blue with flags of the same colour so racers can distinguish them quickly at high speeds. As long as ski tips of the skier cross the line between the slalom poles, there is no penalty for knocking down a gate. If a competitor misses a gate, he must stop and climb back up to ski through it, or face disqualification.

Each set of slalom gates has an official gatekeeper who is responsible for ensuring that each competitor passes through the gate correctly.

## Giant Slalom

The giant slalom is a large-scale slalom and consists of two runs on two different courses for men, and one run only for women.

Giant slalom courses are a minimum of 30 metres wide. Turns on the giant slalom course are prepared as for a slalom event with gates alternately marked with red or blue flags. The 8 metre width of the giant slalom gates is wider than the slalom, and the gates are also set further apart on the course.

The maximum vertical drop of 372 metres of the giant slalom run at Nakiska will determine the number of gate combinations prepared for the Olympic event. The length of the men's run is 1,175 metres and the women's run 849 metres.

The winners in the men's event are determined by the aggregate time in two runs, on two different tracks, on two different days.

## Super Giant Slalom

The Super Giant Slalom (or Super-G) event consists of one run for both men and women.

The Super-G course is prepared as for a downhill, but where slalom gates are placed, they are prepared as for a slalom race. Because of the width of the gates and the greater distances between them, mainly single gates are set in the Super-G.

Where possible, the entire width of the hill is used and marked with alternate red and blue gate flag combinations. The large bumps and rollers on the terrain for the Super-G event somewhat resemble a downhill course, but Super-G skiers never reach the speeds of a downhiller.

If the visibility for the Super-G is poor, as was the case in 1984 at Sarajevo, red directions flags will be set down the left side of the course and green flags will be set on the right side for both giant slalom and Super-G events. The best giant slalom and Super giant slalom racers in the world make few mistakes, but if they do, the Super-G event is less forgiving.

Skiers have just one run for a medal in the event and the lowest time determines the winner. The event will be included in the Olympic format for the first time at the 1988 Olympic Winter Games.

## Alpine Combined

The Alpine combined is a combination of the downhill technique in one race, and slalom technique in the other.

# The Equipment

Skiers do not look back with nostalgia at the ski equipment of the good old days.

Indeed, the modern ski racing equipment of today would boggle the mind of the racer from the baggy-pants days of yesteryear. The natural wool fibres of the baggy tweeds met Greenpeace standards, but didn't do much for racing results. The first stretch pant was designed by Maria Bogner of Germany in the late 1950s, and heralded a new era in racing chic.

Racers who took part in the events of the 1948 Olympics brought their best pair of hickory wood skis to the Winter Games, and used them for all three Alpine races. Competitors first moved away from wood skis after the 1960 Olympic Winter Games when Jean Vaurnet of France won a gold medal in the men's downhill. He wore the first pair of metal skis ever used in Olympic competition.

Today, most Alpine racers have at least ten pairs of skis with various waxes applied to the bases to match radically different snow conditions. The best pair of skis is reserved for race day, and used or scratched ones are demoted to training skis or warm-up skis for inspection runs.

Alpine skis are designed to match the appropriate discipline, and are narrower at the waist than at the tip or the tail.

The waist (sidecut) of the slalom ski is the narrowest of

all three Alpine ski designs. The narrow sidecut gives the ski optimum edging and manoeuvrability to suit the tight quick turns of the slalom event.

The giant slalom ski has a wider waist than the slalom ski, and combines maximum sliding with the preferred degree of flex to enable the giant slalom skier to carve big arc turns.

Downhill skis are almost straight-cut from tip to tail. The small sidecut at the waist allows the ski to track well and hold a straight flat line at high speeds. Downhill skis are the longest of all Alpine ski designs and measure approximately 221-225 cm. Surprisingly, these long skis turn easily for the downhiller travelling at 130 kph.

A new design in downhill skis was introduced at the Olympic Winter Games at Innsbruck, Austria. A hole the size of a tennis ball was sculptured into the front tip of the downhill ski. The hole reduced the mass of the ski tip and also stopped the ski tip from vibrating at high speeds. Austria's Franz Klammer gave the new ski his seal of approval, but did not use them when he won his downhill gold medal at the 1976 Games. Since then, the Canadian National downhill team has gained success with the new design, and most members wear the ski for competition.

New levels of sophistication in racing boot design and ski bindings offer an increased degree of safety and protection to the Alpine racers.

The straight, lightweight ski poles used by slalom skiers have been virtually replaced by a new streamlined model used only for downhillers. Despite being the same length as the slalom ski pole, the downhill pole is bent halfway down the shaft and is moulded to the skier's body.

During the 1960s, the FIS imposed mandatory use of racing helmets that guaranteed free visibility and helped safeguard downhillers from serious head injury.

# Calgary Preview

## Men

For a new generation of Canadian downhill specialists, it's a tall order to follow in the footsteps of the Crazy Canucks.

Veteran World Cup racer Todd Brooker's spectacular crash at Kitzbuhel during the 1987 season signalled an end to his competitive career. Brooker's retirement from the national team pegs Rob Boyd, Brian Stemmle, and Felix Belczyk as the racers to watch as the countdown to the 1988 Olympics begins.

Boyd, the youngest racer in the World Cup's first seed (he will turn twenty-two during the Olympics on February 15) finished in first place at Val Gardena's World Cup in 1986. He followed that up with several top placings during the pre-Olympic season, and represents Canada's hope for an Olympic medal.

Thanks to Sport Canada's "Best Ever" funding program, an increased emphasis on slalom and giant slalom has aided in rebuilding Canada's National Team with a new group of contenders for Olympic selection. Jim Read of Calgary heads the roll call of Mike Tommy from Wakefield, Quebec, and Alain Villiard of Ste.-Adele, Quebec.

Read, considered Canada's top giant slalom racer, will have his work cut out for him as he competes against the 1987 World Giant Slalom Champion, Pirmin Zurbriggen of Switzerland. In fact, the Swiss team is almost unbeatable in every discipline of Alpine skiing. Zurbriggen is the main medal threat for Switzerland in the Giant Slalom and the Super-G. Both he and compatriot Peter Müeller are consistent winners in the downhill. The junior development program in Switzerland produces tremendous team depth, and once racers graduate to an Olympic berth, the in-team competition pushes each member to top results. The unprecedented success of the Swiss team during the pre-Olympic season is a direct result of the grass roots development system within the country.

It's a matter of record that downhill bronze medalist Anton Steiner was the only medal winner for Austria at the 1984 Olympic Winter Games. The slopes once resounded to Austria's famous names in downhill, and the 1988 ski team will be attempting an Olympic comeback. But their team has been taking its lumps lately from Andreas Wenzel of Liechtenstein and new rising star Marc Girardelli. Austria-born Girardelli races for Luxembourg and could be a strong medal contender, but unfortunately may not be allowed to compete as he does not hold a Luxembourg passport.

It appears that United States downhill gold medal winner Bill Johnson's career may have peaked at Sarajevo in 1984. Since the last Olympics, Johnson's results have been disappointing and he has been sidelined with back and knee surgery. Unhappily for the Americans, the rest of their slalom and giant slalom team is not in Phil and Steve Mahre's league. However, hope still rests with Felix McGrath, one of America's top technical skiers.

The one, two slalom finish of the Mahre twins at Sarajevo in 1984 put Didier Bouvet of France in third spot for the bronze medal. The retirement of the Mahre brothers and possible ineligibility of Sweden's Ingemar Stenmark make Bouvet the only French slalom skier in contention at Calgary. His improved ranking since 1984 proves he performs well under pressure and he could easily rise to the gold medal challenge in 1988.

Italy's downhiller Michael Mair could cause the Swiss and Canadian teams some trouble in the race at Nakiska at Mount Allan. Mair has a sound technical base in the event and has emerged as a downhill power in his 1987 World Cup season.

Olympic medal hopes for West Germany rest on giant slalom champion Markus Wasmaier. Sweden's Jonas Nilsson and Yugoslav Rok Petrovic also bear watching, especially Petrovic. In 1986 he wrapped up his and Yugoslavia's first World Cup season title. With a banner pre-Olympic year, Rok Petrovic will be heading for the winner's circle at Calgary in 1988.

## Women

Laurie Graham of Inglewood, Ontario, now heads the women's national team, which has four members who are ranked in the top twenty of one of the disciplines. Of those, Graham is ranked in the first fifteen in downhill. Her impressive first-place finish at the 1986 World Cup competition at Val d'Isère, France, came just a few hours before Rob Boyd did the same thing, on the same day for Canada at Val Gardena, Italy. Considering Graham's racing experience and her leading edge on the international circuit, she has established her credibility as Canada's best medal hope. With a little savvy and luck in her pre-Olympic races, her technical know-how could put her in the top three in 1988.

Next to Gerry Sorensen, Liisa Savijarvi of Bracebridge, Ontario, was the top-ranked Canadian woman at the Olympics at Sarajevo in 1984. Her ninth-place finish in the Olympic giant slalom indicated great things to come, but her 1986/87 season proved to be a personal disappointment. Savijarvi shattered her right knee and crushed two vertebrae in her back following a horrendous crash during a downhill training run in March 1987 at Vail, Colorado. Whether she will ever ski competitively again is questionable.

After the 1984 Olympics, Canada's top-ranked skier in the discipline of slalom was Andrea Bedard of Sutton, Quebec, but her season last year was hampered by knee problems. Team-mate Josee Lacasse has first-rate credentials in giant slalom and successfully defended her Canadian women's giant slalom ski championship last year at Rossland, British Columbia. Lacasse will join other promising newcomers, Karen Percy of Banff, Alberta, and Kerrin Lee of Rossland, British Columbia, in contention for Olympic team selection. Karen Percy of Banff in proving to be one of the best all-round skiers Canada has produced in a long time.

As expected, Switzerland's Maria Walliser is one of the leaders in the women's downhill World Cup standings, and along with team-mate Michela Figini, winner of the 1984 Olympic downhill gold medal, poses a threat to their main rivals. The pair look formidable as do Brigitte Oertli in slalom and giant slalom veteran Vreni Schneider. World champion Schneider's comments after her first-place finish in the 1987 Worlds typifies the positive attitude of the entire Swiss team. At a press conference after the race, she said: "My victory in the world championships has only increased my motivation. I have full confidence and I am skiing at my maximum."

The leader of the Austrian women's Alpine ski team is twenty-one-year-old downhill star Katrin Gutensohn. The aggressive downhiller has proved she is capable of several World Cup wins in a row, and is as talented as she is challenging to coach. Gutensohn has her own way of doing things, and likes to spend her free time pursuing her other favourite sport of hang-gliding. Racer Roswitha Steiner adds depth to the Austrian team.

Debbie Armstrong and Diane Roffe of the United States are skiing moderately well and, barring injury, will enter the Games as contenders. Armstrong is anxious to defend her 1984 Olympic gold medal in giant slalom. Downhiller Pam Fletcher looks like a hot prospect for the American team next season and must be considered as she will be racing close to home.

The West Germans have hit the top fifteen positions in World Cup women's Alpine ski standings with downhillers Michaela Gerg, Regine Mosenlechner, and Marina Kiehl. Gerg and Kiehl have proven themselves winners in the Super-G standings along with team-mate Traudl Hacher. Marina Kiehl's giant slalom performance is only topped by Hacher, and both introduce a West German team loaded with talent.

Italy's 1984 slalom gold medalist Paoletta Magoni-Sforza has an advantage over the rest of the field in technique and experience. She and team-mate Michaela Marzola, a strong Super-G racer, will be a tough combination to beat in the slalom events.

There's always a chance for an upset in Olympic competition despite the fact that the top-seeded favourites are often the medal winners. Watch for Spain's lone entry in the top fifteen in the giant slalom event, Blanca Fernandez-Ochoa, and a young talent, Martija Svet of Yugoslavia. Svet took silver medals in both super giant slalom and giant slalom events at the 1987 World Championships.

France could be well represented by Catherine Quittet, who is strong in both downhill and super giant slalom. Sweden could feature with a strong finish in slalom by Camilla Nilsson.

# Canadians at the Olympic Winter Games:
# ALPINE SKIING

## 1924 Chamonix — I Olympic Winter Games

Not held.

## 1928 St. Moritz — II Olympic Winter Games

Not held.

## 1932 Lake Placid — III Olympic Winter Games

Not held.

## 1936 Garmisch-Partenkirchen — IV Olympic Winter Games

Butler, L.R., Gordon-Lennox, D., Miller, M.

**WOMEN**

*Combined, Downhill & Slalom*
15. Lois Reid Butler
28. Marjory Miller
29. Diana Gordon-Lennox

## 1948 St. Moritz — V Olympic Winter Games

Clifford, H., Irwin, A., Irwin, W., Jolbert, P., Laferte, L., Sutherland, H., Wurtele, R., Wurtele, R.

**MEN**

*Downhill*
28. Harvey Clifford (tie)
28. Hector Sutherland (tie)
56. Albert Irwin
60. Wilbur Irwin

*Slalom*
23. Harvey Clifford
25. Hector Sutherland
33. Wilbur Irwin
61. Albert Irwin

*Special Slalom*
19. Harvey Clifford
28. Hector Sutherland
37. Albert Irwin
50. Wilbur Irwin

*Combined, Downhill, and Slalom*
21. Harvey Clifford
23. Hector Sutherland
36. Wilbur Irwin
49. Albert Irwin

**WOMEN**

*Downhill*
37. Rhona Wurtele

## 1952 Oslo — VI Olympic Winter Games

Bertrand, A., Griffin, J., Hewson, J., Merry, G., Morrison, G., Richardson, R., Schutz, R., Wheeler, L., Wurtele-Eaves, R.

**MEN**

*Downhill*
18. Robert Richardson
31. Gordon Morrison
32. John Griffin
40. André Bertrand

*Slalom*
25. André Bertrand
26. Robert Richardson

*Giant Slalom*
34. Robert Richardson
36. André Bertrand
37. John Griffin
46. Gordon Morrison

**WOMEN**

*Downhill*
8. Joanne Hewson
14. Rosemarie Schutz
20. Rhoda Wurtele-Eaves
27. Lucile Wheeler

*Slalom*
13. Joanne Hewson
19. Rhoda Wurtele-Eaves
26. Lucile Wheeler
37. Rosemarie Schutz

*Giant Slalom*
9. Rhoda Wurtele-Eaves
23. Rosemarie Schutz
27. Lucile Wheeler
30. Joanne Hewson

## 1956 Cortina Ampezzo — VII Olympic Winter Games

Bertrand, A., Heggtveit, A., Kruger, C., Seguin, G., Tommy, Andrew, Tommy, Art, Wheeler. L.

**MEN**

*Downhill*
25. André Bertrand

*Slalom*
50. André Bertrand

*Giant Slalom*
39. André Bertrand

**WOMEN**

*Downhill*
3. Lucile Wheeler
22. Anne Heggtveit (tie)
22. Carlyn Kruger
33. Ginette Seguin

*Slalom*
18. Ginette Seguin
23. Carlyn Kruger
30. Anne Heggtveit

*Giant Slalom*
6. Lucile Wheeler
29. Anne Heggtveit
36. Ginette Seguin

## 1960 Squaw Valley — VIII Olympic Winter Games

Anderson, V., Bruneski, D., Brunet, J.G., Greene, E., Greene, N., Heggtveit, A., Holland, N., Lessard, J., Tommy, F.

**MEN**

*Downhill*
22. Verne Anderson
26. Jean-Guy Brunet
27. Frederick Tommy
28. Donald W. Bruneski

*Slalom*
19. Verne Anderson
22. Donald W. Bruneski
25. Frederick Tommy
34. Jean-Guy Brunet

**WOMEN**

*Downhill*
12. Anne Heggtveit
17. Nancy Holland
22. Nancy Greene
32. Elizabeth Greene

*Slalom*
1. Anne Heggtveit
12. Nancy Holland
24. Elizabeth Greene
31. Nancy Greene

*Giant Slalom*
24. Verne Anderson
26. Jean-Guy Brunet
28. Frederick Tommy
31. Jean Lessard

*Giant Slalom*
12. Anne Heggtveit
26. Nancy Greene
28. Elizabeth Greene
29. Nancy Holland

## 1964 Innsbruck — IX Olympic Winter Games

Batistella, G., Brunet, J.G., Crutchfield, L., Dokka, K., Duncan, P., Greene, N., Hebron, R., Henderson, S., Holland, N., Rutledge, V., Swan, R.

**MEN**

*Downhill*
25. Jean-Guy Brunet
28. Garry Batistella
30. Rod Hebron
34. Peter Duncan

*Slalom*
19. Peter Duncan

*Giant Slalom*
26. Peter Duncan
27. Jean-Guy Brunet

**WOMEN**

*Downhill*
7. Nancy Greene
24. Linda Crutchfield
28. Karen Dokka
34. Nancy Holland

*Slalom*
15. Nancy Greene
16. Linda Crutchfield

*Giant Slalom*
16. Nancy Greene
31. Nancy Holland
32. Linda Crutchfield
34. Karen Dokka

## 1968 Grenoble - X Olympic Winter Games

Clifford, B., Crawford, J., Dokka, K., Duncan, P., Greene, N., Hebron, R., Henderson, S., Henderson, W., Leinweber, J., McKay, B., Rinaldi, G., Shepherd, K., Swan, R.

**MEN**

*Downhill*
27. Wayne Henderson
31. Gerry Rinaldi

*Giant Slalom*
18. Peter Duncan
21. Scott Henderson

**WOMEN**

*Downhill*
10. Nancy Greene
20. Judi Leinweber
22. Karen Dokka
23. Betsy Clifford

*Slalom*
2. Nancy Greene
15. Karen Dokka

*Giant Slalom*
1. Nancy Greene
16. Karen Dokka
25. Judi Leinweber

## 1972 Sapporo — XI Olympic Winter Games

Barrington, R., Crawford, J., Hunter, J., Kreiner, K., Kreiner, L., Oughton, C., Pratte, D., Robbins, D.

**MEN**

*Downhill*
20. Jim Hunter
32. Reto Barrington
38. Derek Robbins

**WOMEN**

*Downhill*
18. Carolyne Oughton
20. Laurie Kreiner
27. Judy Crawford
33. Kathy Kreiner

*Slalom*
19. Jim Hunter
23. Reto Barrington

*Giant Slalom*
11. Jim Hunter
20. Reto Barrington

*Slalom*
4. Judy Crawford
12. Laurie Kreiner
14. Kathy Kreiner

*Giant Slalom*
4. Laurie Kreiner
15. Diane Pratte
24. Judy Crawford
29. Carolyne Oughton

## 1976 Innsbruck — XII Olympic Winter Games

Clifford, B., Hunter, J., Irwin, D., Kreiner, K., Kreiner, L., Murray, D., Read, K., Safrata, R.

**MEN**

*Downhill*
5. Ken Read
8. David Irwin
10. Jim Hunter
18. David Murray

*Slalom*
23. Jim Hunter
27. Robert Safrata

*Giant Slalom*
22. Jim Hunter

**WOMEN**
16. Laurie Kreiner
19. Kathy Kreiner
22. Betsy Clifford

*Slalom*
14. Laurie Kreiner

*Giant Slalom*
1. Kathy Kreiner
22. Betsy Clifford
27. Laurie Kreiner

## 1980 Lake Placid — XIII Olympic Winter Games

Graham, L., Irwin, D., Klettl, L., Kreiner, K., Murray, D., Podborski, S., Read, K.

**MEN**

*Downhill*
3. Steve Podborski
10. David Murray
11. David Irwin

**WOMEN**

*Downhill*
5. Kathy Kreiner
11. Laurie Graham
13. Loni Klettl

*Slalom*
15. Kathy Kreiner

*Giant Slalom*
9. Kathy Kreiner

## 1984 Sarajevo — XIV Olympic Winter Games

Athans, G., Bedard, A., Brooker, T., Graham, L., Haight, D., Podborski, S., Read, J., Savijarvi, L., Sorensen, G., Stemmle, K., Tommy, M.

**MEN**

*Downhill*
8. Steve Podborski
9. Todd Brooker
26. Gary Athans

*Giant Slalom*
24. Jim Read

*Downhill*
6. Gerry Sorensen
11. Laurie Graham
18. Liisa Savijarvi
22. Karen Stemmle

*Giant Slalom*
9. Liisa Savijarvi
17. Diana Haight
33. Laurie Graham

# Biathlon

Canmore Nordic Centre
February 20, 23, 26

*Mathieson, Calgary*

A once-in-a-lifetime opportunity to represent my country at the Olympic Winter Games motivated me to respond to a military newspaper advertisement at RCAF Station Summerside, Prince Edward Island, where I was stationed with the Royal Canadian Air Force in September 1965.

Two-and-one-half years later, Esko Karhu, George Ede, James Boyde, Knowles McGill, and I left Canada as members of the first Canadian Olympic biathlon team ever assembled, and headed to Grenoble, France, to compete at the 1968 Olympic Winter Games.

The road to the Olympics was a tremendous challenge for all of us. After our initial team had been selected for permanent full-time training, we became a highly mobile unit and never spent more than three or four months in one place. We trained at military units from Val Cartier, Quebec, to Camp Borden in Ontario, and radar bases at Kamloops, British Columbia, and Sioux Lookout in Ontario. In 1965, we pioneered the entire Kananaskis area and where Mount Allan stands, we built one of our first biathlon ranges.

During the spring, summer, and fall months of the year, our training consisted of cross-country running, road racing, rifle shooting, circuit and weight training, volleyball, soccer, and swimming. Once snow was on the ground, we concentrated on cross-country skiing and rifle shooting. We trained all day long, five days a week in the summer, and seven days a week in the winter. Each year the competition tour started in early January with travel to Western Europe and Scandinavia and ended in early March. By December of 1967, a team of five biathletes were chosen from the original applicants and made up the official Olympic team for 1968.

From our initial Olympic team, the growth and development of the sport in the Armed Forces took a downturn and for years biathlon was practised only at unit levels within the Canadian Armed Forces. Nevertheless, by 1984 a viable national team of biathletes had been assembled in Canada in hopes of competing at the XIV Olympic Winter Games at Sarajevo, Yugoslavia. But, to meet the selection criteria of the Canadian Olympic Association, any Olympic team must prove its ability to place in the top half of the international field, and the Canadian biathlon team did not. A decision was made to disallow the team to participate in the 1984 Olympics and the national team in Canada was bitterly disappointed.

During the time I practised biathlon, the Canadian Forces Base at Val Cartier, Quebec, was a major biathlon centre in Canada. It is most gratifying to now have a western counterpart to Val Cartier at the Canmore Nordic Centre.

I sincerely hope that spectators will focus some of their time and attention on the sport of biathlon during the 1988 Winter Games. They can be assured that they will find biathlon a fascinating discipline. I welcome you to the sport and I welcome you to the 1988 Olympic Winter Games.

Sergeant George W. Rattai
*Canadian Forces Base*
*Petawawa, Ontario*
*Member of the 1968 Canadian Olympic Biathlon Team*

## The History

The history of the biathlon is based in Scandinavia, particularly Norway, where rock carvings illustrating skiers hunting animals date back 4,000 years.

In 1767 the first biathlon ski race was recorded. A contest of skiing and shooting skills took place among the winter hunters of Scandinavia and demonstrated the use of weapons in nature. Scandinavia became very dependent on the protection that was provided by the ski troops, and eventually biathlon became a military discipline. As time passed, the proficiency of Finland's ski troops increased to the point the Finns were able to defeat the Russian invasion of their country in 1939.

The military ski patrol was a regular training exercise and team competitions became a frequent pastime for the infantry troops. However, biathlon competitions were not introduced into the Olympic Winter Games until 1960. The anti-military concerns that were prevalent after World War II resulted in International Olympic Committee President Avery Brundage declaring that he felt the Olympic Winter Games were no place for a military event.

The Greek word "biathlon," meaning a "dual test," was given to this new Olympic sport as it combined the accuracy of marksmanship and the endurance of cross-country skiing.

Initially, the 20 kilometre was the only race in the Olympic biathlon format. Super Swede Klas Lestander won the premier event finishing in just over an hour and a half (1:33:21.6). By 1964 the eastern bloc countries were making their powers felt and Vladimir Melanin of the Soviet Union won the event in a time of 1:20:26.8. The pendulum swung back to the Scandinavians at Grenoble, France, in 1968 when Norwegian Magnar Solberg finished in an Olympic time of 1:13:45.9. The thirty-one-year-old policeman shot a perfect target score for the first time in his life in the Olympic event, and was the surprise winner of a gold medal. He was too exhausted to pose for photographers at the finish line and said, "I am very, very happy, but just too tired to smile."

Canada's strong bid to host the 1968 Olympic Winter Games initiated an interest in the sport of biathlon in this country.

The Canadian Olympic Association agreed that the hosting nation should have an entry in each event. Since the biathlon fell within the framework of the military forces in other countries, the Armed Forces were chosen as a vehicle for establishing a Canadian team. The approval of the Minister of National Defence was sought and obtained.

Notices were posted throughout the three services for young men interested in a crash course on the biathlon. By 1965 over one hundred applicants reached headquarters and seventy men were tested for the team. Eventually nine were chosen for final training; three from the navy, three from the army, and three from the air force. Ranging in age from twenty-one to twenty-nine, the servicemen ranked from experts in bomb demolition, to ski coaches, to rifle coaches, to parachutists, to sailors. Regardless of their backgrounds, they all went into training for the 1968 Olympic Winter Games at Grenoble, France. The training became part of the NORAD radar watchdog chain at the Canadian Forces station at Sioux Lookout, Ontario.

Skiing an average of 30 miles (48 km) a day and then working out on the rifle range, they would finish their day off with weight-lifting sessions in the gym using drills that would directly benefit skiing muscles and breathing development. Statistics showed that some of them lost up to an average of five pounds a day, and burnt up 5,000 calories in the process.

In 1968, Canada sent its first and only biathlon team to the Olympic Winter Games. The team consisted of Esko Karu, George Ede, Knowles McGill, James Boyde, and George Rattai. The team competed in the relay event and the 20 kilometre race, with Esko Karu's 1:32:42.9 finish time Canada's best effort. It was almost a Scandinavian sweep in 1972 at Sapporo, Japan, when Norway's Solberg repeated his gold medal finish in 1:15:55.5 and Lars-Goeran Arwidson of Sweden won the bronze. The single breakthrough for the Communist nations was a silver medal for East Germany.

Magnar Solberg's second consecutive gold medal win in 1972 exemplified the superb physical conditioning of an Olympic biathlete. With four years added to his age in between the two Olympic Winter Games, Solberg's finish times were, nevertheless, almost identical. The extra two penalty minutes were added for two missed targets.

Although the 20 kilometre event has been an Olympic medal see-saw between the Communist bloc countries and the Scandinavians, there has been no contest with the Russians since the four-man relay event was introduced into the Games in 1968. However, in 1972 and 1976, Finland's biathletes were able to break the Communist bloc monopoly with consecutive silver medal finishes.

World champion Heikki Ikola of Finland entered the 1976 Olympic Winter Games as the biathlon favourite in the 20 kilometre event but lost the gold to Nikolai Kruglov of the Soviet Union. Both biathletes drew two-minute penalties for missed targets but the Russian army lieutenant proved himself the stronger skier by edging out the Finn with a time of 1:14:12.26.

Nikolai Kruglov of the U.S.S.R. is thrown into the air by team-mates after the Soviets finished first in the biathlon relay at the 1976 Olympic Winter Games. *Keystone Presse Agentur, Switzerland*

In 1980 thirty-three-year-old Alexander Tikhonov won his fourth gold medal when his team took their fourth consecutive Olympic relay event at Lake Placid, New York. East Germany bumped Finland out of the silver medal spot and the West Germans wound up with the bronze.

Soviet biathlete Anatoli Aljabiev finished the 20 kilometre race with an Olympic record time of 1:08:16.31 and a perfect target score.

Another biathlon event was added to the Olympic programme in 1980 at Lake Placid. The 10 kilometre race was won by East German Frank Ullrich, who also won a silver in the 20 kilometre.

The virtual monopoly of the Olympic biathlon events by the Soviet Union and East Germany ended at Sarajevo, Yugoslavia, in 1984. It was fitting that the country which had originated the biathlon would produce a sensational biathlete to break the medal stronghold of the Communist superpowers.

Norwegian Eirik Kvalfoss became a national hero with his gold medal win and Olympic record time of 30:53.8 in the 10 kilometre event. Another breakthrough was the silver medal win of West German Peter Angerer beating out Markus Jacob of East Germany who finished with a perfect target score and the bronze medal. And, to continue his biathlon success at Sarajevo, Angerer went on to win a gold medal in the 20 kilometre event. The young West German completed his race in a record time of 1:11:52.7.

The 30 kilometre relay event produced the best relay team of 1984 with the Soviets taking the gold medal, Norway the silver, and West Germany the bronze.

# The Venue

The Olympic biathlon events will take place within Alberta's Kananaskis Country at the Canmore Nordic Centre.

Situated approximately 100 kilometres west of Calgary, Canmore was a former coal mining centre in the 1900s. The expected five thousand spectators and two-hundred-and-fifty athletes attending the events will be transported to the Nordic Centre via the Trans-Canada Highway.

The three Olympic biathlon events consist of 10 and 20 kilometre individual races and a 30 kilometre four-man relay. The competitors race the course and stop at the firing range to shoot at stationary targets.

The combined cross-country and biathlon stadium has start and finish lines for both sports. Although they share the same location, the events have separate facilities. Athletes will frequently pass through the stadium area, on a limited number of short loops, to give spectators a close-up view of the Nordic events.

The stadium is located adjacent to the biathlon shooting range. The shooting area is approximately 50 by 90 metres and provides competitors with thirty-two targets in all. The firing range faces due north which ensures that the sun will be behind the biathletes when they are shooting.

Biathlon trail systems are designed to satisfy the requirements of Olympic calibre competition and cover approximately 20 kilometres of trail corridor. The design of the trails allows racers to gradually raise their heart rates after leaving the start area and challenges them at key intervals throughout the course. A gradual ascent, rather than a steep incline to the finish line, avoids too many tied races. This feature ensures that the strongest athlete will finish first.

Snowmaking capacity is an Olympic requirement at all Olympic venues, and is provided for at the Canmore Nordic Centre.

Permanent features of the complex as a legacy after the 1988 Olympic Winter Games will include the 1,000-square-metre day lodge, the biathlon shooting range, 20 kilometres of competitive biathlon trails, approximately 32 kilometres of competitive cross-country trails, and 10 kilometres of recreational ski trails.

The internationally acclaimed facility at the mountain village of Canmore is the best Nordic centre Canada has ever had.

## The Technique

The biathlon's extremes of cross-country ski racing and rifle marksmanship make strange bedfellows.

Concentrating on firing a rifle accurately with a pulse racing with fatigue is tremendously stressful for the athlete, and a challenge to self-composure. In the biathlon event, the biathlete is penalized for poor shooting skills. Therefore, the winners of the biathlon are not always the fastest cross-country skiers or the best marksmen, but those who finish with the least amount of penalties added to the total time. A case in point at the Olympic Winter Games at Sarajevo in 1984, was East German biathlete Markus Jacob who finished the 10 kilometre event with a score of ten perfect bull's-eye shots on the target range, and a bronze medal.

In the Olympic biathlon program there are three races, of 20 kilometres, 10 kilometres, and a 4 x 7.5 kilometre relay.

The target range holds the key to victory in the biathlon event and getting in and out of the shooting range quickly is crucial to the biathlete.

In approximately thirty seconds, an Olympic class biathlete can align himself up with the target in a prone or standing position, sling the rifle off his back, shoot five shots, and return the rifle to the back harness.

Although wind affects marksmanship in the biathlon event, a fall on the cross-country track loses time, and may clog the rifle sight with snow and result in the competitor getting hit on the head with a ten pound rifle!

The sports psychology skills of the biathlete make it possible for him to utilize various techniques to gain control of his level of mental consciousness. Taught to use mental imagery and

Norwegian biathlete Magnar Solberg, gold medal winner at the 1968 and 1972 Olympic Winter Games. *Deutsche Presse-Agentur GmbH*

visualization, the biathlete quickly attempts to convert his "mental-set" once he has entered the shooting station. Using mind control enables the athlete to perform as in slow motion with calm, collected concentration.

Being in top physical condition and using patterned breathing techniques, the biathlete can reduce his heartbeat on the target range by sixty beats, from the first to the final shot, in a period of thirty seconds.

Studies of the shooting technique indicate that the shots are fired between heartbeats in the respiratory cycles of one breath in for two seconds, and one breath out for two seconds. During this respiratory cycle there is a pause when the lungs are relaxed, and it is at that precise moment that the shot is fired.

A steady hand shoots well; however, for the biathlete, breathing and concentration must also be synchronized with eye focus within a five-second time frame. It is pointless to centre the eye on the actual rifle sight circle until the proper respiratory cycle is achieved. Keeping the eye moving around the small dotted circle in the rifle sight is paramountly important as eye focus is at a maximum for only five to seven seconds.

A world class biathlete is an exceptional competitor.

Norwegian Eirik Kvalfoss demonstrates the prone technique used by Olympic biathletes. *Aftenposten, Norway*

## The Rules

The biathlon was added to the Olympic Winter Games in 1960. The event consisted of a 20 kilometre individual race, skied in five segments interspersed with four rounds of target shooting.

Shooting rounds alternate from a prone position to a standing position. The prone position offers a steady, stable platform for the marksman, and because of this he must shoot at a 115 mm circular metal target with a 45 mm inner circular scoring mark. This is the smallest of all biathlon targets and is about the size of a Canadian Olympic Coin. In comparison, the standing position affords an 115 mm metal target with a larger scoring mark. The five metal targets are placed 215 mm apart in a straight row and face the competitors from a distance of 50+

metres. The biathletes shoot five bullets each time they enter the target area and a missed shot draws a one minute penalty that is added to the final time.

After the biathlete is finished his shooting round, the mechanical targets are lowered into a judges' pit that has been constructed below the ground. There, the targets are closely inspected before results are posted. Because most biathlon officials value their lives, they choose to remain underground and out of range.

Penalty loops of 150 metres are added for each target missed in the 10 kilometre event that was added to the Olympic Winter Games in 1980. The penalty circle is often lined with a mob of cheering spectators who enthusiastically count the penalty laps for the competitor. Nicknamed "the box" by the biathletes, the penalty loop is a fenced-in cross-country track near the target area. The 10 kilometre race has just two shooting stops interspersed with three racing segments. In both the 20 kilometre and 10 kilometre races, competitors start one minute apart at the starting gate.

An added attraction to the Olympic biathlon format is the four-man relay, first held in 1968. The relay event requires 7.5 kilometres from each of the team members. A mass-start of the men out of the starting gate makes for an exciting first leg of the race. The event has only two shooting station stops and racers are allowed three extra rounds, over and above the regulation five in the other two biathlon events. In all races, the first five bullets used are inserted together on the target range and fired in rapid succession. Having eight bullets to shoot five targets in the relay event is a definite advantage, but each of the last three bullets must be loaded into the open bolt of the rifle as a single shot.

As the biathlete completes his leg of the relay race and enters into the 30 metre length of cross-over track, he must place his hand firmly on his team-mate's body to ensure that contact has been made. A hand-to-hand passover is not allowed.

Women have never competed in any Olympic biathlon events. However, in 1978 the full-bore military rifle fired at 150 metres was replaced in competition with a smaller bore rim-fire rifle which was fired at 50 metres. This rule change opened the doors to women and youth competitors in the biathlon.

Spectators watching the biathlon events at the Canmore Nordic Centre will be reminded again that the sport requires skill and determination.

## The Equipment

"Skinny Skis" are designed to be lightweight and flexible. The skis are half the width of an Alpine ski and have no metal edges on the bases.

Competitive clothing is so thin for the biathlete that serious problems would result, particularly in extremely cold weather, if the racer did not have the opportunity to warm up gradually once he is on the course. Traditionally, biathlon track design avoids long downhill runs directly after the start line.

All rifles used in the Olympic biathlon event must be non-automatic and the weight of the small-bore rifle is about ten pounds. Different athletes prefer different makes of rifles, and many of the .22 calibre foreign models are designed especially for the biathlon event.

The rifles are slung on the back of the athlete and worn like a knapsack. It is almost impossible to secure the rifle harness tightly so that it is snug against the back. Russian studies have shown that the biathlete must compensate the body angle with a decrease in forward position to adjust to the added weight of the rifle. Extension and bending of the knee and hip are slightly restricted and once again demonstrate the difficulty of this unlikely combination of cross-country skiing and rifle marksmanship.

The biathlete is prohibited from continuing on to the next firing range unless his rifle has been unloaded.

# Calgary Preview

It seems the gods have been vacationing elsewhere as far as Canadian involvement in the Olympic biathlon is concerned.

In fact, the Canadian Olympic Association chose to bypass the event for the XIV Olympic Winter Games at Sarajevo, Yugoslavia, in 1984. Never having entered a biathlete in the 10 kilometre event at the Winter Games, Canada's best finish in international competition was in the 20 kilometre race. Esko Karhu's forty-sixth-place finish at Grenoble, France, in 1968 is Canada's only Olympic Winter Games record in biathlon.

The biathlon is a national participatory winter sport in Norway and so it was appropriate that a Norwegian biathlete won a gold medal at Sarajevo in 1984. Eirik Kvalfoss clocked the fastest time of 30:53.8 and his expert rifle marksmanship put him in top place in the 10 kilometre event. West German Peter Angerer pushed Kvalfoss all the way and finished a silver medalist with a time of 31:02.4. East German Matthias Jacob shot a perfect score at the shooting station, and finished with a time of 31:10.5 as the bronze medalist. Look for continued dominance of the 10 kilometre event by the Germans and Scandinavians at Calgary. The 1987 World Cup leader is Fritz Fisher of East Germany.

The Soviets have produced some brilliant racers who will be challenging the field in 1988 at the Canmore Nordic Centre. Last year, at the first biathlon World Cup ever staged in North

West Germany's gold medal winners Peter Angerer and Fritz Fisher demonstrate how the hand must be firmly placed on the team-mate's body at the end of a relay lap. *Deutsche Presse-Agentur GmbH*

Five-time Canadian National Champion, Corporal Eric Rauhanen, at the shooting range. He trains an average of forty hours a week with the co-operation of the Department of National Defence. *Athlete Information Bureau/Canadian Olympic Association*

America, the rifle range at Canmore Nordic Centre was tested by the best in the world. The Soviets, who choose their top biathletes from an estimated sixty thousand Russian competitors, were represented by top finishers Valeri Medvedtsev in the 20-kilometre individual race, and Yuri Kachkarov, who won the 10-kilometre event, setting a World Cup record in the process.

Compared to the Soviet Union, Canada is getting close to the one thousand mark in active biathlon competitors, up nearly two hundred from a couple of years ago. Mainstays of Canada's national biathlon team are Charles Plamondon of St. Augustin, Quebec, Glenn Rupertus of Camrose, Alberta, Paget Stewart and Garet Coyne of Canmore, Alberta, Ken Karpoff of Edmonton, Albert and Jamie Kallio of Deep River, Ontario. Their 1988 Olympic team participation will be based on their selection races and performances on the World Cup tour. Although he collapsed from exhaustion at the finish line at the pre-Olympic event in 1987, Paget Stewart was the top Canadian finisher at the 1987 World Cup. His forty-seventh-place finish was an incredible achievement for the six-man Canadian team.

The formidable athletic prowess of biathlete Peter Angerer of West Germany took him to a first-place finish, and a gold medal in the 20 kilometre biathlon event in the 1984 Olympics. The 1987 season signalled his return to top ranking in international biathlon competitions after an eleven-month suspension for drug use. Angerer is a clean shooter and superb athlete, but will be challenged by East Germany's Frank-Peter Roetsch, Harri Eloranta of Finland, Sverre Istad, and Eirik Kvalfoss from the Norwegian team. The training regimen followed by the Soviets, Germans, and Scandinavians indicates few surprises or upsets for medalists at Calgary in 1988. They are the ones to beat.

The 30 kilometre biathlon relay event produced the best relay team of 1984 with the Russians taking the gold medal. The silver medal was won by the Norwegians and bronze won by the West German team. The Soviet team's solid lead in the relay events during the pre-Olympic year will provide very tough competition for the other teams at the Canmore Nordic Centre in 1988. However, there is an outside chance that the persistence of the Nordic nation's attitude and national character could upset the Soviets' medal prospects at the XV Olympic Winter Games.

Norway's Eirik Kvalfoss, gold medal winner of the 10 kilometre at the 1984 Games. *International Olympic Committee Archives*

Peter Angerer of West Germany slings his rifle off his back to prepare for one of his shots in the 20 kilometre race at the 1984 Games. He won a gold medal in this event. *European Press Photo Union*

# Canadians at the Olympic Winter Games
## BIATHLON

Canada has participated in the biathlon once at the Olympic Winter Games.

### 1968 Grenoble — x Olympic Winter Games

Boyde, J., Ede, G., Karu, E.K., McGill, K., Rattai, G.

46. Esko K. Karu
51. George Ede
53. James Boyde
54. George Rattai

# Bobsleigh

Canada Olympic Park
February 20, 21, 27, 28

*Photo by Vanessa Emery*

Having made presentations on behalf of CODA (the Canadian Olympic Development Association) to the International Bob and Luge Federations since the early 1960s and to the IOC in 1966, it gives me particular pleasure to write the introduction to a sport which has finally been established on Canadian soil, some twenty years later, here in Canada's Olympic Park. This introduction also gives me the opportunity to dispel some of the myths about bobsleighing.

When I was bobsleighing, ours was still very much an amateur sport. There were no refrigerated tracks. The season was consequently short and one could participate at an international level with only a few weeks of training and racing each year, so long as you had a good feel for ice, were strong, fast, and competitive in spirit, and felt that the excitement was worth the risk of accidents, which befell us all at one time or another. It was a marvellous period to be practising the sport each winter in a different country, with a great deal of camaraderie amongst the teams which competed on a very even footing with similar equipment, the best invariably victorious and applauded by the rest.

As for most of the Olympic sports, times have changed. Now endless research into bobsleigh design, coupled with countless hours of practice year-round and a full winter season, are the order of the day for a team wishing to be competitive. It was unreasonable to expect Canadians ever to be in contention again without a home track. Now that we have it, we can hope.

In spite of the basic change from amateur fling to full-time commitment, bobsleighing as a sport has changed surprisingly little over the years. It has always been a terrific thrill, a bit akin to a three-dimensional roller coaster without a fixed track to get to the other end. It has always relied heavily on the skill of the pilot to steer the swiftest (and safest) course. And, particularly since 1952, when a weight limit was imposed on both the four and two-man crews, it has come to rely increasingly on the athletic prowess of the entire team, the initial thrust from the starting blocks being a very important contribution to the bobsleigh's speed until gravity takes over.

The thrill has always been in the rapid and frequent changes of direction and, of course, trying to go faster than everyone else. The speeds have become a little faster but so, coincidentally, have the tracks become a little safer with overhanging walls and the greater control possible through modern equipment on smoother (refrigerated) ice. Contrary to popular belief, the winning sled has never been determined by raw courage, but rather by the combination of technically efficient equipment, the thrust at the start, and the pilot's skill at weaving through the labyrinth of curves and straights as perfectly (and safely) as possible. Unlike other hazardous speed sports, however, one does not have to worry about brakes or acceleration because the brakes are not used until after the finish and one has at least a little time to absorb the force of gravity.

The Calgary 1988 bobsleigh track encompasses all that has been learned about bobsleighing to date and will provide tremendous excitement to spectators and sliders alike. Because it does this, while really challenging the pilot's skills, it will endure for many world championships to come and perhaps other Olympics. At the ultimate level, there is really nothing that can quite match this sport.


Victor Emery
*Pilot of Canadian bobsleighs for ten years from 1956 culminating in gold medals in the four-man bobsleigh at the 1964 Olympics and 1965 Worlds as well a bronze in the 1965 World Two-Man Championships.*

## The History

It was the innovative Eskimo who first harnessed the sled to a team of dogs to transport the hunter over the vast silent ice of the Canadian north.

Montrealers first pointed the toboggan downhill on the famous Tuque Bleue slide in the 1870s, but it was the Swiss who later attached a steering mechanism to the toboggan. From then on, riders have been offered hair-raising changes of direction while they negotiate corners in a bobsleigh.

With the increase in length of the smaller handsled, the longer vehicle offered greater speed, more excitement, and room for more riders. Thrill-seekers, willing to try anything once, included the Swiss and free-spirited English vacationing in Switzerland. The craze for the new daredevil sport lured sportsmen away from the smaller skeleton sled and converted them to bobsleigh enthusiasts.

As many as six men or women riding on one sled, all lying on their stomachs, would career recklessly headfirst down the mountains. Soaring off the rudimentary courses into space, the riders found themselves performing spectacular aeronautical manoeuvres. To put an end to this athletic lunacy, courses with high banks were constructed and sledders adopted a sitting position for more control.

This modification in body position also permitted new, more streamlined designs with either wheel or rope steering, and brakes for the last person in tandem.

The new design of sled also initiated a new name for the sport.

It evolved from the high embankments on the curves of the course. Once the driver had entered the turn and reached the precise line of maximum speed and height on the wall of the curve, he would dive the sled back down into the chute. To gain more speed as the sled exited from the bend onto the straightaway, the riders would bob forward with their heads and simultaneously shove backwards with their seats. This practice eventually stopped when the faster speeds of the modern sleds made it ineffective.

The bobsleigh, named by a wild brigade of speed demons, was to become one of the most popular events in the Olympic Winter Games.

Nineteenth-century bobsleigh racing rules originally specified that two members of the four or five-member teams must be women. Although the disadvantages of wearing long skirts may have hindered their riding ability, the women performed admirably in these early competitions.

The first bobsleigh courses were fashioned by snow banking the edges of the natural tracks. As interest in the sport grew, the design of the race courses became more and more technical with the addition of ice and water. The ice was cut from adjacent lakes, hauled up the mountainsides of the Alps by teams of horses, packed piece by piece into the bobsleigh course, and then watered down. Eventually the bobsleigh runs were nothing more than steep troughs of solid ice.

With the increasing speed of the sleds and the high accident rate on the dangerous courses, a decision was made by the Swiss in 1904 to design and construct a bobsleigh run. Today,

"The Spill", ca. 1889. Tobogganing on the park slide, in Montreal, Quebec. *Notman Photographic Archives, McCord Museum*

the famous bob run at St. Moritz is still considered one of the premier race courses in the world and one of the few remaining which relies on freezing temperatures as opposed to artificial refrigeration. By 1914 there were over one hundred bobsleigh courses with varying levels of sophistication in Europe.

The sport came to Canada more slowly. In 1911, a young Swiss ski instructor and bobsleigh enthusiast was imported to the Laurentians. Emile Cochand not only built the first ski resort in Canada, but founded the first bobsleigh club in the country at the exclusive Seignerie Club in Montebello where some of the banks can still be seen in the forested hillside leading down to the Ottawa River. His name is perpetuated today in the popular Chalet Cochand resort, at Ste.-Marguerite, Quebec.

In 1923 the Fédération Internationale de Bobsleigh et de Tobogganing (FIBT) was founded. It ruled that women be disallowed from the bobsleigh event and as a result women have never competed in the event at the Olympic Winter Games.

When the Olympic Winter Games were inaugurated at Chamonix, France, in 1924, the bobsleigh event consisted of a four and a five-man competition. The Swiss team dominated the competition and won the gold medal, with Great Britain winning the silver, a fitting tribute to the freewheeling vacationers of the preceding generation.

St. Moritz, Switzerland, home of the notorious Cresta Run, was the site of the second Olympic Winter Games in 1928. The skeleton (or cresta) event was one of the more dangerous events to be introduced. The 40-60 lb. (18-27 kilo) vehicle with fixed steel runners is ridden in a headfirst prone position and steered by subtly shifting body weight to negotiate the curves on the course. By dragging the inside foot, both steering and braking are introduced quite necessarily on occasion, as the Cresta run cannot be taken flat out.

The bobsleigh event at St. Moritz in 1928 on its specially designed track marked the first international Olympic bobsleigh competition with the United States entered in the race. The race was won by Billy Fiske, an American who steered his five-man sled to a gold medal victory ahead of fellow countryman John Heaton, who picked up the silver. Fiske became the wonderboy of the bobsleigh at the Games in 1928, winning his gold medal at eighteen years of age.

Construction of the first bobsleigh run in the Western Hemisphere was initiated after the selection of Lake Placid, New York, as the site of the third Olympic Winter Games in 1932. The Lake Placid run was to become one of the most challenging in the world, and in fact has claimed a number of lives over the years. Other precedents set were the ruling that crews

This roller was filled with hot water and used to flatten the course for sled races on the Davos-Klosters Road in Switzerland. *Courtesy Roger Gibbs*

The Swiss, including Emile Cochand, came to Ste.-Agathe-des-Monts, Quebec, in the early 1900s to teach Canadians the sport of bobsleigh. *Notman Photographic Archives, McCord Museum*

Women bobsleighers take the corner at Davos, Switzerland, in the early 1900s. *Courtesy Roger Gibbs, London, England*

of only four men would make up the bobsleigh event and the introduction of a two-man boblet event.

The Olympic Games were opened by New York Governor Franklin Delano Roosevelt and spectator concern for the safety of bobsleighers soon became a major issue at the bobsleigh course on Mt. Van Hoevenberg. The concern inspired the wife of the Governor, Eleanor Roosevelt, to go down the run in a bobsleigh to show the public how safe the sport had become—an Olympic Winter Games historical record by anyone's standards.

American engineering ingenuity, with newly invented V-shaped steel runners, produced gold medals once again for the United States in both the four-man and two-man competitions. The new runners were designed to clamp onto the slow wooden slats of the bobsleigh. However, after official protests from other countries about the ''razor blade surgery'' on the track, the V-shape of the runner was declared illegal by race officials. A new steel runner, however, with a rounded surface, was given FIBT acceptance.

Billy Fiske again piloted the American bobsleigh team in 1932 to a gold medal. Due to a slow track caused by a thaw, the competition was limited to two runs. One of Fiske's crew members was the Yale and Oxford-educated Eddie Eagan, the 1920 Olympic Heavyweight boxing champion. The gold medal win by Eagan demonstrates one of the unique traits that runs like a common thread through the backgrounds of bobsleigh athletes—the sport attracts athletes from other sport disciplines and Eagan was no exception. Eddie Eagan, the future chair-

man of the New York Boxing Commission, distinguished himself as the only person in Olympic history to win a gold medal in both Olympic Summer and Winter Games. Eagan and Fiske, both legends in Olympic bobsleighing, never again raced together in the Olympics. Billy Fiske, one of the first American pilots to join Britain's Royal Air Force when war broke out, was shot down over Germany in 1939, dying at twenty-nine years of age.

Despite heavy rainfall and a slow track at the Winter Games at Garmisch-Partenkirchen, Germany, in 1936, two American brothers, Bill and Bob Linney, won the gold in the two-man competition. In the four-man event, the Swiss won both gold and silver, and Great Britain the bronze.

St. Moritz, Switzerland, was the site of the fifth Olympic Winter Games in 1948, the first Games after World War II. The cresta event was held again with fifteen competitors from six countries. Appropriately, the gold medal winner was Nino Bibbia, an extraordinarily talented rider from Italy, who for the decades since has won innumerable trophies on the Cresta, still competing as a top class rider, though now into his sixties. The winning bobsleigh teams in 1948 were the Americans and the Swiss.

Andreas Ostler of Germany proved that weight means speed in Olympic bobsleighing at the sixth Olympic Winter Games at Oslo, Norway, in 1952. The gold medal teams of the 1952 Winter Games were the last of an era of momentous heavyweights in the sport. The sturdy Germans carried a net weight of 236.6 kg in the two-man contest, and with two equally stalwart teammates, had a combined man weight of 472.5 kg in the four-man race. Ostler became the first man in Olympic history to pilot gold medal sleds in both the two-man and four-man bobsleigh events.

Race officials and judges from the FIBT were subjected to such a barrage of complaints from other bobsleigh teams against the gold medalists that a new ruling was introduced by the Federation after the 1952 Olympics. Maximum weight limitations for the combination of man and sled were imposed which brought the sport back to being an athletic contest. Since 1954, the weight combination of the two-man sled and riders cannot exceed a total weight of 390 kg with the four-man sled combination not exceeding 630 kg.

With bobsleighers now averaging 80-90 kg, the weight factor is equalized and men with the build of football half-backs have proven to be the best combination for an athletic start and a fast run on the track.

Cortina d'Ampezzo, Italy, was the site of the seventh Olympic Winter Games in 1956, and was the first time that Canadian Victor Emery saw the sport of bobsleighing. Emery, a keen Alpine and Nordic skier, was living in Europe at the time. He decided to cross-country ski over the mountains from St. Moritz, Switzerland, where he was doing some Cresta, to watch the Winter Olympics in Italy. Switzerland took the gold in the four-man bobsleigh piloted by forty-six-year-old Franz Kapus. Italian Eugenio Monti, a former alpine skiing star, won silver medals in both the two-man and four-man races.

Already a legend in bobsleighing at the age of twenty-eight, and equipped with a new Podar bob, Eugenio Monti went on to win eleven World Championships from 1957 to 1968. Monti is considered to be the greatest driver in the history of bobsleighing, but it was not until twelve years after his Olympic silver medals in Cortina that the Italian finally won Olympic gold medals at Grenoble, France, in 1968 in both the two and four-man events.

Immediately following the Winter Games at Cortina d'Ampezzo, Victor Emery, from London, Ontario, returned to St. Moritz with the British bobsleigh team and took his first rides there in competitions on the bobsleighs of the famous Marquis di Portago, who had just taken fourth place in the Olympics for Spain. Unfortunately, Portago was destined for a fatal car crash a year later in the famous Mille Miglia.

Emery also rode with Keith Schellenberg, captain of the British sled, who became a life-long friend and loaned Emery equipment to get started as a bobsleigh driver. Schellenberg also helped him to find brakemen from among spectators by suggesting that Emery was longer in experience and skill than was the reality. After a one-run "hair-raiser" behind pilot Emery, the "cannon fodder" brakeman rarely remained with him for a second run.

In exasperation, Emery telephoned London to his old university friend, Lamont Gordon, to come to St. Moritz for a try and convinced him they could spell each other off as brake-

The German gold medal heavyweights in the four-man bobsleigh event at the 1952 Games in Oslo, Norway. Weight restrictions were later imposed in the bobsleigh events. *Deutsche Presse-Agentur GmbH*

man and driver for the remainder of the season. Gordon agreed, and went on to pilot sleds for Canada until 1965, achieving a fourth place in the four-man World Championships in Garmisch-Partenkirchen, Germany, in 1962 at the zenith of his career.

Eugenio Monti's gold medal plans were frustrated in 1960 by a decision made by organizers of the eighth Olympic Winter Games at Squaw Valley, California, not to build a bobsleigh run. With only nine countries interested in competing in the event, the construction of a bobsleigh run was considered too expensive. Thus bobsleighing endured an eight-year layoff as an Olympic event until being included in the 1964 Games at Innsbruck, Austria, by which time a number of World Champions were champing at the bit.

In 1964, Eugenio Monti, with six consecutive two-man boblet World Championships and three World Championships in four-man to his credit, entered the ninth Olympic Winter Games at Innsbruck, Austria, as the gold medal favourite. But Monti's run for glory was effectively destroyed by his personal demonstration of great sportsmanship. The Olympic ideal of fair play needed no better example than Eugenio Monti's contribution to gold medal wins by the British and Canadians.

In the two-man competition at the completion of his run, track officials informed Eugenio Monti that the British team was in trouble up at the start house. As Nash and Dixon prepared for their second run, they had discovered that an axle bolt on their sled had sheered and broken off. Instantly, Monti whipped a bolt off his own sled and rushed it up to the British team at the top of the start area.

With that good deed, the British men were able to slide again within the time limit, and Monti denied himself his coveted gold medal by finishing third. The gesture was not out of character and Monti's unselfish nature was illustrated when he said, ''Tony Nash won the gold medal because he was the best two-man driver in the Games. . . .'' Eugenio Monti went on to be the first recipient of the Pierre De Coubertin Fair Play Trophy in May of 1965. A true gentleman in the tradition of Olympic sportsmanship, Monti became the first holder of the Olympic award. The trophy is not necessarily awarded every year, but when merited, is presented to an amateur athlete whose career or good sportsmanship justifies an award of special distinction.

''The biggest upset in Olympic bobsleigh history'' was what one coach called the phenomenon of the Canadian team in 1964. The Canadians, like the British, had been working their way up through the ranks in world competitions since 1959. With the help of the Italians in training and competition, the Canadian crew came through with a gold medal victory unexpected by the outside world.

Dubbed the ''intellectual sled'' by the bobsleigh fraternity, the Canadian four-man bobsleigh was piloted by Harvard MBA Victor Emery, his brother John Emery, a plastic surgeon, geologist Peter Kirby, and teacher Douglas Anakin. Other members of the contingent were Lamont Gordon, driver of Canada 2, Gordon Currie, David Hobart, and Christopher Ondaatje. The team was coached by Doug Connor, a former Cresta champion and managed by Charles Rathgeb, a well-known businessman and valued sports enthusiast from Toronto.

To warm up for the bobsleigh event, the fun-loving contingent entered Doug Anakin and John Emery in the luge competition. The luge event was introduced as a Winter Olympic sport that year. But after the death of one British luger and three serious injuries to others, coach Doug Connor decided to withdraw his Canadians and save them for the premier event—the four-man bobsleigh competition. As warm weather threatened the track, Olympic officials opted to start the bobsleigh competition a day early at the Games.

On the first run of four-man competition, the Canadians astounded everyone by establishing a track record. This performance was no fluke, as the two-man boblet competition with twenty-two entrants had been very successful for Canada. Victor Emery and his brakeman, Peter Kirby, had led after the first heat and narrowly missed a bronze medal in finishing fourth. The team had been expected to do better in the fours and had consistently been among the top sleds in the trial runs leading up to the competition.

The phenomenal time of 1:2.99 for the first heat, never to be reached again on the Igls track, was achieved in spite of a back axle seizing near the end of the run, threatening to force the Canadians out of the race before the second heat.

Once again, the Italians came to the fore, and Eugenio Monti's mechanics swarmed over the Emery sled, adjusting it suffi-

Charles Rathgeb, Jr., the general manager of the bobsleigh team in 1964, and Lamont Gordon, who piloted the first-ever Canadian entry in international competition. *Courtesy Charles Rathgeb*

Italian Eugenio Monti (right) is interviewed together with British gold medal winners in the two-man event. Tony Nash (centre) and Robin Dixon (left). Monti was awarded the Pierre de Coubertin Trophy at the 1964 Games. *Deutsche Presse-Agentur GmbH*

ciently to partially free the axle for the second heat. At the end of the second run, the Canadians were comfortably ahead of the field, over half a second in the lead, having placed second in that heat.

As the weather turned cooler at Igls, the competition was extended for an extra day, one heat being run on each of the second and third days.

The extra day proved fortunate as Victor Emery came down with a tetanus shot reaction in the middle of the night and was barely able to make his way to the track for his third run. After a second-place finish for the Canadians, John Emery, the only one to know of the problem, slipped his brother away to the hospital until the next day's final heat.

The Canadian fours dominated the finals the following day. Their first-place finish in the fourth heat put them exactly one second ahead of the next sled, an extremely large margin by bobsleigh standards. The all-out effort by the crew produced a total time of 4:14.46 and the gold medal. Austria won the silver and Emery's friend and mentor, Eugenio Monti, won the bronze just as he had done in the two-man event.

At the Sport Hotel in Igls, the Canadian team's victory party became a legend of its own in the annals of Olympic history. Back at Olympic Village in Innsbruck, the party ended with a swap of attire with the medal-winning Swedish hockey team.

"Now I can retire a happy man," said forty-year-old Eugenio Monti, the master of his sport at the tenth Olympic Winter Games at Grenoble, France, in 1968. Driving both two-man and four-man sleds to medal victories, the celebrated red-haired Italian finally had achieved his twelve-year dream.

Left out of the medal standings at Grenoble in 1968, the Canadian crew nevertheless had retained its place in international bobsleighing for two years after the 1964 Olympics. In spite of a shoulder injury from a training-run spill, Victor Emery and Michael Young took a bronze medal in the 1965 World Championship two-man boblet event at St. Moritz, Switzerland, the following year and the four-man team of Victor Emery, Peter Kirby, Michael Young, and Gerald Presley won the gold medal by the huge margin of two seconds.

In 1966 the team went on to the World Championships in Cortina d'Ampezzo, Italy, and was heading for a medal once again in the four-man competition when the track started to break up and disaster struck the German team when one of its drivers was killed and another seriously injured. The race was cancelled halfway through the event.

By 1967 three of the Emery crew had married and the team retired from international competition.

Both Canadian and American bobsleigh teams went to the Olympic Winter Games at Sapporo, Japan, in 1972 at a definite disadvantage. Lake Placid's bobsleigh run at Mt. Van Hoevenberg provided the only bobsleigh practice facility in North America, and it had been closed by the State of New York due to budget cutbacks. The interruption in training for both the Americans and the Canadians contributed to both teams failing to place any sled in the top ten. Germany won the gold in the two-man event, and Switzerland won the gold medal in the four-man event with a time of 4:43.07.

For the twelfth Olympic Winter Games at Innsbruck, Austria, in 1976, the prior bobsleigh and luge runs were replaced by a first-ever combined track at Igls. Denver, Colorado, had withdrawn as host city of the 1976 Games and the International Olympic Committee, on very short notice, had accepted the invitation to host the Winter Games from Innsbruck.

The suggestion from the organizing committee to combine the bobsleigh and luge tracks was based on financial obligations that the Games would be held in Innsbruck at a reasonable cost. The proposed combination facility, although not ideal, was a compromise track, shorter than the FIBT regulation 1,500 metres for the bobsleigh event, with fewer curves and less gradient. Luge athletes expressed concern about the heavy bobsleighs, with combined weight of riders and four-man sled at 630 kg, causing track damage when running the course. Built primarily for the luge with its rudimentary steering capabilities, the track proved too little a challenge for the bobsleighers. However, the construction was completed and the combined track provided a reasonable compromise for the contestants.

The German Democratic Republic had only three years to practise the sport of bobsleigh before entering the Games at Innsbruck for the first time, yet ended up winning both gold medals in the event. Meinhard Nehmer, a staff sergeant in the German army, distinguished himself as the third driver to pilot two gold medal sleds at the same Olympics. It was a combination of fast starts and sled innovations which gave the medal winners the edge. At the age of thirty-five, the former javelin thrower joined the elite company of double gold medal winners, Germany's Anderl Ostler and Italian Eugenio Monti. West Germany took the silver medal in the two-man bob and the bronze in the four-man event. Switzerland, in the opposite order, took silver in the four-man and bronze in the two-man competition. Canada once again finished well out of medal contention.

Mt. Van Hoevenberg's original bobsleigh track, built for the 1932 Olympic Winter Games at Lake Placid, New York, was reconstructed for the XIII Olympic Winter Games in 1980 to

The Canadian gold medalists at the 1964 Games: (l. to r.) Victor Emery, Douglas Anakin, John Emery, and Peter Kirby. *EPU*

make it one of the fastest in the world. It was also very challenging. During the two-month run up to the championships, bobsleighers, setting record times on practice runs, were involved in forty-five accidents that put twenty-four of them into the hospital.

Setting the pace on the first run of the Olympic event, the two-man Swiss team of Erich Schärer and Josef Benz clocked a course record of 1:01.87. The Olympic record time on their first run, combined with their next three runs, won a gold medal for Switzerland in the event with a total time of 4:09.36. The honours in the bobsleigh event at Lake Placid went to G.D.R. Air Force Lieutenant Meinhard Nehmer once again. By retaining the title he won at Innsbruck in 1976, he became the first man to win an Olympic bobsleigh gold medal twice running since Billy Fiske did so on the same track at the Winter Games in 1932.

Canada's performance on the one-mile course was less than spectacular. The four-man sled, driven by Alan MacLachlan of Toronto, finished its second run on its side, and the team withdrew from the event on the final day.

Overlooking picturesque Sarajevo, Yugoslavia, Trebevic Hill was the location of the bobsleigh and luge course for the XIV Olympic Winter Games in 1984. The 1,245 metre combination track incorporated thirteen curves, several of which prompted concern by the bobsleighers during their practice runs. A build-up of thick ice on the curves had caused the track to break up on three bends, while the fifth bend on the course developed a hole in the ice that forced cancellation of some training sessions. Track damage from the heavy bobsleighs and snowstorms in Sarajevo caused many interruptions in both training and competition.

The one group of individuals that appeared unaffected by the wind and snow were the crews from East Germany who dominated the events with their new innovative sled design. The equipment breakthrough on the sled was the shock suspension built over each runner which allowed the pilot to drive the sled more steadily on the course than anyone else. Wolfgang Hoppe and Dietmar Schauerhammer led in all four runs of the two-man bob and picked up the gold medal with a time of 3:25.56. The four-man event was also won by Wolfgang Hoppe, who piloted his crew to victory in a record time of 3:20.22. Alan MacLachlan of Toronto and Bob Wilson from Montreal placed fourteenth in the two-man event with an aggregate time of 3:30.74 and in a field of twenty-four competitors, the four-man Canadian team placed eighteenth.

Once again, at Sarajevo, bobsleighing went through a transition. Until 1952, unlimited weight restrictions made it an unequal contest for the lighter teams. From 1956 to 1980, the contest was basically equal for all, although the importance of the initial push had become crucial due to more gradual start-

Meinhard Nehmer, a staff sergeant in the German Democratic Republic Army, leads his team to a gold medal win at the 1980 Games. *Deutsche Presse-Agentur GmbH*

ing chutes and some of the driving challenge had been eliminated due to the smoothness of the ice on the new artificial tracks.

By 1984, new engineering designs by the East Germans, Russians, and Swiss produced superior equipment compared to the rest of the field, and once more introduced an inequality into the sport. The FIBT is currently addressing this problem in hopes of eliminating these differences by 1988.

With the exception of the gold medal win in the four-man bobsleigh in 1964, Canada has been riding a losing record in the Olympic bobsleigh event. However, if the differences in sleds are eliminated by the FIBT, the construction of the spectacular bobsleigh and luge run at Canada Olympic Park should allow the Canadians, given their home-track advantage, to feature once again in the Olympic bobsleigh event.

The distinctive "wishbone" design of the combined bobsleigh and luge facility is the first ever constructed in the world with separate starts and built to Olympic standards.

## The Venue

Canada Olympic Park, a ten-minute drive from the core of downtown Calgary, is the site of the XV Olympic Winter Games bobsleigh event in 1988.

Constructed by the Government of Canada at approximately $18 million, the 1,480 metre long course contains fourteen curves built into the reinforced concrete track. The run is completely refrigerated at a constant temperature of –4°C.

In addition to training elite athletes, the bobsleigh run at Canada Olympic Park features a junior training start point with a length of 810 metres that will allow a maximum practice speed of 87 kph. Also featured is a start point at the 435 metre mark on the track for tourist enjoyment.

Bobsleighs weighing up to 630 kilograms will reach speeds of up to 125 kph as over twenty thousand spectators and media crowd into the viewing areas to watch the Olympic event. Closed circuit television along the full length of the course will cover the race and the event will be monitored with Swiss timing equipment.

A tribute to the precision engineering and design, the track will have an average gradient of 8 per cent. After the bob crews push off from the start house, the sled will pass through the starting gate and break the electric eye as the sled moves along the straightaway at the top of the course. Travelling to corners one, two, and three, the riders enter the steepest part of the track between corners four, five, six, and seven as the course gradient increases to 15 per cent. Corners seven and eight are called the Omega curve, and as riders enter this "S" bend, the intermediate split time will give a good indication as to who is leading the field. A 270 degree change in direction awaits the bobsleighers as the sled enters the Kreisel corner which swings back under itself, subjecting riders to nearly maximum 4.5 G-forces in the six seconds it takes to go through it. Spectators inside the enclosed circular viewing area will be treated

Pilot Wolfgang Hoppe of the German Democratic Republic drives his four-man bobsleigh to a gold medal win at the 1984 Games. *Deutsche Presse-Agentur GmbH*

to a close-up look at the daredevil sport of Olympic bobsleighing. The Labyrinth section encompasses curves ten and eleven as the sled then enters corner twelve (left) and corner thirteen (right) which flow into finish corner fourteen, past the electronic score board, and straight up to the finish line.

An educated spectator knows that one mistake on a bobsleigh run, and it's all over. Racing fans also know that if they want spectacular thrills and spills, the Olympic bobsleigh event at Canada Olympic Park will be where the action is in 1988.

## The Technique

It takes approximately one minute for world class bobsleighers to make a descent on a bob run.

On the tighter corners of the track, riders are subjected to G-forces of up to four and one half times the weight of gravity. This is the point at which blackouts begin to occur.

The sport of bobsleigh is a test of strength and running speed of the entire crew as well as driving skill and cool nerve on the part of the pilot. Success on the track depends on the mechanical perfection of the sled, the initial thrust given by the entire crew at the start, and the expertise of the driver on the way down.

Technical execution in moving the sled through the high (up to 6 metres) curved embankments has been described by Olympic gold medalist Eugenio Monti as "a feeling" that is an inherent instinct many world-class bobsleigh pilots possess.

The decision of how to take the curve lies solely in the hands of the driver of the bobsleigh. If he takes the curve too high, the sled could flip right over or fly off the course into the blue yonder; too low, and the sled may turn over at the end of the corner or slam violently into the opposite wall as it is propelled out of the bend. Between high and low is a judgement call depending on how the sled entered the corner, and at what speed.

Depending on the requirements of the corner, the driver attempts to take it at the right apogee (highest point of the curve) and then gain maximum G-drop by knifing the sled at the appropriate moment into the next straight. For the driver, this type of clean exit is akin to threading a needle on the trot.

While every member of the crew is important for the thrust at the start, the brakeman is the last man to get in, and therefore should be the strongest and fastest runner.

Although he never applies the brakes until the race is over and the sled past the finish line, the brakeman is also in the best position to assist the driver should the sled run into difficulty on the descent. Because he can best feel whether the sled is skidding up or down going in the curves, the brakeman also helps the driver assess each run.

Spotters on the side of the track are important and communicate with the driver as he walks the course between runs.

After their initial thrust at the start, the two middle riders in the four-man bob maintain stability in the sled during the descent. They are subjected to violent jerks from every direction all the way down and, being in the middle, it is paramountly important that they absorb these in a manner that keeps their weight central on the sled—not an easy task when they are literally on a roller coaster in three dimensions, without an exact trackline.

The Olympic bobsleigh event is visually dramatic in every way, from the unique rhythmical push-pull start to the finish.

Holding onto the push-bar handles, a four-man bob crew can lull viewers into a trance as they rock their bobsleigh back and forth across the ice at the starting gate. The slow steady build-up of rhythm is a study of timing and motion that ends abruptly with an explosive running push start as the driver hollers: "Go!" On this signal, the crew thrusts the sled out of the push grooves and the crew races forward in unison as they begin the 40 metre accelerating sprint down the start track. From this standing start, the bobsleigh speeds forward accompanied with an outburst of cheering from the fans lined up along the railings on both sides of the course.

The sled is positioned for the flying start 15 metres back of the electric eye. The driver gets in first and grabs hold of the steering ropes, as the number two and three men mount the sled and fold in the push bars. The last man on the sled, the brakeman, jumps on just as the front cowl crosses the 50 metre line.

At the early stage of the run, there is very little traction on the ice. The challenge of maintaining the sled on a true line at this point is an extremely delicate task for the driver. In fact, nobody shifts his initial seating position until the sled arrives at a corner where it begins to cut ice.

Despite the size, weight, and speed of sled acceleration at the start, the spectator will observe the extreme care and finesse the brakeman uses when he takes his upright position at the back—like someone sitting down on a dozen eggs might accurately describe the graceful motion. A delicate manoeuvre for a brakeman, who perhaps is a former football player, or decathlon champ converted into an Olympic bobsleigher.

From then on, it is mainly up to the driver (or pilot) who must allow the sled to seek the natural and truest line on the straights with a minimum of time-losing skids. Conversely, the driver must have enough control to take over at the crucial moment in each curve to bring the sled safely back into the next straight.

# The Rules

Women have never competed in the Olympic bobsleigh event.

There are two events included in the Olympic bobsleigh format. Each country is eligible to enter two teams in each of the two-man and four-man events. A bobsleigher is also permitted to enter both events.

Olympic bobsleigh competition provides four or five international judges and some ten to twenty officials. A draw is held to determine the starting lineup order before each event. Although the first few competitors may find the track slow compared to a team with a later draw this is usually equalized by the draw which changes the order for each descent.

The flying start takes place 15 metres above the starting line and the crew is allowed to accelerate beyond the line for any distance they wish.

Swiss timing will monitor the race electronically and will start to record the time the instant the front cowl of the sled crosses the starting line. The competition consists of four heats in both events, and the aggregate time of the four individual runs determines the placings.

Total combined weight of crew and sled may not exceed 390 kg for the two-man and 630 kg for the four-man bobsleigh. If the sled is below the maximum weight restrictions, additional ballast in the form of lead weight is admissible, but overweight means disqualification.

Mechanical accelerating devices are prohibited on the sled. Each sled is equipped with a serrated rake brake at the back. The crew is disqualified if the brake is applied on the course during a race. By that time all racers are expected to be going full-out after several practice runs at building up speed.

The combined luge and bobsleigh run at Calgary meets the FIBT ruling of minimum length of 1,200 metres with an average gradient of at least 8 per cent and a maximum of 15 per cent.

Bobsleigh is a sport that has taken its share of lives, and with the potential for an injury always present, the medical team at Canada Olympic Park will be highly visible during the Olympic Games.

# The Equipment

More effective steering and better control of skidding are two reasons why the European rope steering method has replaced the driver's steering wheel on most bobsleighs used in Olympic competition today. The steering ropes are attached to the front runners of the sled. The front runners have a 67 centimetre clearance between them on both four-man and two-man bobsleighs. The maximum length is 270 centimetres for the two-man and 380 centimetres for the four-man.

During the years of Olympic competition, the bobsleigh has evolved from its humble beginning as a fundamental wooden sleigh, into the 340.9 kg of metal and fibreglass racing machinery of the four-man sled that speeds down the bobsleigh course like a runaway truck.

As of March 1985, the standardization of all bobsleighs was enforced by the FIBT. The new ruling did away with the suspension over the front runners that had served the East Germans so well in their gold medal finishes at Sarajevo, Yugoslavia, in 1984. The new rules for design should put all competitors on an equal footing, once again pitting man against man.

Racing helmets are mandatory wear for bobsleighers in Olympic competition. The drivers and most crew members also wear goggles. The tight-fitting racing uniform is made from a stretch material and some riders wear elbow pads over the racing suit. Most drivers wear gloves, although some have been known to go without them for extra sensitivity with the ropes.

Bobsleighers wear racing shoes with small flexible spikes on the soles that look like file cleaners. The spikes give the necessary traction on the ice for the flying start.

Most bobsleighs used in international competition are made in Italy.

## Calgary Preview

For the first time in the history of Canadian bobsleighing, the team will not have to leave the country to train for the entire season during an Olympic year. The performances of Canada's two-man and four-man bobsleigh teams have improved considerably in international competition since the construction of the 1,480 metre track at Canada Olympic Park.

Based on results at the 1987 World Championships, as well as the 1987 European Championships, Canada has pre-qualified its top three bobsleigh drivers for the 1988 Olympics. Which two of the three will actually compete will not be known until

Two Swiss Olympians on an early design of bobsleigh. *Foto Plattner of St. Moritz*

official training at the Games is almost finished. This is standard practice for all countries participating. The top three drivers are Chris Lori, Dave Leuty, and Greg Haydenluck. Haydenluck, an Olympic-calibre track and field athlete, distinguished himself by being one of the first bobsleighers to open the new Calgary track in March of 1986. He would also like to distinguish himself by equalling cross-country skier Pierre Harvey's Olympic record (1984) by competing in the 1988 Olympic Winter Games and the 1988 Olympic Summer Games in track and field.

Leuty's sports background is somewhat typical of many athletes who have adopted the sport of bobsleigh. He was captain of football, and named Most Valuable Player of the team while attending high school at Upper Canada College in Toronto, Ontario. He was also the Ontario junior silver medalist in the decathlon, and played competitive ice hockey during high school and as a student at the University of Toronto. As grandson of Lionel Conacher, "The Big Train," Canada's finest all-round athlete, Leuty could add to the family laurels with an Olympic bobsleigh victory in 1988.

The Canadian sleds will be loaded with talent, and should include Clarke Flynn, brakeman Lloyd Guss, and crewmen Kevin Tyler and Steve Hall.

The G.D.R. continues to dominate the Olympic bobsleigh event. The East Germans possess a tremendous depth of training combined with good driving skills and superb starts. They are usually at the top of the international bobsleigh field. Driver Wolfgang Hoppe returns to four-man bob Olympic competition after his 3:20.22 gold medal victory at Sarajevo, Yugoslavia, in 1984. Along with brakeman Andreas Kirchner and riders Roland Wetzig and Dietmar Schauerhammer, the team is unquestionably the best bet for another gold medal performance in 1988. The Number Two and Number One two-man sleds from East Germany finished up with gold (3:25.56) and silver (3:26.04) in the medal standings on Trebevic Hill at Sarajevo. With continued success in European and world championships since 1984, drivers Detlef Richter or Bernhard Lehmann could easily repeat their medal performances again at Calgary in 1988.

Another contender in the four-man event could be the Swiss team piloted by Hans Hiltebrand. Swiss pair Ralph Pichler and Celest Poltera could give both the Soviets, and East and West Germans a good run for the money in the two-man competition. Pichler and Poltera won the 1987 World Championship at St. Moritz, Switzerland.

The United States won many medals in the earlier Olympic Winter Games, but has not taken a medal since 1956 when Tom Butler, Jim Lamy, Arthur Tyler, and Bill Dodge picked up the bronze medal in the four-man event. The Number One American entry in Calgary will be a four-man bob driven by pilot Matt Roy and his crew, who placed first in the 1987 World Cup standings, and with many American fans attending the

Canada's four-man bobsleigh team head onto the track at the 1984 Games at Sarajevo, Yugoslavia. *Athlete Information Bureau/Canadian Olympic Association*

Games to cheer him on in Calgary, he must not be underrated. Austria, Italy, Great Britain, and the U.S.S.R. are also expected to give strong performances at the XV Olympic Winter Games bobsleigh competition at Canada Olympic Park in 1988.

## Canadians at the Olympic Winter Games
## BOBSLEIGH

### 1924 - 1960

Canada did not participate.

### 1964 Innsbruck — IX Olympic Winter Games

Anakin, D., Currie, G., Emery, J., Emery, V., Gordon, L., Hobart, D., Kirby, P., Ondaatje, C.

**TWO-MAN**
4. Victor Emery, Peter Kirby
11. John Emery, Gordon Currie

**FOUR-MAN**
1. Victor Emery, John Emery,
   Doug Anakin, Peter Kirby
14. Lamont Gordon, Chris Ondaatje,
   David Hobart, Gordon Currie

### 1968 Grenoble — X Olympic Winter Games

Faulds, A., Gehrig, H., Goetschi, H., McDougall, P., Storey, R., Young, M.

**TWO-MAN**
19. Purvis McDougall, Bob Storey

**FOUR-MAN**
17. Purvis McDougall, Andy Faulds,
   Bob Storey, Michael Young

### 1972 Sapporo — XI Olympic Winter Games

Blakely, P., Faulds, A., Gehrig, H., Hartley, M., Nelson, C., Richardson, D., Storey, R., White, V.

**TWO-MAN**
14. Robert Storey, Michael Hartley
18. Hans Gehrig, Andrew Faulds

**FOUR-MAN**
13. Hans Gehrig, Andrew Faulds,
   David Richardson, Peter Blakely

### 1976 Innsbruck — XII Olympic Winter Games

Dunn, W., Frank, C., Kilburn, J., Lavelley, J., Martin, C., Nelson, C., Smith, M., Stehr, T., Vachon, B., Veale, D.

**TWO-MAN**
18. Colin Nelson, Jim Lavelley
23. Joseph Kilburn, Brian Vachon

**FOUR-MAN**
17. Colin Nelson, Thomas Stehr,
   David Veale, Jim Lavelley
21. Christopher Frank, William Dunn
   Christopher Martin, Brian Vachon

### 1980 Lake Placid - XIII Olympic Winter Games

Cantin, S., Glynn, M., Kilburn, J., MacLachlan, A., Vachon, B., Wilson, R.

**TWO-MAN**
13. Joseph Kilburn, Robert Wilson
20. Brian Vachon, Serge Cantin

### 1984 Sarajevo — XIV Olympic Winter Games

Flynn, C., Leuty, D., MacLachlan, A., Wilson, R., Carr, J., Rice, D.

**TWO-MAN**
14. Alan MacLachlan, Bob Wilson

**FOUR-MAN**
18. Alan MacLachlan, Bob Wilson,
   Dave Leuty, Clarke Flynn

# Figure Skating

Olympic Saddledome
February 16, 20, 22, 23, 25, 27, 28

Stampede Corral
February 14, 18, 21

Father David Bauer Olympic Arena
February 17, 24

I hadn't really planned on becoming a figure skater. Like many Canadian boys, when I started skating, I played hockey. Figure skating came later when I was trying to improve my rather mediocre hockey skills with skating lessons. After a few sessions, however, I realized that I was more suited to figure skating than hockey and enjoyed it more, so at the age of nine, I abandoned my hockey career for what was to become a life-long commitment to figure skating.

Although I seemed to have a gift for my new sport and it certainly came more naturally to me than putting a puck in a net, there was still a lot of really hard work. Long hours, early mornings . . . but isn't that the life of any amateur skater? Across Canada, thousands and thousands of young skaters have put aside a ''normal'' life for one of 5 A.M. practices in cold, dark arenas, full school loads crammed into half days between practice sessions, parents cutting back to pay for more skating lessons, and loneliness as we watch our classmates go off to parties and outings with friends, while we head for the rink for another late-night practice. It's hard work trying to be your best, but at the end of it is always the dream. The dream of standing on the podium, perhaps in a strange country, with your heart pounding as you listen to your national anthem being played.

I had a taste of that feeling at the 1984 Olympics when I won the silver medal. As I stood on that podium far away in Sarajevo, my mind carried me back home and I felt pride not only for myself and my family, but for all the young Canadian skaters whose dream I was living.

It was a privilege to be there representing Canada. It was an honour to be a medalist and I did not take it lightly. I felt that I was a symbol, a representative of all our young dedicated skaters, most of whom will never see glory outside their hometown rink. I stood there for them, as well as myself.

Now, looking toward 1988, it is with great pride that I introduce the sport of figure skating to the Calgary Olympics, not only as an Olympic medalist, but as importantly,

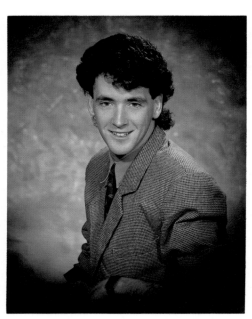

*Studio Two, Orillia, Ont.*

as just one member of the vast Canadian skating community. Welcome to the Olympics. Welcome to figure skating.

Brian Orser, O.C.
*Seven-time Canadian Senior Men's Figure Skating*
*Champion*
*1984 Olympic Silver Medalist*
*1987 World Champion*

## The History

Jackson Haines and the cup presented to him by the Vienna Skating Club, about 1865. *The Golden Age of Canadian Figure Skating, Summerhill Press, 1984*

Louis Rubenstein of Montreal, Quebec, was the first figure skating champion of the Dominion of Canada in 1883.
*Notman Photographic Archives, McCord Museum*

Skating is the world's oldest winter sport.

The Swedes, Norwegians and Finns were the first to use animal bone skates as a means of winter travel, and the Dutch used the word "schaats" to name the sport.

Ironically, it was the Scots who emerged as the initiators of the sport of skating as we know it today. The Scots invented an all-iron blade in 1572 and in 1642 the Skating Club of Edinburgh was founded.

Skating made its way to Canada via the Scots, and the skate blade was further refined in Philadelphia by an American, E. W. Bushnell, in 1848. Bushnell introduced a steel blade that could hold a sharper edge and was considerably lighter than the cumbersome iron blade. The new curved steel blade revolutionized the sport and soon pleasure skating became a fashionable winter activity on the frozen lakes and rivers of North America.

The all-steel blade with toe picks allowed skaters to cut sets of figures, people's names, and intricate flower designs onto the ice surface.

Throughout Europe and North America, skaters assembled a repertoire of skating routines which included the cross-foot spin, the Philadelphia twist, the grape-vine, the inside edge, the cross-roll backwards, and the double forward locomotive step.

In 1862, the famous Victoria Ice Rink was built in Montreal, Quebec, and the Victoria Skating Club was founded. One year before the skating club was formed, a young boy was born in Montreal who would grow up to become the first recognized world figure skating champion.

Born in 1861, Louis Rubenstein was the son of a well-established Jewish family. The family had a membership at the Victoria Skating Club, and as a young boy Rubenstein became intrigued with ice skating. He would practise for hours on the rink that gained fame as the birthplace of ice hockey in Canada.

During this time, ice skating was a freestyle form with no particular pattern or technical style to it. Louis Rubenstein, however, had heard of a new form of ice skating being popularized throughout Europe and North America by a man named Jackson Haines.

Haines, an expatriate Canadian, was a figure skater and a ballet master who had gone to Vienna, Austria, in 1864 to study ballet and music. In Austria, the Viennese were waltzing to the tunes of Lehar and Strauss.

With brilliant foresight, Jackson Haines blended the beauty of ballet, ice skating, and the Viennese waltzes into a new art form that would eventually become the single most popular competition at the Olympic Winter Games.

Inspired by Haines' reputation, Louis Rubenstein went to Europe to learn the art of figure skating from him in 1870. Jackson Haines so greatly influenced the young Canadian's skating style that when the first official figure skating competition was held at the Montreal Winter Carnival in 1883, Louis Rubenstein was declared the first figure skating champion of the Dominion of Canada.

He retained the title until 1889. He was the U.S. Champion in 1888 and 1889 and in 1890 won the World Championship at St. Petersburg (now Leningrad) in Russia. Rubenstein founded

North America's oldest skating association in 1878 when the Amateur Skating Association of Canada was formed.

The first international figure skating competition was held in Vienna in 1882. Compared to the fun-filled Montreal Winter Carnival, the competition in Vienna was far more serious. The requirements of each competitor were twenty-three compulsory school figures. In addition, each skater gave a four-minute free-skating demonstration and performed one special figure of his own choice.

From 1896 until 1905, the world championships were held for men only. Nevertheless, by 1906 a women's programme had been included in world competition. In 1908, both men and women made their Olympic debut in the skating events at the Olympic Summer Games at London, England.

Ulrich Salchow of Sweden, a legendary sportsman, won the gold medal in the men's singles and gave his name to the famous jump still seen in competition today. For top skaters, the double or triple Salchow jump is a compulsory requirement in Olympic ice skating events.

As there was no artificial ice rink available at the fifth Olympic Summer Games at Stockholm in Sweden, an ice skating programme was not included in 1912. And, as Europe moved toward the turmoil of World War I, the Games of the sixth Olympiad at Berlin, Germany, were cancelled.

Figure skating was again included in the format of the Olympic Summer Games at Antwerp, Belgium in 1920. Ulrich Salchow defended his title at age forty-three, but lost to fellow Swede Gillis Grafström.

Inauguration of the Olympic Winter Games in 1924 marked the second of three consecutive gold medal wins by Gillis Grafström in men's singles.

Canada's first pairs team, fifteen-year-old Cecil Smith and Melville Rogers of Toronto, placed seventh in the standings.

In the archival records of the Olympic Winter Games, few athletes have done more to glorify their sport than Sonja Henie from Oslo, Norway. Just eleven years old when she made her Olympic debut at the 1924 Winter Games the tiny Norwegian blonde placed last out of a field of eight skaters.

In spite of her place in the medal standings, Henie became a cause célèbre as the youngest competitor taking part in the 1924 Winter Games and the first ice skater precocious enough to wear a short skirt for her performance.

During the four years between the Winter Games of 1924 and 1928, Sonja Henie pursued an Olympic gold medal with determination. She studied skating and ballet with the best teachers in Europe and by 1927 had won the world championships in Oslo. Henie entered the Olympic Winter Games at St. Moritz in 1928 laden with honours. She had four straight Norwegian titles and a World Championship to her credit and was unquestionably the gold medal favourite.

For most skating spectators today, it is impossible to imagine ice skating without the magic of music, jumps, spins, and spirals seen in Olympic competition. But, until Sonja Henie's performance at St. Moritz, solo performances were as methodical as the drill of the changing of the guards at Buckingham Palace, and a good deal less interesting.

Sonja Henie changed all that with her performance at the second Olympic Winter Games. The fifteen-year-old glided onto the ice at St. Moritz resembling a doll-like character from a Hans Christian Andersen fairy tale. Her performance as the "dying swan" in the finale of Tchaikovsky's "Swan Lake" elevated free-skating to new Olympic standards. Henie was awarded her first of three consecutive gold medals and a historic skating career was launched.

Gillis Grafström, the illustrious Swede, won his third straight Olympic gold medal at St. Moritz. The pairs competition was won by the beautiful Andrée Joly and her partner and husband-to-be Pierre Brunet of France.

There was a medal in men's singles for Canada at the 1932 Winter Games at Lake Placid, New York. Montgomery Wilson won the bronze in the men's division, Canada's first Olympic medal for figure skating.

The reign of Sweden's Gillis Grafström came to an end with a gold medal win by Karl Schäfer of Austria. Pairs gold was won by Andrée and Pierre Brunet of France. The Brunets retired from Olympic competition after the 1932 Games and Pierre Brunet eventually coached Canada's Don Jackson to an Olympic bronze medal in 1960.

Sonja Henie was the unanimous choice as the gold medal winner in the women's singles. She also announced that she would retire from Olympic competition after the fourth Winter Games at the twin towns of Garmisch-Partenkirchen, Germany, in 1936.

Entering her third Olympics, Sonja Henie had become so popular that throngs of adoring fans pushed forward to see her wherever she skated.

Hoping to close out her Olympic career by winning her third gold medal, Sonja Henie was surprisingly tense before the competition began. Her cause for concern was young fifteen-year-old British prodigy Cecilia Colledge whose talent was

Canada's first Olympic pairs skaters, Melville Rogers and Cecil Smith, practise in London, England, before leaving for the 1924 Games at Chamonix, France. *The Golden Age of Canadian Figure Skating, Summerhill Press, 1984*

becoming a threat to her skating supremacy. Yet, even her crowd-pleasing Nazi salute at centre ice prior to her performance could not convince officials to award her higher marks than Henie. Sonja Henie was virtually unbeatable. Colledge won the silver medal for Britain, and Henie bade farewell to her amateur status after winning her third and final Olympic gold medal.

One week after the Winter Games ended at Garmisch-Partenkirchen, Henie chalked up her tenth consecutive world championship title in Europe. And, blessed with a good head for business, her sense of timing proved perfect for turning professional in March 1936. Henie established her fabulously successful ice show in New York and inspired an unparalleled number of children to learn to figure skate. The success of her ice show venture led to movie contracts with Twentieth Century-Fox in Hollywood. She made ten movies in California and popularized ice skating throughout North America and Europe.

Unfortunately, Sonja Henie's life did not have a fairy tale ending, and she died at fifty-seven years of age of leukemia in 1969.

During her superlative career she won three Olympic gold medals and ten consecutive world championships, accumulated over one thousand figure skating awards, married three times, and became a successful film star in America. At the time of her death, her personal fortune was estimated at over $47 million.

As Europe moved toward the global conflict of the Second World War, an eleven-year-old Canadian girl won the junior figure skating title at the national championships in Canada in 1939. Barbara Ann Scott, a little blonde charmer from Ottawa, was the youngest skater in the history of Canadian figure skating to hold the title.

During World War II, the Olympic Winter Games were uncelebrated and unawarded. After the war, a new generation of figure skaters took over. The sensation of the figure skating competition at the seventh Olympic Winter Games at St. Moritz, Switzerland, in 1948 proved to be Canada's Barbara Ann Scott.

Scott had trained diligently during the war years and had won the Canadian senior championship title in 1945, 1946, and 1947. During the summer she would put in nine hours a day of practice, six days a week. Training at the Ottawa Minto Skating Club in the winter and the Shumacher Arena during the summer, Scott had over twenty-thousand hours of practice ice time to her credit when she won the World and European Championships in 1947.

After the 1947 European championships, Barbara Ann returned to a jubilant home-town welcome. The citizens of Ottawa presented a brand new canary yellow convertible to their figure-skating heroine.

Avery Brundage, the indomitable President of the International Olympic Committee, was quick to point out that the only obstacle that stood between Barbara Ann and the shiny new sports car was the possibility of an Olympic gold medal. To accept the car would put her amateur status in jeopardy.

Sonja Henie retired after the 1936 Olympic Winter Games after winning three Olympic gold medals and ten consecutive World championships. *Oslo Skoyteklubb, Norway*

Barbara Ann Scott won Canada's first gold medal in figure skating at the 1948 Games. *Canada Sports Hall of Fame*

If ever a Canadian figure skater deserved a reward for all her hard work and dedication to her sport, it was Barbara Ann Scott. But for competitors who take part in the Olympic Games, the International Olympic Committee represents the powers that be. President Brundage insisted the little convertible had to go back, and back it went.

The winners' circle at the 1948 Olympic Winter Games was proof that Sonja Henie's influence had contributed to the new look of North American figure skaters.

Harvard University freshman Dick Button dazzled judges and spectators with his spectacular double axel jump in his free-skate performance. He was awarded first place and the gold medal in the men's singles event. By 1949, the nineteen-year-old held the European, Olympic, World, North American, and United States titles. Button was the first man to hold all five international skating titles.

Micheline Lannoy and her partner Pierre Baugniet of Belgium won the gold in the pairs competition, and a young Canadian pairs team won the bronze.

Suzanne Morrow and Wallace Deistelmeyer of Toronto were both strong individual skaters. Deistelmeyer held the 1948 Canadian men's singles title and Morrow won the 1949-1951 Canadian women's singles title after the Olympics. As a pairs team they were Olympic bronze medalists, the 1948 North American Pairs Champions, and the 1948 Canadian Dance Champions.

Morrow and Deistelmeyer were the first pairs skaters to ever perform the spectacular Death Spiral in international competition in 1948. Suzanne Morrow is also Canada's only woman figure skater to win senior championships in the three disciplines of singles, pairs, and dance.

On January 14, 1948, Barbara Ann Scott won the European Championships at Prague, Czechoslovakia. Three weeks later she was at St. Moritz, Switzerland, at the fifth Olympic Winter Games.

The eighteen-year-old skated onto an outdoor ice rink that had been badly chewed up from the preceding hockey game. Skating skillfully around the ruts and bumps, her flawless performance put her in first place for the gold medal. Her win was the first figure skating gold medal in Canadian history.

"If only one of our children could some day skate like that," a woman in the audience whispered to her husband. Jarmilla Jelinek, wife of influential industrialist Henry Jelinek of Prague, Czechoslovakia, had always loved figure skating. Her grandfather had been the manager of the Czechoslovakian National Exhibition and had overseen the construction of the first ice stadium at Prague.

The Jelineks and their five children were a family dedicated to ice skating. The two eldest sons had been singled out and given figure skating lessons at an early age.

One day at the ice arena, the figure skating coach told Jarmilla Jelinek that all his efforts were a waste of his time and her money. "Your sons have talent, but no interest. They both prefer ice hockey to cutting figure eights," he said reluctantly. As he spoke he scanned the busy arena and pointed out a little boy and girl happily absorbed in their skating practice. "Those two little ones over there have something very special. They have both talent and interest. If I could concentrate on them, I could make them into world champions." Jarmilla Jelinek looked toward the direction he was pointing and smiled. "But those are also my children," she said as she watched Otto, aged six, and Maria, aged four.

Otto and Maria skated during the turbulent postwar years in Czechoslovakia, and made their pairs performance debut in 1947 at the Prague ice stadium.

But there had been little time for skating in a country filled with political crises. There were times of crisis ahead for the Jelinek family, but the memory of Barbara Ann Scott's Olympic performance would sustain Jarmilla Jelinek through the next difficult years.

Barbara Ann Scott returned to Ottawa after the 1948 Olympic Winter Games as the golden girl of Canadian figure skating. She was showered with awards and gifts and, having announced she was turning professional, she could accept them.

Among her presents was the little convertible, but it was no longer yellow. Barbara Ann had waited patiently for her new sports car, and this time around she wanted it painted in her favourite colour, pale blue.

One month after the 1948 Olympic Winter Games had ended, the world learned that the Communists had taken over

Maria Jelinek and Otto Jelinek at the 1955 Canadian Championships in Toronto, Ontario, where they won the Canadian Junior Pairs Championship. *Courtesy Henry Jelinek*

Czechoslovakia. Henry Jelinek's cork manufacturing plant was among the industries confiscated behind the Iron Curtain.

On May 15, 1948, a frightened and exhausted mother, accompanied by four of her five young children, successfully managed a harrowing escape across the Czech border. Jarmilla Jelinek, her children Richard, Otto, Henry Jr., and little Maria would join her husband and eldest son, already safe in Lausanne, Switzerland.

Bidding a sad farewell to their Czech heritage, the Jelineks began their search for a new adoptive country. Their bitter exile ended with a new beginning in Canada. Safe in Oakville, on the shores of Lake Ontario, Otto and Maria Jelinek began their skating career in earnest.

The sixth Olympic Winter Games were held at Oslo, Norway, in 1952. Jeanette Altwegg won the gold medal for Great Britain in the women's singles.

Dick Button, in his senior year at Harvard, executed his triple loop jump, making three complete revolutions in the air. He won his second gold medal and announced he was turning professional to join the Ice Capades.

Frances Dafoe and Norris Bowden from Toronto entered their first Olympics as the 1952 Canadian Pairs Champions. Coached by Sheldon Galbraith, the same man who trained Barbara Ann Scott, Dafoe and Bowden had invented their own spectacular variety of routines.

Their emphasis on lifts and jumps was criticized internationally for being "too athletic" and partisan judging lost them the World Championships in 1953. Nevertheless, their determination to get to the top finally won them the World Championships in 1954. Frances Dafoe and Norris Bowden were Canada's first World pairs champions.

While Dafoe and Bowden were enjoying their year of sovereignty, three young figure skaters burst on the Canadian figure skating scene in 1955.

Fourteen-year-old Don Jackson from Oshawa won the 1955 Canadian junior men's title. Coach Sheldon Galbraith called Jackson "the greatest natural skater I have ever seen."

At the same National Championships in Toronto, Otto and Maria Jelinek, representing the Oakville Figure Skating Club, won the 1955 Canadian Junior Pairs Championship.

The Jelineks' win initiated an invitation from Vienna, Austria, to attend the World Championships immediately following the Canadian Championships. At that time, Vienna was under the rule of the four Allied powers of France, Britain, the United States, and Russia. Henry and Jarmilla Jelinek said it was out of the question to risk exposing their children to the Communists. The invitation was sadly declined.

Frances Dafoe and Norris Bowden represented Canada at the 1955 World Championships at Vienna and successfully defended their title. The one remaining title for Dafoe and Bowden to win was an Olympic gold medal at the 1956 Olympic Winter Games at Cortina d'Ampezzo in Italy.

Olympic figure skating judging is a complicated and often unenviable task. At Cortina d'Ampezzo, a controversial judges' decision gave the gold medal to Austrian pair Elisabeth Schwarz and Kurt Oppelt. Frances Dafoe and Norris Bowden, the popular

Don Jackson of Oshawa, Ontario, was a natural showman on ice, and won the bronze medal at the 1960 Games at Squaw Valley, California. *Canada Sports Hall of Fame/Gilbert A. Milne*

world champions, finished up in second place with the silver medal for Canada.

When it was announced that a Hungarian pair had beaten out the popular young German team of Marika Kilius and Franz Ningel for the bronze, the grumbling about the judging erupted into an uproar. Spectators pelted officials and judges with oranges and it took almost an hour to clean off the ice.

Tenley Albright won the gold medal for the United States in the women's event, and the men's singles finished with a one, two, three sweep for the United States. Hayes Alan Jenkins and his brother David from Colorado won the gold and bronze respectively. It was the first time in Olympic figure skating history that brothers had stood on the winners' podium together.

Silver medalists Frances Dafoe and Norris Bowden retired after the 1956 Olympics, and the door of figure skating acclaim opened for Barbara Wagner and Bob Paul of Toronto.

Competing in their first Olympic Winter Games, the Canadian duo had finished in sixth place at Cortina. The year after the Olympics, Wagner and Paul captured four consecutive figure skating titles in Canada and the United States. Within the short space of sixteen days, the remarkable young Canadian pair won the Canadian junior and senior pairs, the North American pairs, and the Worlds.

In 1958, Barbara and Bob both decided to quit school and launched into an intensive eight-hour-a-day training regimen under Sheldon Galbraith.

Wagner and Paul entered the eighth Olympic Winter Games at Squaw Valley, California, in 1960 with three World crowns, two North American titles, and five Canadian Senior Championships to their credit.

Their breathtaking performance was unprecedented in Olympic figure skating history, and earned the Canadians seven firsts from seven of the nine judges. Barbara Wagner and Bob

Robert Paul and Barbara Wagner, gold medal pairs skaters at the 1960 Games. They were the last non-Soviet couple to win the pairs gold medal at the Olympics. *Canada Sports Hall of Fame*

Paul skated into Olympic history as the first North Americans to win the pairs event. They were also the last non-Soviet couple to win the event.

The Canadian team at Squaw Valley had a reserve pair of skaters who were eager to reach for top honours. Otto and Maria Jelinek had shown promise in their pre-Olympic years. They had placed third in the 1957 Worlds and had taken third spot again at the Worlds at Paris, France, in 1958.

The comely brother-and-sister team were in top form for their Olympic debut and skated with superb artistry and precision. Yet, in spite of their excellent performance, the judges displayed marks that put them in fourth place in the medal standings.

Otto Jelinek was totally demoralized. But his parents had taught their children well, and Otto and Maria put the past behind them. The next morning, they were out on the rink again, practising for their next competition, the Worlds in Vancouver.

Another figure skating distinction for Canada at the 1960 Olympic Winter Games came in a diminutive five-foot-four package of talent. Don Jackson from Oshawa, Ontario, was a natural showman on ice and trained under Otto Gold in Ottawa and Pierre Brunet in New York.

In 1959 Jackson captured the Canadian senior men's title and the North American championships. In the 1959 World Championships, he placed second. He was eighteen years old when he entered his first Olympic competition at Squaw Valley and won a bronze medal.

America's David Jenkins won the gold in the men's singles event. Carol Heiss of the United States won the singles event and after the Olympics married 1956 gold medalist Hayes Alan Jenkins.

The World Championships were held in Vancouver immediately following the 1960 Olympic Winter Games. Don Jackson performed his spectacular delayed double axel, stopping dead in mid-air before making two complete revolutions above the ice. His free-skating display brought ecstatic fans to their feet and once again he placed second in the championships.

Otto and Maria Jelinek, skating in front of most of the same judges who, perhaps, had underrated them at the Olympics, earned their rightful second-place finish behind Wagner and Paul.

Figure skating promoters and fans were beginning to lose patience with the scoring system, and again judges and referees were faced with intense criticism at the Worlds.

By 1960, the Canadian public began to take notice of a little Canadian champ waiting her call to figure skating fame. Petra

Burka was born in Amsterdam in 1947 and was given her first skating lessons by her mother and coach, Ellen Burka.

Ellen Burka held the 1945 Dutch figure skating title, and after the family emigrated to Toronto in 1951, she became one of Canada's top figure skating coaches. Eventually she would coach Canada's Toller Cranston to a 1976 Olympic bronze medal.

At thirteen years of age, Petra Burka won the Toronto senior women's title. The making of a champion had begun.

Figure skating, like many Olympic sports, has a set series of steps up the competitive ladder which must be followed for national and international success. In order to win the World title, it is an unwritten rule that a figure skater must have won either a European or North American championship in the same year. North American Championships are held only every second year, and in 1961 the competition was scheduled for Philadelphia.

World Champions Barbara Wagner and Bob Paul retired from the amateur ranks after the 1960 Olympic Winter Games. It looked like there was room at the top for Otto and Maria Jelinek. But, if they wanted to try to win the 1961 World title, it was essential that they place first at Philadelphia.

The city chosen for the 1961 World Championships was announced and the competition was scheduled to take place in Prague, Czechoslovakia. "You are not going," Henry Jelinek said sadly, "If you crossed the border into Communist Czechoslovakia, you could be arrested and used as hostages."

According to the Czechoslovak regime, the Jelineks were still considered citizens of Czechoslovakia. Once Otto and Maria

were behind the Iron Curtain, the Canadian government could do nothing on their behalf to ensure their safety.

But the years of persecution by the Gestapo and his later exile had made Henry Jelinek clever and resourceful. He contacted the Minister of Foreign Affairs in Ottawa. The only solution, explained the Minister, would be to persuade the Communist government in Prague to release Maria and Otto from their Czechoslovak citizenship. To accomplish this task, Henry Jelinek secured the backing of the Canadian Skating Association and contacted the headquarters of the International Skating Union at Davos, Switzerland. With twenty-eight nations affiliated with the prestigious association, the ISU was in a position to make the Czech skating organization an ultimatum.

The proposal was very clear: Otto and Maria Jelinek were to be guaranteed a protected arrival and stay while in Prague, and a safe journey back to Canada. It was pointed out to the Czechs that if skaters from the West could not be guaranteed safe conduct, the 1961 World Championships would be held in Germany or Italy.

Having spent millions to arrange for the competition to be held in Prague, the offer was one the Czechs couldn't refuse. Otto and Maria were summoned to Montreal and the documents that released them from their Czechoslovak citizenship were presented to them by the consul general of the Socialist People's Republic of Czechoslovakia.

To celebrate their new citizenship, the Jelineks entered the 1961 Canadian Senior Pairs Championships at Montreal, and won, as Canadians.

The following February, Don Jackson won the men's singles event at the 1961 North American Championships in Philadelphia, and Otto and Maria Jelinek won the pairs event.

Immediately after the 1961 North American Championships, the Canadian and American figure skating teams left Philadelphia for Prague, Czechoslovakia.

But Otto and Maria Jelinek's return to the city of their birth was to be regretfully brief. On February 15, 1961, the plane carrying the entire American figure skating team to the World Championships at Prague crashed near Brussels, killing seventy-three people. Among the casualties were eighteen figure skaters, five coaches, and the team manager. There were no survivors.

Out of respect to the memory of the American skaters, the 1961 World Figure Skating Championships were cancelled. The competition was re-scheduled for 1962 in Prague.

During the twelve-month interval between the scheduled World Championships, Otto and Maria achieved the apex of their skating talent under the expertise of coach Bruce Hyland, and at the Toronto Skating Club under the aegis of coach Sheldon Galbraith, Don Jackson intensified his campaign to win a World Championship medal.

Before leaving again for Prague, the Jelineks and Jackson competed at the fifty-first Canadian Figure Skating Championships at the Toronto Varsity Arena.

Although they won their events, the real show-stopper was a fifteen-year-old girl who captivated the audience with spectacular jumps which, until then, had only been managed by male skaters.

Petra Burka captured a bronze medal for Canada at the 1964 Games at Innsbruck, Austria. *Canada Sports Hall of Fame/ICE Photographer*

At the 1962 Canadian Figure Skating Championships, Petra Burka performed the first triple Salchow in the history of women's figure skating. The Salchow is a jump named after the Swedish Olympic champion Ulrich Salchow. To execute a Salchow, the figure skater takes off on the front skate, rotates in a complete circle in the air, and lands on the back outside edge of the opposite skate.

Although Salchow was the originator of the jump, he only made one mid-air rotation while performing it. Petra Burka executed the three mid-air revolutions of her triple Salchow as part of her solo performance, and with her amazing accomplishment, she stole the show.

In 1962 Otto, aged twenty-two, and Maria not quite nineteen, returned to Prague as young Canadian ambassadors to compete in the World Figure Skating Championships. The Czechoslovak government had little tolerance for defectors, and the press had made no mention of the young expatriates at the championships. Yet, as they acknowledged the thunderous applause from the audience after their performance, it was obvious the popular brother-and-sister team were the symbol of freedom to the Czechs. Against their formidable Russian rivals, Ludmila Belousova and Oleg Protopopov, the Jelineks skated the performance of their lives and were announced as the 1962 Champions of the World.

Barred from Czechoslovakia, Henry and Jarmilla Jelinek watched their son and daughter on television from Davos, Switzerland. They saw the final chapter of their story unfold in the ancient ice stadium at Prague, where Grandfather Zizka and all the Jelineks had learned to skate.

At the same competition in Prague, Don Jackson won the first men's singles world title in Canada's history. 1960 Olympic silver medalist Karol Divin of Czechoslovakia had outskated Jackson in the compulsories. Jackson knew he had to skate superbly to win the world title, and his last-minute pep talk with coach Galbraith gave him the competitive edge he needed.

Jackson's skating was so superb that even the referees admitted they had never seen anything like it. He electrified the figure-skating fraternity with a repertoire of triple Salchows, three double axels, and the first triple lutz ever performed in the history of figure-skating competition. His come-from-behind record hasn't been equalled in singles since.

Seventeen-year-old Canadian skater Donald McPherson of Windsor, Ontario, skated into the record books at another World Championship. In 1963 at Cortina d'Ampezzo, Italy, he distinguished himself as the youngest man to ever win the gold medal at the Worlds.

Before the 1964 Olympic Winter Games at Innsbruck, Austria, Donald Jackson and the Jelineks had turned professional, along with Don McPherson. Conscious of the financial sacrifices their families had made for them, all of them had decided to leave the amateur ranks to accept starring professional roles—Jackson in the Ice Follies, the Jelineks in the Ice Capades, and McPherson in a European skating show, Holiday on Ice.

Petra Burka entered the ninth Olympic Winter Games as the Canadian Senior Champion after a fierce battle with Wendy Griner for the championship. Burka's dazzling Olympic solo

Canadian pair Debbi Wilkes and Guy Revell, the bronze medalists who ended up as silver medal winners in the record books, as they compete at the 1964 Games. *The Athlete Information Bureau/Canadian Olympic Association*

performance captured the bronze for Canada behind gold medalist Sjoukje Dijkstra of the Netherlands.

Former roller-skating champion Manfred Schnelldorfer won the men's singles event. Fourteen-year-old Scotty Allen of Smoke Rise, New Jersey, won the bronze medal. A tribute to the rebuilding of a grief-stricken American team, Scotty Allen was the youngest athlete to ever win an Olympic Winter Games medal.

The 1964 Games marked the entry of Soviet domination in the Olympic pairs event. The first Russian pair of distinction were Oleg Protopopov and his wife Ludmila Belousova from Leningrad. They were a love affair on ice, and skated in perfect harmony, in their gold medal performance.

The bronze medal was won by Canadian pairs Debbi Wilkes and Guy Revell, who ended up making Olympic history through the misfortune of the silver medalists. Marika Kilius and her partner Hans-Jurgen Bäumier of Germany were awarded the silver medal. Later, it was discovered the German pair had signed a professional contract and had taken part in an ice revue before the Olympics. The professional contract infringed on Olympic rules, and the medals were withdrawn in favour of the Canadians.

Women's singles gold medalist Sjoukje Dijkstra retired after the 1964 Winter Games and cleared the way for an outstanding year for Petra Burka. In 1965 she won the Canadian title, the North American championship, and the World crown in Colorado. Burka was selected as Canada's outstanding woman athlete in 1965.

A key entry at the 1966 Canadian championships was a thirteen-year-old figure skater from British Columbia. Karen Magnussen made her first public skating appearance as a six-year-old snowflake in a Vancouver winter carnival. When she was nine, Karen won the B.C. women's novice trophy. At thirteen, she entered the Canadian Figure Skating Championships and placed fourth.

By 1967 Magnussen was skating internationally at the World

Championships in Vienna. Her crowd-pleasing free-skate performance put her in seventh place, but only twelfth overall in the final standings. During the span of her fifteen-year skating career, Karen Magnussen would witness the modernization of the archaic judging methods that plagued her early performances.

The Canadian Figure Skating Championships were held in Vancouver prior to the 1968 Olympic Winter Games at Grenoble, France. There, a rising young figure skating star, who was an art student at the Ecole des Beaux Arts in Montreal, made a desperate bid for a berth on the Canadian Olympic team. Trailing behind in the compulsory figures, Toller Cranston skated like a madman in his come-from-behind solo performance. His outrageously extroverted free skate was a combination of originality and artistry which, until that time, had only been explored in men's figure skating by Jackson Haines.

Haines, the father of modern skating, was born in Canada. His hobby of painting provided him with a creative counterbalance to his interest in figure skating. When he first blended figure skating, ballet, and music in Vienna, very few people understood what he was attempting to do.

Although his audiences loved his performances, exponents of the staid "Victorian" school misunderstood him and laughed at him. The night before he died in 1876 he wrote in his diary, "I predict a hundred years will pass before my dreams for artistic skating will come to be realized." Given the free will to return to Canada a century later, Jackson Haines perhaps could have seen himself reincarnated in the country's ultimate crowd pleaser, Toller Cranston.

Cranston had never received a greater reception than when the Vancouver audience gave him a standing ovation after his performance. But the judges, dumbfounded by what they saw, gave Toller such low marks that his hopes of making the Olympic team were ruined. Spectators were infuriated by the marks, and the controversy that was to surround all of Cranston's performances had begun.

When the marks came up, the tears welled up too, and as he left the ice he skated right into the arms of a woman he had never seen before. She took his arm and pulled him aside into a private room. "Stop crying," she said. "Go out there again and meet them with your head up high. Be proud, because you are the most artistic skater in the world." Ellen Burka, mother of 1964 Olympic bronze figure skating medalist Petra Burka and one of Canada's top figure skating coaches, knew quality when she saw it.

The following year, eighteen-year-old Toller Cranston packed up his art supplies and skates, and moved to Toronto to train with Ellen Burka at the Toronto Cricket Club.

Austrian figure skater Emmerich Danzer headed into the 1968 Olympic Winter Games at Grenoble, France, as World Champion. Despite having top scores in the free-skating competition, he placed only fourth in his compulsories, and fourth overall. The fact that the reigning World Champion did not win an Olympic medal indicated that a change in the judging system was long overdue.

Petra Burka's surprise announcement that she would retire at age nineteen from amateur competition before the 1968 Olympics opened the niche at the top of Canadian women's figure skating.

At fifteen, Karen Magnussen entered the 1968 Winter Olympics as Canada's first western Canadian Champion. Again her free skating was exceptional. She placed a creditable fourth in the competition, and seventh overall.

Canada's 1960 gold medalist Bob Paul coached America's Peggy Fleming to a gold medal in the women's singles event.

The exceptional rapport and obvious love that Ludmila Belousova and Oleg Protopopov had for each other fascinated audiences as the Soviet twosome skated to their second Olympic gold medal. Later Protopopov remarked, "These pairs of brother and sister, how can they convey the emotion, the love, that exists between a man and a woman? This is what we try to show."

During the 1969 European Championships, Belousova and Protopopov were dethroned by a younger Soviet pairs team who had developed a new style. The performance marked the beginning of nineteen-year-old Soviet pairs skater Irina Rodnina's skating career which would match Sonja Henie's medal accomplishments.

Where Belousova and Protopopov had been elegant and fluid on the ice, Irina Rodnina and Aleksei Ulanov dazzled audiences and judges with their athletic virtuosity. They performed complex lifts and spectacular jumps, and placed first in the medal standings.

But, by the time of the 1972 Olympic Winter Games at Sapporo, Japan, romantic problems had disrupted the harmony of the gold medal pair. The high-spirited Irina suffered disappointment at the Olympics when it was discovered that her adored partner had fallen in love with the beautiful Lyudmila Smirnova of the No. 2 Soviet pair. Despite winning the gold medal, Rodnina's heart was broken, and she left the ice in tears after the medal presentations.

Following the 1972 Winter Games, Lyudmila Smirnova and Aleksei Ulanov were married, and not seen in Olympic competition again. Back in the Soviet Union, the search began for Irina Rodnina's new skating partner.

Karen Magnussen was forced to relinquish her Canadian figure skating crown due to stress fractures in both legs, and watched the 1969 Canadian Championships from a wheelchair. She recaptured her Canadian title in 1970 and won her first international award in 1971 at the Worlds in Lyons, France. Magnussen beat out her arch-rival Janet Lynn of the United States for the bronze medal.

Unquestionably, the women's figure skating event at the 1972 Olympic Winter Games influenced the adoption of a new scoring system. A case in point was Austria's Trixi Schuba. Schuba was a superior and highly schooled compulsory figure skater, and built up a commanding lead with her six figures. Although she placed seventh in the free skating with a precise but lacklustre performance, she won the gold medal.

Janet Lynn and Karen Magnussen, both superb free skaters, battled it out for the silver medal. Janet Lynn eliminated herself from a second-place finish with two falls in her short programme, and a fired-up Karen Magnussen won the silver with her incredible performance. The medal was Canada's only one at the 1972 Winter Games.

Records are made to be broken, and Czechoslovak figure skater Ondrej Nepela's unbroken record was no exception to the rule. He had not fallen during a skating competition for four years, but saved his big tumble for his Olympic performance at Sapporo. Despite his fall, he was the unanimous choice of all the judges for the gold.

Toller Cranston was the 1972 Canadian Senior Champion when he attended his first Olympics at Sapporo. He finished up in ninth place, and had a few choice words for the judges. Forced to accept the criticism of his unique skating style, the outspoken Cranston could give back as good as he got. "Skating itself is not a joke," he said. "The joke is the actual officiating, which is incomprehensible to any rational person." Never at a loss for words, Cranston's remarks did not do much for his status with the international judging establishment. But he didn't lose any sleep over it. His greatest happiness was to transcend the judges and reach his always appreciative audience.

In fact, no one could skate like Toller Cranston. He was so artistically superior and so popular after the 1972 Olympics that when he was working on his programme for the debut of Leoncavallo's *I Pagliacci* in Munich, Germany, he was amazed to see over two thousand people in the arena just to watch him practise.

Following the Olympics at Sapporo, the International Skating Union modernized the scoring system in favour of the free skater. The new rules gave only thirty per cent of the total mark to the compulsory school figures. The other twenty per cent went to the basic free-skating exercises, and the remaining fifty per cent to the free-skate performance. The change was long overdue.

Gold medalist Trixi Schuba retired from amateur competition, and Karen Magnussen, competing under the new rules, made history by winning the 1973 World Championships at Bratislava, Czechoslovakia. Karen was the first western Canadian to win a gold medal at the Worlds. She won gold (overall), gold (free skate), and gold (compulsory figures).

At the end of the 1973 season, Karen Magnussen turned professional and signed a $300,000 three-year contract. It was the largest contract the Ice Capades had ever given to a skater.

Toller Cranston held the Canadian championship title for six successive years from 1971 until 1976. In 1974 and 1975, he won the gold medal for his free skating at the Worlds.

Cranston entered the 1976 Olympic Winter Games at Innsbruck, Austria, as a strong medal favourite but he had a couple of obstacles to contend with. One was the reality that the Soviet and Eastern bloc judges considered his skating style too balletic, and they did not approve of the way he expressed his ire toward them so blatantly.

Cranston's second obstacle was John Curry from Birmingham, England. The European press had described Toller Cranston as "the skater of the century." John Curry, who had been inspired by Toller Cranston, was headlined as "the Nureyev of the Ice."

Both skaters' elegant styles had been criticized as being "too

unmasculine" by the Communist judges, and John Curry chose to supplement his performance with a repertoire of more orthodox jumps. The Soviet judge, finding no fault with his more traditional skating, awarded Curry second place in the free skate, and gave first place to Soviet skater Vladimir Kovalev.

Toller Cranston, the man who had made an indelible imprint on the face of men's figure skating, was not about to compromise his unique style for his Olympic performance. His uninhibited free-skating exhibition was the best of the Games and the response from the audience was a jubilant ovation. He placed third and won the bronze medal. John Curry won the gold. Cranston's medal win was, nevertheless, a triumphant breakthrough that would stir new beginnings in men's figure skating. The judges' decision to award him an Olympic medal indicated that his unorthodox technique had, at last, been internationally accepted.

The 1976 Olympic Winter Games marked Toller Cranston's last amateur performance, and he ended the speculation about his future by announcing he would turn professional. He launched his own successful ice show and entered an entirely new era of his dramatic skating career.

Irina Rodnina returned to the 1976 Olympic pairs competition as if nothing had happened. Her new partner and husband was Aleksandr Zaitsev of Leningrad. They skated easily into first place for the gold medal.

Ice dancing made its debut at the 1976 Winter Games, and the Soviet dancers dominated the competition. Husband-and-wife team Lyudmila Pakhomova and Aleksandr Gorshkov were awarded first-place votes by all nine judges.

Under the tutelage of Canada's Robert Paul, an adorable nineteen-year-old Dorothy Hamill enchanted the sellout crowd at the arena, and won the gold for the United States in the women's singles event.

In 1979, seventeen-year-old Brian Orser of Penetanguishene, Ontario, landed the first triple axel ever seen in Canadian competition at the novice championships. The triple axel, a three-and-a-half mid-air rotation jump, is considered the most difficult in figure skating.

At nine years of age, Orser had teamed up with the newly hired pro at the Mariposa School of Skating, twenty-year-old Doug Leigh. Thirteen years later, they were still together at the 1984 Olympic Winter Games, and could claim modern skating's longest lasting skater-coach relationship.

Orser's win at the 1979 Novice Championships increased pressure from skating experts to move to Toronto to be coached by Canada's top trainers, but the soft-spoken Brian was a small-town boy at heart, and refused to leave his favourite coach. Eventually, Orser would prove that a figure skater could remain at his home club with his original coach and still move up in the international ranks.

Top scores in the compulsories again affected the outcome of the women's singles event at the 1980 Olympic Winter Games at Lake Placid, New York. East German Anett Poetzsch won the gold by gaining a large lead in the compulsory figures. America's Linda Fratianne, the two-time world champion, was

Gold medalist John Curry, of Great Britain, silver medalist Vladimir Kovalev of the U.S.S.R., and bronze medalist Toller Cranston of Canada at the 1976 Games. *Deutsche Presse-Agentur GmbH*

unable to close the gap with her superb free skating, and settled for the silver.

It could have been the same story in the men's singles event, as Robin Cousins of Great Britain, acknowledged as the best free skater in the world, got off to a poor start in the compulsories. Trailing in fourth place, Cousins' breathtaking free-skating performance took him up to the gold medal, the second successive Olympic championship for Britain.

Two other British skaters finished in the top ten in the ice dance competition. Nottingham's Jayne Torvill and Christopher Dean, comparatively unknown fifth-place finishers, had begun their meteoric ascent of the international skating ladder.

By 1978 Russia's Irina Rodnina had won her tenth consecutive World Championship. The birth of her first child gave the couple a year off, during which time the World title was captured by Tai Babilonia and Randy Gardner of the United States. Spectators hoping to see a fierce Olympic competition between the young Californians and the Soviets were destined for disappointment. Randy Gardner suffered a groin injury shortly before he arrived at Lake Placid, and the pair withdrew from the event.

By capturing the gold medal at Lake Placid, Rodnina joined Sonja Henie in the record books. Both women had won three Olympic gold medals, and ten World Championships.

The year after the Olympics, Brian Orser won his first Canadian Championship. His win dethroned three-time Canadian champion Brian Pockar of Calgary. Pockar had been coached

by Winnie Silverthorne, and had won a bronze medal in the 1982 Worlds.

Five-time Canadian Champions Sandra and Val Bezic had done the choreography that took Ontario's Barbara Underhill and Paul Martini to the 1979 and 1980 Canadian Senior Pairs title. Competing in their first Olympics at Lake Placid, the six-foot Martini of Oshawa and petite five-foot Underhill from Woodbridge, Ontario, were satisfied with their ninth-place finish.

By 1983, Underhill and Martini had progressed to a bronze medal at the 1983 Worlds at Helsinki. Ranked third in the world, the talented pair were well-known for Martini's treacherous and highly scored triple-twist throw jumps that sent the tiny Underhill spinning through the air.

The Ontario pair entered the 1984 Olympic Winter Games at Sarajevo, Yugoslavia, as one of the pairs good enough to be Olympic champions. But they were in trouble almost as soon as they started their short programme.

Two faltered throws and one jump into their performance, Underhill was executing one of the simplest moves in the programme, and fell backwards while skating into a sit spin. Four years of training for the Olympic medal came tumbling down as Barbara slid to the ice, and her partner crumpled on top of her.

Later at a press conference, her voice strained, Barbara Underhill said, "What's happened may seem like the end of the world but we'll get it back into perspective in a hurry." The words were courageous, but the disappointed pair never

British figure skaters Jayne Torvill and Christopher Dean, the best-ever Olympic ice dancers, perform their gold medal debut.
*Deutsche Presse- Agentur GmbH*

fully recovered psychologically from the disastrous fall, and ended up in seventh place.

Underhill and Martini's fall opened the field to many others, including America's Kitty and Peter Carruthers.

Adopted separately at birth, they had progressed as an extraordinarily talented brother-and-sister team to their second Olympics at Sarajevo. Tied for second place coming into the long programme, Kitty and Peter faced the most dramatic moment of their skating career. When the chips were down, they did it. Their flawless performance moved them into second place for the silver medal behind Elena Valova and Oleg Vasiliev of the Soviet Union.

Their win for the United States was the most successful Olympic pairs performance since the tragic plane crash at Brussels in 1961.

Some people thought that Raleigh bicycles had been the best thing to come out of Nottingham, England, until they saw Jayne Torvill and Christopher Dean skate at the 1984 Olympics. On Valentine's Day Nottingham's most famous ambassadors were joined by world television audiences and a capacity crowd at Sarajevo's Zetra Ice Hall for a history-making pairs performance. Mesmerizing their audience while they skated to the romantic strains of Ravel's "Bolero," Torvill and Dean set a record unlikely to be broken for years to come in Olympic competition. Their charismatic performance earned them an unprecedented string of perfect 6.0s across the board from all nine judges. They were also the first non-Soviets to win the event since it was added to the Olympic format in 1976.

The four-time world ice-dancing champions turned professional after their Olympic year and launched their own unique ice show in London, England. During the span of their amateur career, Jayne Torvill and Christopher Dean were awarded perfect scores from figure skating judges no less than 126 times.

Eighteen-year-old skater Katarina Witt of East Germany was the synthesis of femininity and athleticism in the women's figure skating competition. The classical beauty skated the most technically difficult programme of all the skaters in the free skate. Throughout her gold medal performance, she would break into her radiant smile as she flirted saucily with her television and live audience. Her upbeat style was most unusual for the more traditionally staid Eastern European skaters and placed her first in the medal standings.

United States Champion Rosalyn Summers, age nineteen, finished in second place, and the bronze medal was won by Ira Ivanova of the Soviet Union.

At 5'3", diminutive Scott Hamilton of the United States was the giant of classic skating technique, and the overwhelming medal favourite in the men's singles event.

Since September of 1980, Hamilton had won seventeen consecutive competitions, and breezed through the compulsories in first place. But his short and long programmes were marred by a cold and ear infection that he developed at the Games.

If Hamilton's standards were slightly off at Sarajevo, Canada's Brian Orser's were more than on. The three-time Canadian champion had been the bronze medal winner in the 1983 Worlds

1984 Olympic gold medalist Katarina Witt of the German Democratic Republic, winner of the women's singles event. *Deutsche Presse-Agentur GmbH*

but was trailing in seventh place in the compulsories at the Olympics.

Whereas Hamilton excelled at the school figures, Orser excelled at free skating. Hamilton knew the twenty-two-year-old Canadian was his man to beat. Brian Orser's win in the short programme at Sarajevo was Scotty Hamilton's first loss since 1982, and brought Orser up to fifth place. In the long programme, his five triple-jump format left the crowd roaring with approval at his knockout performance. Orser's eleven 5.9s compared to Scott Hamilton's six indicated that he had solidly beaten the American in two out of three events.

But Scotty Hamilton coasted to a gold medal victory with his large lead in the compulsories. Brian Orser, nevertheless, had cracked the top ranks with his runner-up silver medal. Orser's silver medal was the best Canadian performance in the men's singles event since the first Olympic Winter Games in 1924.

The Olympics at Sarajevo finished, Barbara Underhill and Paul Martini returned to Toronto to prepare for the 1984 World Championships in Ottawa.

At the lowest ebb of their skating career, the popular pair considered turning professional. Their coaches, however, had other ideas. They persuaded Underhill and Martini not to discount their last chance at international distinction by withdrawing from the prestigious championships. This proved to be the most fortuitous decision of all for the Ontario couple.

After a disappointing seventh-place finish at the Olympics, Barbara Underhill had admitted that her new figure skates were not working for her. For their last amateur performance, Paul Martini urged her to wear a favourite pair of skates that she had retired over a year ago. And, wearing her dependable old figure skates, Barbara Underhill gave a dazzling pairs performance with Paul Martini.

Three days after the championships began, tears spilled down Barbara Underhill's face as she and Paul Martini stepped up on the winners' podium at Ottawa's Civic Centre to receive their 1984 World Championship gold medal.

Barbara Underhill and Paul Martini's gold medal win, along with Brian Orser's Olympic silver medal win, were not the only things the Canadian skating establishment had to boast about in 1984.

In September, 1984, newly elected Prime Minister Brian Mulroney introduced his first cabinet to Canadians. Among the Ministers was a former Olympic pairs skater, who had been a Member of Parliament since 1972.

The Honourable Otto John Jelinek was appointed as Canada's Minister of Fitness and Amateur Sport.

Tears of joy from Barbara Underhill, as she and her partner Paul Martini skate up to the podium to receive gold medal in the 1984 World Championships in Ottawa. *Canada Wide Feature Services Limited*

# The Venue

The figure skating events at the 1988 Olympic Winter Games will be held under the world's largest elliptical roof, at Calgary's Olympic Saddledome.

Be it classical or jazz, the sound of the music used by the figure skaters will be improved by the six thousand acoustic panels that cover the interior of the roof.

Constructed on a grand scale, the Saddledome includes a private club and thirty-three private boxes, a first-class restaurant, a 120-seat press box, a media lounge with five separate interviewing rooms, ten dressing rooms for Olympic figure skaters, and the dressing rooms of the National Hockey League Calgary Flames.

The tiered deck system for seating inside the arena can be expanded to hold a maximum crowd of approximately nineteen thousand people.

The 1956 Olympic Winter Games in Cortina d'Ampezzo, Italy, were held without benefit of computers. Nerve-racked figure skaters were forced to wait eight hours before their Olympic results were compiled.

The state-of-the-art computer facility at the Olympic Saddledome can, nevertheless, only process what the judges feed it. Results will be spewed out in record time and scores will be posted on the electronic scoreboard overhead at centre ice.

The 8.5 x 5.3 metre scoreboard will feature scores and full-colour animation on all four sides. It is operated by over two hundred and fifty computer files and is lighted with almost forty thousand light bulbs.

The Saddledome's new "jet ice" machines purify water before it is made into ice, and the resulting surface is faster and harder for figure skaters. The Olympic Saddledome has refrigeration equipment rated at two hundred and sixty tons, more than double the amount the veteran Stampede Corral has.

Adjacent to the Olympic Saddledome, the Corral will be used as a second Olympic ice surface for the figure skating events. The Stampede Corral seats approximately six thousand, and was the home arena for the 1968 Olympic Winter Games Canadian bronze medal hockey team coached by Father David Bauer. Compulsories will take place at the Father David Bauer Olympic Arena.

Accessibility for Olympic visitors to the Olympic Saddledome and the Stampede Corral will be facilitated by the Light Rail Transit station at Stampede Park.

Bus terminals are located on the northeast side of the building, and up to twelve buses can be loaded simultaneously. By using public transportation, ten thousand Olympic spectators can leave Stampede Park within thirty minutes of the end of an Olympic figure skating event.

Of the estimated six hundred million people throughout the world who will watch the Games on television, many will watch the best figure skaters in the world compete for Olympic medals in 1988.

Calgary's centrepiece of the Games, the unique Saddledome, awaits the 1988 Olympic Winter Games figure skating event.

# The Technique

The magic of figure skating has a language all its own.

According to the official ice skating format, spectators will be seeing flying camels inside the Olympic Saddledome at the 1988 Winter Games. Along with the camels, there will be triple Salchows, double loops, sit spins, and death spirals.

Ticket holders of the sought-after skating finals are the envy of most spectators at the Games. Nevertheless, there is another side to the glamorous spectacle of the free skating competition.

The least publicized and seemingly mysterious school figure event is held in the early morning hours in a half-empty and silent arena. There, under the eagle eye of the judges, the skaters show their craftsmanship by executing the difficult and tedious compulsories.

Depending on the figure drawn, the compulsories require three or four tracings on each foot of one original figure. Judges look for a clean first print, with perfectly round and equal circles. Three exact and symmetrical repetitions of the original print are what they want to see.

A skate blade has an outside edge and an inside edge. By skating on the inside or the outside edge of the blade, a figure skater draws one line on the ice. The compulsory figures are always done on the edges. Skating on a flat blade and making two lines on the ice is not allowed.

Perfection on the ice is not the only thing judges want to see. While tracing the figure, the flow and lean of the body carriage is judged, along with the steadiness of edge change as the skater moves from one blade to another. In the compulsories, accuracy and concentration are the name of the game.

Gone are the days of the staid single Salchow jump. In fact, women figure skaters began to take on such gymnastic feats that in 1983, the International Skating Union imposed several restrictions on jumps, somersaults, and backflips.

No one could perform a butterfly jump or a Russian split jump like Canada's Toller Cranston. Petra Burka's specialty was the triple Salchow jump. The waltz jump, the Salchow, the cherry flip, the axel, and the lutz are some of the spectacular jumps that Olympic figure skaters perform.

The two categories of jumps are edge jumps and toe jumps.

The Salchow is an example of an edge jump in which the skater takes off from an edge only.

The lutz jump is a toe jump. The skater takes off from a curved or straight line and uses the toe pick of the free leg skate for take-off. Perfect timing is essential for the lutz jump. The skater must wait until the skating foot is pulled in closely toward the toe-pick foot so take-off is upward. Pitching forward in the air or keeping the feet crossed too long during the lutz are mistakes that are dangerous.

A good landing from a jump is straight up, not too deep a knee bend, arms outstretched, and back arched. Most of the trouble begins for a skater if a good landing is not sustained and a two-footed landing does not win a skater any points. Accidents are only seconds away, and no skater is immune to a mishap.

The three basic types of spins are the camel spin, the sit spin, and the upright spin. The variations of the three spins are endless.

Some of the more common spins are the camel spin, in which the skater jumps from one skate to the other during the spin, the flying spin, and the sit spin. To perform the dramatic lay back spin, the skater spins on one leg in an upright position and then leans the body backward or to the side. The free leg is held high behind the skater, and the arms are extended over the head. Toller Cranston's genius on ice was demonstrated superbly in his experimentation and innovative variations of the spins.

The jumps and spins are connected on the ice by intricate dance steps. Free-skating programmes are loaded with mohawk turns, bracket turns, rocker turns, chassé steps, and slide chassés. Other moves such as spirals, spread eagles, and pivots flow from superb edge control and add speed to the connecting steps.

The names of the pairs moves aren't exactly household words. Helicopter lifts, split triple twists, tango camels, and side-by-side triple toe loops take years of constant repetition and costly lessons to perfect.

The pairs event incorporates singles requirements and designated pairs lifts and jumps. Both partners must be powerful individual skaters who can work together in unison. The only time spectators will see the woman lifted up off the ice is in the pairs event.

Audiences watch the pairs event, mesmerized by the waltz, tango, or jazz music while the skaters perform with seemingly effortless grace. But, behind the quiet and calm exteriors are two intensely competitive and finely tuned athletes. Both skaters must develop tremendous stamina along with their acrobatic skills. The women are no strangers to falls from high above the ice, broken jaws, and concussions.

Nevertheless, during an Olympic performance, both partners must smile and look confident and relaxed, no matter how nervous they feel.

Ice dancing is similar to ballroom dancing, with precise, rhythmical steps skated to orchestral music. Ice dancers strive to shadow skate with each other in perfect unison, as they swing into symmetrical curves in time with the music. Good body carriage is extremely important, and all actions of the dancers should be harmonious and flowing, not jerky or rushed.

If the dancers are separated on the ice, which is seldom the case, the distance allowed is only two arm lengths away from each other. During the free skating performance, five low dance lifts may be performed but the male partner never raises his hands past his shoulders. The five dance jumps permitted are basically used to change the foot or direction of travel.

The skating technique in character with the ice dance event incorporates harmony, elegance, and grace all expressed by the movements of the skater through the music.

Brian Orser, 1984 Olympic silver medalist, demonstrates the skills of a champion at the 1984 Games at Sarajevo. *Athlete Information Bureau/Canadian Olympic Association*

# The Rules

The Olympic figure skating events include individual skating for men and women, pairs skating, and ice dance.

The all-important school figures count for thirty per cent of the singles competition. The school figures gave the sport its name, and are the basis of the Olympic competition.

During the nineteenth century, figure skaters were required to draw their chosen figure on paper for a competition, and then "trace" it on the ice while skating. Tracing competitions were won by the skater who performed the most difficult and intricate design. These figures were eventually replaced by forty-one official figures included in the modern Olympic format. All forty-one figures are based on the figure eight.

Today, there are six predetermined figures that skaters practise for a singles competition. But not until a few days before the actual competition are the contestants told what three figures will be required for the judges. By setting a high score in the compulsories, the figure skaters set themselves up for seeding (the drawing of positions) in the free-skating portion.

The prescribed short program is a maximum of two minutes and has seven required elements in it. The short program is performed to music chosen by the skater, and is worth twenty per cent of the total score for singles, and twenty-five per cent for pairs.

In contrast to the compulsory short program, the long freestyle program has no required elements. The long program is worth fifty per cent in singles, and seventy-five per cent in pairs. The singles and pairs skaters are free to show off new spins, jumps, and dance movements. The program lasts for approximately four minutes.

The nine judges compute the degree of difficulty (technical merit) along with the artistic impression of the performance, and display the first set of marks on large cards held in front of them. The second set of marks for artistic impression are displayed on the scoreboard.

For instance, after all couples have skated the short program in the pairs event, they have been awarded two sets of marks. The maximum score in each set is 6.0. The marks are then divided by 2.5.

More importantly, the skaters are ranked from best to worst by the judges. "Ordinals," the term used for the numerical equivalent of ranking (1 for first place, 2 for second, etc.) are assigned by all nine judges.

Although the scoring of figure skating may seem unintelligible to Olympic spectators, the key to being declared the winner is having a majority of ordinals (first-place votes).

The psychological warfare that both skaters and judges encounter throughout competitions make the task of figure-skating judging extremely complex. In the final analysis, the marks are awarded by nine very human judges, but the exercise of global powers over them was marked on a rare occasion at the Olympics at Sarajevo in 1984.

International politics being what they are, a political coup might be described as a unanimous agreement of nine major world powers.

At the 1984 Winter Olympics, all it took was the ice dance performance of Britain's Jayne Torvill and Christopher Dean. Judges from the Soviet Union, Italy, Switzerland, Japan, the United States, Canada, Austria, Hungary, and Great Britain simultaneously displayed their marks for Torvill and Dean's artistic impression.

6.0   6.0   6.0   6.0   6.0   6.0   6.0   6.0   6.0

The nine 6.0s across the scoreboard provided an unforgettable milestone in the history of Olympic figure skating.

Ice dance was introduced to the Olympic format in 1976 and consists of compulsory dance (thirty per cent of the total mark), original set pattern dance (twenty per cent), and free dance (worth fifty per cent).

In the compulsory dance, the skaters are required to skate three repetitions of one dance that utilises the entire ice surface. Ice dancers are marked on their accuracy of repetition, timing, and rhythm.

The original set pattern marks are divided into sections of composition and presentation. Each couple can choose their own music, but the competition is not a free dance as there are some restrictions. All dance moves must conform to the rules of the International Skating Union, and costumes must be simple and modest. No show costumes are allowed in the event.

The free dance program is a four-minute showcase of originality and personal expression for the ice dancers.

Show costumes are worn, no compulsory moves are required, and all types of music are permitted. If the music is judged to be unsuitable, or more than three changes in music tempo occur during the performance, the couple is penalized. Judges also penalize an ice dance couple if they appear to skate as if in the pairs competition by performing feats that attempt to show physical strength. The treacherous throw jumps are very highly scored in the pairs event, but would be severely penalized by judges in the ice dance competition.

To simplify the figure skating rules, the following should be remembered: each skater appears three times in singles and ice dance, and twice in the pairs event.

# The Equipment

Speedskating was the only form of skating possible until the invention of the new lightweight metal blade in 1848. The metal blade was fixed to the skate boot with screws and was further refined when the blade was curved upward at the front and toe picks added to it.

Today, figure skaters who compete in the singles events need two pairs of skates.

For the compulsories, a razor-sharp blade makes cutting figure eights more difficult than a duller blade. In fact, skaters who perform in the compulsories may only sharpen their skates once or twice a year. The bottom toe pick on the skate blade is removed for the compulsories.

For the freestyle event, the sharper the skate blade, the better. A sharp blade makes a solid and steady jump landing, particularly in the singles and pairs events. The jumps, spins, arabesques, and pivots wear down the blade and figure skaters, like hockey players, are continually sharpening blades.

The picks, located on the front of the blade, are extremely important to aid the skater in the toe-assisted jumps.

Boots and skate blades are purchased separately. Leather boots are traditionally black for men, and beige or white for women.

Most skate blades are made in England and are solid Sheffield steel.

Sonja Henie was the first figure skater to wear a short skating skirt in the Olympic competition in 1924. Since then, skating costume design has come a long way.

Nevertheless, clothing worn in the compulsory figures, the compulsory dance events, and the compulsory freestyle short program must be tasteful and appropriate.

In the longer freestyle event, the figure skaters put on the ritz. The most expensive skating costumes for women are the fashionable beaded dresses. White fur made an appearance in the free dance performance of the ice dancing event at the 1984 Olympics. Seventeen-year-old Soviet beauty Marina Klimova was one of the prettiest figure skaters at the Games, and wearing a dress with white fur trim, skated off with the bronze medal with partner Sergei Ponomarenko.

When Canadian figure skater Robert Paul won his Olympic gold medal at Squaw Valley, California, in 1960, he wore the popular modified version of the tuxedo, complete with black tie. Those days of formality for men have ended although the occasional tux is still seen in ice dancing competitions. Men today wear as colourful a spangled skating costume as they wish, but the rules of tastefulness and appropriateness still apply to the compulsory events.

# Calgary Preview

## Men's Singles

The Olympic figure skating events at Calgary in 1988 will highlight as talented a field of young skaters as any Olympic Winter Games ever.

Canada's only world champion entry into the official Olympic events will be 1987 World Figure Skating Champion Brian Orser. Orser, who lost out on the world championship the previous year, placing a close second to Brian Boitanno of the United States, collected his dues at Cincinnati, Ohio at the 1987 Worlds. Being another year older, Orser appeared remarkably calm and had quieted his nerves in preparation for his flawless freeskate performance. He was right on target for the world title. "It was a special feeling," said Brian Orser after the competition, "I knew it before I went out there." And, with Toller Cranston and Don Jackson of Canada in the audience, Orser eclipsed all other figure skaters in Cincinnati to become third man in Canada, along with Donald Jackson and Donald McPherson, to hold the World title.

Orser will face strong challenges from arch-rival Alexander Fadeev of the Soviet Union and Josef Sabovcik of Czechoslovakia.

Known as Mr. Marlboro, Jozef Sabovcik's heavy smoking habit doesn't seem to have an effect on his figure skating performance, which has steadily improved since his bronze medal win at Sarajevo in 1984.

The Americans have a skater who could capture a medal in Brian Boitano. Boitano, like Brian Orser, excels at the triple axel jump and is an exciting free skater to watch. Boitano turned in a solid performance at the 1984 Games at Sarajevo, and placed second at the 1987 World Figure Skating Championships.

Vacancies on the Canadian Olympic figure skating team could easily be filled by Kurt Browning and Michael Slipchuk of Edmonton's Royal Glenora Club.

## Women's Singles

In 1987, Jill Trenary of Minnetonka, Minnesota, capped a remarkable comeback from cut muscles and arteries in her left leg (sustained in a freak accident two years before) by upsetting World Champion Debi Thomas. Trenary won the women's crown at the 1987 U.S. figure skating championships by beating defending champ Thomas, a medical student at Stanford University.

Thomas consistently places well in the compulsories, short, and free skating performances, and with 1987 World Champion Katarina Witt of East Germany right on her heels, has her work cut out for her in 1988 at the Olympics.

West Germany has produced a brilliantly successful singles skater in Claudia Leistner, a former world champion roller skater turned figure skater. Leistner is giving veteran team-mate Manuela Ruben a run for her money and won the German championship last year. At seventeen, Leistner won the silver medal in the 1983 Worlds at Helsinki and set her career in motion. Since then, she has finished in the top ten at the World Championships and trains both in the United States and West Germany, skating up to thirty-five hours a week.

A Soviet skater worth watching is Elena Vodorezova, who excels at the compulsories. Elena is coached by the famous Stanislav Zhuk and in her spare time helps with the productions of the Bolshoi Ballet. The U.S.S.R. gold champion performs like a ballerina on the ice and is well known for her seemingly weightless jumps and superb program choreography.

Anna Kondrashova is also a promising young figure skater from the Soviet Union. Her short program and free skating continually impress international judges. Kondrashova is able to perform four different triple jumps in her daring free-skate performance.

The retirement from the amateur ranks of both Rosalynn Sumners and Elaine Zayak of the United States opened the field for a battle between Californian Tiffany Chin and another promising newcomer, Caryn Kadavy. Chin, an ethereal beauty, performs with a delicate charm combined with surprisingly strong athletic ability considering her weight of only 40.4 kg. Since her 1984 Olympic debut, Chin has emerged as a threat to the reigning supremacy of both top women skaters, Katarina Witt and Debi Thomas. Chin and Kadavy will battle it out for top international rankings before the 1988 Olympics in Calgary.

Elizabeth Manley of Ottawa and Patricia Schmidt, of

Edmonton's Royal Glenora Club, head the Canadian women's team. Manley captured the 1987 Canadian championship after losing it in 1986 to Tracey Wainman. Wainman's skating career has been nothing short of traumatic. She won her first national senior title as a tiny thirteen-year-old in 1981, lost her Canadian title to Torontonian Kay Thomson in 1982, finished seventh in the 1983 Nationals in Montreal, and did not compete in 1984 because of tendinitis. Attempting a comeback, Tracey Wainman won the 1986 Canadian Championships. She turned professional in 1987 and is now performing with Holiday on Ice in Europe.

## Ice Dancing

In 1985 at Tokyo, Canada's top ice dancers Tracy Wilson from Port Moody, British Columbia, and Rob McCall of Halifax, Nova Scotia, won a bronze medal, the first Canadians to win a World Championship medal since 1964. Since then, they have placed third at the 1987 World Championships and are considered potential Olympic champions. Canada's other pair are brother-and-sister Rod and Karyn Garossino of Carstairs, Alberta, who are currently training in Toronto.

The Olympic competition, however, will be tough against the European and World Champions Natalya Bestemianova and Andrei Bukin of the Soviet Union. 1984 Olympic bronze medalist Marina Klimova and Sergei Ponomarenko are also to be reckoned with. To date, there are no British replacements for Jayne Torvill and Christopher Dean, who turned professional after the 1984 Winter Games. The United States has an ice dancing pair that could feature in 1988 with Suzanne Semanick and Scott Gregory.

## Pairs

In the past twenty years of the World figure skating champion-ships, the Soviets have won the pairs title eighteen times. It hasn't been much different in the Olympics.

The last non-Soviet couple to win the Olympic pairs event were Canada's 1960 Olympic gold medalists Robert Paul and Barbara Wagner.

The Americans came close in the 1984 Winter Games, when popular brother-and-sister Peter and Kitty Carruthers won the silver medal. Since the retirement from the amateur ranks of the Carruthers in 1985, the American pair of Jill Watson and Peter Oppegard have made steady progress in international and European competitions, but whether they can make it into the winners' circle against the Soviets is the big question.

The East Germans have a strong pair in their national champions but they are constantly beaten by the 1984 Olympic gold medalists Elena Valova and Oleg Vasiliev of the Soviet Union. Another outstanding Soviet pair are World Champions Ekaterina Gordeeva and Sergei Grinkov.

Most sports have their cycle, but not pairs skating for the Soviets. They will be the ones to beat at the Olympics in Calgary in 1988.

After winning the 1984 World Championships, Canada's Barbara Underhill and Paul Martini turned professional and passed the Canadian pairs title on to the defending champions Cynthia Coull and Mark Rowsom. They cracked the top ten at the Worlds last year, and the win was a big confidence-booster for the Canadian pair. Unfortunately, Coull and Rowsom split up in the summer of 1987 because Rowsom underwent surgery and might not recover in time to train for the Olympics. Expecting to be competing in Calgary in 1988 are Denise Benning and Lyndon Johnston who train at the National Pairs Centre in Preston, Ontario.

# Canadians at the Olympic Winter Games
# FIGURE SKATING

## 1924 Chamonix — I Olympic Winter Games

**MEN, INDIVIDUAL**
7. Melville Rogers

**WOMEN, INDIVIDUAL**
6. Cecil Eustace Smith

**PAIRS**
7. Melville Rogers,
Cecil Eustace Smith

## 1928 St. Moritz — II Olympic Winter Games

Eastwood, J., Smith, C., Smith, M., Wilson, C., Wilson, M.

**MEN, INDIVIDUAL**
12. Montgomery Wilson
16. John Eastwood

**WOMEN, INDIVIDUAL**
5. Cecil Eustace Smith
6. Constance Wilson

**PAIRS**
10. John Eastwood,
Maude Smith

## 1932 Lake Placid — III Olympic Winter Games

Bangs, C., Claudet, F., Fisher, E., Littlejohn, M., Reburn, S., Rogers, I., Rogers, M., Wilson, M., Wilson-Samuel, C.

**MEN, INDIVIDUAL**
3. Montgomery Wilson

**WOMEN, INDIVIDUAL**
4. Constance Wilson-Samuel
13. Elizabeth Fisher
15. Mary Littlejohn

**PAIRS**
5. Constance Wilson-Samuel,
Montgomery Wilson
6. Frances Claudet,
Chauncy Bangs

## 1936 Garmisch-Partenkirchen — IV Olympic Winter Games

Bertram, L., Garland, A., Reburn, S., Sweatman, F., Wilson, M., Wilson-Samuel, C.

**MEN, INDIVIDUAL**
4. Montgomery Wilson

**PAIRS**
6. Louise Bertram, Stewart Reburn
12. Audrey Garland, Fraser Sweatman

## 1948 St. Moritz — V Olympic Winter Games

Deistelmeyer, W., Morrow, S., Take, M., Scott, B.A.

**MEN, INDIVIDUAL**
12. Wallace Deistelmeyer

**WOMEN, INDIVIDUAL**
1. Barbara Ann Scott
12. Marilyn Take
14. Suzanne Morrow

**PAIRS**
3. Suzanne Morrow,
Wallace Deistelmeyer

## 1952 Oslo — VI Olympic Winter Games

Bowden, R.N., Dafoe, F., Firstbrook, P., Morrow, S., Smith, M., Smith, V.

**MEN, INDIVIDUAL**
5. Peter Firstbrook

**PAIRS**
5. Frances Dafoe,
R. Norris Bowden

**WOMEN, INDIVIDUAL**
6. Suzanne Morrow
9. Marlene Smith
13. Vera V. Smith

## 1956 Cortina d'Ampezzo — VII Olympic Winter Games

Bowden, R.N., Dafoe, F., Johnston, A., Pachl, C.J., Paul, R., Snelling, C., Wagner, B.

**MEN, INDIVIDUAL**
8. Charles Snelling

**WOMEN, INDIVIDUAL**
6. Carole Jane Pachl
9. Ann Johnston

**PAIRS**
2. Frances Dafoe,
R. Norris Bowden
6. Barbara Wagner,
Robert Paul

## 1960 Squaw Valley — VIII Olympic Winter Games

Griner, W., Jackson, D., Jelinek, M., Jelinek, O., McPherson, D., Paul, R., Tewkesbury, S., Wagner, B.

**MEN, INDIVIDUAL**
3. Donald Jackson
10. Donald McPherson

**WOMEN, INDIVIDUAL**
10. Sandra Tewkesbury
12. Wendy Griner

**PAIRS**
1. Barbara Wagner,
Robert Paul
4. Maria Jelinek,
Otto Jelinek

## 1964 Innsbruck — IX Olympic Winter Games

Burka, P., Carpenter, N., Griner, W., Kenworthy, S., Knight, D., Neale, W., Revell, G., Snelling, C., Strutt, F., Ward, L., Watters, J., Wilkes, D.

**MEN, INDIVIDUAL**
9. Donald Knight
13. Charles Snelling
16. William Neale

**WOMEN, INDIVIDUAL**
3. Petra Burka
10. Wendy Griner
12. Shirra Kenworthy

**PAIRS**
3. Debbi Wilkes,
Guy Revell
14. Faye Strutt,
Jim Watters
16. Linda Ward,
Neil Carpenter

## 1968 Grenoble — X Olympic Winter Games

Carbonetto, L., Cowan, L., Forder, A., Humphrey, J., Hutchinson, S., Magnussen, K., McGillivray, D., McKilligan, B., McKilligan, J., Stephens, R.

**MEN, INDIVIDUAL**
7. Jay Humphrey
16. David McGillivray
22. Steve Hutchinson

**WOMEN, INDIVIDUAL**
7. Karen Magnussen
13. Linda Carbonetto

**PAIRS**
16. Anna Forder,
Richard Stephens
17. Betty McKilligan,
John McKilligan

## 1972 Sapporo — XI Olympic Winter Games

Bezic, S., Bezic, V., Cranston, T., Hubbell, J., Hutchinson, R., Irwin, C.L., Magnussen, K., Petrie, M.

**MEN, INDIVIDUAL**
9. Toller Cranston

**WOMEN, INDIVIDUAL**
2. Karen Magnussen
13. Cathy Lee Irwin

**PAIRS**
9. Sandra Bezic,
Val Bezic
15. Mary Petrie,
John Hubbell

## 1976 Innsbruck — XII Olympic Winter Games

Alletson, K., Berezowski, B., Bohonek, S., Carscallen, S., Cranston, T., Fraser, D., Gillies, E., Jones, C., Nightingale, L., Porter, D., Shaver, R.

**MEN, INDIVIDUAL**
3. Toller Cranston
14. Stan Bohonek

**WOMEN, INDIVIDUAL**
9. Lynn Nightingale
14. Kim Alletson

**PAIRS**
14. Candace Jones,
Donald Fraser

**DANCE**
10. Barbara Berezowski,
David Porter
13. Susan Carscallen,
Eric Gillies

## 1980 Lake Placid — XIII Olympic Winter Games

Dowding, J., Kemkaran, H., Martini, P., Pockar, B., Wighton, L., Underhill, B.

**MEN, INDIVIDUAL**
12. Brian Pockar

**WOMEN, INDIVIDUAL**
15. Heather Kemkaran

**PAIRS**
9. Barbara Underhill,
Paul Martini

**DANCE**
6. Lorna Wighton,
John Dowding

## 1984 Sarajevo — XIV Olympic Winter Games

Beacom, G., Eggleton, J., Eisler, L., Johnson, K., Johnston, L., Kunhegyi, M., Manley, E., Martini, P., Matousek, K., McCall, R., Orser, B., Thomas, J., Thomson, K., Underhill, B., Wilson, T.

**MEN, INDIVIDUAL**
2. Brian Orser
11. Gary Beacom
20. Jamie Eggleton

**WOMEN, INDIVIDUAL**
12. Kay Thomson
13. Elizabeth Manley

**PAIRS**
7. Barbara Underhill,
Paul Martini
8. Katherina Matousek,
Lloyd Eisler
12. Melinda Kunhegyi,
Lyndon Johnston

**ICE DANCE**
8. Tracy Wilson,
Rob McCall
12. Kelly Johnson,
John Thomas

# Ice Hockey

Olympic Saddledome
February 13, 14, 15, 16, 17, 18, 19, 20, 21, 22, 24, 25, 26, 27, 28

Stampede Corral
February 13, 15, 16, 17, 18, 19, 20, 21

Father David Bauer Olympic Arena
February 22, 23

# Olympic Hockey: "Make Use of Technique, but Let the Spirit Prevail"

*Mathieson, Calgary*

The history of Canadian interest in Olympic hockey is a paradoxical one. For a long period Canada dominated this sport in the Olympics, but never had much interest in it, perhaps because there was not much competition. Since 1952, on the other hand, Canada has not won a gold medal in Olympic hockey, but the interest in it has been much greater.

What this seems to mean is that Canadians are not just interested in winning. They are interested in good hockey. They love to win, naturally enough, but winning only has meaning when the competition is worthwhile, when the hockey is worth playing and worth watching. And that, it may be noted, is a good expression of the Olympic ideal.

We may, I think, assume that hockey is worth watching when it is worth playing. When, then, is it worth playing? Canadians have played hockey for generations and have certainly found it worthwhile; but if you asked them why, they would often be hard put to answer.

Perhaps we can find an answer from outside Canada. No one has looked at Canadian hockey more carefully than the Europeans, and from what they have learned by observing, they have built the success of their teams in world hockey.

There are, in the eyes of the Europeans, four major elements in hockey. There is first the element of skill, both individual and collective. Skating, stick-handling, passing, shooting, fore-checking, back-checking, goal-tending: these are among the basic skills in hockey that distinguish good teams, and good games, from bad. A second element is that of sheer physical capacity: given equal skill, that team will normally prevail that has the better physical conditioning, the one whose players can keep skating, shooting, and checking for the whole game and the whole series. These first two elements are mainly matters of preparation. They are set before the game begins. There is also, however, and this is a third element, the area of strategy and tactics. It is not enough to have skills and to be in perfect shape; one must also know how and when to use those skills and make use of one's capacities. This is an element which must be both thought out beforehand and applied in the midst of the contest. And finally there is a fourth element which honest observers could not fail to note. Besides skill and conditioning and strategy or tactics, there is the element of spirit—drive, eagerness, enthusiasm, spontaneity, and desire; this, showing itself in the course of a contest, will often determine victory or defeat.

These four elements, in the European view, are the determining ones in international competition in hockey (and, one might note, the same would apply to many other areas as well). Dominance in all four elements is unlikely to be achieved by any one team, any one nation; but a team, a nation, which could establish pre-eminence in three of these elements might well dominate international and Olympic competition for a long time. The observers recognized from the beginning that their teams could not overcome the Canadians in the area of spirit, but they felt that skills could be learned by practice and conditioning developed by discipline and that good coaching could supply the strategy and tactics. And who, at this date, would judge such observers to have been mistaken?

All of this, unquestionably, has a significance for Canadians. For us, however, the issue must be a different one: we have experienced the frustration of spirit being defeated, but, we still must ask, is victory itself worthwhile without spirit? Once the question is put in this way, the answer, I think, is obvious.

The challenge of Olympic hockey for Canadians is evident. We must, as Joe Primeau—the only man ever to coach teams to victory in the Memorial Cup, Allan Cup, Alexander Cup, and Stanley Cup—used to say, "Make use of technique, but let the spirit prevail." We must—and recent results in world competitions at the midget and junior levels as well as in the last Canada Cup seem to show that we are doing this—develop the skills, the conditioning, the strategies and tactics needed for victory; but we must do this in such a way that the spirit of the game and the players who play it will be strengthened. To win in any other way will not satisfy Canadians.

Such a challenge goes far beyond hockey. It involves moral and spiritual issues in Canada and the world. Can our society, by what is best in it—by that in it which can be seen, not at its deepest, no doubt, but perhaps at its most evident, in the sort of spirit that can animate our teams—develop also our skills and disciplines in all areas of our life so as to make them useful for our best national purposes? This is not something which can be accomplished in Olympic hockey alone, but our experience there may provide a stimulus for an effort which will carry Canada and the whole world much further.

Father David W. Bauer, CSB, O.C.

# The History

The game of hockey is regarded by many Canadians as a national birthright.

In fact, soldiers of the Royal Canadian Rifles organized Canada's first ice hockey team in 1885 at Kingston, Ontario. During the long cold Canadian winters, teams from Kingston, Montreal, and Halifax joined in the popular new sport to play in the first recorded hockey league in the world.

The origin of Canada's national sport dates back to ancient Greece where athletes practised a form of field hockey. The Roman conquerors took the game from Greece to France where it was named "hocquet." Eventually the game made its way across the English Channel to Britain, and ended up in Canada via the Scottish settlers who re-named the game "shinny."

Canadian youngsters, enduring winter temperatures of -30°C and -40°C, were quick to adapt the game from playing field to outdoor ice. Canadian farm boys played hockey with their young shins wrapped in Eaton's mail-order catalogues, held on with sealer rings from their mothers' kitchens. Many National Hockey League stars had humble beginnings on the frozen countryside ponds of Canada.

In 1893, the sixth Governor-General of Canada, Lord Stanley, donated a fifty dollar trophy to the Canadian Amateur Hockey Association for the best team in the country. During the following years, high speed ice hockey grew into a spectator favourite. By 1924, Boston, Detroit, New York, and Chicago had joined forces with Montreal and Toronto to form the National Hockey League. The Stanley Cup was now awarded to the best professional ice hockey team, and the National Hockey League eventually encompassed over twenty teams. Today the Stanley Cup has become a skyscraper of a trophy. The trophy is awarded annually to the top team and is the most coveted prize in professional hockey, inscribed with the names of every player of every team that has ever won it.

**TORONTO GRANITES**
Olympic Hockey Champions—1924

Back Row—left to right: H. McMUNN    B. McCAFFREY    R. SMITH    B. RAMSEY    E. COLLETT    S. SLATER    J. CAMERON

Front Row: P. CAMPBELL    H. WATSON    W. HEWITT    D. MONROE    F. RANKIN (Coach)

The Toronto Granites, the Olympic hockey champions in 1924. *Hockey Hall of Fame, Toronto*

When the game was introduced as an event in the Olympic Summer Games at Antwerp, Belgium, in 1920, Canada was represented by an amateur team, winners of the Canadian Championship, the Winnipeg Falcons. And, to no one's surprise, the team dominated the tournament, winning the first gold medal ever presented for Olympic ice hockey.

From the initial introduction of ice hockey into the Olympic Games, Canada's Olympic ice hockey teams won four consecutive gold medals. Their 1920 win was followed in 1924, at the first formal Olympic Winter Games at Chamonix, France, in 1928 at St. Moritz, Switzerland and in 1932 at Lake Placid, New York. It was not until 1936 at Garmisch-Partenkirchen that the pattern was broken, surprisingly by Great Britain. The Olympic Winter Games resumed after World War II, and Canada once again reigned supreme in 1948 in St. Moritz, Switzerland, and in 1952 in Oslo, Norway. The U.S.S.R. competed in the Olympic Winter Games for the first time in 1956, and fielded its first Olympic hockey team at Cortina d'Ampezzo, Italy. With Soviet representation in hockey, the Canadian hockey dynasty came to an end.

Ironically, the game from ancient Europe that had been adapted to Canada's winter environment had once again made its way back across the ocean to become the favourite spectator winter sport of the Soviets. The Soviets had been watching the hockey technique of the masters, the Canadians. Refining a European style of hockey, the Soviets lived, trained, and played together for most of the year.

In their Olympic ice hockey debut in the Games in 1956, the U.S.S.R. won the gold medal and Canada the silver. From their first appearance in the Olympic Winter Games in 1956, the U.S.S.R. has failed to win gold medals in ice hockey only twice. Both times the Soviets were denied gold medals by the United States—at the Olympic Winter Games at Squaw Valley, California, in 1960 and at Lake Placid, New York, in 1980—proof that home-ice has its advantages.

As the Russian hockey expertise increased, so did the frustration of Canadian amateur hockey players and their coaches. Canada possessed most of the best professional hockey players in the world, but they were ineligible for amateur Olympic competition. Ice hockey is one Olympic sports discipline that has been particularly plagued by the amateur-professional conflict in the history of the Olympic Winter Games.

Aspiring collegiate and junior hockey stars are lured away from amateur ranks by large salaries and the prestige of National Hockey League contracts. The trend to assemble teams of young, inexperienced hockey squads within six months of Olympic Winter Games competition ended in disappointing results, with Canada being left out of medal contention.

Coincidentally, these extenuating circumstances provided the impetus for Canadian ice hockey coach Father David Bauer to undertake an experiment with amateur players. A Basilian priest from Notre Dame School at Wilcox, Saskatchewan, Father Bauer dedicated himself to salvaging Canadian hockey prestige by devising a youth plan. Assembling a group of school teachers and unknown university players to train and live together while teaching or attending school, Father Bauer hoped to regain Canadian hockey supremacy. The establishment of a permanent Olympic ice hockey team, dedicated to "Father" and the Olympic amateur movement would prove its worth.

Four years later, the Canadians were back to play the favoured Soviets once again in the Olympic Winter Games at Innsbruck, Austria, in 1964. The U.S.S.R. was victorious against Canada; however, Canada led twice in the tense final championship that ended with a 3-2 score. Placing fourth behind Sweden

The 1928 Canadian Olympic hockey team. *Hockey Hall of Fame, Toronto*

## THE WINNIPEG HOCKEY CLUB
### Olympic Hockey Champions—1932

Back Row—left to right: D. G. THOMSON (President)  N. W. LESLIE (Vice-Pres.)  E. A. GILROY (President, Man. A.H.A.)
Second Row: C. CROWLEY  N. MALLOY  H. SUTHERLAND  R. HENKEL
A. DUNCANSON  F. WOOLLEY  V. LINDQUIST  A. WISE  K. MOORE
First Row: G. GARBUTT  R. RIVERS  H. SIMPSON  W. COCKBURN (Capt.)
S. WAGNER  W. MONSON
Seated: W. J. ROBERTSON (Mgr.)  J. L. HUGHES (Coach)  C. C. ROBINSON (Olympic Rep.)  W. BOWMAN (Trainer)
J. E. MYERS (Secretary-Treasurer)

The 1932 Olympic Ice Hockey Team. *Hockey Hall of Fame, Toronto*

(silver) and Czechoslovakia (bronze), Canada lost out in its bid for an Olympic medal by a goals-scored percentage. Still, for the Canadians, after years of discouraging Olympic ice hockey results, the Bauer Team concept was a pivotal approach to Olympic ice hockey in Canada. To the credit of coach Father David Bauer, the Canadians earned the bronze medal at Grenoble, France, at the Olympic Winter Games in 1968 and proved Canada was capable of working its way back into medal contention in Olympic hockey.

Having shown such promise in 1968, it was unfortunate Canada chose to withdraw from the Olympic ice hockey event for the XI Olympic Winter Games at Sapporo, Japan, in 1972. Canadian ice hockey officials faced a major controversy with disputes over definitions of professional and amateur status. Failing to arrive at a compromise in the dispute, Canada ended up boycotting its own national sport at the Olympic Winter

Games in Japan. Hockey Canada officials had grown tired of seeing Canadian amateurs being trounced in the Olympic Winter Games hockey event, and they demanded to use the best team that Canada could produce. That meant professionals, and that meant ineligibility in Olympic Games competition. This dilemma ended with the national team being disbanded in 1970.

Calgary lawyer Joseph Kryczka was the president of the Canadian Amateur Hockey Association in 1972 following the dispute over player eligibility. As president of the CAHA, Kryczka played an important role in setting the stage for Canadian professional hockey stars to challenge the U.S.S.R. to an historic eight-game series in 1972. The long-awaited hockey event sparked a national hockey craze in Canada and captured attention of hockey fans throughout the world. The hearts of Canadian hockey fans burst with pride when Canada won the series in the final game in Moscow. This tournament became a model

# R.C.A.F. FLYERS-OTTAWA—1948

Back: G. McFAUL    A. LaPERRIERE    F. DUNSTER    L. LeCOMPTE    R. SCHROETER    H. BROOKS    A. GILPIN

W. HALDER    G. MARA    I. TAYLOR    Dr. A. G. WATSON    FRANK BOUCHER

Front: M. DOWEY    E. HIBBERD    O. GRAVELLE    A. RENAUD    R. FORBES    P. LEICHNITZ    P. GUZZO    R. KING

The RCAF Flyers from Ottawa, gold medal winners at the 1948 Olympic Winter Games. *Hockey Hall of Fame, Toronto*

of outstanding international ice hockey, and Justice Joseph Kryczka was inducted into the Alberta Amateur Hockey Association Hall of Fame in 1984.

Having shunned two consecutive Olympic Winter Games, at Sapporo, Japan, in 1972 and Innsbruck, Austria, in 1976, Canadian Olympic ice hockey would have disappeared from the world scene if it had not been for a group of Calgary businessmen and Hockey Canada. Reviving the Bauer concept, an Olympic hockey team was established in Calgary during the year preceding the XIII Olympic Winter Games at Lake Placid, New York, in 1980. Donated oil drilling trailers were set up outside the veteran Stampede Corral (seating capacity six thousand) for the young hockey players to live in until the Games were held in February at Lake Placid. Living together and working out together, the players received a $50-a-month training allowance and a $215-a-month living allowance. Father David Bauer was the unpaid coach, and a federal grant of $300,000 along with corporate donations made up a $700,000 budget for the Olympic hopefuls.

Despite the dedication of the group of juniors, college kids, and quasi pros, the Olympic hockey team fell behind in the tournament at Lake Placid in 1980 and lost out in its attempt to advance to the final round. Canada finished with a 3-2 average at the Games. The Soviet Union once again won five games straight, including a 6-4 win over Canada in the preliminary round. Canada ended up in sixth place in the medal standings, but the country was back in the Olympic Winter Games thanks to Father David Bauer, who said, "Because Canada might not win in the Olympics is no reason not to proceed again."

One of the biggest upsets in the history of Olympic sports was the "Miracle on Ice" when the U.S.A. beat the U.S.S.R. in hockey at Lake Placid, New York, in 1980. The boycott of the Olympic Summer Games in Moscow by the U.S.A. had left the Americans with only the Olympic Winter Games as a vehicle for national pride. Team U.S.A. was not among the medal favourites, but managed to sweep all five games in the preliminary round by beating Sweden, Czechoslovakia, Norway, Romania, and West Germany. Advancing to the finals in

The 1952 gold medal Olympic ice hockey team: George Abel, John Davies, William Dawe, Robert Dickson, Donald Gauf, William Gibson, Ralph Hansch, Robert Meyers, David Miller, Eric Paterson, Thomas Pollock, Allan Purvis, Gordon Robertson, Louis Secco, Francis Sullivan, Robert Watt. *Hockey Hall of Fame*

Father David Bauer interviewed after Canada's victorious opening game against Sweden at the 1964 Olympics. The bruise on Bauer's forehead was the result of a broken hockey stick hurled at him by a player from the Swedish team; never one to hold a grudge, Bauer took the Swede to the Soviet hockey game the following night. *Deutsche Presse-Agentur GmbH*

the other division, the Soviets had won all five preliminary games, including the win against Canada. With Canada failing to make it to the final round, Canadian hockey fans turned their loyalties toward the U.S.A. In front of a sellout crowd of over eight thousand the American hockey team skated on to the ice to face the team that had established itself as the best in the world. The excitement in the hockey arena increased with every shot at American goalie Jim Craig, whose record of thirty-nine saves in the game was a phenomenon. At the 10 minute mark of the third period the score was 4-2 for the U.S.A. and the wild cheering of the fans filled the arena until the last seconds of the game had ticked off. When the game ended in victory for the U.S.A., the euphoria of the charged-up fans even had the Soviet players smiling as they congratulated their American rivals. Team U.S.A. advanced to the final round against Finland, and won the tournament and the gold medal

at the XIII Olympic Winter Games at Lake Placid. The victory by the Americans represented the second time the Soviets had been beaten in Olympic ice hockey—both times by the Americans, and both times on American home ice.

The hockey event at the XIV Olympic Winter Games at Sarajevo, Yugoslavia, in 1984 began with an official protest from Finland that Canada had professional players on its team. The crux of the issue was the fact that two players in the Canadian line-up had signed contracts and played games with the NHL, forfeiting their amateur status. The question of eligibility had once again surfaced in the Olympic Winter Games.

The International Olympic Committee's definition of an amateur was expanded in 1984 to include any player who had never played on an NHL team. Therefore, players in the AHL or players who had signed a professional contract but never played in the NHL were eligible. Although the re-definition of the rules was considered an anachronism by many international hockey officials, the ruling made the IOC able to decide who was eligible to compete in the hockey event at the Games.

With the lowering of the NHL draft age to eighteen, it would seem evident that North American professional hockey players do not fully support the concept of amateur Olympic ice hockey teams. Conversely, every hockey team in the eastern bloc countries is supported by the government or a state-owned industry, while maintaining that they are not professional hockey players. The inability of the organizations to patch up their differences produces hockey representatives working at cross-purposes. This problem is handed over to the IOC at the Olympic Winter Games on a regular basis, every four years. The eligibility muddle at Sarajevo in 1984 was eventually settled by the IOC. The two Canadian team members in question were declared ineligible to play in the Olympic tournament as both had played games in the National Hockey League.

The XIV Olympic Winter Games hockey event began at Sarajevo's Zetra Arena with pressure on Team U.S.A. to repeat the 1980 gold medal performance. Liberated by defeat in their first game, the U.S.A. lost to the Canadians 4-2. From then on Canada became Team Cinderella of the Games, and a group of carping Canadian sports pundits who had predicted Team Canada would be humiliated by defeat finally had to face their come-uppance. Buoyed by the victory over the Americans, the Canadians went on to win three more games against Austria, Finland, and Norway and found themselves in the elite unbeaten company of the Soviets and the Czechs. Canada's pendulum of fortune changed as Team Canada went on to face the formidable opponents with losses to the Czechs (4-0), Soviets (4-0), and Swedes (2-0). Placing a credible fourth, after the bronze medal match against Sweden, the Canadians performed extraordinarily well against some of the world's best hockey teams at Sarajevo, Yugoslavia, in 1984.

Head Coach Dave King stated, "I just hope Canada is proud of these kids. They didn't win a medal, but they gave it their whole effort." After the 1984 Games, the Olympic hockey team supplied the NHL with a number of outstanding players including James Patrick (New York Rangers), Pat Flatley (New York Islanders), Mario Gosselin (Quebec Nordiques), Kirk Muller

(New Jersey Devils), Russ Courtnall (Toronto Maple Leafs), Carey Wilson (Calgary Flames), Doug Lidster (Vancouver Canucks), Craig Redmond (Los Angeles Kings), and Kevin Dineen and Dave Tippet (Hartford Whalers).

In October of 1986, the International Olympic Committee set a new ruling on one of sport's most controversial issues. Surrendering to modern times, the IOC voted unequivocally to allow hockey professionals to lace up for the Olympics.

The new decision was welcomed by ice hockey officials, but with words of caution. The about-face by the International Olympic Committee raises uncertainty regarding player eligibility versus availability. It could be that the new ruling may have little effect on Canada's Olympic team as it is highly unlikely that the top NHL players will be available for the competition.

The fact remains that the National Hockey League's first priority is to their ticket holders. Talented players on NHL teams mean money in the bank, and even more money for a team that makes the playoffs.

The decision made by IOC in October of 1986 forced NHL players to operate under the rules of the International Ice Hockey Federation for the Olympic tournament. That meant that the rules would revert back to those voted on at the 1985 World Championships in Prague, Czechoslovakia. The parameters of the Prague rules were that only professionals under twenty-three years of age and only those who had not played pro-hockey after September 1, 1987, would be eligible for the 1988 Olympic Winter Games.

But, another new ruling voted on before the 1987 World's in Vienna, Austria opened the Olympic tournament up to all professional hockey players, with no restrictions. Now young players benefit by having the option to start their professional careers without giving up the dream of representing their country on an Olympic team.

## The Venue

The majority of the Olympic ice hockey event for the XV Olympic Winter Games will take place in Calgary's unique coliseum, the Olympic Saddledome.

Featuring the graceful "saddle" design, the Olympic Saddledome boasts the largest free-span concrete roof in the world. The coliseum was built specifically for professional hockey and Canada's Olympic Team, and includes both NHL and Olympic size ice surfaces.

The record $309 million (U.S.) payment for television rights that the XV Olympic Winter Games Organizing Committee negotiated with the American Broadcasting Corporation was directly related to a schedule that stretched the 1988 Olympics out to sixteen days instead of the traditional twelve.

The 1988 Olympic ice hockey tournament will be a longer fifteen-day tournament instead of the traditional eleven-day format. Most hockey games involving European teams will be played in the morning and games involving the United States or Canada will take place in the evening, during each country's prime time.

A win in any game is worth two points, a tie one point. Total points won make up a team's final standing. In the event of a tie, the team with the most goals scored is the winner.

Several other games will be played at the Stampede Corral and the Father David Bauer Olympic Arena.

## The Technique

The Olympic Saddledome's ice surface meets the International Ice Hockey Federation rule book specification of 60 metres by 30 metres.

The red line (neutral zone) divides the ice rink into three 60 foot (18 metre) divisions. Each team has its own blue line. The nets are regulation size of four feet (1.22 metres) wide and are placed ten feet (13.5 metres) from each end of the ice. The new 160 pound (72.48 kilo) D-shaped steel Megg-Net is held in place by magnets that give way on impact of any player over 185 pounds (84 kilos)—much safer than the net that put Dave Hindmarch of the Calgary Flames in a wheelchair for four weeks after knee surgery in 1983. Hockey players will no longer be colliding with the old stationary net previously used by the NHL. Invented by Dennis Meggs, of Waterloo, Ontario, the new net was introduced to the NHL at Toronto's Maple Leaf Gardens in 1983.

An ice hockey team is composed of twenty players, six of

Canadian Olympic team head coach Dave King. *Calgary Herald*

whom play on the ice at one time—a centre, two forwards, two defencemen, and a goaltender. The wings covering the sidelines of the rink and the centre covering the wide middle lane make up the team's offensive line. The opposing team's forwards and centre must be kept from breaking through the offensive line to avoid a two-or-three-on-one approach to the goal. For the offensive line, scoring ability must match defence ability. To aid the forward line, two defencemen are behind them covering a radius of 20 yards (18.29 metres) in front of their goaltender. The cardinal rule for the defencemen is that the goalie must never be left unprotected. If a defenceman does leave his position to join the attacking forward line, one of the wings must fall back and cover the defenceman's territory. Since the slapshot has been allowed in Olympic hockey, it is not unusual to see a defenceman score. The U.S.S.R. had devised an entire offensive game plan using the dual role of the defenceman.

During play, the forward line has unlimited substitution and is changed about every 45 seconds. A defensive line has a shift of 45 seconds and both lines change without play being stopped.

Skating technique is an art to an Olympic hockey player. Fast starts, bone-jarring stops, and quick turns must be combined with the ability to break away and get the puck moving as a play develops. Puck control and stick handling take years of practice to perfect. An Olympic hockey star can pass a puck from man to man with unbelievable precision.

The ice hockey event will be a challenge to the spectator's ability to watch the puck, and to know who is on and off the ice as the lines change in rapid succession, and the graceful high-speed game flows back and forth over the ice.

Ice hockey, Canada's national sport, is the fastest game played by man.

A demonstration of perfect goalie technique by Canadian Mario Gosselin at the 1984 Games. *Athlete Information Bureau/Canadian Olympic Association*

The moment of victory for the American team at the 1980 Games at Lake Placid. *United States Olympic Committee Photo*

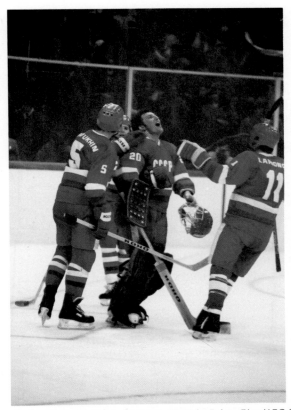

Exultant Soviet goaltender, Vladislav Tretiak. *Robert Riger/ABC Sports*

# The Rules

The rules of the game were developed in Canada in 1875.

John George Alwyn Creighton, author of the first set of hockey rules, was a young engineer working in Montreal, Quebec, when the Grand Trunk Railroad was being constructed in 1875. A superior athlete, Creighton's favourite sport was rugby. A difficult sport to play at the best of times, the rugby season was shortened by the long cold winter months in Quebec. Several of his friends, who played lacrosse, faced similar problems trying to maintain physical fitness when playing fields were buried under snow. These were the days before indoor arenas and sports clubs.

The circumstances provided the incentive for eighteen young men to invent a new winter game that would become Canada's national sport. Appearing at the Victoria Skating Rink in Montreal on a cold March day, the young sports enthusiasts brought along a medley of equipment from their favourite sports—bandy sticks from field hockey, ice skates, and a lacrosse ball.

The person who designed the 60.96 metres (200 feet) by 25.91 metres (85 feet) dimensions of the Victoria Park Skating Rink probably had no idea that the rink dimensions would become the standard maximum size for Olympic rinks all over the world.

Pleasure skaters fled the Victoria Rink that day in Montreal as the young men took to the ice. With bandy sticks flying

An early ice hockey game at Victoria Ice Rink, Montreal, Quebec. *Notman Photographic Archives, McCord Museum*

and the lacrosse ball bounding skyward and everywhere, it did not take long before someone cut away the round ends. The first hockey "puck" was in existence. This madness on ice was orchestrated by young George Creighton hollering rugby rules at the skaters. The first game of hockey in the world was taking place.

For those who have had the opportunity to play rugby, the first rule of the game is to survive the experience. The second rule of rugby is for the players to stay onside, with the ball behind the offensive line. Creighton transferred this rule to hockey, and as a result, the forward pass was not allowed in ice hockey for another fifty years.

To date, Olympic hockey has been governed by the rules of amateur hockey which are very close to professional rules. The cardinal rule of hockey still applies to both codes and that is the puck must precede an attacker across the blueline. If it doesn't, an offside is called, and a faceoff takes place outside of the offensive blueline.

The format for the twelve-team Olympic ice hockey format is a division of the teams into two separate groups—the A and B pools.

An ordered numbering system that reflects the final standings at the 1987 World Ice Hockey Championships in Vienna, Austria, determined who would play whom in the preliminary round robin. The A pool is comprised of ice hockey teams that finished in the first, fourth, fifth, eighth, ninth and twelfth positions at the tournament. These teams are Sweden (1), Canada (4), Finland (5), Poland (8), Switzerland (9) and France (12). The B pool is comprised of those hockey teams that finished in the second, third, sixth, seventh, tenth and eleventh posi-

tions. These teams are the U.S.S.R. (2), Czechoslovakia (3), the Federal Republic of Germany (6), the U.S.A. (7), Norway (10) and Austria (11). Both the A and B pool teams play separate round robin tournaments—(i.e., each of the six teams will play each other once).

The top three teams from each pool will then carry forward their points acquired against the other teams advancing from their pool round. In the medal round each team will cross over to play the three teams from the other pool. The gold, silver and bronze medals will go to the three teams with the highest points totals upon completion of the medal round tournament.

Due to the nature of the separate A and B pool round robin tournaments in the preliminary round, it is possible Canada will not play the U.S.S.R., the U.S.A., Czechoslovakia or any other B pool team. Canada will meet these B pool opponents only if it places among the top three positions in the A pool tournament and advances into the medal round.

A hockey game consists of three 20 minute periods of play and teams change ends at the start of each period.

The officials for Olympic hockey are appointed by the International Ice Hockey Federation and include seven international referees and thirteen linesmen, nine international. One official is selected from each country represented in the tournament.

## Penalties

Many of the differences between the rules of amateur and professional hockey involve infractions that result in penalty calls. Penalties in Olympic play are divided into four categories, and generally are more severe than the professional penalty codes.

# Official Referee Signals

**BOARDING**

Pounding the closed fist of one hand into the open palm of the other hand.

**HIGH-STICKING**

Holding both fists, clenched, one above the other at the side of the head.

**ROUGHING**

A thrusting motion with the arm extending from the side.

**CHARGING**

Rotating clenched fists around one another in front of chest.

**HOLDING**

Clasping the wrists of the "whistle hand" well in front of the chest.

**SLASHING**

A chopping motion with the edge of one hand across the opposite forearm.

**CROSS-CHECKING**

A forward and backward motion with both fists clenched extending from the chest.

**HOOKING**

A tugging motion with both arms, as if pulling something toward the stomach.

**SPEARING**

A jabbing motion with both hands thrust out in front of the body.

**DELAYED CALLING OF PENALTY**

Referee extends arm and points to penalized player.

**INTERFERENCE**

Crossed arms stationary in front of chest with fists closed.

**TRIPPING**

Strike the right leg with the right hand below the knee keeping both skates on the ice.

**ELBOWING**

Tapping the elbow of the "whistle hand" with the opposite hand.

**MISCONDUCT**

Place both hands on hips.

**UNSPORTSMAN-LIKE CONDUCT**

Use both hands to form a "T" in front of the chest.

Official Referee Signals. *Provided by the Calgary Flames Hockey Club*

Holding on to the puck or an opponent too long, or substituting a player too soon, are all minor infractions punishable by two minutes in the penalty box. Tripping, charging, cross-checking or holding on to a player to prevent a score, are considered minor infractions as well and also carry a two-minute penalty. Any player who uses foul language or is particularly abusive to an official is given a ten-minute misconduct penalty. Expulsion from the game is the result of any player deliberately attempting to injure an opponent, or starting a fight. The Olympic movement takes pride in discouraging the violent aspects of ice hockey from dominating the game.

In the event that a penalty is called against the goalie, another player can serve the time. A goalie can be pulled out of the game, leaving the net open and another player can be added to the team. A hockey team can never play more than two men short at any one time. A penalty shot is awarded to a team if their player is deliberately interfered with when going in on goal "in the clear."

The battle for the puck in Olympic hockey produces intense physical contact between players, particularly along the boards. Shoving, high sticking, and the occasional flying fist are not exclusive to professional hockey. An Olympic hockey player is never pleased to be banished to the penalty box. If the opposing team scores within two minutes of a faceoff, the penalized player can return to the game instantly. However, a player is not allowed out of the penalty box within the two-minute span, even though the other team does score within two minutes of the faceoff, if he has been involved in the major infraction of fighting. No matter how many goals the offending team scores while a player's team-mates play shorthanded, a five-minute penalty must be served.

Watching the concentration and excitement in the eyes of the hockey player in the penalty box is worth a second look to the spectator. Nothing else matters more to this young Olympian at that moment than to get back on the ice and into the action with his team-mates. The moment his penalty is over and he leaps out of the penalty box and scrambles over the boards, all the years of self-discipline, determination, and sheer joy for the love of hockey seem to hit the ice with him.

# The Equipment

In the early days of ice hockey, players never considered wearing hockey helmets. Hockey Hall-of-Famer Eddie Shore played eighteen years as a defenceman and from 1926 to 1940 broke his nose fourteen times, his jaw five times, and accumulated 978 stitches overall. The International Ice Hockey Federation didn't like statistics like that and ruled helmets compulsory for the juniors that moved up through the ranks into the pros. By the 1960s, even the toughest ice hockey players wore helmets in Olympic competition.

Quebec native Jacques Plante, a superb technical goalie, played for the Montreal Canadiens when they won the Stanley Cup six times, including a record five straight times. During a game in November of 1959, he was struck in the face with a puck, and then became the first goalie to regularly wear a protective mask. Doug Grant, a native of Cornerbrook, Newfoundland, was the first goalie to paint his mask. In 1974 when playing goal for the Detroit Red Wings, he painted some red lightning bolts on it. For years it was considered a ritual by all goalies to paint their masks in outrageous designs.

Clint Benedict, who played hockey from 1917 to 1930 and who broke his nose during one of his games, designed the first goalie mask in the world made out of leather which protected his eyes and his nose. Toronto's Hockey Hall of Fame, home of Benedict's first rudimentary mask, boasts the most extensive goalie mask display in the world.

One of the unsung heroes of the Canadian ice hockey history was a harness maker by trade, Hamilton's Emile "Pops" Kenesky. As a teenager, he worked sewing stitches at 30 cents per 1,000. In 1917, he purchased a store with a downpayment of $15 and made the first pair of goalie pads there out of an old pair of cricket pads.

Kenesky used to watch the Catholic league hockey players in Ontario and realized that the goalies needed more protection than was provided from the cricket pads they wore during the games. He took a cricket pad and increased the width to twelve inches. The Hamilton Tigers of the NHL asked him to make some for their team, and "Pops" Kenesky was launched into a lifetime career which would span three generations of excellence. The Kenesky goalie equipment is still made in Hamilton, Ontario, today by his four sons and his grandson. The long-

Emile "Pops" Kenesky, the Canadian who invented the goalie pad.
*Hockey Hall of Fame, Toronto*

est and heaviest goalie pads (7 pounds each) ever made by Kenesky's were for professional Ken Dryden, one of the tallest goalies in the history of ice hockey.

One of the basic methods of separating a hockey player from the puck is the body check. Legally, a body check can be executed from the side or the front of a player, but never from the back. To protect players from the force of his opponent he wears shoulder pads, elbow pads, padded hockey gloves, padded hockey pants, shin pads, and knee pads. Hockey helmets are mandatory in Olympic competition.

Recently, a new concept in skate design resulted in the black plastic skate support seen on many hockey skates today. The steel blade is mounted into the plastic support and attached to the sole of the skate. The result is a lighter skate and a much sharper blade.

Good stick work can keep the opposition off-balance, and during last year's season, Canada's Olympic hockey team used over 170 dozen sticks during their pre-Olympic year.

Team Canada will go through at least 30 dozen of them during the series at the 1988 Olympic Winter Games in Calgary.

# Calgary Preview

With a maximum seating capacity of nineteen thousand, the Olympic Saddledome offers the spectator unobstructed, pillar-free viewing of the 1988 Olympic Winter Games ice hockey tournament.

Despite the fact that the Soviets finished in third place at the 1985 World Championships at Prague, Czechoslovakia, and were defeated by the Canadians, their teams have dominated competitions for decades.

Unquestionably, the U.S.S.R. brings the top hockey team into the Olympic Winter Games at Calgary in 1988. Fans of international hockey may well remember the XIV Olympic Winter Games at Sarajevo, Yugoslavia, in 1984 as the fourth and final Olympics for the brilliant Soviet goaltender, Vladislav Tretiak. The Soviet national team star infused his team's line-up with an attitude of excellence that made scoring against the Russians virtually impossible. Outscoring their opponents 48-5 at Sarajevo's Zetra Arena, Tretiak allowed only four goals against the Soviets during the tournament. Revered by his countrymen and at the pinnacle of his game, the cat-quick Tretiak achieved shutouts in the two medal rounds against Canada (4-0) and Czechoslovakia (2-0). Returning to the Olympics in 1988 for the Soviets will be the "K.L.M." line of forwards Vladimir Krutov, Igor Larinov, and Sergei Makarov. The best-trained defenceline includes Viacheslav Fetisov and Alexei Kasatonov. Evgeni Belosheikin replaces Tretiak in goal. Watch for twenty-two-year-old Valeri Kamensky, the new child prodigy of Soviet ice hockey.

Other medal favourites are the Big Three, the Swedes, the Czechoslovakians, and the Canadians, who figure to give the Soviets their stiffest competition at Calgary. Realistically, Sweden's bronze medal win at Sarajevo in 1984 and its world championship in 1987 stand the team in good stead to give the Russians their greatest difficulty in winning the gold medal. Coached by Jan Starsi, the Czechs have lost several of their 1984 Olympic team members to the NHL, but have managed to develop a group of young sharp-shooters for their Olympic squad.

Back to challenge Team Sweden after losing the bronze-medal match at the Zetra Icehall at Sarajevo in 1984, Team Canada will be gunning for a medal at Calgary in 1988. Returning to coach the Olympic hockey team is Team Canada's head coach Dave King. The innovative coaching staff also includes veterans Guy Charron and Ron Smith. Their expertise, combined with King's, could put Canada into medal contention.

"Discipline is the name of the game", assesses King, who emphasized European skating and conditioning skills to his highly disciplined twenty-man squad. With the change in eligibility rules, an Olympic team line-up is difficult to predict as the presence of the National Hockey League could have a major impact.

One possible solution to the thorny issue of NHL player availability may be for the Olympic team to have access to its alumni. Graduates of the 1980 and 1984 Olympic hockey teams, now playing with the NHL could clear waivers and be excused from their teams in the short term. By allowing the former Olympic players to return to the national team program for six months, the NHL teams could maintain the competitive balance in the league. A small number of ex-Olympians would enhance, not defeat the purpose of the ongoing national hockey program. This workable compromise could supplement the 1988 Olympic hockey team, instead of parachuting an entire group of NHLers onto the team a day before the Opening Ceremonies, and obliterating the permanent national team.

Heading into Calgary, the Soviet Union and Sweden are definite favourites to qualify for the medal playoffs. However, given the set of circumstances that led to the major upsets by Team U.S.A. at the Olympic Winter Games in the United States in 1960 and 1980, the fact remains that every team has a chance.

The first gold medal that Canada ever won for Olympic ice hockey was at the Summer Games in 1920. Despite the fact that the Winter Games started just four years later, Canada's first Olympic gold hockey medal was unfortunately not counted as an official medal in the record books. If it was, Canada would enter the XV Olympic Winter Games ice hockey event tied with the Soviet Union for gold medals.

# Canadians at the Olympic Winter Games
## ICE HOCKEY

### 1924 Chamonix — I Olympic Winter Games

1. Granites of Toronto

Jack Cameron, Ernie Collett, Albert McCaffery, Harold McMunn, Duncan Munro, W. Beattie Ramsay, Cyril Slater, Reginald Smith, Harry Watson

### 1928 St. Moritz — II Olympic Winter Games

1. University of Toronto Graduates

Charles Delehay, Frank Fisher, Grant Gordon, Dr. Louis Hudson, Norbert Mueller, Bert Plaxton, Hugh Plaxton, Richard Plaxton, John Porter, Frank Sullivan, Joseph Sullivan, Ross Taylor, Dave Trottier

### 1932 Lake Placid — III Olympic Winter Games

1. Winnipeg Hockey Club

William Cockburn, Clifford Crowley, Albert Duncanson, George Garbutt, Roy Hinkel, Victor Lindquist, Norman Malloy, Walter Monson, Kenneth Moore, Romeo Rivers, Harold Simpson, Hugh Sutherland, Stanley Wagner, Alston Wise

### 1936 Garmisch-Partenkirchen — IV Olympic Winter Games

2. Maxwell Deacon, Ken Farmer, Hugh Farquharson, N. Friday, James Haggerty, Walter Kitchen, Raymond Milton, Dinty Moore, Herman Murray, W. Arthur Nash, David Neville, G. Saxbury, Alexander Sinclair, Ralph St. Germaine, William Thompson

### 1948 St. Moritz — V Olympic Winter Games

1. Hubert Brooks, Murray Dowey, Bernard Dunster, Roy Forbes, Andrew Gilpin, Orval Gravelle, Patrick Guzzo, Wallis Halder, Ted Hibberd, Ross King, André Laperrière, Louis Lecompte, Julius Leichnitz, George Mara, Albert Renaud, Reg Schroeter, Irving Taylor

### 1952 Oslo — VI Olympic Winter Games

1. George G. Abel, John F. Davies, Billie Dawe, Bruce Dickson, Donald V. Gauf, William J. Gibson, Ralph L. Hansch, Robert R. Meyers, David E. Miller, Eric E. Paterson, Thomas A. Pollock, Allan R. Purvis, Gordon Robertson, Louis J. Secco, Francis C. Sullivan, Robert Watt

### 1956 Cortina d'Ampezzo — VII Olympic Winter Games

3. Kitchener-Waterloo Dutchmen

Denis Brodeur, Charles Brooker, William Colvin, James Horne, Arthur Hurst, Byrle Klinck, Paul Knox, Kenneth Laufman, Howard Lee, James Logan, Floyd Martin, Jack McKenzie, Don Rope, George Scholes, Gerry Theberge, Robert White, Keith Woodall

### 1960 Squaw Valley — VIII Olympic Winter Games

2. Robert Attersley, Maurice Benoit, James Connelly, Jack Douglas, Fred Etcher, Bob Forhan, Don Head, Harold Hurley, Ken Laufman, Floyd Martin, Robert McKnight, Cliff Pennington, Don Rope, Robert Rousseau, George Samolenko, Harry Sinden, Darryl Sly

### 1964 Innsbruck — IX Olympic Winter Games

4. Henry Akervall, Gary Begg, Roger Bourbonnais, Kenneth Broderick, Richard Broadbelt, Raymond Cadieux, Terrence Clancy, Brian Conacher, Paul Conlin, Gary Dineen, Robert Forhan, Marshall Johnston, John MacKenzie, Seth Martin, Ross Morrison, Terrence O'Malley, Donald Rodgers, Rod Seiling, George Swarbrick, John Wilson

### 1968 Grenoble - X Olympic Winter Games

3. Roger Bourbonnais, Ken Broderick, Ray Cadieux, Paul Conlin, Gary Dineen, Brian Glennie, Ted Hargreaves, Fran Huck, Marshall Johnston, Barry MacKenzie, Bill MacMillan, Steven Monteith, Morris Mott, Terry O'Malley, Danny O'Shea, Gerry Pinder, Herb Pinder, Wayne Stephenson

### 1972 Sapporo — XI Olympic Winter Games

No team entered.

### 1976 Innsbruck — XII Olympic Winter Games

No team entered.

### 1980 Lake Placid — XIII Olympic Winter Games

6. Glenn Anderson, Warren Anderson, Ken Berry, Daniel D'Alvise, Ronald Davidson, John Devaney, Robert Dupuis, Joseph Grant, Randall Gregg, David Hindmarch, Paul MacLean, Kevin Maxwell, James Nill, Terrence O'Malley, Paul Pageau, Bradley Pirie, Kevin Primeau, Donald Spring, Timothy Watters, Stelio Zupancich

### 1984 Sarajevo — XIV Olympic Winter Games

Warren Anderson, Robin Bartel, Russ Courtnall, Jean Jacques Daigneault, Kevin Dineen, Dave Donnelly, Bruce Driver, Darren Eliot, Pat Flatley, Dave Gagner, Mario Gosselin, Vaughn Karpan, Doug Lidster, Darren Lowe, Kirk Muller, James Patrick, Craig Redmond, Dave Tippett, Carey Wilson, Dan Wood

# Luge

Canada Olympic Park
February 14, 15, 16, 17, 19

*Mathieson, Calgary.*

Because luge is somewhat misunderstood in the shadow of its counterpart, the bobsleigh, I am pleased to provide an introduction to the sport for the 1988 Olympic Winter Games in Calgary.

"You have to be crazy to luge, don't you?" a sports reporter asked United States luge team member Bonny Warner at the 1984 Olympic Winter Games at Sarajevo, Yugoslavia. Warner's answer impressed me when she replied, "Crazy people don't make it in luge. You'll find that good luge athletes tend to be very sane people."

Luge was a mystery to me when I first became involved in it. But in November of 1970, a unique set of circumstances put me on a luge sled at the track in Königssee, West Germany. There, through the urging of three other Canadian athletes, I learned the basics of luge.

Once on the run, I was committed to driving the fastest track in the world, or accepting the alternative—crashing! After I left the start, the most breathtaking experience of my life unfolded before me. The pounding of my heart reverberated throughout my helmet as hundreds of memories were implanted on my brain. When I crossed the finish line, my immediate reaction was that it had been a great run, and I couldn't wait to go again.

One of the fringe benefits of my first year of luge training was an array of bruises that surpassed my total lifetime accumulation. But I pursued my training and race schedule diligently and by the end of the season I had competed in the 1971 World Championships.

In retrospect, the more I participated in luge, the more I learned. Admittedly, my first experiences in luge were frightening at the time. The fear was due to the dangerous aspects of the sport, but also to my own uncertainty as to my ability to perform well under the circumstances.

While I was competing in luge, the danger factor involved appeared to be much more predominant than it is in luge competition today. The safety of the athlete has been a top priority in the design and construction of the new bobsleigh and luge track in Calgary. Because it is also one of the fastest tracks in the world, the lugers will be presented with an equal challenge of technically sound sled driving.

A top athlete, while training and competing, will realize the value of good physical and mental training and conditioning. All luge athletes face the same demand of becoming confident in their own ability. You can bet that luge athletes competing for the medals in 1988 will be directing their concentration toward this challenge as well as toward the glory of an Olympic victory.

For me, competing in the sport of luge offered tremendous personal rewards and an opportunity to make lasting friendships with people from many nations. My involvement with luge opened the door to the privilege of representing Canada at the 1972 and 1976 Olympic Winter Games. It was a great honour.

Welcome to the 1988 Olympic Winter Games, and welcome to the sport of luge.


Doug Hansen
*Olympic participant—1972, 1976*
*Olympic luge coach—1984—Sarajevo*
*Chairman—OCO'88 luge committee*

# The History

Canada, as host country to the XV Olympic Winter Games, can claim some of the credit for luge and tobogganing being included in the Olympic format.

Undoubtedly, the polar bear ancestors of Games mascots Hidy and Howdy "belly-whopped" down the snowcovered hillsides of Newfoundland decades ago. Long before people were sliding in Europe, the sport was a popular pastime with the Coughnawaga Indians of Ontario. In fact, the word "toboggan" is a North American Indian name given to the sledges used to transport supplies between camps in the winter.

In the 1870s a toboggan slide was constructed on the southwest corner of Mount Royal at Montreal, Quebec. The notorious Tuque Bleue track was 412 metres long and frightened the daylights out of everybody who went down it.

Europe was introduced to the sled by the Romans who travelled from one alpine legion station to another on it. The Swiss named the sled the "handschlitten" and it became an integral part of life in the Alps.

Although tobogganing was a popular pastime during the Canadian winters, Switzerland is considered the birthplace of competitive sliding. From the early slide races, three competitive sports developed and have taken their place in the Olympic Winter Games: *bobsleigh*, on the Olympic program since 1924; *skeleton* sled racing, which appeared on the Olympic calendar only at St. Moritz, Switzerland, in 1928 and 1948; and *luge*, which, although the oldest of the three, did not become an official Olympic event until 1964.

The famous Tuque Bleue toboggan slide circa 1910, Montreal, Quebec. *Notman Photographic Archives, McCord Museum*

Ironically, the Swiss villages that were to become world famous as winter sport capitals started out as health spas for Britons and Europeans who were ill, tired, or retired.

British author and critic John Addington Symonds retired to the mountain air of Davos at the end of the nineteenth century, due to poor health. During the winter months, he began to consider the "handschlitten" as a potential racing vehicle and generated enough local enthusiasm to develop sled racing as a competitive winter sport for both men and women.

By 1879, Symonds had overseen the construction of the first two winter-sport facilities at Davos. The two sled runs initiated the popular new "Schlittelpartie." At the crack of dawn, guests would leave the hotel and travel four kilometres up the mountain by horse-drawn sleighs to the little village of Klosters. After a baronial Swiss lunch on top of the Alps, the well-fuelled British took to the sleds for a hair-raising ride down the course to Davos.

On February 12, 1883, the "Great International Sled Race" was held for the first time at Davos.

The eighteen competitors did, in fact, form an impressive international slate. There were twelve local enthusiasts from Davos, two Germans, one Dutchman, two Australians, and one Canadian. The race ended up in a tie between Swiss sledder Peter Minsch from nearby Klosters, and John Robertson, an Australian studying at Oxford. Both men covered the 4 kilometre course from Klosters to Davos in 9 minutes and 15 seconds. But, Robertson declined the Fr.100 prize and insisted that it should go to Minsch because he represented the local Swiss sledders.

The sled race was such a success that the Davos Toboggan Club was formed in 1883 and, to no one's surprise, John Addington Symonds was elected president.

The riding position initially taken by sledders on the "handschlitten" was, and still is, an upright sitting position. But, south of Davos, at another Swiss resort, a British sportsman was getting his thrills by careening down the mountainsides in a head-first prone position.

Major S. H. Bulpett, who owned a chalet at St. Moritz, joined forces with Christian Mathis, the village blacksmith, and together they modified the design of the wooden "schlittli" into a steel sled. The new sleek racing machine was a mere shadow of its poor wood relation, and was re-named the "skeleton" by the Englishmen.

The sportsmen soon discovered that the head-first prone position, as opposed to the seated position on the schlittli, increased their speed on the new sled. The new skeleton revolutionized the sport of sledding and the craze, accelerated by the British, soon caught on in Switzerland. It wasn't long before the early sledders were seen hurtling down the mountainsides with their chins mere inches above the ice and snow.

Visitors soon challenged local sledders to skeleton races held on the road from St. Moritz down to Celerina. Local traffic was tied up for hours when the races took place. But eventually, the local villagers, fearing somebody would inevitably be killed in what was considered the most dangerous of near-airborne adventures, announced the road was barred to any further bloodthirsty pursuits.

It was then that Major Bulpett's wisdom prevailed and with the help of local Swiss ingenuity, he devised Switzerland's first

Women were always encouraged to take part in this sport. The hand-held stocks were used to "peg" furiously on the curves of the Davos-Klosters Road. *Courtesy Roger Gibbs, London, England*

A luge race in 1904 at Murzzuschlag. *Courtesy Bert Isatitsch, Austria*

rudimentary sled-run. The course was constructed from St. Moritz and zigzagged three-quarters of a mile down to the crest of the valley below. The tiny village of Cresta, just above Celerina, was at the finish line, and the name of the run stemmed from the little community. From this point in time, the skeleton sled was often referred to as the "cresta." The famed Cresta Run at St. Moritz holds the distinction of being the site of the first Grand National Race in 1885. The Cresta Run is still in use today.

The St. Moritz Tobogganing Club was formed in 1887, and several of the founding members were women. One of the more legendary performances in the 1919 Ladies' Grand National was that of Mrs. Bagulary from England who beat her husband's fastest time of the year by one tenth of a second. A formidable accomplishment for a young woman wearing a full-length skirt.

Skeleton sledding competitions continued in Switzerland for the next twenty years without a fatal accident. It wasn't until 1907 that Captain H. S. Pernell VC and Comte de Bylandt of Belgium were both killed from injuries sustained while racing on the Cresta Run. The daredevil sport was evolving into such a dangerous operation that by 1923, it was felt women should no longer be allowed to compete on the Cresta.

When the first Olympic Winter Games were held at Chamonix, France, in 1924 there were two reasons why the skeleton race was not held as an Olympic event. One was the lack of an adequate skeleton track at the resort, and the other was the introduction of a thrilling new sport with more devotees to it.

Bobsleighers had earned their place on the racing circuit after the blacksmith from the little village of St. Moritz invented a new idea in sledding.

Welding two small sleds together, making the back sled rigid and the runners on the front sled movable, Christian Mathis had turned the simple clipper-sled into a new racing vehicle. This basic principle is hardly different on the bobsleighs that are built today, and with several people on the sleigh at one time, the degree of excitement was increased for the riders.

The second Olympic Winter Games were held at St. Moritz in 1928 and for the first time a special race track was available for the skeleton riders. A small field of ten entries from six countries took part in the race. The Heaton brothers of the United States made headlines by recording the two fastest times in each of the three heats and won the gold and silver medals. David Northesk managed to fly the Union Jack for Great Britain on the victory stand and picked up the bronze medal—a tribute to the brigade of daredevils from his country that had preceded him in the past era of sledding.

The small entry field of skeleton riders at the 1928 Olympic Winter Games gave rise to concern from the International Olympic Committee. Games requirements state that a sport must be well recognized and practised by many of the participating countries in order to be included in the Olympic Winter Games. In comparison to the small skeleton event, the popular sport of bobsleighing was well attended in the 1928 Games with twenty-three bob crews from fourteen countries.

The new innovative bobsleigh, with a sleek aerodynamic front body and crews of two or four men, was gaining in popularity. The heavy bobsleighs were shoving aside the small skeleton sleds and relegating the lonesome riders to second-class citizenry. Pushed out of the big time, small sled racing remained out of the Olympic competition for nearly twenty years.

After World War II, interest in the small skeleton sled was revived and several international sledding events were held in Europe. The renewed interest in the sport led to the event being reintroduced at the fifth Olympic Winter Games held at St. Moritz in 1948.

The 1948 Games witnessed the Olympic debut of Italian Nino Bibbia, the all-time great of the skeleton event. Bibbia won the Olympic gold medal at St. Moritz and over the span of his career won the Grand National Race no less than eight times. His name was inscribed on almost every trophy presented to the winner of the skeleton event for more than two decades of international sledding history. His last Grand National trophy was won in 1973.

Bibbia narrowly beat out the sentimental favourite at the Games, John Heaton of New Haven, Connecticut. Heaton won his first Olympic silver medal in the skeleton event at nineteen years of age in 1928 and his second silver medal twenty years later, at age thirty-nine in 1948.

The skeleton, or cresta event, has only been held at the Winter Games in 1928 and 1948. The event was discontinued after the Games of 1948 and will only be held if the Games are staged, if ever again, at St. Moritz, Switzerland.

The luge, as we recognize it today, evolved from the wooden "handschlitten" used by the earliest sledders from Davos, Switzerland.

Despite the sport never being part of the Olympic Games, interest in sliding spread from its humble beginnings in Switzerland to the German speaking countries. The Austrians and Germans used the name "Rodel" (sleigh) for their newly adopted sport, and "Rodelverbaende" (Toboggan Clubs) mushroomed throughout the two countries.

By 1913, the Germans were ready to host their national championships in Ilmenau for both men and women. The following year, the first European Championships were held on the Jeschken, in Reichenberg, Austria (today Liberec, Czechoslovakia) and over thirty thousand spectators came to watch the daring new sport of "rodel." Although women did not take part in the first European Championships, they were always encouraged to compete on the regional and local level.

Not surprisingly, the development of sliding was interrupted by the outbreak of World War I. Yet, once peace had been declared, the popularity of the sport was again revived and by 1927 the International Tobogganing Federation was established. In 1935, the International Bobsleigh Federation (FIBT) joined forces with the International Toboggan Federation and the sport of sliding took on the name "luge," a French word for Swiss toboggan.

For centuries, the "handschlitten" used in the Alps was a lightweight model with curved front runners made from one long continuous piece of wood. Then, in the early 1900s, the

Bert Isatitsch, President of the Fédération Internationale de Luge de Course, is congratulated by Juan Antonio Samaranch, now President of the International Olympic Committee, after luge was accepted as an official Olympic event. *International Olympic Committee, Switzerland*

Bavarians invented the revolutionary Oberaudorf design and although it was greeted with laughter from the others, they had the last laugh by winning all the races.

The essential difference between the two sleds was that the runners of the Oberaudorf sled tilted inward, compared to the flat runners of the earlier models. Constructing the runners with angled outside edges gave the sled more flexibility and the Bavarians more leg and foot manoeuvrability.

After World War II, the sled was again modified and streamlined to look more like the luge seen in Olympic competition today.

In 1954, a school superintendent from Rottenmann, Austria, was elected as president of the "Section de Luge" of the International Bobsleigh and Tobogganing Federation. From 1946 onward, Bert Isatitsch's campaign efforts on behalf of his favourite sport would eventually be rewarded by having luge recognized as an official Olympic event.

Shortly after Isatitsch had been elected president, luge separated itself from the International Bobsleigh and Tobogganing Federation and became an autonomous sport governing body. The International Luge Federation (FIL) was formed and the first luge World Championships were held in 1955 at Oslo, Norway.

The championships at Norway were held on a Naturbahn course, a snow track constructed on natural terrain. It was after the championships that an alternative to the Naturbahn was deemed necessary by officials.

It was because of this that a Kunsteisbahn (artificial ice track with steeply banked curves) was specified by the International Olympic Committee when luge was finally accepted as an Olympic discipline in 1959. But, the Olympic debut of luge was delayed until the Winter Games of 1964 because there was no track for either bobsleigh or luge at the 1960 Games at Squaw Valley, California.

Luge was formally introduced at the ninth Winter Games in Igls at Innsbruck, Austria, and a total of thirty-eight men and seventeen women from twelve countries competed for the first set of Olympic medals awarded.

With the reputation for being one of the most dangerous of winter sports, many critics voiced the opinion that luge should not be included in the Olympic format. Support for those concerns increased with the news that Polish-born Kazimierz Kay-Skrzypeski, a member of the British luge team, had been killed while practising on the Olympic run at Igls two weeks before the Games were to begin.

The casualty rate was high at Igls and once the Games began, both United States and German teams narrowly escaped serious injuries in separate luge accidents.

Bobsleighers Doug Anakin, John Emery, and Purvis McDougall of Canada decided to prepare themselves for their bobsleigh event by practising with the luge teams. But, after witnessing the accidents and injuries on the luge track, Canadian bobsleigh coach Doug Connor pulled his boys out of the luge practice runs. A fortuitous decision that, if not taken, could have affected the gold medal outcome of the four-man Canadian bobsleigh team at Innsbruck in 1964.

Top honours at Innsbruck went to the Germans who won five out of the six possible medals in the singles luge event. German slider Ortrun Enderlein placed first in the women's event and Thomas Kohler won the men's singles. The only one that got away from the Germans was the gold medal in men's doubles won by Josef Feistmanti and Manfred Stengl of Austria.

The 1964 Winter Games represented the first and last time

East Germany's Thomas Kohler won the first Olympic gold medal ever presented for the men's singles event. *Deutsche Presse-Agentur GmbH*

the two Germanies would enter an Olympic event as one country.

Women's singles defending champion Ortrun Enderlein became the centre of an Olympic controversy at the tenth Winter Games at Grenoble, France, in 1968. The East German luger, along with her team-mates, aroused suspicion after their third run. The women appeared at the track at the last moment before competing, and vanished as soon as they were finished. The President of the Jury of Appeal, Lucian Swiderski of Poland, requested a close-up look at the East German's sled runners. It was soon discovered why the German women had so consistently placed in the top four spots on each run. They had been heating the metal runners on their sleds, an illegal practice in luge competition. All three women were disqualified.

The disqualifications presented a medal opportunity to Italian luger Erica Lechner who went on to win the gold. Austrian Manfred Schmid won the men's singles and East Germans Klaus Bonsack and Thomas Kohler won the two seater event.

Canada entered its first official luge team at the 1968 Winter Games at Grenoble, France. Victor Emery, Lamont Gordon, and Doug Connor had introduced Canadians to luging in 1957 at a ski area in Quebec and Emery was the first Canadian champion. Later a better run was built at St. Donat in Quebec where the first North American championships were held. Several western Canadians who travelled across the border to a small luge club in Lola Hot Springs in Montana were eventually promoted to positions on Canada's Olympic luge team. By 1967, the Canadian amateur bobsleigh and luge association was founded and Cliff Powell of Montreal was the first president.

At the 1968 Winter Games at Grenoble, France, the best finish for the men's team was thirty-first place for Roger Eddy with a combined time of 3:01.39. Linda Bocock's twelfth-place finish of 2:32.46 was the Canadian women's team's best time, and a best-ever placing by a Canadian woman in Olympic competition.

At the eleventh Olympic Winter Games at Sapporo, Japan,

in 1972, IOC President Avery Brundage and the International Luge Federation encountered a unique jury dispute in the men's doubles event.

There are two heats in the two-seater event. The first run at Sapporo was won by Paul Hildgartner and Walter Plaikner of Italy. It was not until all contestants had taken the first run that officials discovered a malfunction up at the start gate. As a result, a re-run was called. The Italians protested the decision arguing that all racers had been subjected equally to the same problem and that the original times should be counted. The Jury of Appeal denied the protest. The next two official runs produced the problem of a tie between Horst Hörnlein and Reinhard Bredow of East Germany, and the Italians.

Brundage met with jury officials to consider the dilemma and, for the first time in Olympic luge competition, gold medals were awarded to both teams.

The East Germans also picked up the gold in the men's and women's singles events. By winning the gold medal, Anna-Marie Muller reinstated the East German women as the world's best lugers after the scandal of disqualification in 1968.

Canadian luge doubles team members Doug Hansen of Calgary and Larry Arbuthnot of Montreal competed at Sapporo under the burden of the limited funding the Canadian Olympic Association could provide for the team.

As a doubles team, Hansen and Arbuthnot subscribed to the theory that two heads are better than one and took it one step further by inventing a new starting technique at Sapporo that is still used in doubles luge competition today.

Before the Winter Games in 1972, the start technique for the two-seater event was for the frontman (driver) to push off from the handles unassisted. The backman (rider) only moved his upper body in unison with the frontman to help maximize on the driver's push-off. To assist in this manoeuvre, the backman held straps with his hands that secured the driver's position on the sled.

With an old second-hand junker of a Polish sled, the Canadian doubles team was hard-pressed to build up much speed once headed down into the first turn of the course.

Hansen and Arbuthnot concluded it would be a better idea for the bottom man to also be pulling to direct as much force on the start handles as possible. But, how to do it? Their search for an aid to a better start technique ended with an old pair of skate laces.

During one of their practice starts, Arbuthnot tried intertwining a couple of old laces between his fingers on both his right and left hand. He then extended the long free ends of the two laces back to his elbows to Doug Hansen behind him on the sled. Hansen made a loop at the end of each skate lace for handgrips. With the team rocking the sled back and forth in unison, the tandem pull-off shot the team out of the start ramp like a slingshot.

Something of a curiosity, the new grips proved to be a definite advantage for the Canadians. The skate lace handgrips actually worked so well on their first official run that Larry Arbuthnot pulled the start handles loose from the ice at the start line as they took off. Hansen and Arbuthnot distinguished themselves by having the race delayed for the next-up Americans while race officials froze the start handles back into the track.

Finishing up in sixteenth place in the two-seater event Doug Hansen later remarked, "Maybe we didn't win the event, but we figured we were the fastest sled on the track for the first 50 metres. . . ."

Eventually, the design of the grips was modified, and handgrips were accepted as standard equipment for the two-seater event. Today the leather handgrips are located on the speed suits at the elbows of the top rider.

East German lugers continued to dominate the events at the 1976 Olympic Winter Games at Innsbruck, Austria. Most of the sports venues at Innsbruck had been used for the 1964 Winter Games, but the combined bobsleigh and luge run was one of the few new facilities built specifically for the 1976 games.

With a history of three separate bobsleigh and luge tracks expensively constructed for the Olympic Winter Games in 1964 (Innsbruck), 1968 (Grenoble), and 1972 (Sapporo), the International Olympic Committee agreed with a suggestion from the organizing committee for the XII Games at Innsbruck in 1976. A proposal was made to hold the luge and bobsleigh events on the same run at Igls, near Innsbruck. Although financially very acceptable, the proposal was not at all popular with the Fédération Internationale de Bobsleigh et de Tobogganing (FIBT). A compromise track would have to be constructed that would be shorter than the usual bobsleigh run length of 1,500 metres, with fewer curves and less gradient. The lugers were unhappy, claiming that the heavy bobsleighs would ruin the track for their smaller, lighter sleds and that a bob track favoured heavy competitors and provided little challenge for lugers. Even though the problems remain the same today for both disciplines, the FIBT relented and a combined track was built at Igls in Austria. All five events were held on the same run, three for luge and two for bobsleigh. This decision established a precedent

Canadians Doug Hansen and Larry Arbuthnot demonstrate their "skate lace invention", which initiated the design of handgrips, now a standard part of the equipment. *Courtesy Doug Hansen*

for future track construction at Sarajevo, Yugoslavia, in 1984 and Calgary in 1988.

In 1976, Dettlef Gunther and Margit Schumann won the luge single events, and the fastest time of the two-seater race went to Hans Rinn and Norbert Hahn, all from the German Democratic Republic.

There was little improvement in Canada's standings at Innsbruck. Carole Keyes finished in the women's event in twenty-second place and Larry Arbuthnot in thirty-first place in the men's. In a field of twenty-five teams, doubles team Arbuthnot and Hansen finished in seventeenth place.

The Soviets, on the other hand, relative newcomers to the luge events, entered their first teams at the 1976 Winter Games at Innsbruck. By 1980 the U.S.S.R. had already won a gold medal in the women's singles event at the Olympic Winter Games at Lake Placid, New York. In each of the four heats, Soviet luger Vera Zozulia clocked the fastest time, and for the first time since the luge event was introduced to the Olympics in 1964, the East German women were beaten out for the gold medal.

Nevertheless, Vera Zozulia's gold medal was the only one to get away from the East Germans, Bernhard Glass winning the gold in men's singles, and Hans Rinn and Norbert Hahn repeating their 1976 gold medal performance in men's doubles.

Bruce Smith of Mississauga, Ontario, turned in Canada's best performance ever in 1980, finishing in eleventh place with a combined time of 3:01.074.

Like tennis, it's the prestige of the luge singles title that everyone really wants.

The Italians, who for years had unsuccessfully battled the Germans, Austrians, and Soviets for a medal, had their best chance at the title in 1980 at the Olympic Winter Games at Lake Placid, New York.

Ernst Hapsinger of Italy was leading by half a second in his first three runs and was well on his way to the gold medal luge victory. With just one run to go, Italy's hopes were destroyed when Hapsinger lost control on one of the final turns

and crashed near the end of his final run. Sadly for Italy, he finished up in twenty-first place.

By 1984, Italian Paul Hildgartner had vowed to avenge Hapsinger's defeat at the Olympic Winter Games at Sarajevo, Yugoslavia. Thirty-one-year-old Hildgartner was the sentimental favourite and a veteran competing in his fourth Olympic Winter Games. This was to be his last Winter Games and his last chance to fulfill his Olympic dream of a gold medal. He was leading in his first three runs and didn't want the same thing to happen to him that had happened to Hapsinger four years ago.

Lucky enough to have the luge track swept just before his dramatic fourth run in a heavy snowfall, Hildgartner won the gold medal with a winning time of 3:04.26.

The East German women again swept the women's event with gold, silver, and bronze, sledder Steffi Martin winning the gold with a combined time of 2:05.65. West German doubles Hans Stangassinger and Franz Wembacher won the two-seater race.

For Paul Hildgartner, who had luged to school in northern Italy from the age of nine, the gold medal in 1984 at Sarajevo signified Italy's finest hour in the Olympic sport of luge.

## The Venue

Prior to the construction of Calgary's combined bobsleigh and luge track, the sport of luge rivalled jai alai for media attention in Canada.

But now Canadian luge enthusiasts have something to boast about at Canada Olympic Park. The 1,260 metre luge track correlates the required gradient, speed, and centrifugal forces that combine to produce speeds up to 125 kph. The track occupies approximately 20 acres of the 200 acre Olympic Park site and is made out of concrete. It is kept at a constant -4°C by an ammonia gas refrigeration system. Built above the ground, the track has an average gradient of 10 per cent, embraces fourteen curves, and is 1.5 metres wide.

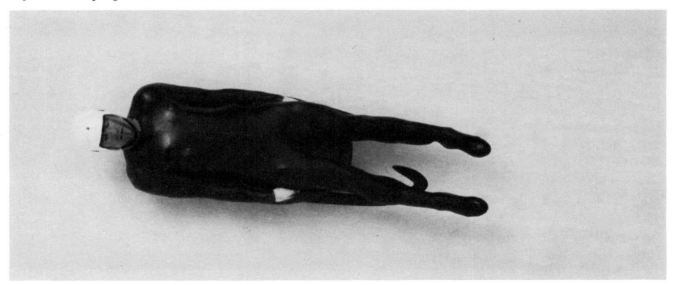

Italian Paul Hildgartner slides to victory in the men's singles event at the 1984 Games. *Deutsche Presse-Agentur GmbH*

Lightning-quick corners one, two, three, and four take men's singles riders from their separate start house onto the combined track at corner five. At this point the riders will have reached their average speed of 115 kph. The women's and men's double teams start down the track, just above corner four at the 1080 metre mark of the course, and head past their first curve onto the track and into the Omega corner. Here electric eye timers will take split times to indicate who is leading the pack. The 270 degree Kriesel track corner will swing back under itself, subjecting the riders to four G-forces in the five or six seconds it takes to negotiate the curve.

After holding quick, tight corners up to the Labyrinth section of the track, the sledders will travel to the finish corner past the electronic score board.

A special feature of the luge run at Canada Olympic Park is that it can be divided into five starting points for advanced, intermediate, and beginner luge practice.

Canada's national luge team members train five months a year on ice from November to the end of March. Canada is one of the twenty-six countries that will be participating in the Olympic Winter Games luge event in Calgary in 1988.

# The Technique

Luge is considered to be one of the most dangerous of all the Olympic Winter Games sports. Riders are always on the thin edge of disaster and the sport has tremendous spectator appeal.

From the initial sitting position of the early sledders, different positions have been adapted by riders over the years. The upright posture on the sled that was once preferred by the Austrians eventually evolved into the flat-on-the-back position. This body position offers similar advantages to the luge rider as the EGG or racing tuck position does to the downhill ski racer. To help stay on board in this position, some racers go so far as to use pieces of sandpaper to keep themselves from shifting position on the sled.

Being a gravity sport, combined with speeds up to 125 kph, one of the main things for the luge racer to possess is a strong neck. Strong legs are also important to guide the sled down and sideways. Because of its flexibility, the sled is so manoeuvrable that a slight movement of the head or shoulders can change the rider's direction. Steering or braking devices on the sled are restricted.

The initial starting position for the singles event has the rider's body tightly contracted on the luge with knees drawn up close to the body. The athlete grasps the start handles, head down, elbows bent, knees wide, and begins the rocking motion back and forth to build up forward momentum. Once off the starting platform, the paddling action with the hands begins. This motion helps to increase speed at the top of the course. The rider then scoots forward at the hips and assumes the prone position on the luge. This start is one of the most critical manoeuvres for the luger.

The luge must leave within 30 seconds of being given the start signal or the riders face disqualification. A fast start is vital. Even one tenth of a second lost at the start could cost a full second or more at the bottom. Pushing off from the fixed start handles, the racer breaks the electric beam at the bottom of the starting ramp to start the clock.

Once on the course, a good line is all-important. Like bobsleigh races, luge races are won or lost on the curves. Because a race consists of lowest combined time of four heats, rock-steady consistency is essential. Often the best lugers are calm and almost nerveless. If a rider tries to correct a small error too quickly or change the line of descent too rapidly, the luge could go out of control.

In the doubles event, the responsibility for maintaining the correct body position on the luge lies with the bottom rider. The doubles starting technique requires the upper competitor to belt himself onto the sled with a strap at the hips. Then, with both lugers in a sitting position on the sled at the start ramp, the bottom rider grasps onto the handgrips attached to the partner's elbows. The push-pull motion at the start handles begins, and as the sled is pushed off, the two riders assume the prone position and take up the rein.

The riding technique requires expert symmetrical handling of the sled runners. Legs and feet on the track during a run may put the sled out of control and even result in broken or twisted ankles. The ball and heel are the only part of the foot that should ever touch the ice at the finish ramp for braking and stopping. There is only one position for feet during the run, and any other way is dangerous.

The outcome of the luge race is influenced by the capabilities of the athlete. Technical expertise, physical conditioning, and a good psychological attitude aid the luger in pre-visualizing the course and executing a smooth run. An Olympic calibre sledder must be able to adapt to changing conditions on the track and, by virtually using a sixth sense, be able to detect and correct errors in a matter of tenths or hundredths of a second.

# The Rules

There are three events in Olympic luge competition, the men's and women's singles and the men's double race. Each has minimum requirements for track lengths in international racing: 1000 metres for men's singles and 750 metres for women's singles and men's doubles.

The required weight of the singles sled is 22 kilograms and 25 kilograms for the doubles sled. Luge is a gravity sport, and for this reason, a competitor may compensate for weight differences by wearing a weight vest which increases weight up to a maximum of 13 kilograms for men and up to 10 kilograms for women.

Helmets are mandatory for lugers and the plastic wind protector "bubble" attached to the helmets lets riders see where they are going at 125 kph.

Runners on the sled must be made of steel and, because of the cost, are usually only laminated on the bottom with alloyed steel. The runners can be waxed, but not heated.

The examination of luges and equipment begins prior to the race. Body weight, additional weight, weight of race clothing, and total weight are noted and entered in the official record. At the start area, the temperature of the steel blades is taken. The temperature of each runner at the start area must be within plus 5°C of the air temperature. After the temperature examination, the luge may not be exchanged nor the runners warmed. At the finish line, the weight of the luge and weight of the athlete are checked again, along with a re-check of runner temperature.

Four heats are run in the singles events, and two heats are run in the doubles event. The runs are timed to the nearest one thousandth of a second and the winner has the lowest aggregate time after four runs in the singles, or two runs in the doubles.

It is mandatory that the men's two-seater racers take their two runs on the same afternoon. In all singles events there are four timed runs, normally one per day and one run taking place at night under the lights. However, in Calgary at the 1988 Olympic Winter Games there will be no night runs but two runs per day for two days.

Competitors in the Olympic luge event must be at least sixteen years old and the same rider can compete in both singles and doubles events.

The luge course must be travelled from the start to the finish in a seated or reclining position, and the competitor must cross the finish line in contact with his/her luge.

## The Equipment

There is no typical luge in Olympic competition.

In fact, the East Germans are so secretive about their sled design that they have been known to station security guards around their sleds at races to prevent their rivals from analyzing the luge construction.

There is no restriction on the length of the sled, but most sleds used in Olympic competition are about 1.2 metres long. For safety reasons, it is mandatory that sleds have only one set of runners with rounded outer edges. The distance between the inside edges of them can be no more than 45 centimetres. The runners are anchored to the sled bridges or main frame utilizing rubber grommets, which give flexibility to the sled.

FIL rules state that the singles sled can weigh no more than 22 kilograms and the doubles sled no more than 25 kilograms. Since the early 1980s, the canvas seat on luge sleds has been replaced with an aerodynamic fibreglass ''wind-slip.'' According to the rule book, the fibreglass shell or lining must not extend

The conical shaped helmets used by the Germans in 1976 were disallowed in future Olympics. *Deutsche Presse-Agentur GmbH*

past the shoulders in the rear, and must not extend past the knees in the front.

A close look at the gloves of the luger makes a spectator think that the athlete may be looking for a street fight instead of a sled race. Steel spikes are sewn into the fingers of both gloves. These spikes are used to dig into the ice on the track for fast start paddling once the sled leaves the starting gate. Protective elbow and knee pads, and a kidney belt can be worn but are not mandatory. Specialized footwear, governed by the rule book, is used for aerodynamics.

Until the Olympic Winter Games at Innsbruck, Austria, in 1976, race helmets could be of any design. Several ideas were incorporated including a conical shape that has since been disallowed. The FIL now requires all competitors to wear helmets that correspond to the shape of the head.

Considering the potential degree of danger in the Olympic luge event, the amount of protective equipment worn by a sledder appears to be minimal.

# Calgary Preview

## Men
The innovative luge skills of the Germans, Italians, and Soviets in speed, riding technique, and sled construction have made them the teams to beat in Olympic luge competition.

"Anything is possible, even at my age," says veteran luger Paul Hildgartner of Italy, who at age thirty-four has no intention of retirement even though he won a gold medal at Sarajevo. He will be back at the Olympics in 1988 along with his team-mate Norbert Huber, who placed second in the World Cup at Canada Olympic Park in 1987. The men's singles event will a tough rematch between Huber and Rene Friedl of the German Democratic Republic, the young nineteen-year-old who won the 1987 pre-Olympic event.

In fact, the sledders from the G.D.R. are so gifted technically and their skills so perfected, it is debatable whether anyone else can beat them. Both their men's and women's teams cleaned up in the 1987 pre-Olympic events. The Austrians could feature with Markus Prock, and the Soviets are still placing well. The 1984 Olympic silver medalist Sergei Danilin could be in the top five, along with fellow countryman Valeri Dudin.

Canada's top medal contender at Sarajevo in 1984 was the 1983 World Champion Miroslav Zajonc, who defected to Canada in 1982. However, the Czechs had complained when they learned that Zajonc intended to race for Canada at the Games, and after some discussion, Olympic powers declared the Czech ineligible. Disillusioned, the former member of the Czechoslovakian national luge team withdrew his name and has since moved to the United States to wait the required three-year period before naturalization. Zajonc will be back in full force by 1988 for the Americans and will bear watching.

Zajonc was definitely Canada's loss, especially for a country that is attempting to build an international-calibre luge team. For a young field of Canadian sliders, the 1988 Olympics are a mixed blessing. Pressure to perform at top international levels must be measured with the reality that the sport is still in its infancy in Canada. "It's tough when you get your best times ever and still have time to make up," said Canadian coach Carole Keyes. Still, with many promising lugers coming up through the ranks, a viable Olympic team may be in existence for Canada in 1988. To date, Chris Wightman of Ottawa, Ontario, and Quebec's Nil Labrecque, who won the 1987 Canadian championship, have already qualified for Olympic team selection in the singles event. Doubles team Bob Gasper from Lloydminster, Alberta, and partner André Benoit of Lapraire, Quebec, look like Canada's best hopes in that event.

The Soviets again have some excellent doubles racers, including 1984 Olympic silver medalists Evgueni Belousov and Alexandre Belyakov. For the G.D.R., Jorg Hoffman and Jochen Pietzsch could be a medal winning doubles team. With Canada's national luge team showing marked improvement, a full team could take to the Olympic track for the first time in Canadian history. Canadian Olympic Association officials will be looking for results from lugers in the top half of the demanding international circuit during the year leading up to the 1988 Olympic Winter Games.

## Women
The woman to watch on the luge track in 1988 will be reigning world champion Cerstin Schmidt. Schmidt and team-mates Gabrielle Kohlisch and Ute Oberhoffner finished in a one, two, three sweep of the World Cup in Calgary in February, 1987. Of the three, Schmidt particularly enjoys the long curves on the Canada Olympic Park track as they suit her fluid luge style.

The Italian women continue to slide well, and Marie-Louise Rainer may be in the winner's circle at the Olympics. For the Americans, it looks like Bonnie Warner is still their best bet.

Canada's veteran rider Carole Keyes will attend her fourth Olympic Winter Games in 1988 as the national team coach. An athletic therapist and teacher, Keyes is from Montreal, Quebec, and is one Canada's most respected sledders. For the Canadian women's team, both Leanne Schade of Osgoode, Ontario, and Marie-Claude Doyon of Sherbrooke, Quebec, look promising. Doyon finished in sixth place overall on the 1985-86 World Cup circuit, and won the 1987 Canadian championship. For Marie-Claude Doyon, the victory represented her third national title in as many years.

# Canadians at the Olympic Winter Games
## LUGE

### 1924 - 1960

Events not held.

### 1964 Innsbruck — IX Olympic Winter Games

No team entered.

### 1968 Grenoble — X Olympic Winter Games

Arbuthnot, L., Bocock, L. C., Coulson, D.J., Diplock, M., Eddy, R.E., Nelson, C.R., Walter, P.

**MEN**

*Singles*
31. Roger E. Eddy
33. Larry Arbuthnot
37. Colin R. Nelson
47. Darcy Coulson

**WOMEN**

*Singles*
12. Linda Crutchfield-Bocock
18. Martha Diplock

### 1972 Sapporo — XI Olympic Winter Games

Arbuthnot, L., Hansen, D., McComb, D., Neilsen, P.

**MEN**

*Singles*
25. Larry Arbuthnot
35. David McComb
38. Douglas Hansen

*Doubles*
16. Larry Arbuthnot, Douglas Hansen

**WOMEN**

*Singles*
Canada did not participate.

### 1976 Innsbruck — XII Olympic Winter Games

Arbuthnot, L., Bowie, M.J., Chase, J., Hansen, D., Keyes, C., McComb, D., Michaud, D., Shragge, M.

**MEN**

*Singles*
31. Larry Arbuthnot
35. Michael Shragge

*Doubles*
17. Larry Arbuthnot, Doug Hansen
22. David McComb, Michael Shragge

**WOMEN**

*Singles*
22. Carole Keyes
23. Mary Jane Bowie
26. Julie Chase

### 1980 Lake Placid — XIII Olympic Winter Games

Keyes, C., Jensen, M., Nadeau, D., Smith, B.

**MEN**

*Singles*
11. Bruce Smith
17. Mark Jensen

**WOMEN**

*Singles*
18. Carole Keyes
22. Danielle Nadeau

### 1984 Sarajevo — XIV Olympic Winter Games

Keyes, C., Rossi, S.

**MEN**

*Singles*
Canada did not participate.

*Doubles*
Canada did not participate.

**WOMEN**

*Singles*
22. Sue Rossi
24. Carole Keyes

# Nordic Skiing

## Cross-Country Skiing and Nordic Combined

Canmore Nordic Centre
February 14, 15, 17, 19, 21, 22, 25, 27/Cross Country
February 28/Nordic Combined Cross Country
February 24/Team Cross Country

Canada Olympic Park (70 Metre Ski Jumping)
February 27/Nordic Combined
February 23/Team

"Times are changing. Today we see real genuine Indians in the ski tracks! And it was a beautiful sight. The delightful Indian twins, Shirley and Sharon Firth, charmed everyone as they diagonaled around the 5 kilometre course."

*Ajtenposten*, Oslo, Norway
1969

"Both in the girls' and boys' classes, the Canadians won everyone's heart. They became the spectators' favourites everywhere they went, and must have signed at least a thousand autographs."

*Kirunen*, Falun, Sweden
1969

*Bob Wilson/Yellowknife Photo Centre*

These newspaper quotes, and many others like them, were just the beginning of our careers as competitive cross-country skiers.

From six years of age, when our parents sent us to Sir Alexander Mackenzie School, our life has revolved around skiing. It was there in 1967 that Father Mouchet introduced us to Bjorger Pettersen, a man who would have a tremendous impact not only on our lives, but on the lives of many other students from the District of Mackenzie. That year, when we were just thirteen years old, Bjorger showed us photographs of world-famous cross-country skiers like Norway's gold medalist Hallgeir Brenden. He told both of us that if we trained hard for one year, we could go to Scandinavia to race and he would introduce us to all the cross-country skiing stars.

At that time, neither one of us ever dreamt that we would eventually represent Canada in four consecutive Olympic Winter Games.

For us, cross-country skiing has been the perfect sport. Not only does it suit our emotional temperament, but it provided us with an opportunity to reach the highest fitness level possible. But more than that, cross-country took us places, introduced us to wonderful people, and gave us the privilege of representing Canada throughout the world.

The life of an Olympic athlete is not always an easy one. For our Métis and Eskimo team members, and for many Canadians who still compete in Europe each year, the distances travelled take their toll. While we lived out of suitcases during the race season in Europe, the Europeans could go home to their families between events on the circuit. We missed our own people of the North, and longed to return to familiar surroundings. Yet it never occurred to either one of us to quit or give up. Instead, we set our goals ahead of us and worked toward them.

To those of you who cross-country ski every year, and never hope to stand up on the victory podium, it is worth remembering that it is fun to keep physically fit by participating in one of the greatest winter sports of all time— cross-country skiing.

And to those skiers who race, may we encourage you to continue and follow your dream which may take you to the Olympic Games.

We would like to welcome all the competitors to the XV Olympic Winter Games in Calgary in 1988, and wish them the best of luck in the Nordic events at the Canmore Nordic Centre.

Sharon Firth
*Nineteen-time Canadian Champion*
*Four-time Olympic Team Member*
*Winner of the John Semmelink Memorial Trophy\**

Shirley Firth Larsson
*Twenty-nine Canadian Championship gold medals*
*Four-time Olympic Team Member*
*Winner of the John Semmelink Memorial Trophy*

*John Semmelink, a young medical student at McGill University and member of Canada's national ski team in the 1960s, was killed at Garmisch-Partenkirchen, Germany, when he careened off a cliff during the Arlberg-Kandahar race. The John Semmelink Memorial Trophy for skiing excellence has been awarded to such outstanding athletes as Horst Bulau, Steve Podborski, and the Firth twins.

# The History

No other winter sport can claim an older example of its equipment than Nordic skiing.

In 1921, the "Hoting Ski" was discovered buried in a bog at Hoting, Sweden. It is the world's oldest ski. Made of pine, the ski measures 111 cm long and has a groove carved into the centre of it to hold the foot onto the ski by a retaining strap. The ski is estimated to be about 4,500 years old.

For centuries, the cross-country ski has been an integral part of life in Scandinavia. It is a matter of intense national pride to all Scandinavians when one of their racers crosses the finish line first in the Olympics. Two of the world-renowned races held annually in Norway and Sweden are based on the ancient sagas of Scandinavian heroes.

During the civil uprising in the year 1206, members of the King's Guard secured the Norwegian line of kings by escaping from Oslo to Osterdal (480 kilometres away) with two-year-old Prince Haakon Haakonsson, heir to the throne of Norway. The heroic legend was the inspiration for the 56 kilometre "Birkebeiner" cross-country race which follows a portion of the route taken in 1206. The race has been held since 1932, and in 1987 a Canadian would beat over five thousand participants to become the first Canadian in history to win the prestigious ski marathon.

Political assailants chased King Gustaf (Vasa) Eriksson out of Salem, Sweden, in 1521. He fled on cross-country skis to safety in Mora, a distance of 85 kilometres. To commemorate the successful escape, the Vasaloppet race, inaugurated in 1922, is held every year and retraces the route skied by the King.

Despite the fact the Scandinavians used the ski for hunting and touring, people in other parts of the world remained uninterested in cross-country skiing until a Norwegian invented a new ski binding. Sondre Norheim attached a leather heel strap on a pair of skis in 1840. The heel strap, combined with the existing toe strap, radically changed the control and turning precision of the ski.

Norheim first attempted a ski turn by placing one ski far forward of the other, and gradually angling the tip of the forward ski inward, in the direction to be turned. His demonstration of the new bindings took place in the small Norwegian county of Telemark. Today, the Telemark turn is one of cross-country skiing's most useful manoeuvres.

Norwegian Fridtjof Nansen marked a milestone in the history of cross-country when he skied across Greenland and lived to write a book about it in 1890.

It was some time before cross-country skis were used in Canada, though. During the late 1700s, surveyor David Thompson explored the country in the winter months wearing North American Indian snowshoes, never skis. But when the Gold Rush hit North America in the mid-1800s, miners and loggers came from all directions, including Norway. With the Norwegians, came cross-country skis.

Rossland, British Columbia, was one of the biggest boom towns of all, and it was there that "Norwegian Snowshoes," as they were called, made an appearance in the ski jumping event of Canada's first winter carnival held in 1898. Despite the popularity of ski jumping as it spread across Canada, cross-country advocates slowly began to outnumber their airborne counterparts.

Ottawa and Montreal staged cross-country competitions in 1914. The Canadian Amateur Ski Association, still governing skiing today, was formed in Montreal in 1920. By the late 1920s, ski trains loaded with cross-country skiers from Montreal were travelling to the quaint French Canadian villages in the Laurentians. In the West, too, cross-country skiing was thriving at Banff, Skoki Valley, Sunshine Village, the interior of British Columbia, and Grouse Mountain on the West Coast.

Canadian cross-country skiers did not take part in the first Olympic Winter Games in 1924 at Chamonix, France. The Scandinavians dominated the events by taking the first eleven places with Thorlief Haug winning three gold medals for Norway and a bronze medal for jumping.

Canada had two cross-country skiers in the Games at St. Moritz, Switzerland, in 1928. William Thompson and Merrit Putman placed thirty-seventh and fortieth respectively, in the 18 kilometre race. A Swede, Per Erik Hedlund, crossed the finish line almost one minute ahead of the silver medalist. Hedlund's margin of victory still stands today in Olympic record books.

Before the Olympic Winter Games took place at Lake Placid, New York, in 1932, Canada's best known cross-country pioneer and legendary trail cutter, Herman Smith-Johannsen, settled permanently in the Laurentians, where he made his living hunting and fishing.

Born in Oslo, Norway, in 1875, Johannsen graduated in engineering from the University of Berlin in 1899, emigrated to America, and worked in Cleveland, Ohio, for a company that sold heavy machinery. His work took him to Canada and he discovered the beauty of Northern Ontario and Quebec. Herman Smith-Johannsen was to become one of the legends of Canadian sport, but his nickname was given to him by the Cree Indians.

According to an Indian legend, Johannsen was so admired by the Cree Indians who met him in the bush during the construction of the Grand Trunk Railway in 1902, that they named him "Okamacum Wapooes," or "Chief Jackrabbit." When he lost everything in the Depression, Johannsen moved to Canada for good.

A tireless worker and already in his mid-fifties, he pioneered the development of cross-country skiing in Quebec and Ontario. From Labelle to Shawbridge he blazed and cut the trail that would eventually go all the way north to Mont Tremblant. The Maple Leaf Trail and the Lachute-Ottawa cross-country marathon trail were two of his famous contributions to the sport in Canada. In 1972 Jackrabbit Johannsen was awarded the Order of Canada and in 1982 was the first cross-country skier in Canada to be inducted into the Sport's Hall of Fame. Jackrabbit Johannsen's ski career mellowed only when he broke his leg at ninety-six years of age. Jackrabbit Johannsen died in 1987 at one hundred and eleven years of age. At the time of his death, he was Canada's oldest citizen.

Most of the cross-country events of the 1932 Olympic Winter Games were held in a raging blizzard at Lake Placid, but it

The arrival of Number 15 at the finish line heralds another Scandinavian sweep of the medals at the 1928 Olympic Winter Games at St. Moritz.
*The International Olympic Committee Archives, Lausanne, Switzerland*

The "Birkebeiner" race is held annually to commemorate the escape by a two-year-old prince over the Lillehammer Mountains in 1206.
*The Lillehammer Olympic Development Association*

didn't seem to stop the Scandinavians from winning all the medals.

Fifteen Canadian cross-country racers participated in the 1932 Games, with a best-ever sixteenth-place finish by Kaare Engstad, of Burns Lake, British Columbia, in the 50 kilometre. Engstad's respectable finish was the best Canada would see in Olympic competition for a long time.

One of the problems was that Jackrabbit Johannsen's training run for the team he was coaching ended right at the bottom of Big Hill in Shawbridge. After his racers had crossed the finish line, Jackrabbit would encourage them to practise their Telemark turns on Alex Foster's rope tow on the hill. Often, that was the last Jackrabbit Johannsen saw of his cross-country racers. "Foster's Folly" offered them more thrills with less effort, and for 25 cents a day, converts by the dozen took up Telemarking.

Rope-tow fever was not the only significant event to contribute to the demise of cross-country skiing in Canada. In 1935, a new front-throw cable ski binding, which held skiers' heels down onto the skis, was invented. The "Kanadahar" binding dramatically improved the downhill skiers' performance.

To cater to this new generation of skiers, Canadian ski pioneers began to build ski resorts that offered groomed slopes, rope tows, and ski lifts. Some legendary developers were Mike Dehouck at Mont St.-Anne, Joe Ryan at Mont Tremblant, John Clifford at Camp Fortune, Cliff White in Banff, and Rudolph Verne on the West Coast. "This epidemic of rope tows will ruin cross-country skiing in this country," bemoaned Jackrabbit Johannsen, and he was right.

The Scandinavians swept all the medals again in the Nordic events at Lake Placid, including the Nordic Combined. The Combined is a two-day Olympic competition consisting of a 70 metre jump on one day, and a 15 kilometre cross-country race on the next. Each athlete makes three jumps, with his two best leaps counting toward his final score.

In the early days of Olympic competition, the event was not considered an odd combination, but today it is. Not many men are good at it.

In 1936, Canada had a Nordic Combined skier William G. Clark, who competed in what was then the 18 kilometre race and placed forty-seventh. His best of three jumps off the 70 metre put him in thirty-ninth place in the Nordic Combined standings at the Olympic Winter Games at Garmisch-Partenkirchen, Germany. Nevertheless, the Norwegians excelled at the Nordic Combined and in fact, took gold, silver, and bronze medals in the event in every Olympics from 1924 to 1936.

A 4 x 10 kilometre relay race was added to the Nordic for-

The 1932 Olympic ski team. *Canadian Ski Museum*

mat at the 1936 Winter Games and the Finns provided a spectacular finish to the new event. When Finland's anchor man Kalle Jalkanen started the final lap he was 82 seconds behind the last Norwegian, and overtook his opponent by 18 metres as he skied into the stadium to be greeted by a cheering mob of spectators. From the time it was inaugurated, the relay race was an immediate favourite with Olympic fans, and still is today.

Nordic skiing came to a standstill in Canada during World War II, and when the Winter Games began again in 1948, a small four-man Nordic team went to the Olympics at St. Moritz, Switzerland. It was another medal sweep by Sweden in all Nordic events at the Games. The only one that got away from the Swedes was the Nordic Combined, won by Heikki Hassu of Finland.

A four-man Nordic team represented Canada at the 1952 Olympic Winter Games at Oslo, Norway, but the Scandinavian countries provided a field of Nordic medal winners again. Norway captured two more gold medals with victories by Hallgier Brenden in the 18 kilometre race and Simon Slattvik in the Nordic Combined. Veikko Hakulinen of Finland won the 50 kilometre race, but the big news was the first women's cross-country event, a 10 kilometre race won by Finland's Lidiya Wideman.

At the Oslo Olympics, Norway's skiing ace Stein Eriksen helped establish Alpine skiing as a North American favourite, and there seemed no way to reverse the trend. Interest in cross-country skiing slipped into the doldrums in Canada, except for a hard core of supporters which included Alberta's "Little Norway."

Camrose, Alberta, 95 kilometres southeast of Edmonton, is a rich, mixed-farming area located on the banks of Stoney Creek which flows through the centre of town. Clarence and Irvin Servold's Norwegian parents were one of the many Scandinavian families that settled in the area in the early 1900s, and formed one of Canada's first ski clubs in 1911. During the long winter months, cross-country skiing was a way of life for the Servold family. Almost before the little brothers could walk, they began to ski using barrel staves as skis, and popular tree branches for poles.

The boys attended Camrose Lutheran College, a school established by the Norwegian community. Apart from the standard Canadian school curriculum, the school offered two extra courses. One was the study of the Norwegian language, and the other was a compulsory physical education in cross-country skiing. Physical Education soon became the Servold brothers' favourite subject. After school, the brothers would head out the back door of their house, slide down the creek banks onto the ice, and ski for miles on the frozen surface of Stoney Creek. As they followed the Stoney Creek valley south, the banks became steeper and steeper.

It was Irvin's idea to build the jump. By today's standards, it wasn't much, but the homemade wooden trestle was enough to help Irvin Servold reach his dream of becoming a skiflyer. And, while Clarence cross-country skied back and forth on the ice below, practising for his races, his little brother practised ski jumping.

By the time Clarence was twenty years old, he had won every major cross-country race in western Canada, and his teenage brother had won everything there was to win in ski jumping competitions.

In 1955, the Canadian Olympic Association invited the

brothers to put together a three-man Nordic team to represent Canada at the seventh Olympic Winter Games at Cortina d'Ampezzo, Italy. The one condition was that the Servolds had to pay their own way to the Games. That one condition could have been the end of their Olympic dream if it hadn't been for the fierce Nordic pride of the people of Camrose. By February, the Camrose community had raised the money for their hometown boys, and Clarence and Irwin Servold left for the Games in Cortina with Jacques Charland from Quebec.

The Servolds weren't the only newcomers at the Winter Games in 1956. The Russians made a long-delayed entry into the Olympics and won both the 4 x 10 kilometre relay and the women's 10 kilometre. The 18 kilometre race was officially changed to the 15 kilometre and was won by Norwegian Hallgeir Brenden, who successfully defended his 1952 title. His teammate Sverre Stenersen won the Nordic Combined, and Sweden's Sixten Jernberg won the first of his three Olympic gold medals in the 50 kilometre race.

Two new events were introduced to the Nordic format at Cortina—a 30 kilometre race for men, and the popular 3 x 5 kilometre women's relay, won by a team from Finland.

Four years later, the Servolds were back at the Olympics at Squaw Valley, California. Clarence Servold's second-place finish in the 15 kilometre race of the Nordic Combined still stands as Canada's top Nordic record at the Olympics. It also put him in contention for Canada's first Nordic Olympic medal. But his ski jumps the next day were flawed by the wrong choice of wax, and because the final results are based on the highest combined points for both the cross-country race and the ski jump, Clarence Servold finished out of the medals, and so did Irvin.

It was a bitter disappointment for Clarence and Irvin Servold, but both brothers have a unique second chance to have the Servold name in the record books.

Watch for cousins twenty-six-year-old Dave, and twenty-seven-year-old Jon, of Camrose, Alberta, the two highflying sons of Clarence and Irvin Servold, members of the Canadian Nordic Combined ski team who could be competing at the 1988 Olympic Winter Games in Calgary.

A solid break in the Nordic Olympic records was recorded in 1960 at Squaw Valley, when the first non-Scandinavians won two events. Germans Helmut Recknagel and Georg Thoma won the ski jump and the Nordic Combined, but the rest of the medals were divided among Norway, Sweden, and Finland.

Sweden's "King of the Skis," Sixten Jernberg, won a gold medal in the 30 kilometre, Haakon Brusveen of Norway took the 15 kilometre race, Kalevi Hamalainen of Finland won the 50 kilometre and the Finns were also victorious in the 4 x 10 kilometre relay. In the women's events the U.S.S.R.'s Maria Gusakova won the 10 kilometre race and Sweden the 3 x 5 kilometre relay.

Meanwhile, back in Canada in 1959, the remote village of Aklavik, Northwest Territories, situated fifty miles away from the Arctic Ocean, had slowly begun to sink into the mud of the Mackenzie River delta. The government of Canada made a decision to build a new village for the people of Aklavik which would also be a centre for government agencies. The Firth family was one of the one hundred families that were moved to the new site, named Inuvik, one hundred miles above the Arctic Circle.

Relocating his wife and children to Inuvik was a major undertaking for Loucheux-Métis trapper Stephen Firth, but with the stoic determination that typifies the people from the northern tundra, he set up his new Arctic line and began to trap around Inuvik.

To administer to Inuvik's new flock, the Roman Catholic Church transferred Oblate missionary priest Father Jean Marie Mouchet from the Athabascan Indian village of Old Crow in the Yukon, to Inuvik. Born in Chamonix, France, and always a keen skier, Father Mouchet had trained with the French ski troops during World War II, before coming to Canada.

At Old Crow, Father Mouchet had introduced cross-country skiing to the parishioners, and the entire village became involved in the sport. The older members of the community, who were unable to ski, became officers of the Old Crow Ski Club, and in effect, members of the town council.

When he was sent to Inuvik on a leave of absence from Old Crow in 1965, Father Mouchet set up a cross-country ski program for the Roman Catholic students who boarded at Grollier Hall Hostel. The ski program was open to students of Inuvik's Sir Alexander Mackenzie School who numbered approximately four hundred from all areas of the District of Mackenzie. Among the borders were treaty Indian Fred Kelly, John Turo, and Maurice and Ernie Lennie, whose families lived two hundred and fifty miles south of Inuvik at Fort Good Hope. With snow from October until the end of May, cross-country skiing suited the geographic and climatic conditions of Inuvik, and it soon became a way of life with the students.

Two of the students at Sir Alexander Mackenzie school were sisters Shirley and Sharon Firth. With five older and five younger brothers and sisters, the twin girls were born on New Year's Eve right in the middle of the twelve Firth children who lived with their parents in a one-room house, on the north side of town. And all in good time, cross-country skiers throughout the world would recognize the names of the Loucheux-Métis twins from Inuvik.

At the 1964 Games at Innsbruck, Austria, Sixten Jernberg made Olympic history. The thirty-five-year-old Swede was recrowned with his second Olympic gold medal in the 50 kilometre and three days later won another gold medal in the relay race. An exceptional athlete, Sixten Jernberg is acknowledged as the most successful skier in history. No other Olympian has won three individual golds, three individual silvers, one individual bronze, and a gold and a bronze in relays.

The star of both the 15 and 30 kilometre races was Eero Mäntyranta, member of a superb Finnish team that won both events. Norway's Tormod Knutsen won the Nordic Combined, but the Norwegian women were shut out of the gold medals in the women's events. Claudia Boyarskikh of the Soviet Union raced in all three events, including the new 5 kilometre race introduced in 1964, and picked up three gold medals for the Russians. Canada's best finish was fifteenth place in the men's 4 x 10 kilometre relay.

By the spring, Father Mouchet had assembled enough skiing enthusiasts to justify establishing a yearly spring training clinic at Inuvik for 1965 and 1966. The Canadian Amateur Ski Association provided Bjorger Pettersen, a native of Norway, as the coach and director. It was at the spring training camps of 1965 and 1966 that Petterson first noticed the natural talent on skis of two of the youngest participants, Shirley and Sharon Firth, and the competitive spirit that existed between the two of them.

By 1967, Father Mouchet's ski experiment had grown far beyond a simple community project. With over 175 Indian, Eskimo and Métis youths participating on ''les Espoir team'' (the junior team), the ''B'' team and the top Inuvik Ski Team, Father Mouchet applied to the federal government for financial assistance.

In August of 1967, the National Fitness Council of the federal Department of Health and Welfare financed a grant of $25,000 for the establishment of the Territorial Experimental Ski Training (TEST) program in Inuvik. With millions of dollars invested yearly in exploration of the North's other resources, very little had been invested in developing its human resources. In fact, every family in the North annually paid over one hundred dollars for correctional institute operations alone.

The main purpose of the TEST program was to assist in the development of youth, and to raise the outside image of the underdeveloped Northern people. By making the best of their environment and excelling in competitive cross-country skiing at the national and international level, the young people of the North would have the opportunity to reach their maximum potential as they faced a changing world.

Father Mouchet was needed back at Old Crow, so he contacted the most logical person to develop the TEST program in the capacity of full-time coach and director. In October of 1967, Bjorger Pettersen left an executive job in Norway that he had just started, and arrived in Inuvik to begin the most demanding, interesting, and satisfying job in his life.

When training began on the tundra in late October, Pettersen ran five hundred skiers through his program and from them picked the ten-member Inuvik Ski Team. From then on, Pettersen directed most of the TEST effort to the top team. Shirley and Sharon Firth were invited to join the team, and Pettersen's brother Rolf, a member of the 1968 Canadian Olympic Cross-Country Ski Team, joined them to train with them during November.

Sweden's Sixten Jernberg, the most successful cross-country skier in history, competes at the 1964 Games. *Deutsche Presse-Agentur GmbH*

The Inuvik Ski Team: (from left to right) Roger Allen, John Turo, Fred Kelly, Harold Cook, David Cook, Bjorger Pettersen, Roseanne Allen, Anita Pettersen, Sharon Firth, and Shirley Firth. *The Citizen, Prince George, British Columbia*

Being on the top team was no joke, but the hard cold winters had developed the skiers' greatest strength—their toughness—both physical and mental. Bjorger Pettersen mapped out an Olympic calibre training program for his racers that demanded up to 30 kilometres daily, seven days a week, and often had them skiing in the dark Arctic night after school. In his diary Bjorger Pettersen wrote, "I remember one day in January, I wrote on the blackboard in the ski lodge . . . Boys 30 km, Girls 20 km. No questions were asked and the distance was completed by all. Later that day, I found out that the temperature was 45 below."

In December 1967, coach Bjorger Pettersen took the Inuvik Ski Team to their first big race at Anchorage, Alaska.

The older junior boys' class, which the Americans considered their strongest, was won by Fort Good Hope's "Kelly Express." Sixteen-year-old Fred Kelly was the first Canadian skier ever to win a junior class race in Alaska.

In the junior girls' race, Shirley Firth clocked a winning time that matched the same time as Alaska's most outstanding junior women's racer, Barbara Britch. It was the first time Britch's time had even been equalled, let alone by a fourteen-year-old. The medal sweep by the Inuvik Ski Team also included first-place finishes for Rex Cockney of Inuvik, David Cook of Fort Good Hope, and Mabel Kudluk of Sachs Harbour.

From then on, the team concentrated on one race—the 1968 Canadian National Championships scheduled for Port Arthur, Ontario, just after the Olympic Winter Games.

The first event of the 1968 Winter Games at Grenoble, France, provided the first Nordic gold medal for Italy, when Franco Nones won the 30 kilometre race. Granted, Nones had trained in Sweden with a Swedish coach, but for the twenty-seven-year-old skier from the Dolomite Mountains, it was an Italian first.

Norway's three-time silver medalist Harald Grönningen finally beat Finland's Eero Mäntyranta in the 15 kilometre race and won his first gold medal. Ole Ellefsaeter of Norway won the gruelling 50 kilometre race and the Norwegians were victorious in the men's relay.

Toini Gustafsson, a twenty-six-year-old physical education teacher from Sweden, won the 10 and 5 kilometre races in the women's events, and won the silver medal in the relay.

As the Olympic flag was lowered at the Closing Ceremonies in Grenoble, France, back in Canada coach Bjorger Pettersen was preparing his ten-member ski team in Inuvik for its first trip out of the North. Scheduled were ten races in Alberta and Ontario, including the race that could lead to its Olympic debut, the 1968 Canadian National Junior Ski Championships.

The eight-hour trip on the DC-8 Mainliner flight was like a dream-come-true for the Firth twins. Years later, after competing in four Olympics, Sharon Firth recalled that seeing the sparkling lights of the city as the plane approached Edmonton, at one o'clock in the morning, would always remain as one of the highlights of her life.

Success after success followed the Inuvik Ski Team as its members competed against the best Alberta had to offer. But once they had arrived at Port Arthur, the tension increased with the presence of Ottawa's Malcolm Hunter and nineteen-year-old Ed Day from Kimberley, British Columbia, the two top racers in the country.

During his pre-race pep talk to his team, Bjorger Pettersen asked them for the first time to ski all out—to ski until they dropped.

No one in Canada could have followed Fred Kelly on the last 5 kilometres of the Nationals that day. But his race was far from easy and coach Pettersen had taken Malcolm Hunter's time from the 9.25 kilometre mark as he stood on the side of the trail.

Bjorger Pettersen knew that Fred Kelly had to be exactly at that point on the trail at no later than eleven minutes after Hunter in order to tie his time. What does a coach think in such an instance?

The thoughts of Bjorger Pettersen, later recorded in his TEST progress report to the Federal Government, indicate what was going through his mind as he stood there waiting for the Kelly Express.

I swallowed heavily, glanced at my watch . . . ten minutes and fifty seconds. . . . THERE, someone just crossed the mark where I was taking my intermediate times from. My heart stopped for a moment then started to beat violently . . . THERE, running like a clock, relaxed and gliding with the same stride used by the Norwegian Olympic champions and moving FASTER than anyone else, was the Kelly Express. I jumped five feet into the air and screamed at the top of my lungs . . . "You're leading by a few seconds." I only had one ski on but I started running after him to the finish line. When I arrived at the finish area, Fred was standing modestly over with the rest of the team behind the crowds. I rushed over to him, picked him, his skis and poles up in my arms and embraced him . . . the cameras flashed. Harold Cook, John Turo, Maurice Lennie and Roger Allen, who placed 5th, 6th, 9th and 10th respectively, gathered round. We were all happy and on the last 5-kilometers, the boys had proved that there still is a lot of fight left in the Natives of Canada's far North. Racing in what experts term the toughest cross-country field ever assembled in the National Junior Championships, a modest sixteen-year-old Indian boy of the North had become the champion of Canada.

The girls, led by fourteen-year-old Rose Ann Allen of Inuvik, continued to shatter records. A girl with exceptional leadership qualities and a top student, Rose Ann Allen of Inuvik became the youngest Nordic Canadian ski champion in history. Shirley Firth placed second and Sharon Firth third. The team captured the first three places in the relay the following day.

The nationwide press coverage the Inuvik Ski Team received after cleaning up at the Nationals caught the eye of CBC broadcast journalist Jarl Omholt-Jensen who was stationed at Fort Churchill, Manitoba.

Jarl Omholt-Jensen was born in Oslo, Norway, in 1947 and moved to Montreal, Quebec, with his family before he was two years old. Born into a family of Nordic skiers, he started cross-country skiing at a young age and won the Quebec Junior Championship in 1964.

A natural communicator with a magnetic personality, Omholt-Jensen was invited by the CBC to do cross-country ski radio commentary during the winter. After he finished school, he was hired on permanently with the CBC and was transferred to Fort Churchill for his first job in 1967. After researching the history of the success of the Inuvik skiers, Jensen requested a transfer to Inuvik. When his boss asked him why he wanted to go so far North, Omholt-Jensen said, "Because there is a story there." Not only did he find one, but he also gained himself a berth on the Canadian National Team from 1969 to 1973.

One of Jensen's first assignments was to cover the events at the United States Junior Ski Championships at Bozeman, Montana. It was there that Shirley Firth upset the eighteen-year-old

The "Kelly Express", Fred Kelly, at sixteen the champion of Canada.
*Courtesy Bjorger Pettersen*

United States Olympic star Barbara Britch by winning the North American Championship. The most prestigious victory ever by any Northwest Territories athlete had been accomplished by fourteen-year-old Shirley Firth who stood 4'11" and weighed 98 pounds. Twin sister Sharon placed third behind Britch.

Toward the end of the ski season, Bjorger Pettersen gave the Ski Team a questionnaire to fill out. Some of their answers to two of his questions are noted in his progress report.

1. *Name some of the things skiing does for you:*
"I get rid of my shyness" — "I bring pride to the North" — "It makes me feel like another person" — "Makes me healthier" — "Brings me confidence and teaches me things about Canada" — "Gives me fight" — "Keeps me out of mischief" — "Gives me a goal in life."

2. *Name some of the things I did wrong in my coaching of the Inuvik Ski Team:*
"Being too soft-hearted" — "Too generous and not strict enough" — "Not thinking of our religion" — "Too kind to the girls" — "Maybe too many meetings" — "Depending

on Shirley and Fred to win the big meets" — "Being grouchy before the big meets."

Sparkling spring sunshine in late May brought with it mild weather and thawing conditions on the tundra. During the 1967-68 ski season, the team members had skied more than 30,000 kilometres in training and raced a total of forty-five races. The last big race of the season was Inuvik's yearly Top of the World Ski Championships and another clean sweep by the skiers provided an opportunity for a little promotion at home.

Bjorger Pettersen's 1968-69 goal for his team was to qualify them by having them compete with the best, and they did. One of the biggest accomplishments of the TEST program was three years of total medal sweeps by Shirley Firth and Fred Kelly at the 1968, 1969, and 1970 United States Junior Nationals. Another team goal of Pettersen's was to have his team compete on the tough European circuit before the 1970 World FIS Ski Championships were held at Vysoke Tatry, Czechoslovakia. At the end of the season, Canada's first win in an FIS sanctioned race in Sweden had been won by the Kelly Express, along with six Canadian championships and three American championships by the rest of the team.

Shirley and Sharon Firth were among the members of the first Canadian women's team to participate in the World Nordic Championships in Czechoslovakia in 1970. Struggling with the high altitude and the fact that each member entered in each race was the youngest ever in history, the Inuvik skiers made an incredible showing. Top Canadian finish was Shirley Firth in thirty-third place. Next stop was the famous Homenkollen race at Oslo, Norway, the oldest and largest skiing competition in the world. Fred Kelly placed eleventh in the junior men's class with only five Norwegians ahead of him.

During the previous season, the Firth twins had emerged as consistent winners, with Shirley chalking up twenty-one victories and twin sister Sharon picking up eleven firsts. Celebrities at home and abroad, the twins continued their domination of women's cross-country skiing. At the U.S. Junior Nationals at Jackson Hole, Wyoming, Sharon took the gold in the 5 kilometre race and Shirley won the gold medal in the 10 kilometre. By the time the Canadian Senior Nationals had finished in Ontario, Shirley was the first skier, along with Sharon, to share in back-to-back senior women's relay titles.

In 1971, Shirley Firth was the first skier, along with Sharon, to share in three-in-a-row women's national relay titles. Selection for the twins on the Canadian Olympic Team, along with Roseanne Allen and Ottawa's Helen Sander, was assured.

Not only were the twins members of the first Canadian women's cross-country team to the Olympics, the skiers from the far North largely dominated the men's national team at the Olympics in Sapporo, Japan, in 1972. Ottawa's Malcolm Hunter joined up with Inuvik's Fred Kelly, Roger Allen, and Jarl Omholt-Jensen on the relay team for a creditable thirteenth finish in the 4 x 10 kilometre relay.

In the men's events at Sapporo, Sweden won the 15 kilo-

metre race, and Vyacheslav Vedenine became the first Soviet skier to crack the gold medal circle in the 30 kilometre. The closest ever Olympic 50 kilometre race was won by Norwegian Pål Tyldum, and the Soviets won the relay.

The stunning success of the Japanese ski jumpers at Sapporo carried through to the Nordic Combined event when Hideki Nakano placed first in the Ski Jumping. His second half of the two-part event was less than spectacular. He placed last in the 15 kilometre race, and ended up a disconsolate thirteenth overall. His first and last place finishes in the Nordic Combined were an Olympic first for the record books.

At the Winter Games in 1964, Soviet skier Claudia Boyar-skikh captured all three women's Nordic gold medals. In the 1972 Games at Sapporo, twenty-nine-year-old Galina Kulakova did the same thing.

The Canadian women's team had a best-ever Canadian finish in the 4 x 5 kilometre relay. Back in Canada after the Olympics, the Firth twins continued to collect accolades. The twelve event Trans-Am Series between Canada and the United States ended with the largest meet north of the Arctic Circle—Inuvik's annual Top of the World Championships. Sharon Firth finished first overall among North American women with 215 points, and her twin sister finished second with 195 points.

At the end of their Olympic debut year, the Firth twins became the first Nordic skiers to ever be awarded the John Semmelink Memorial Award by the Canadian Ski Association for their contribution to skiing in Canada. Considering the fact that Shirley Firth had contracted hepatitis in November just before the Olympics and was thought to be a doubtful starter at the Games, her accomplishments during the season had been outstanding.

In 1973, Ottawa's Sue Holloway was accepted on the national ski team. During the same year, Quebec's Pierre Harvey was accepted on the national cycling team.

Pierre Harvey and Sue Holloway are the only athletes in the history of Canada to have competed in both Summer and Winter Olympics in the same year.

Sue Holloway always loved sports. As a youngster she cross-country skied with her family, took ballet lessons, and eventually ended up in judo classes at age ten. In high school she was a provincial middle and long distance track and field champion, excelled at volleyball, and did some canoeing in the summer. But, during the winter, nothing interfered with cross-country skiing and Sue had been winning races since she was ten years old.

The Rideau Canoe Club was a five-minute walk away from the Holloway home, and it was there that sixteen-year-old Sue Holloway started to kayak. Two years later she placed first in four events at the 1973 Canadian Kayak Championships during the summer, and in the winter she was accepted on the national ski team.

Unquestionably, it was a challenge for Holloway to keep up with the competitive Firth twins. During the 1973 season, the twins battled it out with each other for the top Canadian ranking. Sharon won the gold in the 5 kilometre race at the

Sue Holloway, the only woman in Canada to compete in both the summer and winter Olympics in the same year. *Ray Pilon, the Canadian Olympic Association*

Pierre Harvey, the only Canadian man to compete in both the summer and winter Olympics in the same year. *Jacques Plante Photograph, St. Lambert, Quebec*

Canadian Senior Championships at Prince George, British Columbia, and Shirley picked up the silver. Later at the North American Championships at Thunder Bay, Ontario, the twins reversed the winning order to gold for Shirley and silver for Sharon in the 5 kilometre.

It was a different story for the team in Europe as coach Bjorger Pettersen chugged between meets in a rented Volkswagen van. Cross-country skiers develop peak form well into their thirties, and the young Canadians were no match for the Scandinavians. Nevertheless, Holloway joined up with the twins and Edmonton's Joan Groothuysen to finish in eighth place in the relay event at the Swedish Ski Games at Falun.

During the 1974 season, Sue Holloway was a member of both the Canadian Senior Championship and North American Championship gold medal relay teams. In her pre-Olympic year, Sue Holloway was on the relay team that made North American history for the Firth twins. At the North American Championships at Mont St. Anne, Quebec, Sharon won the gold in the 5 kilometre and 10 kilometre races. Sharon Firth was the first Canadian woman to sweep all three golds in North America.

In 1976 Sue Holloway accompanied the Canadian National Ski Team to Innsbruck, Austria, for the Olympic Winter Games and six months later became the first woman athlete in Canada to qualify for an Olympic paddling final at the Summer Games in Montreal, Quebec.

After the Summer Games, Sue Holloway realized that com-

peting at two sports at the world level was too demanding, and she was faced with the inevitable decision of choice.

Kayaking proved to be the best of choices for Sue Holloway.

Since deciding on kayaking fulltime, Holloway has collected a string of Canadian, North American, Continental Cup, and World championships that are unprecedented in the history of women's participation in the sport in Canada. A member of the 1980 and 1984 Summer Olympic teams, Holloway, along with partner Alexandre Barré, won an Olympic silver medal in the 500 metre doubles event, and an Olympic bronze medal in the 500 metre kayak-four event at the 1984 Olympic Summer Games in Los Angeles.

Pierre Harvey was born in Rimouski, Quebec, in 1957. A graduate engineer from Laval University and an incredibly gifted athlete, Harvey began his sports career as a swimmer. At twelve, he had won his first championships, but at fifteen gave it all up for competitive cycling. At eighteen, he was accepted on the National Cycling Team just in time to compete in the 1976 Olympic Summer Games in Montreal, Quebec. He placed twenty-fourth in the individual road race, a best-ever Canadian performance in that event.

Fortunately for Canada, Pierre Harvey took up cross-country skiing to keep in shape for cycling.

The Firth twins chalked up another record at the 1976 Olympics at Innsbruck, Austria, as the first female Canadian cross-country skiers to compete in back-to-back Winter Games.

American silver medalist Bill Koch, the first North American man to win a Nordic Olympic medal, competes at the 1976 Games. *Deutsche Presse-Agentur GmbH*

Soviets Nikolai Bazhukov and Sergei Saveliev won the 15 and 30 kilometre events, but American Bill Koch stole the show with his silver medal finish behind Saveliev. The sensational skier from Vermont is the only American to have won an Olympic Nordic skiing medal.

Norwegian Ivar Formo won the 50 kilometre and his countrymen were the surprise silver medalists in the relay. The East Germans had skied a superb first leg of the relay but their second skier, Axel Lesser, collided with a spectator on the course and he abandoned his race. Nevertheless, Olympic team-mate Ulrich Wehling turned in the best performance in the Nordic Combined to give East Germany the medal it had hoped to win in the relay.

The women's events at Innsbruck were clouded with a medical controversy involving nasal spray. Soviet racer Galina Kulakova was bidding for the successful defence of her 1972 Olympic title in the 5 kilometre event, but placed third behind Finland's gold medalist Helen Takalo. After the race Kulakova was disqualified for using the spray which contained a banned drug. Undaunted, she won the gold medal in the relay and a bronze in the 10 kilometre.

The Canadian women's team finished in seventh place, which ranked as Canada's best relay record. But the 1976 Games were to herald the end of an era for the Inuvik Ski Team.

Prior to the Games, Bjorger Pettersen announced he would retire as coach of the National Team to set up a permanent training centre for cross-country skiers at McBride, British Columbia. With him went Ernie Lennie, the boy who at fifteen years of age had raced against and beaten the entire United States Biathlon Team. The retirement of Fred Kelly, Ernie Lennie, and his mentor Bjorger Pettersen left Bert Bullock of Inuvik missing his own people of the North. With the potential of becoming the top Canadian champion, Bullock had placed an unprecedented fourth in the 1974 world junior championships at Autrans, France, and had missed a medal by just one second. Nevertheless, he finished off his year as the most successful of all the racers to come out of Inuvik and the first skier to win the 15, 30 and 50 kilometre titles at the 1976 Canadian Nationals. At the end of the season, Bert Bullock announced that he too would retire from active competition.

No one is sure what started the revival. The first indication that a renewed interest in cross-country skiing would virtually explode in the 1970s was the sudden demand for equipment. Ski shop owners across the country were caught by surprise and hard put to supply their customers with Nordic gear.

The increased interest in the sport could perhaps be ascribed to Alpine skiers growing weary of long lift lines and crowded hill conditions. Jackrabbit Johannsen always recommended "hobnobbing with nature" but undoubtedly one of the biggest factors was the fitness boom that swept the country. The expense of Alpine skiing was also a contributing factor to people moving away from the slopes and onto the cross-country trails. Parents discovered they could outfit the family for Nordic skiing without taking out a second mortgage on the house.

Tens of thousands took up ski touring and it is estimated that by 1988 there will be more than five million cross-country skiers in Canada.

More meaningful to a new generation of Nordic enthusiasts were the continued successes of Sharon and Shirley Firth. After the 1976 Olympics, both girls won gold medals in the relays at the Canadian Senior Championships at Sudbury, Ontario. The twins were the first skiers to give the Northwest Territories four consecutive women's relay titles.

Whitehorse in the Yukon hosted the 1977 Canadian Senior Nationals, and it was Sharon's turn in the winners' circle. She won the gold in the 5 kilometre race, gold in the 10 kilometre, silver in the 20 kilometre, and gold in the relay.

The 1978 Canadian Senior Championships were held at Sault Ste. Marie, Ontario, and it was there that Shirley Firth won all three events. Her goal had been to win three gold medals and she proved to herself she could do it. She was the first Canadian woman in history to sweep all three individual events.

The pre-Olympic year began well for the Firth twins. At the Canadian Seniors, Shirley again won the gold medal in the 10 kilometre, Canada's first skier to win three consecutive 10 kilometre titles. Sharon's gold in the relay event gave her nine titles, the most of any skier in Canadian senior history. At the Winter Games in Brandon, Manitoba, she won two gold medals. But the real show-stopper in Brandon was an Olympic cyclist.

Not only did twenty-one-year-old Pierre Harvey win everything, but along with his team-mates, won Quebec's first cross-country relay medal in thirty years.

A five-woman Nordic team was Canada's only entry in the 1980 Olympic Winter Games at Lake Placid, New York. The Firth twins established another Canadian record at the Games by being the first Canadian or American women skiers to compete in three consecutive Olympics. The relay team finished in eighth place with individual placings in the twenties and thirties.

For the first time in Olympic history, Norway finished without a single Nordic gold medal in 1980, and Finland's Juha Mieto, the 6'5'' "Scandinavian Giant," lost the gold medal in the men's 15 kilometre by one one-hundreth of a second to Sweden's Thomas Wassberg.

A tall, lean Russian took the first gold medal of the Games in the 30 kilometre, and then went on to establish an Olympic record as anchorman on the gold medal relay team and as gold medalist in the 50 kilometre race. Nikolai Zimyatov, who said he sang while he skied, was the first man to win three gold medals in the Nordic events in the same Olympics. Soviet domination of the men's events was reaffirmed by the silver medal win of Vasili Rochev in the 30 kilometre. Ivan Lebanov, a relatively unknown racer, gave Bulgaria its first Olympic medal ever by picking up the bronze.

East Germany's Ulrich Wehling felt right at home atop the 70 metre jump at Lake Placid as he prepared to make his final leap in the event considered the "crown of skiing." Wehling already had two Olympic gold medals in the Nordic combined from 1972 and 1976, and wanted his third before he retired after the Lake Placid Games. His success in the 15 kilometre cross-country race and the 70 metre jump made him the only man in Olympic history to capture three consecutive gold medals in the same individual event.

The Soviets and Finns had dominated the women's relay since the 1972 Games, but a fleet-footed foursome from East Germany outclassed all other teams in the event at Lake Placid. Anchored by Barbara Petzold, the 10 kilometre gold medalist, the East Germans were well ahead of the field by the end of the second lap. Much to the chagrin of the veteran Soviet team, the win by the East Germans was a triumph of youth over experience.

Nevertheless, age had some benefits for two of the Soviet relay members, and their silver medal win added to their already impressive Olympic medal count. Galina Kulakova's total was four gold, two silver, and two bronze, and Raisa Smetanin's count was three gold and two silver.

Although not a participant in the 1980 Winter Olympics, Pierre Harvey was a member of the National Team in 1980 and by 1981 had reached North American championship calibre. He won the North American 3 x 10 relay in 1981, the National 15 kilometre in 1981, 1982, and 1983, and the Sett International Del Fondo 30 kilometre race in 1982. From 1981 through 1984 he was twice fifth in the World Cup 15 kilometre events, and six times among the top eight.

Based on his results, he was accepted on the 1984 Olympic team and "rookie" Pierre Harvey added to his Olympic laurels with a twentieth-place finish in the 50 kilometre race.

The German Democratic Republic's Ulrich Wehling won three consecutive gold medals in the Nordic Combined event in 1972, 1976, and here in 1980. *Deutsche Presse-Agentur GmbH*

The triumph of youth over experience at the 1980 Games gave the gold medal to the women of the G.D.R. instead of the veteran Soviets in the 10 kilometre relay event. *Deutsche Presse-Agentur GmbH*

In the 30 kilometre event, Harvey finished just shy of Canada's record nineteenth-place finish in the 15 kilometre by Clarence Servold at Cortina d'Ampezzo, Italy, in 1956.

Six months later, Pierre Harvey was one of four riders entered in the individual road race at the 1984 Olympic Summer Games at Los Angeles, California. Riding themselves into exhaustion to protect the endurance of their best rider Steve Bauer, the team effort by cyclists Louis Garneau, Alain Masson, and Pierre Harvey produced a silver medal finish for Bauer. It was the first medal for Canadians in Olympic cycling since 1908.

When the Firth twins entered their fourth Olympic Winter Games at Sarajevo, Yugoslavia, in 1984, they held just about every Canadian record imaginable in women's cross-country skiing.

Internationally, Shirley Firth had recorded the best World Cup finish ever by a Canadian woman, with her fourth-place finish in the 10 kilometre event in Czechoslovakia in 1981. In 1982 she was ranked eleventh overall in the World Cup standings.

The women's 20 kilometre race was contested for the first time in the Olympics at Sarajevo and Sharon Firth finished with a Canadian best, in twenty-first place. Twin sister Shirley's twenty-second place in the 10 kilometre race was her best Olympic result. No one could catch Finland's Liisa Haemaelainen. The twenty-eight-year-old physiotherapist reaped the majority of gold medals, only losing out in the relay event to the Norwegians.

The Soviet skiers had been expected to dominate the men's events on Sarajevo's Igman plateau but the Swedes, led by 1977 World Cup champion Thomas Wassberg, won the battle for gold medals. Wassberg won the 50 kilometre, and Sweden's powerful newcomer, Gunde Svan, took the gold in the 15 kilometre followed by two Finns, Aki Karvonen and Harri Kirvesniemi. The Norwegians picked up their first Olympic gold medal in eight years by winning the relay race. The winner of the 30 kilometre was Nikolai Zimiatov, the Soviet triple gold medalist from Lake Placid, who covered the course in 1:28:56:3. After the 1984 Winter Games, the thirty-year-old Firth twins said good-bye to Olympic competition, ending brilliant cross-country ski careers that had spanned almost two decades.

Shirley and Sharon Firth are the only Canadians in the history of the Olympics to have competed in four consecutive Winter Games. Admitting their biggest advantage was the fact they were twins and could spread the pressure between them, Shirley and Sharon also gave credit for their success to their parents, to Father Mouchet, and to Bjorger Pettersen. In an interview with freelance journalist and television commentator Jarl Omholt-Jensen, Shirley Firth stated that neither one of them was disappointed they hadn't won an Olympic medal. "I have no regrets at all," she said. "I wouldn't have changed anything. I've learned and seen so much."

In January of 1986, Bjorger Pettersen took a temporary leave of absence from his ranch in British Columbia to join the management team of the XV Olympic Winter Games Organizing Committee in Calgary to oversee the staging of the Nordic events for the 1988 Winter Games.

# The Venue

The Canmore Nordic Centre, site of the Nordic events for the 1988 Olympic Winter Games, is located approximately 100 kilometres west of Calgary, and immediately northwest of the town of Canmore, Alberta.

Constructed by the Alberta Provincial Government at an estimated cost of $17.3 million, the Nordic Centre meets the International Ski Federation and Olympic standards set for cross-country and Nordic Combined courses.

Although the total competitive trail system comprises less than 50 kilometres, use of the terrain is at a maximum with approximately 10 kilometres of ski trails that will function independently for recreational skiers and provide connectors to the town of Canmore and Banff National Park. Approximately 2.5 kilometres of training track has also been constructed for roller skiing during the summer months.

Cross-country races occur over a predetermined distance and the courses and terrain are extremely challenging.

Bleacher-style standing space will accommodate approximately ten thousand spectators at the Nordic Centre. Separate start/finish areas for cross-country skiing and biathlon events will enhance viewing of both sports by spectators and television viewers during the Games.

A number of temporary facilities required for staging the Olympics will include a variety of media trailers on-site, athlete and officials' services, team waxing trailers, timing facilities, a volunteer centre, and an awards presentation area.

Spectator viewing areas and television camera locations along a significant percentage of the course will ensure that racing fans and media will be offered excellent vantage points to watch the Nordic events. The main scoreboard at the start/finish area is easily viewed by spectators, media, officials, and racers.

To comply with the Olympic requirement, snowmakers will provide snowmaking capability and stockpiling facilities.

The design and construction of the Canmore Nordic Centre exemplifies the key objectives of planners to integrate the competitive needs of cross-country skiers with training and recreational needs.

# The Technique

Cross-country ski racing is one long endurance test and it helps if you enjoy your own company.

Indeed, research studies done in Scandinavia contend that Swedish cross-country skiers live ten years longer than the average citizen in their country. Canadians need look no further than Jackrabbit Johannsen to validate the theory.

The basic forward motion on cross-country skis is similar to walking. With the support of poles for balance, beginners soon learn to shuffle along over the flat terrain of a playing field or golf course.

But, spectators won't be seeing much of the "golf course shuffle" at the 1988 Olympics. The transition from touring to good racing results is directly related to physical conditioning, race experience, mastery of technique, and speed.

In cross-country skiing, a backward kick produces a forward glide. A follow-through of the pole push and a weight change from one ski to the other produce a smooth rhythmical motion for the racer. This kick-glide sequence is known as "the diagonal stride" in cross-country jargon.

In past Olympic years, most racers preferred to use the stride and a single or double pole action to race to the finish line. The snow on the tracks was often loose and soft which enabled the racer to get a good amount of traction between the snow and the ski. However, as race courses became more technical and groomed with two set tracks running down the middle of the trail, the hard smooth surface of the deep set grooves offered less and less traction.

To speed themselves up, racers began to use the "marathon skate." Unlike the diagonal stride, in which both skis remained in the set grooves, the technique of the marathon skate was to have one ski in the groove and one ski out. The skating motion used with the outside ski, along with the double pole stance, accelerated the racer along the straightaways.

Needless to say, racers soon discovered that two skis out of the narrow grooves were faster than one. Racers who had trained for years in the traditional method and advocated the diagonal stride were soon left behind as an entirely new crop of racers began to make themselves felt in the winners' circle. Among the medal winners was American Bill Koch.

Koch, a native of Guilford, Vermont, skated extensively during the 30 kilometre race at the 1976 Olympic Winter Games at Innsbruck, Austria. He stunned the field by becoming the first North American to win an Olympic Nordic skiing medal.

Gaining instant celebrity status and being hounded by the media did not impress Bill Koch, who was an intensely private person. After his silver medal victory, he was asked by a reporter at the finish line if he had lived in Vermont all his life. With a twinkle in his eye and a typical shrug of his shoulders, Koch replied: "Not yet."

Using the skating technique again throughout the 1982 ski season, Koch won the overall World Cup championships and proved North Americans could compete against Europe's best.

Prior to the 1984 Olympics, the International Ski Federation was under pressure from proponents of the "Classic" race format to monitor infractions of the no-skate rule. But, for the Ski Federation, the main problem was that there was no clear-cut interpretation as to the basis of a disqualification. Did skating around a corner constitute an infraction? When did the corner end and the track begin? How many skating strides could a racer take before being disqualified? Was it one, two, or three?

Technical delegates of the International Ski Federation initiated a new ruling which disallowed any skating on the last 200 metres of the race. This ruling, although not ideal, applied to all events except the relay. In the relay race, there was no skating allowed 200 metres before the last baton exchange took place.

Pity Ove Aunli of Norway. He would have placed fifth in the 15 kilometre race at the Olympics if he hadn't forgotten the ruling. Aunli was one of several racers to be disqualified as they skated across the finish line at Sarajevo.

The 200 metre rule will not be used for the 1988 Olympic Winter Games.

Herman Smith (Jackrabbit) Johannsen, the first cross-country skier to be inducted to Canada's Sports Hall of Fame, demonstrates the "diagonal stride". *Canadian Ski Museum*

Canada's Pierre Harvey demonstrates the marathon skate, first used officially at the 1976 Games. *Jarl Omholt-Jensen*

# The Rules

There are four Nordic events for women and four events for men in the Olympic cross-country competitions.

The events for women include a 5 and 10 kilometre individual race, a 20 kilometre event and a 4 x 5 kilometre relay. The men's events include a 15, 30, and 50 kilometre race and a 4 x 10 kilometre relay. For men, each individual lap of the relay is 10 kilometres and for women each lap consists of a 5 kilometre distance.

In the individual events, entrants start at thirty-second intervals, but racers from as many as thirty countries are part of the crowd-pleasing mass start in the relay event.

Each course has a single track set on it and the passing skier has the right of way in competition.

The controversy regarding the constant use of the skating technique, instead of only at designated points on the course, erupted into a full-scale battle for international technical directors by 1986. Athletes who had trained in the classical diagonal method (of keeping the skis in the grooves on the track) supported the ruling that disallowed the skating technique. Skaters, on the other hand, supported the inclusion of the technique because they got to the finish line first and won all the races.

Faced with the dilemma, the International Ski Federation instituted a new ruling after the end of the 1986 ski season. Cross-country races are now divided into two categories of "free-technique" and classical. In the free-technique event, the skier can use any cross-country technique he or she wants to, but only classical technique in the classical race.

The Nordic Combined event consists of a 70 metre jump on one day followed by a 15 kilometre cross-country race on the next day. The two best jumps out of three make up the final score. With two disciplines to master in the Nordic Combined, the racers are subject to a more complex scoring system. The winner of the 15 kilometre race is awarded 220 points. For every minute a racer is behind the winner, he loses nine points. The cross-country points are added to the jumping points to determine the winner.

The masterminds of the Inuvik Ski Team: Father Mouchet (left) and Bjorger Pettersen (right). *Courtesy Bjorger Pettersen*

A new Olympic event will be added to the Olympic Nordic Combined program in 1988. A country will enter a Nordic Combined team of three to jump 70 metres one day and ski in a 3 x 10 kilometre relay race the following day.

In 1988 the Gundersen method of scoring the Nordic Combined will be used for the first time in Olympic competition. Ski jumping distances are converted to times, and with a staggered start, the first racer across the finish line will be declared the winner.

# The Equipment

Technical adaptations of racing skis used in well-prepared tracks have resulted in a lighter and somewhat more fragile ski compared to a recreational model.

Racing skis are made of fibreglass and have polyethylene bases to give maximum slide performance. Unlike Alpine skis, cross-country skis do not have steel edges on the bases.

Most racers have at least two pairs of skis. For dry snow conditions, a soft flexible ski that provides good snow contact and grip at the midsection is preferable. In wet snow, a ski with a stiffer midsection reduces contact with slush and minimizes sticking and dragging of the ski base in the glide.

A good pair of skis with the right wax to suit snow conditions on race day is a racer's most important piece of equipment.

The light, flexible cross-country ski pole is used much more in racing than in Alpine ski racing. In fact, the poles must be strong enough to support the propulsion used to push the racer forward through the tracks of the course.

Cane and bamboo poles have been replaced recently with aluminum and steel alloys. New lightweight plastic baskets on the bottom of the poles are designed to help racers avoid hooking their skis through the basket like Sharon Firth did on the home stretch of the 1969 Canadian Junior Championships.

Racing boots are soft leather and have a thin veneer of rubber or plastic on the leather sole. As the boots are subject to wet snow conditions, most skiers have at least two pairs for training and racing.

"If you're cold, you're not working hard enough," is the way some hard core enthusiasts look at it, but racers must learn to dress for the temperature. Light and windproof clothing is a must—muscle cramps from the cold and frostbite don't do much for race results in the Olympics. One-piece nylon stretch suits are popular with racers, and two-piece suits with knicker socks are comfortable and still used by many competitors. A pair of leather gloves and a woollen toque complete the essential racing gear.

A skilled racer assesses the temperature of the snow and matches his favourite combinations of ski wax to conditions. Snow temperatures lag behind air temperatures and if the temperature is rising rapidly on race day, a skier will wait until the last minute before starting to wax. Waxes vary in their properties, are complicated to apply, and often make the difference between winning and losing a race.

# Calgary Preview

To win an Olympic medal in the Nordic events a competitor doesn't have to be a Soviet or a Scandinavian, but it helps.

All eleven gold medals awarded in the cross-country and Nordic Combined events at Sarajevo were taken home by the Norwegians, Finns, Swedes, and Soviets.

## Men

Gunde Svan, Thomas Wassberg and Torgny Mogren of Sweden, Finland's Harri Kirvesniemi and Aki Karvonen, and Norway's Vegard Ulvang were the dominant cross-country racers last year.

Svan, however, is by far the favourite, and if last year's pre-Olympic races at the Canmore Nordic Centre are any indication of things to come, he will definitely be the one to beat.

Other solid contenders are Soviets Vladimir Smirnov and Alexandre Batuk, relay silver medalists at Sarajevo in 1984. Czechoslovakia, France, Switzerland, Italy, Yugoslavia, Austria, and Spain will also enter the men's events in 1988.

Despite the absence of retired silver medalist Bill Koch, American Jim Galanes will be back for another Olympic try.

Canada's National Champion, Pierre Harvey, chalked up two fourth-place finishes on the 1985 World Cup circuit, and was ranked ninth in the world in 1986. Being the first Canadian to break into the top ten in World Cup standings, Harvey established himself as a power to be reckoned with. His Olympic cycling team-mate, Alain Masson of Laval, won Canada's first international cross-country medal with a third-place bronze finish at the University Games in Belluno, Italy, in 1985.

Richard Weber (now retired) and Yves Bilodeau were members of the Quebec foursome that specialized in the 30 kilometre relay, and Bilodeau will be back for the Olympics in 1988. Their history-making gold medal relay performance in an International Ski Federation sanctioned meet at Le Revard, France, in 1986, was Canada's first gold ever at a European championship.

Then last season, the Canadians posted their best ever relay finish at the World Nordic ski championships at Oberstdorf, West Germany, in February. Yves Bilodeau, twenty-five, of Quebec City had a time of twenty-five minutes, 53.7 seconds in the first leg; Wayne Dustin, twenty-one, of Sault Ste. Marie, Ontario, completed the second with a strong showing of 25:09.5; Alain Masson, twenty-five, of Laval, Quebec, who fell during his run, had a time of 25:20.7; and Pierre Harvey, twenty-nine, of St. Lambert-de-Levis, Quebec, raced the anchor leg in 25:03.3. The win guaranteed both Masson and Dustin a berth on the 1988 Olympic team, along with Pierre Harvey and Yves Bilodeau, who had already been selected for Olympic participation due to previous top results. Canada's eighth-place finish in the 4 x 10 kilometre cross-country, freestyle-technique relay race at Oberstdorf was a morale boost for the men's team in 1987. Head coach Marty Hall was looking for more top results and he got them the next month.

On Saturday, March 7, 1987, at Falun, Sweden, Pierre Harvey became the first Canadian to win a World Cup cross-country ski race, beating his closest rival by more than one minute. Harvey, whose best previous high in a World Cup race was a fourth-place finish, set a blistering pace in the 30 kilometre, freestyle-technique event and clocked one hour, seventeen minutes and 46.5 seconds. Alexei Prokirorov of the Soviet Union was second in 1:18:58.4, while Torgny Mogren of Sweden was third in 1:19:08:2.

"This is the best day of my life in skiing," said twenty-nine-year-old Pierre Harvey. "To be first here in Sweden is really exciting for me because all the best competitors were here today and it was a very strong field."

Just one week after Pierre Harvey made history at Falun, Sweden, newspaper headlines read "Harvey Wins Again" as he came from behind to pass some 2,000 of the 5,900 skiers in the 50th Norwegian Birkebeiner event. Harvey covered the 55 kilometre distance between Lillehammer and Rena in a winning time of three hours eight minutes and 30 seconds to become the first Canadian to ever win the world-famous Birkebeiner event.

With a certain degree of "host country luck," there may be some reshuffling of names at the top during the 1988 Olympic Winter Games in Calgary. When asked what the Olympics mean to him, Pierre Harvey remarked, "The Olympic Games are the dream of every athlete, and the Winter Games are a once-in-a-lifetime situation when they occur in your own country. Nothing can replace the feeling of representing your country in front of the world, and all the training you can do is worth it just for the hope of going up to the podium."

No one could catch Finland's Liisa Haemaelainen at the 1984 Olympic Winter Games, as she reaped the majority of the gold medals in the women's events. *Deutsche Presse-Agentur GmbH*

## Women

The double gold medal winner from the 1984 Olympics, Liisa Haemaelainen of Finland, has retired, but her team-mate Mario Matikainen, winner of both the 1986 and 1987 World Cups, could easily feature at the 1988 Olympic Winter Games. The Swedes headed the roll call in 1987; nevertheless Swedish racer Marie-Helen Westin, Christina Bruegger of Switzerland and Anette Boe of Norway will be attempting to hold off a strong challenge from the Soviet women. Two Soviets in particular, Anfisa Rezcova and Larisa Ptitsyna, are outstanding competitors, and took silver and bronze medals respectively at the world Nordic ski championships in 1987 at Oberstdorf, West Germany.

The Czech women are skiing well, and so are the Norwegians, especially the relay team. The Swedes' chief competition could come from Norway's Brit Pettersen, who won the gold medal in the relay event at the 1984 Olympics. Berit Aunli, Anne Jahren, and Marianne Dahlmo make up the rest of the powerfully balanced Norwegian team.

Other prominent competitors include veteran Olympic competitor Sue Long who heads the American team.

After participating in four Olympics, no one could say that the Firth twins didn't have staying power. With their recent retirement, the field has opened up to some promising new Canadian skiers. National team member Angela Schmidt-Foster will be back to head the women's team. Schmidt-Foster took some big bows after the 10 kilometre classic event held at the Canmore Nordic Centre in 1987 when she raced to a third-place finish, the first ever for a Canadian in World Cup competition.

The next day she paced the Canadian team of Carol Gibson, of Camrose, Alberta, Jean McAllister of Ottawa, Ontario, and Marie-Andre Masson of Victoriaville, Quebec, to a second-place finish in the relay event. At no other time in the history of cross-country skiing in Canada had there been such a victory for Canadian Nordic athletes. "I think this has proven we can be competitive with the world, and that we belong at the top," said Angela Schmidt-Foster, after the race.

Among the recruits vying for Olympic team selection will be Ottawa skier Lorna Daudrich and one of Canada's most promising junior skiers, Jane Vincent of Ontario.

## Nordic Combined

Canadian Nordic Combined hopefuls are Jon and Dave Servold of Camrose, Alberta, and John Hieghland of Thunder Bay, Ontario. First cousins Jon and Dave Servold live and train fulltime in Canmore, Alberta, site of the 1988 Olympic Nordic events. Another top contender for the Canadian team was Hugh Pomeroy of Quebec who was tragically killed near Lake Placid, New York, in the autumn of 1986, while training on the highway on rollerskis. He was a member of the National Nordic team.

United States champion Kerry Lynch nearly broke into the Olympic winners' circle at Sarajevo with his third-place finish in the 15 kilometre race. Unfortunately, his ski jumps didn't match his cross-country skiing accomplishments, and he lost out in his bid for a medal. Both Lynch and national team member Pat Ahern will be back for another bid for the medals in 1988.

The 1984 Olympic Nordic Combined title went to Norway's Tom Sandberg, who finished first in the 70 metre jump and was runner-up to Finland's first-place finisher in the 15 kilometre race, Jouko Karjalainen.

As the Games approach, the top favourites look like Hans Peter Pohl and Hermann Weinbuch of West Germany, Hippolyt Kempf of Switzerland, and Soviet Allar Lewandi. Torbjorn Loekken of Norway, winner of the Combined pre-Olympic competition at Canada Olympic Park and Canmore Nordic Centre, was the tour leader halfway through the 1986/87 ten-event schedule. Loekken will have the Norwegians counting on him in the 1988 Olympic Winter Games in Calgary, especially after winning the World Championship at the end of the 1987 season.

# Canadians at the Olympic Winter Games
# NORDIC SKIING
# CROSS COUNTRY

---

### 1924 Chamonix — I Olympic Winter Games

Canada did not participate.

### 1928 St. Moritz — II Olympic Winter Games

Leohan, L., Putnam, M., Thompson, W.

**MEN**

| *18 kilometre* | *Nordic Combined* |
|---|---|
| 37. William Thompson | 27. Merritt Putman |
| 40. Merritt Putman | |

---

### 1932 Lake Placid — III Olympic Winter Games

Bagguley, H., Ball, W., Clark, W., Currie, J., Douglas, D., Dupuis, G., Engstad, K., Gravel, A., Heggtveit, H., Hogan, J., Lafleur, L., Nordmoe, J., Oliver, B., Pangman, A., Ryan, W., Tache, J., Taylor, J., Wilson, R., Wright, P.

**MEN**

| *18 kilometre* | *Nordic Combined* |
|---|---|
| 35. Arthur Pangman | 10. Jostien Nordmoe |
| 38. William Clark | 24. Howard Bagguley |
| 39. John Taylor | 30. Arthur Gravel |
| 40. John Currie | 31. Ross Wilson |

*50 kilometre*
16. Kaare Engstad

## 1936 Garmisch-Partenkirchen — IV Olympic Winter Games

Baadsvik, K.J., Ball, W., Gagne, N.C., Clark, W., Mobraeten, T.

**MEN**

*18 kilometre*
47. William G. Clark

*Nordic Combined*
31. Tormod Mobraeten
39. William G. Clark
41. Karl Johan Baadsvik
46. William Ball

## 1948 St. Moritz — V Olympic Winter Games

Bernier, L., Dennie, T., Irwin, W., Mobraeten, T.

**MEN**

*18 kilometre*
73. Tom Dennie
81. Wilbur Irwin

*Nordic Combined*
37. Wilbur Irwin

## 1952 Oslo — VI Olympic Winter Games

Carbonneau, J., Charland, J., Laferte, L., Richer, C.

**MEN**

*18 kilometre*
52. Claude Richer
70. Jacques Carbonneau

*Nordic Combined*
Canada did not participate.

## 1956 Cortina d'Ampezzo — VII Olympic Winter Games

Charland, J., Servold, C., Servold, I.B.

**MEN**

*15 kilometre*
19. Clarence Servold

*30 kilometre*
37. Clarence Servold

*50 kilometre*
22. Clarence Servold

*Nordic Combined*
27. Irvin B. Servold

## 1960 Squaw Valley — VIII Olympic Winter Games

Servold, C., Servold, I.B.

**MEN**

*15 kilometre*
35. Clarence Servold
47. Irvin B. Servold

*30 kilometre*
36. Clarence Servold
40. Irvin B. Servold

*Nordic Combined*
25. Irvin B. Servold
28. Clarence Servold

## 1964 Innsbruck — IX Olympic Winter Games

Gartrell, F., Luoma, E., MacLeod, D., Portmann, F., Rautio, M.

**MEN**

*15 kilometre*
34. Donald MacLeod

*4 x 10 kilometre relay*
15. Donald MacLeod,
Franz Portmann,

51. Franz Portmann
61. Eric Luoma
65. Martti Rautio

*30 kilometre*
38. Donald MacLeod
52. Martti Rautio

Eric Luoma,
Martti Rautio

*Nordic Combined*
Canada did not participate.

## 1968 Grenoble — X Olympic Winter Games

Karhu, E., Pettersen, R., Rees, D., Skulbru, N.

**MEN**

*15 kilometre*
56. Nils Skulbru
61. David Rees
63. Rolf Pettersen

*30 kilometre*
52. Nils Skulbru
58. David Rees
61. Rolf Pettersen

*50 kilometre*
46. David Rees

*4 x 10 kilometre relay*
14. Nils Skulbru,
Rolf Pettersen,
Esko Karhu,
David Rees

*Nordic Combined*
Canada did not participate.

## 1972 Sapporo — XI Olympic Winter Games

Allen, R., Allen, R., Firth, S., Firth, S., Hunter, M., Kelly, F., Omholt-Jensen, J., Sander, H.

**MEN**

*15 kilometre*
45. Malcolm Hunter
49. Fred Kelly
50. Roger Allen
52. Jarl Omholt-Jensen

*30 kilometre*
43. Malcolm Hunter
50. Jarl Omholt-Jensen

*4 x 10 kilometre relay*
13. Fred Kelly,
Roger Allen,
Jarl Omholt-Jensen,
Malcolm Hunter

**WOMEN**

*5 kilometre*
26. Sharon Firth
35. Shirley Firth
40. Roseanne Allen
41. Helen Sander

*10 kilometre*
24. Sharon Firth
40. Helen Sander

*3 x 5 kilometre relay*
10. Sharon Firth,
Shirley Firth,
Roseanne Allen,
Helen Sander

*Nordic Combined*
Canada did not participate.

## 1976 Innsbruck — XII Olympic Winter Games

Bullock, B., Day, E., Firth, S., Firth, S., Groothuysen, J., Holloway, S., Lennie, E., Miller, E., Puiras, R., Skinstad, H., Sjolund, K.

**MEN**

*15 kilometre*
33. Bert Bullock
56. Hans Skinstad
59. Edward Day
67. Ernie Lennie

*30 kilometre*
30. Hans Skinstad
31. Bert Bullock
42. Edward Day
56. Reijo Puiras

**WOMEN**

*5 kilometre*
28. Shirley Firth
30. Sharon Firth
31. Joan Groothuysen
34. Esther Miller

*10 kilometre*
28. Sharon Firth
29. Shirley Firth
32. Susan Holloway
34. Joan Groothuysen

*50 kilometre*
22. Hans Skinstad
37. Edward Day
41. Ernie Lennie

*4 x 10 kilometre relay*
12. Bert Bullock,
    Ernie Lennie,
    Edward Day,
    Hans Skinstad

*Nordic Combined*
33. Kurt Sjolund

---

### 1980 Lake Placid — XIII Olympic Winter Games

Firth, S., Firth, S., Groothuysen, J., Miller, E., Schmidt, A.

**WOMEN**

*5 kilometre*
27. Joan Groothuysen
28. Shirley Firth
29. Angela Schmidt
35. Sharon Firth

*10 kilometre*
23. Angela Schmidt
24. Shirley Firth
33. Esther Miller
34. Joan Groothuysen

*4 x 5 kilometre relay*
7. Shirley Firth,
   Joan Groothuysen,
   Susan Holloway,
   Sharon Firth

*4 x 5 kilometre relay*
8. Angela Schmidt,
   Shirley Firth,
   Joan Groothuysen,
   Esther Miller

---

### 1984 Sarajevo — XIV Olympic Winter Games

Harvey, P., Firth S., Firth, S., Schmidt, A.

**MEN**

*15 kilometre*
21. P. Harvey

*30 kilometre*
21. P. Harvey

*50 kilometre*
20. P. Harvey

*4 x 10 kilometre relay*
Canada did not participate.

**WOMEN**

*5 kilometre*
28. Shirley Firth
29. Sharon Firth
39. Angela Schmidt

*10 kilometre*
22. Shirley Firth
29. Sharon Firth
36. Angela Schmidt

*20 kilometre*
21. Sharon Firth
25. Shirley Firth

*4 x 5 kilometre relay*
Canada did not participate.

*Nordic Combined*
Canada did not participate.

---

## Canadians at the Olympic Winter Games
# NORDIC COMBINED

### 1924 Chamonix — I Olympic Winter Games

Not held.

### 1928 St. Moritz — II Olympic Winter Games

27. Merritt Putman

### 1932 Lake Placid — III Olympic Winter Games

10. Jostien Nordmoe
24. Howard Bagguley
30. Arthur Gravel
31. Ross Wilson

### 1936 Garmisch-Partenkirchen — IV Olympic Winter Games

31. Tormod Mobraeten
39. William G. Clark
41. Karl Johan Baadsvik
46. William Ball

### 1948 St. Moritz — V Olympic Winter Games

37. Wilbur Irwin

### 1952 Oslo — VI Olympic Winter Games

Canada did not participate.

### 1956 Cortina d'Ampezzo — VII Olympic Winter Games

27. Irvin B. Servold

### 1960 Squaw Valley — VIII Olympic Winter Games

25. Irvin B. Servold
28. Clarence Servold

### 1964 - 1972

Canada did not participate.

### 1976 Innsbruck — XII Olympic Winter Games

33. Kurt Sjolund

### 1980 Lake Placid — XIII Olympic Winter Games

Canada did not participate.

### 1984 Sarajevo — XIV Olympic Winter Games

Canada did not participate.

# Ski Jumping

Canada Olympic Park
February 14, 17, 20

*Mathieson, Calgary*

On behalf of the Canadian Ski Association Ski Jumping discipline, I am delighted to write the introduction to the exciting sport of ski jumping.

This so-called "crazy" sport is much safer than people tend to believe. And, with better footwear, more aerodynamic suits and faster, more stable skis, ski jumping has given Canadians something to be very proud of.

The sensation of flying on skis is difficult to describe. But, when soaring through the air from a 70 or 90 metre jump with the air pressure forcing against my body and skis, the floating sensation is definitely the ultimate experience for me.

Nevertheless, it is in man-versus-man and man-versus-ski where the real challenge of ski jumping exists. Ski jumpers require not only a great deal of physical strength, but more importantly a great deal of technical skill and mental preparation.

During my eight years as a member of Canada's national team, I have watched the tremendous growth and development of ski jumping in Canada.

Despite the fact that a successful future for ski jumping is virtually assured with the construction of the new facilities at Canada Olympic Park in Calgary, the sport of ski jumping has had difficult times in Canada. After the disastrous 1976 Olympics when most of the team members had either retired or were removed from the team, the sport began a rebuilding process that would eventually produce its greatest ski jumpers who would prepare themselves for the next three Olympics.

Over the past ten years, the sport and the athletes have changed and put Canada on the map in ski jumping. Our young Canadians have done exceptionally well in this sport by winning back-to-back Junior World Championships in 1979 and 1980, in addition to winning numerous World Cup events. With the only major 70 and 90 metre ski jumping complex in Canada located at Thunder Bay, Ontario, Canada has had very respectable results even though the best possible training for Canadian ski jumpers has been limited. The legacy of the 1988 Olympic Winter Games will be the new ski jumping facilities in Calgary that will give Canadians the training centre required in their own country to help strengthen their sport.

Canada has yet to win an Olympic medal for ski jumping. As a Canadian, I feel very fortunate to have the opportunity to compete in my own country at the Olympic Winter Games. As a member of Canada's National Ski Jumping Team, I think we will achieve that gold medal in Calgary in 1988 that we were searching for in Sarajevo in 1984.


Horst Bulau
*Winner of 13 World Cup events, placing second overall in the 1983 World Cup standings, and a member of Canada's Olympic Winter team in 1980, 1984 and 1988.*

# The History

When the Canadian Pacific Railroad was completed from east to west in 1885, the last spike was driven at Craigellachie, located twenty-eight miles west of Revelstoke, British Columbia.

Scandinavian miners and lumbermen were among the new citizens who arrived by train to settle in the little railroad town. Before coming to Revelstoke, many of them had taken their ski jumping skills to snowbound iron mines of Michigan and Minnesota in the United States, and to Eastern Canada where they met with success in Ontario and Quebec.

The first ski club in Revelstoke was formed in 1891 and the membership list read like a Norwegian smorgasbord. During the long winter months, the Olsons, the Carlsons, the Gunnarsens, the Halversons, the Nelsens, the Larsons, and the Christiansons did what they loved doing best—ski jumping.

Most of Revelstoke's ski jumping enthusiasts had learned their favourite sport in Scandinavia where Sondre Nordheim recorded the first officially measured ski jump of 30.5 metres in Norway in 1860.

Many years ago, a farmer scuffed up with his boot what appeared to be an old coin buried on a Norwegian mountainside. Upon closer inspection, he discovered it to be a silver medal inscribed:

CANADIAN SKI CHAMPIONSHIPS
ROSSLAND, BRITISH COLUMBIA—1900

Radio Oslo tried unsuccessfully to find the owner. The medal was then sent to the Canadian Broadcasting Corporation in Montreal and eventually it ended up in the Rossland Historical Museum.

How a medal won by Alex Olson of Revelstoke ended up in Norway is anyone's guess, but at the same Canadian Ski Championships in 1900, the gold medal for ski jumping was won by Rossland's Olaus Jeldness. Jeldness had distinguished himself as the organizer of Canada's first winter carnival in 1898. Born in 1856 at Stangvik, Norway, Olaus Jeldness left for the United States when he was sixteen. During the next ten years, fortune favoured the young Norwegian as he worked his way through the mines of Michigan, Colorado, Oregon, and Montana.

Backed by British capital, Jeldness arrived in Rossland, British Columbia, where he made a fortune selling the Velvet Mine for $250,000. Not only was he wealthy, but Jeldness definitely had a flair for showmanship. When he gave a ski jumping demonstration off the face of Rossland's Red Mountain, the citizens of the tiny mining community lined Columbia Avenue for a glance at their sensational hometown hero.

By the late 1800s, Olaus Jeldness was the best ski jumper in North America, and had the medals to prove it. He was followed in time by British Columbians Torgal Noren and Engwald Engen, and Harvey Lunn from Ishpeming, Michigan.

The intense, but friendly rivalry between Rossland and Revelstoke ski jumpers in the 1920s became a legend of its own, but the fact remained that the city of Revelstoke had the biggest ski jumping hill in North America.

Judge Iverson, President of the Western Canada Ski Associ-

The legendary Olaus Jeldness, organizer of Canada's first winter carnival in Rossland, British Columbia, in 1898, holding his nine foot (275 cm) skis. *Courtesy Sam Wormington*

A ski-jumping demonstration to a crowd of 10,000 in 1921 at the Calgary Exhibition and Stampede Grounds. *Glenbow Archives*

ation, had taken it upon himself to explore the steep slopes around Revelstoke, and it was on Mount Revelstoke itself that he discovered the natural ski jumping site overlooking the city. In 1913, the Chamber of Commerce of Revelstoke donated $1,000 for hill improvements, and the Dominion Government agreed to lease the land to the city for a ski jump.

The Great Ski Hill at Revelstoke had an inrun (approach) that measured over 2,000 feet from top to bottom and the first jumping competitions shattered all existing world records. Henry Hall of Detroit, Michigan, recorded the best professional jump of 229 feet (61.26 metres) and Nels Nelson, captain of the Revelstoke Ski Club, posted the record amateur jump of 201 feet (60.80 metres).

During the annual ski jumping tournaments at Revelstoke, private homes and every hotel in the city were filled with thousands of spectators who came to see the highfliers. To accommodate the overflow, the Canadian Pacific Railroad sidetracked sleeping cars for the duration of the competition.

For the next twenty-five years, ski jumping became one of Canada's most popular winter spectator sports. Ski jumpers crisscrossed the country promoting and developing their sport in British Columbia, the Rockies, and across the prairies to the "cliffs" of Ottawa's Rockcliffe Park and the slopes of Mount Royal in Montreal. Professional ski jumpers and amateurs alike hurtled down wooden trestle jumps to the delight of Canadians everywhere.

One of the wackiest ideas for advertising the Calgary Exhibition and Stampede took place in 1921 for the Canadian Ski Jumping Championships. Promoters erected a wooden ski jump on top of the grandstand and more than ten thousand people showed up at the Stampede Grounds to watch the competition.

Among the top-notchers in the east were Ted Devlin and Sigard and Hans Lockeberg of Ottawa, and Adolf Olsen of Berlin Mills, New Hampshire, who boasted that he did somersaults off the ski hill at Rockcliffe Park in Ottawa, for free. The Governor General was among the ten thousand spectators who watched two university students do a tandem somersault off a ski jump designed by Gunnar Sjelderup at Fairy Lake near Hull, Quebec.

Western Canada produced its share of prominent jumpers including Revelstoke's champion female ski-jumper of the world.

Isabel Coursier had grown up in Revelstoke, and like most children who lived there, she started skiing as soon as she could walk. Each winter she would watch the boys practise their ski jumps and longed to try it, but was never asked. One winter carnival, she was the only girl who entered the "ski-joring" competition, a race in which a skier is pulled behind a pony going full throttle. She beat all the boys. That year she was invited to practise ski jumping on the "Boys' Hill" which was a smaller version of the Great Ski Hill on Mount Revelstoke.

Coursier's best jump of 75 feet (23 metres) was recorded while she was in high school, and after graduation she headed for McGill University to study physical education. Her ski jumping reputation followed her to Quebec, and during her university days she gave exhibitions throughout the Laurentians and the United States.

Isabel Coursier returned to the west to take up her duties

as a physical education instructress at the Provincial Normal School in Victoria, British Columbia. After repeated requests from her admirers in Revelstoke, she agreed to participate in the 1922 winter carnival. It was there that she set the amateur women's world ski jumping record. An article in the *Calgary Herald* described her astonishing accomplishment:

> The champion woman amateur ski-jumper of the world, who has been giving such spectacular exhibitions of the great Scandinavian sport in Montreal and in the recent open amateur ski-jumping competitions at Quebec, is a Western Canadian girl . . . Isabel Coursier of Revelstoke, B.C. Her exhibition record is now 85 feet, but in practice jumps she had made 101 and 103 feet.

Unfortunately for Isabel Coursier, women ski jumpers were not invited to participate in the first Olympic Winter Games at Chamonix, France, in 1924. Indeed, Canada was not represented in the ski-jumping events at the inaugural Games.

Norway provided the star attractions with a clean sweep of the medals by Jacob Thams, Narve Bonna, and Thorleif Haug. Fifty years later, a computation error was discovered in the Olympic record books and fourth-place finisher Andres Haugen of the United States team was informed he had placed third and was awarded his bronze medal at age eighty-three. There was no official protest from Thorleif Haug who had been demoted to fourth place—he had been dead for forty years.

The year following the 1924 Olympics, Nels Nelson made a world record jump of 240 feet off the famous jump in his hometown. His amateur world record stood for six years. But it was another thing to get him over to the Olympics in Switzerland for the 1928 Games.

Nelson fired yard engines for Canadian Pacific Railroad in Revelstoke, and could barely afford to be an amateur jumper, let alone a world traveller. In order to get to the Olympics, he signed up on a tramp steamer with the idea of working his way across the Atlantic.

But when senior Olympic officials found out about his mode of travel to the Games, his trip was vetoed. The consensus: a tramp steamer was not the mode of travel befitting an Olympic athlete. Nels Nelson stayed home and missed the 1928 Olympics.

The 1922 Women's Amateur Champion Ski Jumper of the World, Isabel Coursier, of Revelstoke, British Columbia. *Revelstoke and District Historical Association*

Gerald Dupuis of Ottawa was Canada's first ski jumper to compete in the Olympics in 1928 and finished in a respectable sixteenth place in the 70 metre. It would take more than fifty years for Dupuis' performance to be surpassed, by a fifteen-year-old full-blooded Ojibwa Indian boy.

The Scandinavians continued to chalk up honours at St. Moritz, Switzerland, but Norwegian Jacob Thams suffered a crippling fall while defending his 1924 silver medal. He vaulted 73 metres off the jump which had safely been designed for only a 65 metre leap, and his accident was a grim reminder that ski jumping was not for the faint of heart.

The silver medal was awarded to Birger Ruud, the senior member of three Ruud brothers who were born in the little mining town of Kongsberg, Norway. For years to come, the Ruuds would become the undisputed leaders in the sport of ski jumping, but they would have some competition from Revelstoke, B.C. Unfortunately, it wouldn't be Nels Nelson.

In November of 1932, Nels Nelson accidently shot his left hand off on a duck-hunting trip in Montana. Out of contention for the 1932 Olympic Winter Games at Lake Placid, New York, Nels Nelsen recovered sufficiently to turn his coaching talents toward Revelstoke's Bob Lymburne.

Lymburne began ski jumping in 1925 when he was thirteen years old and by 1927 he had broken the world junior record with a jump of 165 feet. Bob Lymburne led a four-man jumping team into the 1932 Winter Games including Jacques Landry from the Ottawa Ski Club, Arnold Stone from the Grouse Mountain Ski Club, and Leslie Gagne from the Montreal Ski Club. Lymburne placed a respectable nineteenth, as Canada's best finish.

Birger Ruud won the first of two Olympic gold medals in the ski jump and the silver was won by Hans Beck who had grown up with the Ruud brothers in Kongsberg.

In 1931 Birger Ruud held the world record of 76.50 metres until his brother Sigmund broke it during the same season in Davos, Switzerland, with a leap of 81.50 metres. But after the 1932 Olympic Winter Games, Bob Lymburne made good his word that he would bring back the world's ski jumping record to Revelstoke, B.C.

On March 12, 1932, Bob Lymburne did just that, and broke the world's ski jumping record by five feet with a jump of 269 feet (82 metres). Sigmund Ruud, holding the world record of 264 feet (80.47 metres), was relegated to second place in the world standings.

In 1933, Bob Lymburne did it again. He attained the honour of world ski jumping champion for the second year in a row with a jump of 287 feet (87.50 metres) on his home hill, and bettered by six feet the record held by Alf Engen of Salt Lake City, Utah.

No one was more pleased for Bob Lymburne than Nels Nelson. When the distance of 287 feet was announced to the thousands of fans lining the jump, Nelson raised his hat and shouted, "Ladies and gentlemen, you have just seen a new world's record." (*The Revelstoke Review*)

For the first time in ski jumping history, the 300 foot (91.44

metre) mark was passed in Yugoslavia in 1934 by Norway's Birger Ruud who leaped a record 303.5 feet. Not to be outdone by his little brother, Sigmund Ruud's next jump sent him hurtling off the lip at over 160 km an hour. He leaped 313.5 feet (95.56 metres), but fell when he landed.

There would be no re-match for the Ruud brothers and Bob Lymburne at the next Olympics in 1936. Lymburne suffered a bad fall in 1935 at Revelstoke, and his jumping career came to an abrupt end.

Despite the fact that Birger Ruud managed a never-equalled downhill and ski jump gold medal at the Winter Olympics in 1936 at Garmisch-Partenkirchen, Germany, he would have another reason to remember his Nazi hosts at the Games. All three Ruud brothers were destined to spend the war in a German concentration camp.

The best showing by the Canadians at the 1936 Games was a fourteenth-place finish by Tormod Mobraeten of Camrose, Alberta. The results were impressive, despite the team being without Percival Christian "Punch" Bott of Montreal, Quebec.

Percy Bott won the Montreal novice jumping championship at nine years of age and was nicknamed the "Half-Pint Champ of Côte des Neiges" where he was born. He competed for the first time in the 1930 National Ski Jumping Championships in Ottawa at age twelve, and was billed as "The Schoolboy Wonder."

The Canadian Ski Association's ruling on jumping competence overruled restrictions of age in those days, but the International Olympic Committee's rule book read differently. In order to compete in the Olympics, an athlete had to be eighteen years of age. Percy Bott, the boy who had won the Canadian Ski Jumping Championship twice while still attending high school, missed out on the prewar Olympics of 1936, since he was only seventeen.

By 1940, Bott had chalked up eleven national championship medals and would have been Canada's premier hope for a medal at the Olympic Winter Games in 1940 or 1944, if there had been any. But, as "Punch" Bott said, "Hitler got there before I did."

The war took its toll on Canada's young men, including Revelstoke's Hans Gunnarsen, the Dominion Ski Jumping Champion of 1940. Enlisting with a Canadian artillery unit in 1941, Gunnarsen followed the course of battle through France, Belgium, and into Holland, where he was killed in action in 1944.

Norway's Birger Ruud provided a link between the Olympics past and present when he competed in the ski jumping event

Revelstoke's Nels Nelson makes a world record jump of 240 feet off the famous jump in his hometown in 1925. *Revelstoke and District Historical Association*

Bob Lymburne, member of the 1932 Olympic ski jumping team. He achieved the world record for 1932 — 82 metres. *Revelstoke and District Historical Association*

Norwegian Birger Ruud, considered by ski-jumpers as the best jumper in history, demonstrates the "hands-forward" position used by many ski jumpers in early Olympic competition. *Norwegian Olympic Committee*

at the 1948 Olympic Winter Games in St. Moritz, Switzerland. Making an incredible comeback at age thirty-six, Ruud won the silver medal behind gold medalist Petter Hugsted. Teammate Thorleif Schjelderup won the bronze and gave Norway a three-way sweep in the medals.

Among the Canadian ski jumpers at the 1948 Olympics were brothers Albert and Wilbur Irwin. Bert and Bill had started skiing on their home hill in Princeton, British Columbia, a one rope-tow operation managed by their father Benjamin.

During World War II, Bill Irwin moved east to Winnipeg, Manitoba, where he trained the Canadian ski troops. Both brothers were invited to join the 1948 Olympic ski team and competed in the downhill, slalom, and the combined. After the Winter Games, Bill Irwin took charge of the Port Arthur Ski Club and eventually set up Loch Lomond, his own ski resort near Thunder Bay, Ontario. Twenty-five years later, his son Dave would be recruited as one of Canada's daring new downhillers, the Crazy Canucks.

By the end of the 1952 Olympics at Oslo, Norway, the Norwegian ski jumpers had won fourteen of the eighteen medals awarded since the Olympics began in 1924.

Although Arnfinn Bergmann won the gold medal for Norway in 1952, ski jumper Lucien Laferte of Trois-Rivières, Quebec, gave him a run for his money for showmanship.

With the wind at his back, Laferte began his fast descent of the inrun and hurtled off the jump at a hundred kilometres an hour. As he leaned out over his skis, the crowd gasped in disbelief as they watched one of his skis fall off in mid-air. But the imperturbable Laferte glided down to a perfect one-legged landing, did two wide sweeping turns on one ski and came to a stop in front of the enclosure where the Royal Family was sitting. With the aplomb of a champion, the Canadian bowed deeply to His Royal Highness as the crowd roared with approval. In return, Lucien Laferte received a standing ovation from the King of Norway.

It was not surprising that the nation that had established itself as the ski jumping capital of the world would finish up out of the medals at the 1956 Olympic Winter Games at Cortina d'Ampezzo, Italy. A contributing factor to Norway's ski jumping doldrums was the fact that it was resolutely opposed to "monster jumping" (later to become a sport called Ski Flying). Norway discouraged team members from taking part in the competitions and let it be known that it considered the monster jumps a discredit to the sport of ski jumping.

The longer jumps were constructed to make distance performances possible and records were shattered off the new ski jumps at Placia in Yugoslavia (120 metres) in 1948, and on the even bigger jump at Oberstdorf in Bavaria in 1950 (135 metres).

Ski jumpers who competed on the monster jumps made longer jumps and had more time in the air to experiment with different aerodynamic positions. These jumpers soon surpassed the Norwegians and it showed up in the ski jumping results of the 1956 Olympics. For the first time in the history of the Games, Finland won both the gold and the silver medals with

Antti Hyvarinen and Aulis Kallakorpi finishing in the top spots. East German Harry Glass took the bronze.

East German ski jumper Helmut Recknagel finally won a gold medal for his country in 1960 at the Olympic Winter Games at Squaw Valley and was the first non-Nordic to do so. The best finish for Canada was thirty-third place for Jacques Charland of Trois-Rivières, Quebec. Later on, in the mid-1960s, Charland became the first Canadian ski jumper to jump over 122 metres at a ski-flying competition in Yugoslavia.

For the first time in the Olympic ski jumping events, jumps took place on both large and small hills at the 1964 Olympic Winter Games at Innsbruck, Austria. The ski-jumping results in the 1964 Winter Games indicated that the Norwegians had become reconciled with the fact that longer and bigger ski jumps were here to stay. Toralf Engan won the gold medal on the 90 metre jump and a silver on the 70 metre. Since then, his country has ended up out of the medals in Olympic competition.

A change in the ski-jumping format was established at the 1968 Olympic Winter Games at Grenoble, France. During the Innsbruck Games in 1964, ski jumpers had been allowed three jumps for their Olympic competition, but the best two counted toward the score. Unfortunately, many jumpers had taken extra chances and risks, knowing their poor distance mark could be discarded. The scoring had become so complicated for officials that the rule book changed to allow only two jumps in each event.

The Soviets made their long-delayed entry into the gold medal circle when Vladimir Beloussov won the 90 metre event and a Czech broke the Scandinavian-Finnish hold on the event when Jiri Raska won the 70 metre.

The 1972, Japan produced three of the most spectacular ski jumpers to ever go off the 70 metre hill. The host nation of the eleventh Olympic Winter Games recorded a one, two, three medal sweep led by Yukio Kasaya. The 90 metre was won by a Polish ski jumper. Wojciech Fortuna's first jump was so incredibly long that no one held it against him when he finished in a dismal twenty-second place on his second jump. Buoyed by his first jump distance, Wojciech Fortuna won the first gold ever for Poland in ski jumping.

Canada's best-place finish was a seventeenth in the 90 metre jump by Zdenek Mezl, a native of Czechoslovakia who had been training with the Canadians on Camp Fortune's 60 metre jump. Despite the fact that Mezl's placing was admirable, insiders knew that ski jumping had hit the skids in Canada.

The slump had begun in postwar Canada. Many of the Canadian ski-jumping greats didn't make it home from the war, and there was no one left to carry on the tradition. Alpine skiing had also captured the attention of the young generation, and interest in ski jumping in Canada slowly diminished.

Through lack of interest and money, the Trois-Rivières Club closed down, and the old ski jump at the Montreal Ski Club was torn down. Ottawa's Cliffside Ski Jump Hill fell into disuse and so did Revelstoke's Big Hill.

Canada's ski-jumping results at the 1976 Olympic Winter Games were less than spectacular compared to the Austrians who hosted the Games. Karl Schnabl and Anton Innauer won the gold and the silver in the 90 metre event.

After the 1976 Games, Sport Canada and the Canadian Ski Association directors asked the Ski Jumping Association to give them a complete status review on the association. At the end of the season, the budget for the Canadian Ski Jumping Association was cut from $120,000 to nothing. The chairman resigned and the ski-jumping team disbanded. The Canadian Ski Association President called on Fred Morris to be the interim chairman of the Ski Jumping Association.

A plant foreman from Ottawa, Ontario, Morris had been involved with ski jumping in Canada as a young competitor, then as a volunteer and organizer, and finally as the national chairman in 1969 and 1970. He refused to disband Canada's ski jumping team.

Morris called an emergency meeting of the top Nordic experts in the country. Fifteen people sat around a boardroom table in Toronto and discussed the fate of ski jumping in Canada. At the meeting, Fred Morris was appointed the National Chairman, a new constitution was recommended, a new committee structure was established, and an entirely new ski jumping development program was initiated.

A decision was made by the directors that no ski jumper would compete internationally until the jumper's results were at a world-class level. The new program would start at rock bottom with the juniors and would focus on a four-year domestic re-building plan.

A request for interim financing was submitted to the directors of the Canadian Ski Association at their annual general meeting. The good news was that the request was accepted. The bad news was that the funding would amount to only $8,000.

Determined to keep the team together, Fred Morris and his team of volunteers set up a "kitchen table" operation in his home in Ottawa. Morris was the secretary, treasurer, managing director, team director, and program administrator. If you asked Fred Morris what he carried around in his briefcase, he would reply, "The national headquarters of the Canadian Ski Jumping Team."

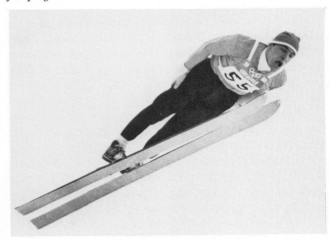

Vladimir Beloussov won the U.S.S.R.'s first gold medal in the 90 metre event at the Games in 1968, at Grenoble.

The incredible sweep of the medals by the Japanese ski jumpers in the 70 metre event in 1972 at Sapporo, Japan: A. Konno (silver), Yukio Kasaya (gold), and Seiji Aochi (bronze). *Deutsche Presse-Agentur GmbH*

Luckily, the Ontario Ski Council chipped in to help fund and establish an Ontario ski-jumping team that would concentrate on the juniors. Another contribution to ski jumping by the Ontario government was the construction of a Nordic training centre at Thunder Bay. Included among the facilities were 70 metre and 90 metre ski jumps, the first ever built that would enable Canadians to train on the same level as the Europeans.

One of the worst things the Canadian Ski Jumping Team had against it was a budget that had been cut from $120,000 to $8,000. But two of the best things the team had going for it were a couple of teenagers who were destined to become Canada's top highflyers.

Steve Collins is a member of the Ojibwa Indian Band and grew up on the Fort William Reserve near Thunder Bay, Ontario. Funded by the Ontario Ski Council, Collins started ski jumping at Mount McKay at eleven years of age and then moved over to "Big Thunder" when the new jumps opened. A natural talent, Steve Collins leaped from obscurity as the youngest competitor to ever compete in a world event in Finland and his record still stands. At fifteen, Steve Collins was a celebrity in Europe after winning three major events.

Horst Bulau grew up in a skiing family and started to ski at two-and-a-half at the Ottawa Ski Club. An accomplished Alpine skier, Bulau was always intrigued by ski jumpers and would wander over to the jumps and watch the older boys go off them. One day he said to the ski-jumping coach, "My Dad says I'm old enough to try to ski jump."

A good coach knows you don't turn down enthusiasm like that, and he started little Horst Bulau off on the 10 metre ski jump hill. He was five years old.

At thirteen, Horst Bulau won his first major competition at the 1975 Shell Cup Juvenile Championships. In 1979, he won the World Junior Championship at Mont Ste.-Anne, Quebec. He placed first in the 70 metre jump.

Bulau gave much of the credit for his wins to his coach, Bill Bakke. Bakke, a former coach of the United States National Ski Jumping Team, had been hired for the 1978-79 season by the Canadian team to coach Steve Collins, Horst Bulau, Ron Richards, and a group of other young hopefuls. His enthusiasm for the sport gave the boys the extra momentum they needed and it began to show up in their results, thus beginning the international success for a new generation of Canadian ski jumpers.

Years later, Horst Bulau would look back to Bill Bakke as the coach and mentor who made him into one of Canada's finest athletes. "Bill Bakke taught me how to be a ski jumper," he said, "but he also taught me about winning and losing and about the dedication and discipline it takes to become an Olympic athlete."

Horst Bulau and Steve Collins were joined by Tauno Kayhko and headed to Lake Placid in 1980 to represent Canada in ski jumping at the Olympics. Kayhko, a top jumper in Finland, had immigrated in 1975 and became a Canadian citizen just in time to take part in the Games.

For the first time in the history of Olympic ski jumping, a tie was declared for second place in the 70 metre jumping event. Manfred Deckert of East Germany recorded jumps of 85 and 88 metres, and Hirokazu Yagi of Japan recorded jumps of 87 and 83.5 metres—both ended up with 249.2 points. Jouko Tormanen of Finland dominated the 90 metre event with the longest jump recorded at the Games at 117 metres.

Steve Collins placed ninth in the 90 metre jump for the best ever Canadian Olympic finish, a record that still stands today. After the Olympics Collins reached the height of his career when he won the 1980 World Junior title, leaping a record 124 metres off the jump at Lahti, Finland (his record still stands),

Bill Bakke, the coach who helped make Horst Bulau one of the best ski jumpers in the world. *Courtesy Horst Bulau*

Finland's Matti Nykaenen, winner of two medals at the 1984 Games in Sarajevo. *Deutsche Presse-Agentur GmbH*

took the Czech ski flying title, and was awarded the Tom Long-boat award and the Viscount Alexander Trophy in 1980.

But Steve Collins' ski jumping career wasn't the only thing up in the air. So was his personal life. Away in Europe all by himself, being a celebrity at such a young age, and missing his familiar surroundings at the Fort William Reserve was too much for a fifteen-year-old to handle. Collins lost his competitive edge and slipped down to sixty-ninth place in the World Cup standings.

Not so for Ottawa's Horst Bulau. He continued to chalk up an impressive array of ski-jumping titles which included first place in the 70 metre and 90 metre jumps at the 1981 U.S. Nationals, third in the overall World Cup standings between 1980 and 1982 and back-to-back first-place finishes on the 70 metre jump at World Cup events at St. Moritz and Gstaad, Switzerland. As Canada's national champion, he battled it out with Finland's Matti Nykaenen for top place in the World Cup standings on the international circuit.

As the 1984 Olympic Winter Games approached, national coach Bill Bakke gave Steve Collins three days to make a decision. Either Collins had to undergo an intensive training and drug rehabilitation program, or he would be thrown off the national team. If ever an athlete loathed a coach for forcing an issue, it was Steve Collins. He phoned his father and told him he was coming home to Fort William. "You have got to

stay, Steve," said his father. "Don't come back to the Reserve now, you'll just hang around and your problem will get worse."

Steve Collins stayed with the national team, and when he entered the 1984 Olympic Winter Games at Sarajevo, Yugoslavia, he out-jumped team-mates Horst Bulau, Ron Richards, and David Brown in the 70 metre competition. Collins finished in twenty-fifth place, a Canadian best in the Olympic event. Not only was Steve Collins a Canadian sports hero after the Olympics, he also became a hero to his own people throughout the country.

It had been hoped that for the first time, Canada would be represented at the 1984 Olympic medal ceremonies by ski jumper Horst Bulau. With seven World Cup wins to his credit, he had been runner-up to the 1983 World Cup title behind twenty-year-old Matti Nykaenen, "The Fly," from Finland. Bulau's standing in the World Cup was a tribute to his courage and strength.

A year before, he had missed half of the season after he had suffered a concussion and broken shoulder blade when he tipped over in the air after leaping off the spectacular 120 metre hill in a ski-flying competition at Harrachov, Czechoslovakia.

But the anticipated duel in the skies over Sarajevo did not take place, and no one was more surprised than Matti Nykaenen, who had openly admitted Bulau was the one to beat for the gold medal. Instead, Horst Bulau finished up in a discon-

Steve Collins shows perfect form in 1980 at Lake Placid, New York, with his left hand catching the wind as he steadies himself high above the spectators. *Canadian Skiing Association, Ski Jumping*

solate tenth place behind winner Matti Nykaenen. It was the most disappointing experience of his ski-jumping career, but he made no excuse for his "off" Olympics.

It was against their own great results of the 1981-83 period that the team had fallen short in Sarajevo. Nevertheless, the 1984 team had performed as well as any other Canadian Olympic ski jump team in history.

In 1980, when Fred Morris gave up his presidency of the Association to become vice chairman of the operations of the Canadian Ski Association's executive committee for ski jumping, the budget for ski jumping in Canada was $200,000.

Today, the Ski Jumping Association is funded by Sport Canada and the Government of Canada through Fitness and Amateur Sport. The annual budget is over half a million dollars.

## The Venue

Two of the most spectacular pieces of construction for the 1988 Olympic Winter Games are the 70 metre and 90 metre ski jumps that tower above the horizon of Canada Olympic Park.

Located within the city limits, Canada Olympic Park has been constructed by the Federal Government for approximately $60 million and is one of the world's leading ski-jump, bobsleigh, and luge training centres. Canada's first quadruple ski-jumping complex includes 30 and 50 metre jumps and the 70 and 90 metre jumps used in Olympic competition. The 30 and 50 metre ski jumps will primarily be used to train juniors.

The year-round training facilities will be covered with a white, fitted plastic matting (much like a carpet). The matting becomes slippery when sprayed with a built-in sprinkler system in the summer months. To reduce friction on the matting, ski jumpers use a special lacquer on the base of their skis during their summer training.

The 90 metre jump rises 30 metres higher than the tallest building in Calgary, the Petro-Canada Tower. Elevators inside the 90 metre tower take spectators to four separate levels—a reception area, a bar and lounge, an observation deck, and the "jump level" where the competitors start their runs.

At the top of the inrun (the approach), ski jumpers will have a choice of between five and ten start gates. The start gates will keep the inrun speed at a safe level in various weather conditions, and prevent ski jumpers from out-jumping the hill.

The steel inruns snake down from the towers of the 70 metre and 90 metre jumps like giant rollercoasters. Undoubtedly it feels like going down one too, when one can compare the vertical drop from the height of the 90 metre inrun to the take-off point to the height of a twenty-story building.

Despite the fact that the two largest towers are separate from each other, the 70 and 90 metre jumps share a common landing area.

Looking up at the landing hill from the thirty-five thousand person "standing room only" amphitheatre, the spectator will see three control point lines drawn on the hill.

A well-designed landing hill is a continuous parabolic curve. The blue line furthest up the hill is called the *norm point* and marks the spot where the landing hill reaches its maximum steepness.

The green line in the middle is called the *table point* and is used to set distance point tables for scoring.

The red line at the bottom of the landing hill marks the point where the contour of the hill changes and begins its pull-out. The red line is important to the jumper because jumps past it are possible, but unsafe. The line is called the *K-point*, named after the German word meaning *critical*.

The five judges will be stationed in the judges' tower located on the side of the landing hill below the take-off.

Scores are based on form as well as distance, and will be displayed on the large electronic scoreboard below the judges' tower.

Traditionally, ski jumping attracts the largest crowds of any Olympic event. An estimated fifty thousand spectators are expected to view the ski-jumping events at the 1988 Olympic Winter Games in Calgary.

# The Technique

The word "commitment" takes on a special meaning to the ski jumper once his skis start moving down the hard smooth grooves of the inrun bordered with "the greens."

The pine bough is the international emblem of ski jumping and small clumps of "the boughs" line both the inrun and the outrun, as well as mark the take-off point. Without the greenery, the jumping area would appear as one big white-out with no depth perception for the ski jumper.

Once the start signal is given the ski jumper, he has exactly twenty seconds to leave the start gate before being disqualified. This ruling was instituted to ensure the competitors will start when told to instead of waiting for a change in the weather. Despite wind being the only real problem in ski jumping, the velocity of it rarely affects the competitor on the inrun.

The tuck position used by downhillers is similar to that used by jumpers on the inrun except that the arms are held back, not forward. On the inrun, ski jumpers can match the speeds of downhillers, but once they take off, their air time is a tad longer than anything a Crazy Canuck would be interested in.

The key to a good flight is a quick, powerful spring off the take-off which propels the jumper forward into a good flying position. A good aerodynamic position on take-off is achieved by closing the gap between skis and body as soon as possible. The stretched-out, parallel position of the jumper over his skis gives height and carry as he squeezes every metre he can out of his flight.

Most ski jumpers lie flat over their skis in flight, but occasionally some will tilt to the side for more sail. Jumpers hold their arms back and to the sides of their body, and steady themselves with their hands.

The flight curve follows the contour of the landing hill, and once the ski jumper is airborne, he is rarely more than ten feet off the ground at any one time.

The ski jumper assumes the Telemark position to absorb the shock of the landing with his knees and hips. The weight is equally distributed on both skis in a Telemark landing. If all the weight is on the front ski, the other ski could drift away and the jumper could fall.

Snow does not inhibit the jumps or slow them down, but to record a good distance, a ski jumper must be lucky with the wind. The direction of the wind and its velocity are monitored by the colourful drogue flag at the top of the inrun. Good steady air is preferred to tricky crosswinds or tailwinds.

# The Rules

There are no jumping competitions for women in the Olympics, but there is nothing in the rule book that states they would not be allowed to take part if one was on a jumping team.

For men, there are three events in Olympic ski jumping—the 70 metre hill, the 90 metre, and a new four-member team jumping event. In each event, men are allowed to jump twice and scores are based on form and distance.

Five judges give the ski jumper his style points. When a jumper moves his skis into the start gate, he has twenty points.

The take-off is no longer judged, but from there the ski jumper can be docked for faults in flight all the way down to a minimum of eight points. The high and low marks of the judges' points are discarded and the three remaining scores are computed along with the distance marks.

In the 1970s, the East Germans experimented with the arms-back position on the inrun instead of the arms-forward position used by most jumpers. Today, the arms are held back and close to the sides for maximum inrun speed and minimum movements on the spring from the take-off.

It wasn't like that in the good old days. Then, ski jumpers looked more like airborne boxers as they made the required three complete revolutions of their arms while in flight, in order to gain their maximum twenty style points.

The jumping distances are measured by a hearty group of OCO'88 volunteers who have been trained and certified by the International Ski Federation as hill markers. Hill markers are stationed one person every metre and stand behind a long tape measure that runs from the top of the outrun to the bottom. The markers watch the feet of the jumper as he lands. Because ski jumpers land in the Telemark position, the mid-point between the front and back foot indicates the distance flown. Working as a hill marker may be one of the coldest volunteer jobs in the world, but it's the best seat in the house at a ski-jumping competition.

Any measuring disputes among the hill markers are resolved by the distance-measuring referee (DMR) who stands behind or across from the volunteers. He acts like a referee and makes the final distance decision before reporting it to the official scorer.

The scoring of ski jumping follows a complex system, but for spectators watching the events, it is helpful to remember that both elements of form and distance are necessary to gain a top score in the Olympics.

Moving the start gate up or down at the top of the inrun will keep the speed at a level that will keep the best jumpers from exceeding the K-point. After competitors take several practice jumps, officials make a decision as to what start gate will be used for the event.

It is possible for the judges to decide to restart the ski-jumping event if winds are sending jumpers too far down the outrun at the Olympics. A jury meeting was called at the 1986 World Cup ski jumping event at Lake Placid, New York, when tricky winds were sending jumpers far beyond the K-point of the 90 metre. The event was restarted after thirty-nine of the sixty-nine competitors from sixteen countries had jumped in the first round. The delay caused the competition to end just before darkness.

## The Equipment

For decades, ski jumping was considered to be a gentleman's sport. Apart from his skis, the jumper's most important pieces of equipment were a shirt and tie, and a V-neck sweater.

The tight-fitting suit worn by today's ski jumper is directly related to how aerodynamically sound the airflight position becomes. Protective helmets and goggles are a necessary safety requirement in Olympic competition.

Jumping skis are half again as wide as Alpine skis and measure approximately 240 to 255 centimetres in length. The skis are made out of wood, fibreglass, and epoxy and each one weighs approximately 2 kilos. The five or six grooves on the ski base keep them straight in the tracks of the inrun, and on the landing. A thin film of wax is applied to the bases before competition.

Jumping boots are made of leather and have high backs and flexible toes which enable the jumper to attain the forward lean position. The skis are attached to the boot by front throw cable bindings with heel springs. Recently a new design, a basic toe clip similar to cross country ski bindings, has proven popular with ski jumpers.

## Calgary Preview

Medal hopes for Canada's ski jumpers will be even more pronounced than usual when the host country boys jump off Calgary's high-flying 70 and 90 metre towers at Canada Olympic Park.

Back to fly for Olympic medals are veterans of seven World Cup seasons, Horst Bulau and, it is hoped, Steve Collins. Other Canadians who will be looking for Olympic competition may include David Brown of Thunder Bay, Ontario, entering his fourth season on the World Cup circuit, Todd Gilman of Thunder Bay, who begins his third year with the Canadian team in 1987, Ian McGrath of Whitby, Ontario, Ron Richards from Oshawa, and Ron Rautio of Thunder Bay.

A couple of jumpers the Canadians would like to beat in 1988 are Yugoslavian student Primoz Ulaga and team-mate Miran Tepes. Ulaga chalked up a double win on the 70 and 90 metre jumps at the 1986 World Cup event at Thunder Bay, marking the second year in a row that one skier has swept the events. The year before, it was Austrian Andrea Felder. Felder will lead a top-notch Austrian team into the 1988 Winter Games along with Ernst Vettori and Franz Neulandtner. Neulandtner excels at the 70 metre jump.

Defending gold medalist Matti Nykaenen hasn't faded from international prominence, although he performed erratically on the World Cup circuit last season, and at one point was sent home by the Finnish federation for disciplinary reasons. One jumper who can give Nykaenen a push is Jens Weissflog, one of the best ski jumpers in the world from the German Democratic Republic. Team-mates Ulf Findeisen and Ingo Lesser also look good.

The Czechs have three talented jumpers in Pavel Ploc, Jiri Parma, and Ladislav Dluhos, along with newcomer Matyaz Debelak. Top American flyer is veteran Olympic competitor Mike Holland. Rick Mewborn and Zane Palmer are also jumping well for the United States.

The Norwegians have four good jumpers who all specialize in the 90 metre event. Both Vegard Opaas and Rolf Age Berg finished well up in the top ten last season, and some of the best stylists around are Ole Gunnar Fikjestol, Jon Inge Kjoerum, and Hjroar Stjernen.

Other ski jumpers who could feature in the medals in 1988 are Poland's Piotr Fijas, Chiharu Nishikata and Masahiro Akimoto of Japan, and Andreas Bauer of West Germany.

Despite Sweden, Italy, France, and the Soviet Union not being as competitive as Czechoslovakia, Norway, and Canada, most jumpers will be at a slight disadvantage as they face Matti Nykaenen, the Austrians and the East Germans.

# Canadians at the Olympic Winter Games
## SKI JUMPING

### 1924 Chamonix — I Olympic Winter Games

Canada did not participate.

### 1928 St. Moritz — II Olympic Winter Games

*Special jump*
16. Gerald Dupuis

### 1932 Lake Placid — III Olympic Winter Games

*Special jump*
19. Robert Lymburne
20. Jacques Landry
29. Arnold Stone
30. Leslie Gagne

### 1936 Garmisch-Partenkirchen — IV Olympic Winter Games

*Special jump*
14. Tormod Mobraeten
35. Karl Johan Baadsvik
38. Norman C. Cagne

### 1948 St. Moritz — V Olympic Winter Games

*Special jump*
39. Wilbur Irwin
44. Tom Mobraeten
46. Laurent Bernier

### 1952 Oslo — VI Olympic Winter Games

*Special jump*
25. Jacques Charland
41. Lucien Laferte

### 1956 Cortina d'Ampezzo — VII Olympic Winter Games

*Special jump*
27. Jacques Charland

### 1960 Squaw Valley — VIII Olympic Winter Games

*80 metre jump*
33. Jacques Charland
35. Gerry Gravelle
44. Alois Moser

### 1964 Innsbruck — IX Olympic Winter Games

*70 metre jump*
43. Kaare Lien
53. John Archibald McInnes

*90 metre jump*
45. Kaare Lien
50. John Archibald McInnes

### 1968 Grenoble — X Olympic Winter Games

| *70 metre jump* | *90 metre jump* |
| --- | --- |
| 53. Ulf Kvendbo | 55. Ulf Kvendbo |
| 55. John McInnes | 57. John McInnes |
| 57. Claude Trahan | 58. Claude Trahan |

### 1972 Sapporo — XI Olympic Winter Games

| *70 metre jump* | *90 metre jump* |
| --- | --- |
| 40. Zdenek Mezl | 17. Zdenek Mezl |
| 44. Ulf Kvendbo | 39. Peter Wilson |
| 48. Rick Gulyas | 45. Ulf Kvendbo |
| 56. Peter Wilson | |

### 1976 Innsbruck — XII Olympic Winter Games

| *70 metre jump* | *90 metre jump* |
| --- | --- |
| 36. Peter Wilson | 45. Peter Wilson |
| 48. Richard Grady | 46. Richard Grady |
| 54. Kim Fripp | 48. Donald Grady |
| 55. Donald Grady | 53. Kim Fripp |

### 1980 Lake Placid — XIII Olympic Winter Games

| *70 metre jump* | *90 metre jump* |
| --- | --- |
| 28. Steve Collins | 9. Steve Collins |
| 30. Tauno Kayhko | 26. Tauno Kayhko |
| 41. Horst Bulau | 29. Horst Bulau |

### 1984 Sarajevo — XIV Olympic Winter Games

| *70 metre jump* | *90 metre jump* |
| --- | --- |
| 25. Steve Collins | 10. Horst Bulau |
| 29. Ron Richards | 26. Ron Richards |
| 38. Horst Bulau | 36. Steve Collins |
| 51. David Brown | 47. David Brown |

# Speed Skating

Olympic Oval
February 14, 17, 18, 20, 21, 22, 23, 26, 27, 28

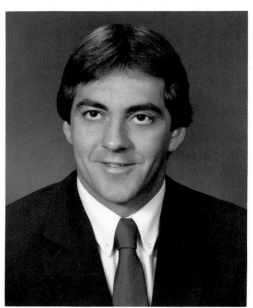

*Mathieson, Calgary*

Having been in the speed-skating sport for sixteen years now and on the National Team for twelve—and still counting—it is with great pleasure I write this introduction to a sport that has remained unknown for too long.

It may come as a surprise to many people but the Canadian Speed Skating Association (CASSA) will celebrate its one hundredth anniversary in 1987. This should coincide with the opening of the magnificent stadium that will be used for the 1988 Calgary Olympics. What a big difference in the sport that could make. Over these one hundred years, very little has changed. In the mid-1970s, after an attempt to develop and increase participation, the whole sport was in serious trouble when a Canadian company producing the only indoor skates available shut down production. Without an artificial track, indoor skating was our only source of developing young skaters. Fortunately enough, creative and enterprising people worked on the problem and managed to overcome it. But that still was not much of an improvement on the sport. Merely a way to stay afloat.

Despite the construction of artificial tracks all over Europe to develop the sport, Canada had to wait until late 1985 when Quebec got sufficient funds to build such a track, facilitating training for more skaters. And everyone knows, that was a direct result of the publicity surrounding my performance at the 1984 Sarajevo Olympics.

It took almost a hundred years for Canadians to realize we not only had the potential to win major races, but were already doing it. How could people forget that speedskating won one of the three medals won at the 1976 Olympics—a silver by Cathy Priestner; one of only two won in 1980—another silver; and three out of four in 1984—two golds and one bronze? How could people forget that Canada had its share of world champions through all these years? Sylvia Burka alone won three (1973, 1976, 1977). In fact Canada is the only country in the world that wins world championship medals without even having its own artificial track to train on.

Over the last ten years, short track (inside an arena) has seen its evolution go to world championship level and since it gained official status in 1981, Canada has won four of the last five championships.

What makes us so good is a mixture of many things: young talented athletes, development programs, a professionally disciplined coaching staff, and numerous other people believing in hard work and success.

The beautiful motion, the ease with which a skater seems to propel himself, the concentration and strength shown on his face along with the euphoria of great speeds on relatively small surfaces are all signs of a beautiful sport that will certainly attract more and more skaters looking for a wonderful experience.

The 1988 Calgary Olympics will give us a chance to show ourselves to all Canadians. A great way to start our second century!

Gaetan Boucher, O.C.
*Triple Medal Winner 1984 Olympic Winter Games*

# The History

The roots of ice skating go back over a thousand years to the frozen canals and waterways of Scandinavia and the Netherlands.

Men laced animal-bone runners onto their wooden shoes and boots and took part in winter hunting expeditions on ice in Scandinavia in the year 1250. During the mid-1600s, round trips between villages had become a useful and enjoyable means of transportation and communications for the Dutch. Throughout the countries of central and northern Europe, people enjoyed the recreational aspects of ice skating and local race competitions. However, though the origins of ice skating are mostly northern European by nature, international speed skating became famous via Scotland.

Golf, ice hockey, and curling are not the only forms of recreation that the sports-minded Scots have introduced to the world. Credit again is directed to the Scotsman who invented the first pair of all-iron skates for speed skating in Edinburgh in 1572. The iron blade, replacing the bone runner, was the spark that ignited the interest in speed skating, which rapidly gained in popularity throughout Europe and Britain. The Skating Club of Edinburgh was formed in 1642 and the first organized speed skating race in the world was held in Britain in 1763, covered a distance of 15 miles (24.14 kilometres).

Skating made its way to North America with the migrating Scots, but interest in the sport remained limited due to the heavy weight of the iron skates and dull blades' need of constant sharpening. A natural step forward for the skate was the invention of a lighter, sharper, and longer all-steel blade produced in Philadelphia in 1850. The initial response to the new sharp-edged steel blade was immediate and by the end of the nineteenth century the mass following of speed skaters spread to many parts of the world.

Canada's first recorded ice skating race took place on the St. Lawrence River between three British army officers who raced from Montreal to Quebec City in 1854. During the next thirty years speed skating races were held in Ontario, Quebec, and the Maritimes, and by 1887 the Amateur Skating Association of Canada was formed. John George Alwyn Creighton of Ottawa, a name synonymous with Canadian ice hockey, was among the five original officers elected at the meeting held at the Victoria Ice Rink in Montreal. Representatives from the cities of Montreal, Toronto, Quebec, Ottawa, Saint John, and Halifax drew up a set of by-laws and a constitution for the Association. The Canadian Amateur Speed Skating Association is the oldest sports association in Canada, and at the inaugural meeting in 1877, the first of many Canadian Governors-General, Lord Lansdowne, was appointed Patron of the Association.

The Amateur Skating Association of Canada sponsored the first official championships of Canada in 1887. The five distances included in the race format were: the 220, 440, and 880 yard races, and a one and a five-mile event. The championships attracted large crowds, who also witnessed a 220 yard hurdle event and an 880 yard backwards race.

Speed skating in Canada and the United States underwent a period of general growth in the late 1800s and many Canadian race records were set at outdoor championships in eastern Canada and the border cities of the United States. Meanwhile,

Jack K. McCulloch, Canada's first speedskating champion and winner of the World title in 1897. *Courtesy John Hurdis*

in the Netherlands, the Amsterdam Ice Club distinguished itself by holding the first World Championships in 1889. The championship title was not won for several years as the champion was declared only if he won all events. Finally, American Joseph Donoghue was announced as the first World speed skating champion at Amsterdam in 1891. He won all four races, including the new five-mile event.

The formation of the International Skating Union (ISU) took place in the Netherlands in 1892. The distances of the four speed skating races were changed to metric by the ISU in 1892 and a ruling was accepted that all international championships in Europe would be held on a double track with the athletes racing in pairs, against the clock.

In North America, on the other hand, speed skaters used the mass-start and did not race in lanes. According to American rules, the lead skater at the front inside edge could be overtaken on the outside.

In 1894 the Amateur Skating Association of Canada became the first non-European association to join the ISU which governs all World competitions and international championships.

When the ISU held the World Speed Skating Championships at Montreal in February of 1897, the three countries who participated were Norway, Germany, and Canada. A Canadian, Jack K. McCulloch of Winnipeg, was declared World Champion, winning two races. Later on that year, McCulloch won the Canadian Outdoor Mass-Start Championship and team-mate W. A. Lockhard of Saint John, New Brunswick, won the 800 yard backwards event.

Participation in speed skating was moving west across Canada and the first championships staged in British Columbia were held at the Annual Winter Carnival at Rossland in 1898.

Involvement in international speed skating became very broad-based during the last years of the nineteenth century. With not only European countries practising the sport, but also Russia, Canada, and the United States, a proposal was made at the inaugural Olympic Congress in Paris, France, in 1894 that speed skating be considered as a demonstration event in the Olympic Games. Speed skating made its Olympic debut in the summer of 1908 at London, England, and again was a demonstration event in 1920 at Antwerp, Belgium, at the Seventh Olympic Games. In 1908, the International Skating Union (ISU) initiated a point system to determine the overall winner in international competition, eliminating the need for a complete sweep of all four events in order to be awarded the title.

Before the introduction of speed skating into the Olympic Games in 1908, the acknowledged masters of the sport were the Norwegians, particularly Oscar Mathisen, who set a world record for the 1,500 metres in 1908.

In 1914 he broke his own World record, in the 1,500 metre race, lowering his time to 2:19.4. This record stood for twenty-three years. After the Olympic Games in 1908, Mathisen set thirteen World records, won the World title five times, and held the European Championship title three times by 1914.

In 1924, the Amateur Skating Association of Canada joined the Canadian Olympic Association just in time to dispatch a single entry in speed skating to the first Olympic Winter Games at Chamonix, France.

Canada's first Olympic speed skater Charles I. Gorman from Saint John, New Brunswick, represented his country and placed seventh in the 500 metre event and eleventh in the 1,500 metre. Charles Gorman also won the World Mass-Start Outdoor Championships later that year and held the Canadian Outdoor Mass-Start Championship title through 1925 and 1926. In 1927 Gorman skated in the World Outdoor Mass-Start Championships and set a world record in the 440 yard event which was only bettered by an American skater in 1942.

The Finns took a commanding lead in the initial Olympic speed skating event at Chamonix. Thirty-year-old Clas Thunberg of Finland won three gold medals in the 1,500 metre, the 5,000 metre and the four races combined. A third-place finish in the 500 metres by Thunberg gave American Charles Jewtraw the first speed skating gold medal won by the United States at the Olympic Winter Games.

Canada entered the second Olympic Winter Games at St. Moritz, Switzerland, with a three-man speed skating team of Charles Gorman, William Logan, and Ross Robinson. Charles Gorman's finish of seventh in the 500 metre event was Canada's best. With entrant William Logan as an Olympic speed skater, the history of a speed skating Canadian family continued. Fred Logan, father of Willy, was an international mass start and North American speed skating champion before the Olympic Winter

Charles Gorman of Saint John, New Brunswick, Canada's single entry in the speedskating events of the 1924 Games. *Courtesy John Hurdis*

Games were restored. His son William Logan became an Olympic medalist and Canadian Champion and his younger brother Frank also won several junior championships in the United States and Canada.

At Lake Placid, Canada was dominated by the superb skating skill of veteran Clas Thunberg from Finland and newcomer Ivar Ballangrud from Norway. A sudden rise in temperature and a thaw in rink conditions forced cancellation of the 10,000 metre event after American skater Irving Jaffee had recorded the fastest time of the first seven of the ten entrants. After a lengthy meeting by officials and judges, a decision was reached that a rerun would be ordered. In the meantime the Norwegians, assuming that Jaffee was the gold medalist, had left for home. The race was then cancelled and declared a non-event (officially not taking place) and the American long-distance star lost out on his bid for the speed skating gold medal.

Canada's speed skating expertise increased tremendously during the years between the 1928 and 1932 Olympic Winter Games. The prowess of skater Frank Stack of Winnipeg, who set a North American Indoor Mass-Start record for the five-mile event in 1930, was demonstrated again in 1931 when he was declared both North American Outdoor and Indoor Mass-Start Champion. Two other members of the men's squad to gain recognition in Canada before the Games in 1932 were Alex Hurd of Sudbury and Herb Flack of Toronto. The select group of "Logan, Flack and Stack" became a Canadian speed skating dynasty during the 1920s and 1930s.

Unfortunately for Canada, women's speed skating did not become an official Olympic event until 1960 at the eighth Olympic Winter Games at Squaw Valley, California. Nevertheless, two women played important roles in the growth of women's speed skating in Canada, and had the sport been a recognized event for women in 1932, the medal count for the Olympic team would have been much higher. Lela Brooks-Potter of Toronto set six World speed skating records in 1925 and was the first all-around World Champion in 1926. Jean Wilson, who was born in Glasgow, Scotland, in 1910 and grew up in Toronto, won all the first all-round Women's North American Championships in 1931.

Entering its third Olympic Winter Games at Lake Placid, New York, in 1932, Canada's speed skating squad included Lela Brooks-Potter, Jean Wilson, Geraldine Mackie, Florence Hurd, and Hattie Donaldson. The Canadian women's team was invited to the Games to take part in the women's speed skating demonstration event. Jean Wilson placed first in the 500 metre and second in the 1,500 metre race. A head-first tumble across the track on the final turn of the 1,000 metre final put Wilson out of contention for another first-place finish, but allowed Canadian team-mate Hattie Donaldson to finish in second place.

The speed skating event at Lake Placid was held under the North American rules with five or six racers in each heat. This ruling so infuriated Olympic champion Clas Thunberg of Finland that he refused to compete in some of the races under the mass-start format. Having not practised mass starts in Europe since 1893, the foreign skating teams were so confused with the North

Canadian Jean Wilson competed in a demonstration event at the Games in 1932. *Canada Sports Hall of Fame*

American rules that, not surprisingly, few qualified in the preliminary heats.

Some sports historians regard the limited European representation at Lake Placid as a contributing factor to a lack of competitive content at the 1932 Winter Games. However, for North American speed skaters, the small field of skaters due to the difficulties and expense of travelling from Europe, represented the route to glory on home ice and they took advantage of their opportunities. John Shea, a popular hometown boy from Lake Placid, took a gold medal in the 500 metre sprint and Canadian skater, Alex Hurd, finished up in third place with the bronze medal. Shea also took the gold medal in the 1,500 metre ahead of a Canadian sweep, including Alex Hurd as silver medalist, William Logan as bronze medalist, and Frank Stack in fourth spot. Long distance American skater Irving Jaffee won the 5,000 metre race and the 10,000 metre event. William Logan placed third for a bronze medal finish in the 5,000 metre race. Frank Stack won Canada's fourth bronze medal for speed skating in 1932 in the 10,000 metre event which was won by Irving Jaffee for the United States.

Canadian speed skaters, who had come of age at the 1932 Olympic Winter Games at Lake Placid, were saddened by the death of team-mate Jean Wilson in 1933. At the peak of her career and only a year after winning two Olympic speed skating titles, Jean Wilson died of a degenerative muscle disease at twenty-three years of age.

The use of the mass start, and the resulting disorientation

William Logan, double bronze medal winner at the 1932 Games at Lake Placid, New York. *Canada Sports Hall of Fame*

of European speed skaters to it, led to a ruling by the IOC that any future Olympic races would be held under the rules of the ISU which stipulated starting in pairs. As a result, the free-for-all mass start in the speed skating event was never again seen in Olympic competition after 1932.

The new IOC ruling produced favourable results for the Scandinavian speed skaters at the fourth Olympic Winter Games in 1936 at Garmisch-Partenkirchen, Germany.

Norwegian Ivar Ballangrud regained his speed skating supremacy in 1936 after his disappointing showing four years earlier at Lake Placid. Ballangrud became the first speed skating triple gold medal winner in the history of the Olympic Winter Games, winning the 500, 5,000, and 10,000 metre events. The Grand Slam that Ivar Ballangrud hoped for was not realized as team-mate and World record holder Oscar Mathisen won the 1,500 metre in an Olympic record time of 2:19.2.

Although Canadian skating ace Alex Hurd won the North American Indoor Mass-Start Championships for the third time in 1936, interest in speed skating was beginning to decline in Southern Ontario in the late 1930s. With the construction of Canada's first ice hockey arena by Conn Smythe MC, in Toronto in 1936, interest in professional hockey by Canadians contributed to the diminishing spectator appeal for speed skating in Ontario. The sport slipped into the doldrums, and suffered a major setback.

The intervening years of World War II were also to take their toll on the Canadian speed skating fraternity, and a generation of speed skaters perhaps sensed that the Winter Games of 1936 might be the last Olympics for several years to come.

Even though the names had changed in Olympic speed skating circles after the war, the Norwegians still reigned supreme and were the ones to beat at the fifth Olympic Winter Games at St. Moritz, Switzerland, in 1948. There were no surprises in the speed skating races, just new faces as Norwegian Finn Helgesen won the 500 metre with an Olympic record, team-mate Sverre Farstad took the gold in the 1,500 metre with another

Olympic record, and fellow countryman Reidar Liakley finished off the triple crown for Norway by winning the 5,000 metre race. Ake Seyffarth of Sweden made it a Scandinavian sweep by winning the 10,000 metre medal.

No Canadian championships had been held during the war years of 1939 to 1945. However, speed skater Frank Stack's loyalty to the sport had paid off in 1946 and 1947 when he won the Canadian Outdoor Mass-Start Championships twice in a row. Stack entered the Winter Games at St. Moritz as a Canadian team member and also as coach of the speed skating squad. He had Canada's best finish in the 500 metre event and finished up in a four-way tie for sixth place.

The sixth Olympic Winter Games were held at Oslo, Norway, in 1952. Canada's speed skating squad was managed by Jim Neil and included Craig MacKay, Ralf Olin, Gordon Audley, and Frank Stack.

Representing Canada in his fourth Olympic Winter Games, Frank Stack paid tribute to the self-discipline and physical qualities of an Olympic athlete. He finished the 500 metre race in a three-way tie for twelfth place at the age of forty-six. Team-mate Gordon Audley placed third in the same event with a three-way tie for the bronze for Canada.

Norwegian truck driver Hjalmar Andersen duplicated fellow countryman Ivar Ballangrud's 1936 Olympic triple gold medal win at the Oslo Olympics. Winning the 1,500, 5,000, and 10,000 metre races, Andersen became the second triple crown speed skater in Olympic Winter Games history, and assured the Norwegians that speed skating supremacy still belonged to Scandinavia.

A new era in Olympic speed skating, starring the Soviets, was ushered into the seventh Olympic Winter Games at Cortina d'Ampezzo, Italy, in 1956. The International Olympic Committee had admitted Russia to membership in the IOC in 1952, but Russia did not attend the Olympic Winter Games that were held that year at Oslo. At the Games in 1956, however, the speed skating event was to become a showcase for the Russians and three out of the four gold medals went back to Moscow. Twenty-four-year-old Yevgeny Grishin from Moscow won the 500 metre event with a world record time and set a world record in the 1,500 metre event. Boris Shilkov captured the gold medal in the 5,000 metre race for the U.S.S.R. and the only medal salvaged for Scandinavia was the gold in the 10,000 metre won by twenty-five-year-old woodchopper Siggee Ericsson of Sweden. For the first time in Olympic Winter Games history, the United States was out of medal contention and Canada would have to wait until 1976 for a medal in Olympic speed skating.

Canada produced many outstanding women speed skaters between the Olympic Winter Games of 1932 and 1960. Although never to have an opportunity to see Olympic competition, skaters Florence Hurd of Toronto, Eileen Whalley and Betty Mitchell of Winnipeg, Pat Lawson of Saskatoon, and Pat Underhill of Edmonton won many Canadian and North American championship speed skating titles before the sport became an official Olympic event for women at the eighth Winter Games.

Would that the big names of the Canadian women's speed

skating Olympic demonstration team of 1932, Jean Wilson, Lela Brooks-Potter, and Hattie Donaldson had not been ahead of their time; they might well have prevailed over the first field of women speed skaters officially included in the 1960 Olympic Winter Games at Squaw Valley, California. The event included races of 500, 1,000, 1,500, and 3,000 metres for women skaters.

Frank Stack accompanied the Canadian speed skating team to Squaw Valley as manager and coach. The first Canadian women's Olympic speed skating squad consisted of Doreen Ryan and Margaret Robb who both skated in all four events with the best finish by Doreen Ryan in ninth place in the 500 metre race.

The Soviet women, from a country with a long speed skating history of its own, won three of the four gold medals in the inaugural event. Twenty-year-old physiology student Lidia Skoblikova of the Soviet team won the 1,500 metre event and set a new Olympic record in the 3,000 metre race. The 1,000 metre race was won by another Soviet, Klara Guseva, and the only medal Russia did not take in the women's speed skating event was the title for the 500 metre race, which was won by Kelga Haase of Germany.

Not to be outdone by the women, the Soviet men also took three gold medals back to the U.S.S.R. Increasing competition from the Soviets did not shut the Scandinavians out of the medal race. Twenty-six-year-old Knut Johannesen of Norway managed to be the first speed skater in Olympic history to finish the 10,000 metre race in less than 16 minutes, setting a new world record of 15:46.6. Roald Aas also won a gold for Norway in the 1,500 metre event, but the undisputed star of Olympic speed skating at the 1960 Games was twenty-eight-year-old Moscow engineer Eugeny Grishin, who tied for a gold medal first-place finish in the 1,500 metre event. His gold medal in the 500 metre race was worthy of attention as he had stumbled and nearly fallen on his final lap, losing valuable seconds as he approached the finish line.

The year 1960 also noted Canada's first (1897) World Speed Skating Champion Jack K. McCulloch (1872-1918) inducted into the Canadian Sports Hall of Fame for his achievements and contributions to speed skating in Canada.

The woman speed skating star to emerge at the ninth Olympic Winter Games at Innsbruck, Austria, was Lidia Skoblikova, who won an unprecedented four gold medals at the Games, and in the process set three new Olympic speed skating records in the 500, 1,000, and 1,500 metre events. Lidia Skoblikova was the first woman to win four Olympic medals at one Winter Games. With nearly everything else going to Skoblikova's team-mates, the Soviet women wound up winning nine out of the twelve speed skating medals.

Skater Terry McDermott, a twenty-three-year-old barber from Michigan, exonerated the United States from twelve years without a medal in Olympic speed skating by winning the 500 metre sprint. He beat out Yevgeny Grishin, the Soviet speedster who held the gold medal in the 500 metre event in the 1956 and 1960 Olympic Winter Games. McDermott's unorthodox skating style of standing almost straight upright was vastly different from the traditional low, hands-behind-the back stance used by most

Gordon Audley admires his bronze medal at the 1952 Games. *Athlete Information Bureau/Canadian Olympic Association*

Frank Stack of Winnipeg, Manitoba, a competitor in three Games, beginning in 1932, and manager and coach of the Olympic team in 1960. *Canada Sports Hall of Fame*

Lidia Skoblikova of the U.S.S.R. won an unprecedented four gold medals at the 1964 Games. *Deutsche Presse-Agentur GmbH*

speed skaters. His unusual technique and a pair of skates he had borrowed from his coach for the race made up the magic combination to give him the gold medal to take back to his hometown of Essexville. Knut Johanessen of Norway broke the Soviet hold on the 10,000 metre with an Olympic record of 7:38.4 and led a gold, silver, and bronze medal sweep of the event for the Norwegians. The Soviet and Scandinavian rivalry continued in the 1,500 metre event with Russia's Ants Antson beating out Rudi Liebricht of the Netherlands. Sweden's John Nilsson skated a remarkably good race and took the 10,000 metre event away from 1960 gold medalist Johanessen.

The poor Olympic showing for Canada in previous Winter Games prompted financial support for training, administration, and speed skating competitions by the government of Canada in 1965.

The 1968 Games marked the fifth appearance at an Olympic Winter Games of speed skating coach Ralf Olin of Calgary, who had been a competitor on Canada's Olympic squads of 1952, 1956, 1960, and 1964. Paul Enock, an Olympic team member from Edmonton, managed Canada's best finish of fifteenth in the men's 10,000 metre race. A four-way split in the final stand-

ings in the men's events kept all the gold medals in Europe for another Olympiad. Erhard Keller of West Germany won the 500 metre sprint, Cornelis Verkerk of Holland won the 1,500 metre in an Olympic record time, Norwegian Fred Anton Maier skated the 5,000 metre in a world record time (7:22.4), and Swedish skater Johnny Hoglin was the surprise winner of the 10,000 metre title in an Olympic record time of 15:23.6.

Speed skating's most talked about finish at Grenoble was the women's 500 metre event. Soviet skater Lyudmila Titova skated a gold medal race in a time of 46.1. However, the gold medalist was upstaged by three American speed skaters who finished just two-tenths of a second behind her in a three-way tie for second place. Twenty-two-year-old Mary Meyers, sixteen-year-old Dianne Holum, and eighteen-year-old Jennifer Fish all received silver medals for their unusual triple tie.

In 1969, a young Winnipeg girl was awarded the Canadian National Junior Speed Skating Championship. A childhood accident had resulted in the loss of one of Sylvia Burka's eyes, but despite her visual impairment she persevered at her speed skating career which would span fifteen years, and three Olympic Winter Games.

At fifteen years of age, Burka attended her first World Championships and was also named "Skater of the Year" by the Canadian Amateur Speed Skating Association in 1970. Her first trip to Europe as an international competitor stood her in good stead for team selection on the Canadian Olympic speed skating squad that entered the eleventh Olympic Winter Games at Sapporo, Japan, in 1972.

With her limited vision, Sylvia Burka was no stranger to falls and disqualifications. Competing in the 500 metre event against sixteen-year-old Anne Henning of the United States, Burka did not see Henning coming into the crossover at the same time she was. To avoid colliding with Sylvia, Henning broke her stride, stood up to let the Canadian skater pass, and lost the race. The United States filed an official protest of interference, Burka was disqualified, and Henning was given another chance to skate the race. On her second run, Henning broke 44 seconds, and won the gold medal with her final time of 43.33. Monika Pflug of West Germany won the 1,000 metre event and Burka, finishing in a respectable eighth place, soon discovered that the rigorous training methods practised by European speed skaters were vastly different to what she had been used to in Canada. Frustrated by never being in the winner's circle, Burka undertook a disciplined approach to her speed skating that would eventually pull her up in the standings, and bring greater speed skating accomplishments.

Dianne Holum of the United States won the first women's medal ever for her country in the 1,500 metre event. She then topped off her victory with a silver medal in the 3,000, losing out to gold medalist Christina Baas-Kaiser of the Netherlands. After an Olympic collection of four medals, Dianne Holum took on the coaching of a promising young skater from Madison, Wisconsin. Fourteen-year-old Eric Heiden would rise to heights in men's speed skating that had never been reached by an American Olympian before, and Holum would coach him on to victory through the 1976 and 1980 Olympic Winter Games.

The real hero of the 1972 Olympic Winter Games at Sapporo was tall, handsome Ard Schenk of Holland. Schenk, who was affectionately known as the "Flying Dutchman," equalled the Olympic speed skating records of Ivar Ballangrud and Hjalmar Anderson by winning three gold medals in a single Olympics.

The only race that eluded Ard Schenk was the 500 metre event. Just four steps off the start Schenk fell and finished up in thirty-fourth spot, proving that nobody's perfect all the time, especially in Olympic competition. However, two weeks after the Olympic Games at Sapporo, Schenk astounded the international speed skating establishment by winning all four events at the World Championships in Norway. His victory matched Norwegian Oscar Mathisen's four-event sweep of 1912.

For Sylvia Burka, the Olympic Winter Games at Sapporo had provided her with an insight into the sacrifices, self-discipline, and dedication that are required from an Olympic athlete. She was tired of being considered by her opponents as the underdog Canadian kid who could never skate anything more than a mediocre race. A self-confident and assertive achiever by nature, Burka refused to accept that she was not

Ard Schenk of the Netherlands, who took three speedskating titles in 1972, all in Olympic record times. *Deutsche Presse-Agentur GmbH*

capable of improving her personal best. Deciding to reevaluate her training routine and mental attitude, Sylvia applied herself single-mindedly to her objective. Just a few weeks after the 1972 Olympic Winter Games, she skated an extraordinary race at the Worlds in Holland and pulled herself up to higher levels of international competition. Sylvia Burka finished her year off by being named "Skater of the Year" by the Canadian Amateur Speed Skating Association.

Burka's 1972 speed skating accomplishments were only a prelude of what was to come. In 1973 Sylvia Burka's rigorous training regimen paid off as she gained prominence for herself and Canada by placing first overall in the Junior World Championships.

Despite a disciplined off-season training schedule and an outstanding year the previous winter, 1974 proved to be full of disappointing results for Burka's speed skating career. Her speed skating slump carried on to a major setback in 1975. Instead of surrendering to her misfortune, the untimely decline in her performance inspired Sylvia Burka to work even harder. An exemplary model for Canadian speed skating hopefuls, Burka stated that rather than being victorious, the lesson learned in overcoming defeat was far more valuable to her as an Olympic athlete.

Unfortunately, Sylvia Burka's second Olympic Games performance at Innsbruck, Austria, in 1976 was another disappointment, with her best finish in fourth spot in the 1,000 metre event.

Sprint skater Cathy Priestner rocketed to a second-place finish in the 500 metre race and became Canada's first woman to win an Olympic speed skating medal.

The nineteen-year-old University of Calgary student's victory was no fluke. Priestner's individual training style was geared strictly toward her proficiency as a sprinter rather than to the longer distances. Choosing to stay in Canada instead of accompanying the rest of the team to Europe, Cathy spent the month of November training at Canada's only regulation-sized speed skating oval in Lethbridge, Alberta. Once in Europe, Priestner got her speed skating season off to an excellent start by gaining

Cathy Priestner of Calgary, Alberta, won an Olympic silver medal in the women's 500 metre in 1976. *Courtesy Cathy Priestner*

triple-header triumphs at international meets during the months preceding the Olympics. "I gave it everything," said the young Calgarian after her Olympic race. Her time of 43.12 seconds paid tribute to her effort as she shattered the Olympic record for the 500 metre event.

In spite of her triumph, Cathy Priestner's moment of glory in first place was all too brief once Sheila Young of the United States skated the same event. Crushing Priestner's short-lived Olympic record, Young finished her final lap with a time of 42.76 to take the gold medal. The first American woman to win a set of three medals in the Olympics, Young took silver in the 1,500 metre and bronze in the 1,000 metre event.

The Canadian men were shut out of the winner's circle in 1976 but Peter Mueller of the United States won the gold medal in the new 1,000 metre race that had been added to the men's events. Norwegian Jan-Egil Storholt celebrated his twenty-seventh birthday by winning the gold medal in the 1,500 metre and team-mate Sten Stensen took the 5,000 metre race. Each event was won by a different man in 1976, with Soviet skater Yevgeny Kulikov winner of the 500 metre and the gold medal going to Piet Kleine of the Netherlands for the 10,000.

A new name appeared on the Canadian Olympic men's speed skating squad in 1976. Seventeen-year-old Gaetan Boucher of the little village of Ste.-Foy, Quebec, finished in a respectable sixth place in the new 1,000 metre men's event, and Canadians would watch his sporting career with pride as his record of consistency increased his stature with the international speed skating establishment.

Several weeks after the twelfth Olympic Winter Games at Innsbruck, in what was to become known as the "Burka Comeback," Sylvia Burka finished first overall in the World Championships held at Gjovik, Norway. The Canadian skater took the title over two skaters who had beaten her in the Olympics just a few weeks before. Gold medalists American Sheila Young and Soviet skater Tatiana Averina lost the 1976 World title to come-from-behind Sylvia Burka. However, more disappointments awaited the Canadian in 1977 as she defended her world title at Keystone, Colorado. Entering the race as the favourite, Burka hit a rut in the ice in the 3,000 metre event and fell, finishing up in fifteenth place in the championships. Two weeks after

her fall in the Worlds, in a typical Burka performance, Sylvia rebounded to win the 1977 World ISU Sprint Championships held at Alkmaar, in the Netherlands. Heartened by her 1977 World title, the victory had restored Sylvia Burka's confidence in her main objective. The one thing left to do in her speed skating career was to win a medal at the thirteenth Olympic Winter Games.

Twenty-one-year-old American speed skater Eric Heiden became a national hero and his name a household word at the Olympic Winter Games at Lake Placid, New York, in 1980.

Unquestionably, Heiden had entered the Olympics as the world's top speed skater, having accumulated numerous international records and winning the World Overall Championships an unprecedented three times in a row. Not only was he the world's best speed skater, he was also capable of racing all distances with equal expertise. Compared to the five different men who won gold medals in their chosen distances at the 1976 Olympic Winter Games, Eric Heiden was an all-round skater, not a specialist.

An impressively strong young man, Heiden's waist measured thirty-two inches, and his thighs each measured twenty-nine inches. He could take any distance given to him and win with his unlimited endurance and skating ability. His remarkable feat of winning every men's speed skating event in an Olympic winter sport that many spectators in the Western Hemisphere felt indifferent to was particularly astounding when skating facilities in North America were compared with those in the U.S.S.R. At the time of the Winter Games at Lake Placid, there were just two Olympic-size speed skating ovals in the United States and one in Canada. In contrast, the Soviet speed skaters had over 1,200 regulation-size rinks in their country.

Ironically, it was the obscurity of the sport of speed skating in the United States that apparently appealed to Heiden. Breaking four Olympic records in the 500, the 1,000, the 1,500, and the 5,000 metre events and establishing a world record in the 10,000 metre event was remarkable in itself, and Eric Heiden became an overnight sensation. Confessing he was uncomfortable with instant fame, "The Great Whoopee," as he called it, Heiden admitted that he liked it better when nobody knew him, and announced his retirement at the end of the 1980 season.

The silver medalist in the men's 1,000 metre event was Canadian Gaetan Boucher. Boucher came into the 1980 Winter Games as a solid favourite with an impressive record of international and Canadian championships to his credit. Paired with Eric Heiden in the first race, Boucher finished in a time of 1:16.68, and for the first time, many Canadians heard or read the name of the speed skater from Quebec who would become Canada's most successful Olympic Games athlete in 1984.

One of six children, Boucher began his speed skating lessons at the indoor hockey rink at Ste.-Foy under the watchful eye of coach Maurice Gagné who is currently the director of the Quebec Speed Skating Federation.

At ten years of age, Gaetan decided to try speed skating to improve his ice hockey game. As he left by himself for his first lesson, his father, never dreaming that one day his son would win an Olympic gold medal, remarked, "I would not

Sylvia Burka, a leading Canadian speedskater, participated in three Olympic Winter Games. *Courtesy Brian Thususka*

count on that too much to improve your skating." And yet, from the moment Gaetan Boucher was on the ice he impressed Gagné immediately with his natural talent on skates. He urged the young boy to continue with speed skating and until he was seventeen years old, Boucher took part in both sports. It was then that Boucher made his total commitment to speed skating.

Beth Heiden, Eric's younger sister, was a World Champion speed skater herself and entered the 1980 Olympic Games as a medal favourite. She won the bronze medal in the 3,000 metre event, losing out to Norway's first woman speed skating gold medalist, Bjoerg-Eva Jensen. Karin Enke, of Dresden, took gold in the 500 metre event, an indication of what was to come from the exceptional East German skater four years later at Sarajevo, Yugoslavia. The U.S.S.R. and Holland won the 1,000 metre and 1,500 metre respectively.

Although she skated well in all her races at the 1980 Olympic Winter Games and finished in the top ten of all events but one, Sylvia Burka's competitive edge seemed to have gone. A medal favourite coming into the Winter Games, Burka's best finish was a disappointing seventh in the 1,000 metre event. Her quest for the Olympic medal she so wanted was over, and she announced that she would retire at the end of the season. During the span of her speed skating career, she had been a source of inspiration to visually impaired athletes, and had accumulated every national speed skating award in Canada, three World titles, and the highest distinction in international speed skating.

After Eric Heiden's retirement in 1980, Boucher had gained

international speed skating honours by setting a world record in the 1,000 metre event and another world record in total points for both the 500 and 1,000 metre sprints. However, his name was still often just seen in his hometown newspaper and, due to illness in February, his seventeenth-place finish at the World Championships in 1983 was less than a newsworthy event. Later on that year a disastrous fall while he was training in a Montreal arena in March sent Gaetan crashing into the boards. He fractured his left ankle and tore all the ligaments. The time he spent in his cast constituted the first training break of more than three weeks that Boucher had taken in eight years of competition.

By the time the Opening Ceremonies took place in the fifty-thousand-seat soccer stadium in downtown Sarajevo, Yugoslavia, in 1984, Gaetan Boucher was twenty-five years old. Taking part in his third Olympic Winter Games, Boucher was selected as the Canadian team's flag bearer at the ceremonies and that honour was a tip-off of good things to come for the speed skater.

One of the most incredible women's speed skating performances of the XIV Olympic Winter Games was by a lanky twenty-two-year-old blonde from Dresden, G.D.R.

Karin Enke had been admitted at age ten to East Germany's top speed skating training team, the Meisterklasse. Enke was a good example of the G.D.R.'s intensively run sports system and had qualified for the 1980 women's speed skating team as an alternate. A star sprinter, Enke came out of nowhere to win the gold medal in the 500 metre event and set an Olympic record of 41.78. To prove that her victory was not a fluke, she carried on to become World sprint champion in 1980, 1981, and 1983. "Let us wait until the Games are over," Karin Enke answered when asked how she felt about being a superstar. However, it was already obvious that she was the queen of women's speed skating at Sarajevo. Enke was the first triple medal winner at the Games winning her third event and establishing a new Olympic record in the 1,000 metre race. Teammate Andrea Schoëne, a twenty-three-year-old mother of a young son, won the silver in the same event, and Soviet skater Natalya Petroseva captured her second bronze.

The G.D.R.'s superstar of speedskating, Karin Enke, winner of four gold medals in 1984 at Sarajevo. *Deutsche Presse-Agentur GmbH*

Gaetan Boucher, Canada's first triple medalist, at the 1984 Games. *Ottmar Bierwagen/Canadian Olympic Association* Inset: Eric Heiden's speed skates, 1980 Olympic Winter Games. *Robert Riger, ABC Sports*

Winning the 1,500 metre and placing second for the silver medal in the 500 metre sprint accelerated Enke's determination to win her fourth Olympic medal in the 3,000. Determined to match the 1964 Olympic four-medal performance by Soviet speed skater Lidia Skoblikova, Karin Enke raced the 3,000 metre two days later. She hit her medal total right on the mark with a silver medal finish in the 3,000 and had to admit after all that she had indeed reached star status.

Having recovered from his broken ankle during the off-season, Boucher looked forward to his Olympic year. The 5'7" 152 pound Boucher knew exactly what he had to do. A few days before the Games began, he started to clock his fastest times of the year during practice sessions. A speed skater with flawless technique and style, Gaetan Boucher was exceptionally good at taking corners in the lanes without a loss of speed. His first race at Sarajevo, the 500 metre, was delayed for five and a half hours because of a heavy snowfall. When the race finally began, Boucher skated the race in the seventh pair and astounded the Canadian public and press with a third-place bronze medal finish just nine-hundredths of a second behind the silver medalist. The gold medal was won by Russian Sergei Fokitchev and Japanese skater Yoshihiro Kitazawa took the silver.

"This is strictly a bonus," said Boucher in response to his win, since he keenly anticipated his next two races, the 1,000 and 1,500 metre events. But, in spite of his talent, Boucher did not start in the top six pairs in the 1,000 metre event at Sarajevo because of his twenty-second-place finish in the World Championships the previous year. He wasn't concerned. The two and one-half laps around the skating oval was his favourite race and the distance was considered his best chance for a medal. He didn't disappoint Canadians watching television at home, or the entire Canadian Olympic hockey team watching from the stands as they cheered him on to his gold medal victory.

As Boucher rounded the final two turns, and the last few seconds remaining ticked away on the clock, the charged-up Canadian contingent broke the euphoric sound barrier as Boucher blew across the finish line in the gold medal time of 1:15.80. The decisive victory was described by Gaetan when he said, "As soon as I crossed the finish line, my coach's reaction told me at a glance everything I needed to know."

Inside the entrance to the Canadian quarters at Olympic Village, the sign went up. "Congratulations, Gaetan—Canada's Greatest Olympian." And, as if it wasn't enough being the first Canadian athlete to win two medals at one Olympic Winter Games since Nancy Greene in 1968, Gaetan Boucher made a prediction. Boucher, matter-of-factly and without a trace of arrogance, said he would be going for gold in the next race, the 1,500 metre. The marketing student from the Université de Montréal knew what he was talking about. The following day he captured his second gold medal in the event, finishing in 1:58.36, beating the two top Soviet skaters Sergei Khlebnikov at 1:58.83 and Oleg Bogiev at 1:58.89.

For Gaetan, whose speed skating hero had been his friend Eric Heiden, the triple medal win was particularly gratifying. Asked if the Olympic medals had taken him out of Eric Heiden's shadow, the soft-spoken Canadian replied, "Winning these medals doesn't take me out of his shadow, they take me out of my own shadow. Instead of always being second, I proved I could be first. I hope I will be recognized for the medals I've won, and maybe I'll be a national hero for a while, eh?"

Owing to the expense of the trip to the Olympic Winter Games in Yugoslavia, Gaetan Boucher's parents were unable to be at Sarajevo to watch their son's golden performance. Nevertheless, the victory brought tears to their eyes, and as he spoke to his son by telephone, Boucher's father seemed to speak for all Canadians when he told him, "Mon bonhomme, tu l'as fait!" My good man, you have done it!

At the victory ceremony at the Skenderija Centre at Sarajevo, Canada's most successful Olympic athlete mounted the podium to receive his second glittering Olympic gold medal. After the Canadian anthem was played and the Canadian flag raised, the moment crystallized into a beautiful memory, as speed skater Gaetan Boucher raised his arms in victory.

In September of 1986, Cathy Priestner moved from London, Ontario, to become the assistant manager of the Olympic Oval on the campus of the University of Calgary.

# The Venue

The speed skating event for the XV Olympic Winter Games will take place in one of the world's first covered speed skating facilities, the Olympic Oval.

A ten-minute ride on Calgary's Light Rail Transit (LRT) will take spectators from downtown Calgary to the Olympic Oval located on the campus of the University of Calgary.

The Olympic Oval was constructed by the Government of Canada at a cost of approximately $39 million. The facility will not only provide the Olympic venue for the speed skating event, but will also be developed as a multi-sports centre as a legacy of the 1988 Winter Games.

The unique roof of the venue is comprised of a number of intersecting concrete arches which have been pre-cast and held in place by buttresses on the outside foundations of the building. The clear-spanned Oval offers excellent viewing for the four thousand spectators who will be watching the speed skating events in 1988.

In the main entrance foyer, the bronze sculptural relief entitled "Brothers of the Wind," will be permanently displayed. Finished by Canadian artist R. Tait McKenzie in 1925, the bronze relief was purchased at a Christie's auction in New York and brought back to Canada in 1984 when it was acquired by the University of Calgary.

Inside the gigantic Olympic Oval, the best men and women speed skaters in the world will compete on the 400 metre track as they race against the clock. The artificial ice surface is a continuous unbroken track consisting of two 5 metre wide parallel lanes. The lanes are divided by movable markers on the straightaways.

The Olympic Speed Skating Format has five races for men and five for women. The 500, 1,000, 1,500, and 5,000 metre distances are common to both men and women. In addition, the women skate a 3,000 metre race and the men a 10,000 metre race.

Countries which participate in the Olympic speed skating event at Calgary in 1988 will be limited to three entries each in the 500 and 1,500 metre men's races, three in the 5,000 metre race, and two in the 10,000 metre. Each of the women's events allows a maximum of three entries.

The maximum number of competitors any country can enter in the Olympic speed skating events is three men and three women.

During the Olympic Winter Games, electronic timing devices will monitor each event at the Olympic Oval and will record times in hundredths of seconds.

The 26,000 square metre Olympic Oval measures 200 metres in length and 90 metres in width. The Olympic venue is so enormous in size that twenty-two tennis courts could be placed inside the 400 metre oval track.

## The Technique

Technique and skating style are two deciding factors that influence the outcome of speed skating races.

The only exception to this rule is in the 500 metre sprint, where the effort expended is one of sheer power. The 500 is definitely an all-out burst of speed, and skaters have been clocked up to 48 kph for the short distance. Statistics indicate that a speed skater is one of the world's fastest self-propelled athletes. An Olympic speed skater can race a mile on a flat surface in approximately two minutes, whereas an Olympic runner takes nearly four minutes to cover the same distance. In the 500 metre event, the winning times are close and often equally matched competitors finish within hundredths of a second of each other.

Longer races require precise technique and concentration on the part of the racer. The starts for the 3,000, 5,000, and 10,000 metre are located at the end of the lane near the turns. For the longer distances, the first moves off the starting line are long strides and the start appears much slower than the sprint start.

Once the skater has built up momentum, he bends forward from the waist and crouches low with his hands behind his back as he glides along the straightaways. As he leans forward into each long stroke, the racer attempts to maintain his stride along an imaginary straight line. The skater tries to avoid swaying from side to side and works to establish a smooth striding rhythm as he moves ahead into the curves.

The ability to master and negotiate the turn is the key to victory for the speed skater. Watching one of the world's fastest skaters scissor-skate around the curves offers the spectator the advantage of seeing the combination of speed, elegance, and power in a superlative athlete.

When skating the longer distances the racer conserves his energy by skating in the hands-behind-the-back position in the lanes. Swinging the arm forward and diagonally across the body, or sweeping the arm straight back as far as possible, is a tech-

nique used by skaters to increase speed and help keep balance through the turn.

Attempting to keep his speed constant as he enters the turn, the racer utilizes the arm swing and crouches low into the cross-over skating action that will take him around the corner.

In addition to technique and skating style, there are climatic elements that determine the final standings in speed skating races.

Until the 1988 Winter Games, Olympic speed skating has been held on an outdoor 400 metre oval. At Sarajevo, the heaviest snowfall the city had experienced in ten years affected the final times for both men's and women's events. For example, none of Eric Heiden's 1980 Olympic speed skating records were broken at the Games in Yugoslavia. However, for Gaetan Boucher, the snowfall during the 1,500 metre men's race worked to his advantage when he skated in the eighth pair for his second gold medal. The ice was scheduled to be serviced after the seventh pair skated, and Boucher was pleased that the maintenance crew was prevented from flooding the ice and making the surface softer and slower. Instead, he skated immediately after the crew had cleaned the ice, and won the event.

Snow is not the only opponent that skaters face on an outdoor rink. Sun can melt the ice and wind can render a speed skater's efforts ineffective as he uses all his strength in an extra effort to fight the sudden gusts or flurries.

The world's finest covered Olympic speed skating oval at Calgary will liberate Olympic skaters from the changes in weather conditions. The world's top speed skaters will enjoy a readily controlled environment for the first time in the history of the Olympic Winter Games.

## The Rules

Start orders and lane selection are decided by a draw the day before the event takes place.

Spectators rarely see two top world-calibre speed skaters race against each other in the Olympic event. Occasionally, two favourites race head to head as did Eric Heiden and Gaetan Boucher, who won gold and silver respectively in the 1,000 metre event at the XIII Olympic Winter Games at Lake Placid, New York, in 1980. In such an instance, the luck of the draw proved fortuitous since extremely competitive opponents often produce the best results.

At the Olympic Oval the speed skaters will race in a counter-clockwise direction, against the clock. Observing the 400 metre speed skating track, it is obvious that the corner radius of the inner lane offers a distinct advantage. To offset this fact, speed skating rules require the racers to cross lanes after each lap. This ruling ensures that an equivalent distance is covered by each pair of racers.

To compensate for the smaller radius of the inner lane, the start lines are staggered for the 1,000, 1,500, 3,000 and 5,000 metre distances.

The cross-overs take place on the entire length of the back-stretch and the rules for the lane changes are very specific.

At the crossing along the straight, interference and collisions frequently result in disqualifications. The right of way belongs to the skater crossing from the outer lane to the inner lane. A collision is considered the fault of the skater leaving the inner lane, unless the other skater causes interference.

With the exception of the first straight of the 1,000 and 1,500 metre distances, skaters must change lanes each time they are on the backstretch. A breach of this rule results in disqualification.

In the event of a fall, the skater is not disqualified and is allowed to proceed in the race.

# The Equipment

The design of speed skates has evolved through the years from the heavy iron skates used in the sixteenth century in Scotland to the lightweight, razor-sharp steel blade skates used in competition today.

Speed skates have long hollow steel blades that enable a racer to power glide smoothly and continuously on one skate and maintain speed on the straightaways and turns.

The front closure of the boot is low-cut compared to an ice hockey skate, the top of the skate reaching just below the ankle to facilitate the forward body lean of the racer and to aid the skater in retaining momentum.

The skater's uniform is skintight, distinctive in bright colour, and made from a four-way stretch nylon fabric to give the speed skater an aerodynamic advantage and also freedom of movement. The hood of the uniform is attached to the suit and covers the head of the skater like a tight-fitting bathing cap.

The only other distinguishing feature of the Olympic uniform for a speed skater is a racing number on an arm band on the right arm. The arm band worn on the left arm identifies the lane the racer is using, white being for the racer starting in the inner lane and red for the racer starting in the outer lane.

# Calgary Preview

### Men
Two major psychological barriers have been removed for promising young Canadian speed skaters since the Olympic Winter Games at Sarajevo, Yugoslavia, in 1984.

Gaetan Boucher's triple medal win at the 1984 Olympic Winter Games triggered an optimistic and enthusiastic outlook for Canadian speed skaters. The second deciding factor has been the construction of Calgary's Olympic Oval.

With fewer than ten speed skating ovals in Canada, all on natural ice, Calgary's indoor oval will now allow skaters to train and attend classes at the University of Calgary at the same time. The Canadian Olympic speed skating team for the first time will be chosen from a field of almost one hundred skaters compared to fewer than twenty in 1984. However, with approximately three thousand competitive speed skaters in Canada, by far the country's best medal hope is still Gaetan Boucher who it is hoped will be competing in 1988 at Calgary. Other

speed skaters who could become medalists in the men's Olympic events are Guy Thibault of Quebec City, Daniel Turcotte one of the best of the younger skaters for Canada, Ben Lamarche of Quebec City, who set a Canadian Junior record in the 500 metre event in 1985 when he was eighteen years old. Lamarche finished in ninth place overall in the 1987 World Championships in the Netherlands.

The speed skating monopoly of the Scandinavian and eastern-bloc countries may continue to dominate the events at the Olympic Oval in 1988. The Norwegians in particular look as strong as ever and skaters Rolf Falk-Larssen, Tom Erik Oxholm, Bjorn Nyland, and Gier Karlstad have all chalked up individual victories in the pre-Olympic events.

Prominent Olympic skater Tomas Gustafson of Sweden has been slightly overshadowed during the past season by veteran skaters Alexander Baranov and Victor Shasherin of the Soviet Union. The performance of the Soviets at all the pre-Olympic speed skating events is impossible to ignore, and with Nikolai Gulyaev and Oleg Bozyev placing first and second respectively in the 1987 Worlds, the speed skaters from the U.S.S.R. look like the medal contenders in 1988.

Throughout the 1986/87 season, the Scandinavian and eastern bloc skaters were joined on the podium by Akira Kuriowa and Yukihira Mitani, two rising Japanese stars. Both should be in peak form for Calgary.

Still in Olympic form are Dutch skaters Leo Visser, Gerrard Kemkers, and Hein Vegeer. If there is a male counterpart to Karin Enke on the team from the G.D.R., he has yet to put in an appearance in international speed skating circles.

The Americans will be represented by sprinter Dan Jansen, who narrowly missed out to Gaetan Boucher in the race for the bronze medal in the 500 metre at Sarajevo in 1984. Other American skaters to watch at Calgary in 1988 are World sprint champions Nick Thometz and Erik Hendriksen.

### Women
Karin Enke will be back in 1988 and that is not the best of news for the field of women speed skaters at Calgary. The speed skating queen at Sarajevo and winner of four Olympic medals in 1984 Kania (née Enke) was married after the 1984 Olympic Winter Games and took 1985 off to give birth to son, Alexandr. Now known as the queen mother, Kania continues to be the dominant force in speed skating since her first World crown in 1980. Her victories, such as her sixth World sprint title at Ste.-Foy, Quebec, in 1987, are always expected and she brings with her the most expertise to the women's event. Being four years older than she was at Sarajevo, Kania may well have to prove herself against her team mates Andrea Ehrig-Schoene, Gabi Schoenbrunn, and Christa Rothenburger.

Canadian Senior Speed Skating Champion Natalie Grenier of Quebec City heads the women's national team. Vying for national team selection will be Nathalie Lambert and Sylvie Daigle from Montreal, and Chantal Coute from Laval, Quebec. Saskatchewan's Shelly Rhead is the only western Canadian on the team.

The girl who gives Karin Kania trouble is American skater Bonnie "The Blur" Blair, who won the 500 metre at the 1987 World Championships at Ste.-Foy, Quebec. Blair finished in second place behind Kania in the 1,000 metre, and she had the East Germans worried. The Soviet skaters could also feature at the Olympics in 1988, and have a good solid team with Irina Kuleshova, Irina Fateeva, Tadianna Kabutova, and Marianne Evgrafova.

## Canadians at the Olympic Winter Games
# SPEED SKATING

### 1924 Chamonix — I Olympic Winter Games

**MEN**

*500 metres*
7. Charles Gorman

*1,500 metres*
11. Charles Gorman

### 1928 St. Moritz — II Olympic Winter Games

Gorman, C., Logan, W., Robinson, R.

*500 metres*
7. Charles Gorman
11. William Logan
14. Ross Robinson

*1,500 metres*
17. Ross Robinson
21. William Logan

*5,000 metres*
22. Ross Robinson
29. William Logan

### 1932 Lake Placid — III Olympic Winter Games

Brooks-Potter, L., Donaldson, H., Flack, H., Hurd, A., Hurd, F., Logan, W., Mackie, G., McCarthy, M., Smyth, H., Stack, F., Sylvestre, L., Wilson, J.

**MEN**

*500 metres*
3. Alexander Hurd
4. Frank Stack
5. William Logan

*1,500 metres*
2. Alexander Hurd
3. William Logan
4. Frank Stack

*5,000 metres*
3. William Logan
7. Frank Stack
8. Harry Smyth

*10,000 metres*
3. Frank Stack
7. Alexander Hurd

**WOMEN**

*500 metres*
1. Jean Wilson
4. Lela Brooks-Potter

*1,000 metres*
2. Hattie Donaldson
4. Lela Brooks-Potter
5. Geraldine Mackie
6. Jean Wilson

*1,500 metres*
2. Jean Wilson
4. Geraldine Mackie
6. Lela Brooks-Potter

### 1936 Garmisch-Partenkirchen — IV Olympic Winter Games

**MEN**

*1,500 metres*
34. Thomas White

*5,000 metres*
25. Thomas White

*10,000 metres*
21. Thomas White

### 1948 St. Moritz — V Olympic Winter Games

Audley, G., Hardy, A., MacKay, C., Stack, F.

**MEN**

*500 metres*
6. Frank Stack
17. Gordon Audley
19. A. Hardy

*1,500 metres*
27. Frank Stack

*1,500 metres (cont'd)*
29. A. Hardy
32. Gordon Audley

*5,000 metres*
14. Craig MacKay

*10,000 metres*
13. Craig MacKay

### 1952 Oslo — VI Olympic Winter Games

Audley, G., MacKay, C., Olin, R., Stack, F.

**MEN**

*500 metres*
3. Gordon Audley
12. Frank Stack
15. Craig MacKay
30. Ralf Olin

*1,500 metres*
16. Craig MacKay
29. Ralf Olin

*5,000 metres*
23. Craig MacKay
25. Ralf Olin

*10,000 metres*
21. Ralf Olin
24. Craig MacKay

### 1956 Cortina d'Ampezzo — VII Olympic Winter Games

**MEN**

*500 metres*
25. Gordon Audley
36. Ralf Olin

*1,500 metres*
41. Ralf Olin
45. John Sands
53. Gordon Audley

*5,000 metres*
33. Ralf Olin

*10,000 metres*
31. Ralf Olin

### 1960 Squaw Valley — VIII Olympic Winter Games

Mason, L., Olin, R., Robb, M., Ryan, D., Sands, J.

**MEN**

*500 metres*
27. John Sands
30. Ralf Olin
41. Lawrence Mason

*1,500 metres*
36. Ralf Olin
43. John Sands
45. Lawrence Mason

*5,000 metres*
28. Ralf Olin
37. Lawrence Mason

*10,000 metres*
27. Ralf Olin

**WOMEN**

*500 metres*
9. Doreen Ryan
17. Margaret Robb

*1,000 metres*
13. Doreen Ryan
19. Margaret Robb

*1,500 metres*
13. Doreen Ryan
20. Margaret Robb

*3,000 metres*
14. Doreen Ryan
16. Margaret Robb

## 1964 Innsbruck — IX Olympic Winter Games

Koning, G., McCannell, D., Olin, R., Ryan, D.

**MEN**

*500 metres*
39. Ralf Olin

*1,500 metres*
37. Ralf Olin
47. Gerald Koning

*5,000 metres*
25. Ralf Olin
35. Gerald Koning

*10,000 metres*
15. Ralf Olin

**WOMEN**

*500 metres*
10. Doreen Ryan
13. Doreen McCannell

*1,000 metres*
11. Doreen Ryan
13. Doreen McCannell

*1,500 metres*
13. Doreen McCannell
16. Doreen Ryan

*3,000 metres*
8. Doreen McCannell
24. Doreen Ryan

## 1968 Grenoble - X Olympic Winter Games

Boucher, R., Enock, P., Hodges, R., McCannell, D., Parsons, M., Thompson, W., Williamson, P.

**MEN**

*500 metres*
25. Robert Boucher
33. Peter Williamson
41. Robert Hodges

*1,500 metres*
26. Robert Hodges
46. Peter Williamson

*5,000 metres*
19. Paul Enock
29. Robert Hodges

*10,000 metres*
15. Paul Enock
23. Robert Hodges

**WOMEN**

*500 metres*
19. Wendy Thompson
23. Marcia Parsons
24. Doreen McCannell

*1,000 metres*
20. Doreen McCannell
21. Marcia Parsons
27. Wendy Thompson

*1,500 metres*
21. Doreen McCannell
24. Marcia Parsons

*3,000 metres*
18. Doreen McCannell
22. Marcia Parsons

## 1972 Sapporo — XI Olympic Winter Games

Barron, A., Burka, S., Cassan, G., Cassidy, J., Gordon, G., Hodges, R., Jackson, J., McCannell, D., Priestner, C., Sirois, K.

**MEN**

*500 metres*
29. Gérard Cassan
30. John Cassidy

*1,500 metres*
23. Robert Hodges
26. Kevin Sirois
36. Andrew Barron

*5,000 metres*
19. Kevin Sirois
25. Andrew Barron

*10,000 metres*
14. Kevin Sirois

**WOMEN**

*500 metres*
14. Catherine Priestner
25. Donna McCannell

*1,000 metres*
8. Sylvia Burka
29. Catherine Priestner
32. Gayle Gordon

1,500 metres
21. Sylvia Burka
27. Gayle Gordon
30. Jennifer Jackson

## 1976 Innsbruck — XII Olympic Winter Games

Appleby, E., Barron A., Boucher, G., Burka, S., Gordon, G., Overend, T., Priestner, C., Vogt, K.

**MEN**

*500 metres*
11. Tom Overend
14. Gaetan Boucher

*1,000 metres*
6. Gaetan Boucher
23. Tom Overend

*1,500 metres*
14. Gaetan Boucher

*5,000 metres*
23. Andrew Barron

**WOMEN**

*500 metres*
2. Catherine Priestner
11. Sylvia Burka
21. Kathleen Vogt

*1,000 metres*
4. Sylvia Burka
6. Catherine Priestner
22. Elizabeth Appleby

*1,500 metres*
9. Sylvia Burka
21. Elizabeth Appleby
23. Kathleen Vogt

*3,000 metres*
8. Sylvia Burka
18. Elizabeth Appleby
23. Gayle Gordon

## 1980 Lake Placid — XIII Olympic Winter Games

Boucher, G., Burka, S., Daigle, S., Durnin, P., Thibault, J., Vogt, K., Webster, B., Webster, C.

**MEN**

*500 metres*
8. Gaetan Boucher
26. Jacques Thibault

*1,000 metres*
2. Gaetan Boucher
20. Jacques Thibault
27. Craig Webster

*1,500 metres*
15. Gaetan Boucher
23. Craig Webster
27. Jacques Thibault

*5,000 metres*
20. Craig Webster

**WOMEN**

*500 metres*
9. Sylvia Burka
18. Kathleen Vogt
19. Sylvie Daigle

*1,000 metres*
7. Sylvia Burka
19. Brenda Webster
24. Kathleen Vogt

*1,500 metres*
10. Sylvia Burka
11. Brenda Webster
16. Kathleen Vogt

*3,000 metres*
11. Brenda Webster
12. Sylvia Burka
23. Patricia Durnin

## 1984 Sarajevo — XIV Olympic Winter Games

Boucher, G., Daigle, S., Grenier, N., Lamarche, B., Pichette, J., Thibault, J., Turcotte, D.

**MEN**

*500 metres*
3. G. Boucher
15. J. Thibault
29. D. Turcotte

*1,000 metres*
1. G. Boucher
19. J. Thibault

*1,500 metres*
1. G. Boucher

*5,000 metres*
36. B. Lamarche
38. J. Pichette

**WOMEN**

*500 metres*
20. S. Daigle

*1,000 metres*
18. N. Grenier
25. S. Daigle

*1,500 metres*
21. N. Grenier
22. S. Daigle

*3,000 metres*
15. N. Grenier

*10,000 metres*
Canada did not participate.

# Demonstration Sports

Curling
Max Bell Arena
February 14, 15, 16, 17, 19, 20

# Curling

**Max Bell Arena**
**February 14, 15, 16, 17, 19, 20,**

The host city for every Olympic Games is invited to include two or three sports that are not official Olympic events, but which are widely practised in the country.

In view of the fact that Canada is the world's dominant nation in the sport of curling, it is hardly surprising that curling was chosen as one of the demonstration sports for the 1988 Olympic Winter Games in Calgary.

There are close to 2 million curlers in Canada compared to about fifty thousand in Scotland, the traditional homeland of this sport. There is more interest from Canadians, both as participants and as spectators, than anywhere else in the world, although curling is popular in France, Italy, Germany, New Zealand, Switzerland, Norway, Sweden, and the U.S.A.

Both Holland and Scotland claim to be the homeland of curling. It was first depicted as a sport by the Flemish painter Pieter Bruegel (c. 1525-69); however, the development of the sport is definitely to be credited to the Scots. The first Scottish Club was formed in 1510 and in 1838 the Grand Caledonian Curling Club was established, although it was renamed the Royal Caledonian Curling Club after an exhibition game for the young Queen Victoria.

Curling was introduced to Canada in 1807; Canadians have been successful at it ever since. At the 1932 Olympics in Lake Placid, New York, the Canadian team from Manitoba, led by J. Bowman, won the exhibition match. The world championship, held since 1959, was won by Canada six times in a row before the U.S.A. (1965) and Scotland (1967) had a chance at the title.

One of the most helpful factors that curling had going for it was the fact that the sport acquired the patronage of many influential Canadians who supported it and were proud of their Scottish ancestry. Among them were the Governors General and more recently, three-time Brier winner Ken Watson of Manitoba, Alberta's Matt Baldwin, and the famous Richardson Rink from Regina, Saskatchewan. Ernie Richardson and his team won four Briers in five years and were among the inaugural teams to take part in the 1959 Scotch Cup, a competition between Canada and Scotland. The ten-nation championship was superseded by the Silver Broom World Championships, which Calgary's Ron Northcott won three times.

The game has been compared to shuffleboard. It is played on a stretch of ice approximately forty-two metres long with a target at each end. The largest concentric circle on the target has a radius of 2.13 metres. A fixed mark in the centre of the circle is known as the house.

Two teams of four players attempt to slide two 20 kilogram granite stones as near as possible to the house. The game has ten ends and is finished when all players have alternately thrown two rocks each. One point is awarded for each stone in the centre of the house and the team with the most stones close to the centre wins.

A unique feature of the sport is the use of a broom to sweep ahead of the running stone to increase the distance the rock will

The famous Richardson Rink from Regina, Saskatchewan, won four Briers in five years. Pictured clockwise from top left: Wes Richardson, Ernie Richardson, Arnold Richardson, and Garnet Richardson. *Canada Sports Hall of Fame*

travel over the surface of the ice. Under orders from the skip, the players sweep in front of the stone, but never touch it. Obviously to sweep out of doors in bad weather was a necessity. The use of the broom moved inside early in the twentieth century when indoor curling rinks were introduced.

The difficulty lies not in launching the stone, but in providing it with the right trajectory. A player can make the stone curl slightly by a movement of his or her wrist on the handle, which accounts for the sport's name.

The most ancient curling stone found to date was discovered in a Scottish marshland near Dunblane. The date written on it was 1551. The first curling stones had fingerholds in them, but by the 1600s, stones with handles were introduced. Today, almost all curling stones are carved out of a special quarry on the island of Ailsa Craig situated in the estuary of Scotland's river Clyde. The quarry produces some fifteen hundred curling stones per year.

Curling has attempted for decades to become honoured as an Olympic sport. It was included as a demonstration sport in the 1924 Olympics and in three subsequent Games.

The 1988 Olympic curling demonstration will be held at the Max Bell Arena. There will be two open competitions, one for men and one for women. Sixteen teams are expected to take part with four curlers per team. Canada's women's world champion Pat Sanders of Victoria, British Columbia, master strategist Ed Lukowich of Calgary, Alberta and the Russ Howard championship rink could dominate the competition.

The two world champion entries to the 1988 Olympic Winter Games are both from Penetanguishene, Ontario. Brian Orser, the 1987 world champion in figure skating is one of them, and the 1987 world men's curling champion Russ Howard is the other one, which is not a bad average for one of Canada's smaller cities.

It is anticipated that curling will put in an all-out effort to be accepted as an Olympic sport as early as 1992.

# Demonstration Events

# Freestyle Skiing

Canada Olympic Park—February 21, 25
Nakiska at Mount Allan—February 22

Freestyle skiing, chosen as a demonstration event in the 1988 Winter Games, has a history that stretches far beyond the "hot-doggers" of the 1970s. While the first flip on skis was noted in 1907, development of the technique in ballet and stunts is attributed to Dr. Fritz Reuel, who in 1929 anticipated a form of skiing related to figure skating and who developed the Reuel ("royal") christie. From 1956 to 1962 Doug Pfeiffer's School of Exotic Skiing taught all sorts of tricks on skis. In the 1960s trick skiing was a popular demonstration for weekend crowds at ski resorts. In 1971 the first National Championships were held in this sport.

Through the 1970s and 1980s, freestyle skiing has been dominated by Canadian athletes such as world champions Greg Athans, Bill Keenan, Peter Judge, Yves Laroche, Marie-Claude Asselin, and the "Zowie" Bowie family.

Freestyle skiing is composed of three events: moguls, aerials, and ballet.

*Mogul* skiing consists of technically correct, aggressive fall line skiing (straight down the main part of a hill), on the steepest and most difficult mogul covered run available. The gradient is 27 to 35 degrees, the length 200 to 250 metres. The run is judged on technical ability, style and time. One of the facets of mogul skiing is "taking air," that is, spontaneous jumps (no flips) performed during the run that lead neither to a loss of time nor rhythm. Canada has been strong in this competition with Bill Keenan of Calgary winning the world championship in 1983.

In the *aerial* event, the skier executes jumps on a specially prepared jump site. The landing hill below the takeoff is 37 degrees in steepness and 30 metres long. The skier performs acrobatic and upright manoeuvres while in the air; the event in fact closely resembles diving. The judges look for height and distance of the jump, the form of the manoeuvre, the landing, and the degree of difficulty. Aerials, like diving, is a spectacular sport and the grace of movement combined with the underlying element of danger makes it particularly popular. The current Canadian champions in this discipline are Jean-Marc Rozon, Lloyd Langlois, and Yves Laroche of Quebec for the men's and Meredith Ann Gardner and Anna Fraser for the women's. Billed as "The Quebec Air Force" Langlois in particular is known for a unique Rudy-Rudy Full—a triple somersault, with four full twists. Last year, Langlois won a World Cup competition in Breckenridge, Colorado, by the largest margin of victory ever recorded in the event.

The *ballet* event can be most easily compared to figure skating. The skier combines a number of intricate manoeuvres in a choreographed routine, performed to music on a gentle slope (gradient of 10 to 14 degrees, distance of 200 to 250 metres). A competition routine combines spins and dance-like steps with double-axel jumps and flips that are executed with the aid of special ski poles. The routine is judged on degree of difficulty, choreography, interpretation of music, as well as the form and line of body. Lucie Barma

Freestyle ski champ Lloyd Langlois, a member of the "Quebec Air Force", demonstrates what being an aerialist means. *Athlete Information Bureau/Canadian Olympic Association*

of Lac Beauport, Quebec, and Chris Simboli of Ottawa, Ontario, are currently the top Canadian skiers in this category.

Freestyle skiing should be tremendously popular with spectators at the 1988 Winter Games because of its high visual appeal. Moguls are scheduled to take place on Nakiska at Mt. Allan, aerials and ballet at Canada Olympic Park.

## Short Track Speed Skating

**Max Bell Arena**
**February 22, 23, 24, 25**

Another first at the Calgary Winter Games in 1988 will be the demonstration event of short track speed skating. For years this sport has been widely practised in ordinary ice hockey arenas throughout Canada.

The differences from speed skating are several: whereas in speed skating the competitor races against the clock, in short track the competitor races against many others in a mass or "pack" start. Speed skating takes place on a 400 metre track which has generally been outside (Calgary's 400 metre covered oval is the world's second; the first was opened in the Netherlands in 1986), whereas short track takes place on a 111 metre indoor track laid out on the surface of a hockey rink.

Quebec's Nathalie Lambert set a world record in the women's 3,000 metre race at the 1987 indoor speed skating championships. *Canapress Photo Service*

High speed and sharp turns make the sport reasonably dangerous and helmets, gloves, and knee pads are mandatory.

In Calgary in 1988 the various competitions—500, 1,000, 1,500 and 3,000 metre, as well as a relay for women (3,000 metres) and men (5,000 metres)—will take place in the Max Bell Arena. A high level of fitness is required in this demonstration event. Each competitor normally skates all distances and relays, often skating through a series of elimination rounds to a final in one day.

Except for British Columbian Eden Donatelli, Canada's eight-member national team comes from Quebec. The men's team consists of former world champion Guy Daignault and his brother Michele, Robert Dubreuil and Louis Grenier, another former World champion. The women's team includes Nathalie Lambert, Ariane Loignon, and Eden Donatelli.

Watch for Bonnie Blair of Champaign, Illinois, to give the tough European field a run for its money. Blair took the 1986 North American Indoor Championships along with the International Skating Union championship in her pre-Olympic year.

## Disabled Skiing Exhibition

**Canada Olympic Park**
**Giant Slalom Exhibition**
**February 21**

**Canmore Nordic Centre**
**Cross-Country Skiing for the Blind**
**February 17**

People with single leg amputations and people who are blind have the same needs for recreation and competition as their able-bodied counterparts.

With adaptions to ski equipment and proper instruction, ski school director Jerry Johnston began to teach both types of disabled skiers at Sunshine Village, Banff, in 1963. By 1975, Johnston's inaugural program had grown into the Canadian Association for Disabled Skiing (CADS) under the auspices of the Fitness and Amateur Sports Branch of the federal government. Since its inception, disabled skiing has expanded to eight provinces in Canada plus the Northwest Territories.

Jerry Johnston was the founding president of CADS in 1976 and during his career with skiing has received the 1974 Alberta Achievement Award for service and in 1979 for excellence and was inducted into the Alberta Sports Hall of Fame as a Builder in 1980 for his work with the disabled.

His Excellency, Dr. Juan Antonio Samaranch, President of the International Olympic Committee, was instrumental in developing sports for the disabled in Spain. During the 1984 Olympic Winter Games at Sarajevo, Yugoslavia, President Samaranch invited disabled skiers to give a demonstration of their sport for the first time in the history of the Olympics.

The demonstration was so well received that a wheelchair race for the disabled was staged at the 1984 Olympic Summer Games in Los Angeles, California.

Again in 1988, the elite of the disabled skiers have been invited to stage an exhibition of their sport at the Olympic Winter Games in Calgary. The two exhibitions will include a giant slalom race for amputee skiers, and a cross-country race for totally blind skiers.

The cross-country event for the blind will take place after the women's 5 kilometre Olympic event at the Canmore Nordic Centre. Each blind racer will be accompanied by a guide who will ski beside or behind the racer to enable the racer to hear their voice. Cross-country skiing for the blind was started in Norway and has spread all over the world. Spectators at the Canmore Nordic Centre will see the top blind cross-country skiers in the world at the 1988 Olympic Winter Games.

The giant slalom race for amputee skiers will take place before the freestyle aerials event at Canada Olympic Park.

United States Disabled Ski Team Coach Danny Pufpaff is an example of the courage many disabled skiers demonstrate. When he stepped on a land mine in Vietnam and had his leg blown off, part of his rehabilitation was learning to ski on one ski at Colorado's Winter Park Resort.

The envy of disabled skiers throughout the world, Winter Park was designed as a national disabled sports and recreation area, and some of the best amputee skiers in the world are trained in the disabled ski program there. Today, very few able-bodied skiers could keep up with Danny Pufpaff on a race course, but one of the skiers who can beat him is his star pupil Greg Mannino. Mannino is one of the hottest amputee racers on the circuit and will be a competitor in the exhibition during the 1988 Olympics.

Canada's national champion Lynda Chyzyk demonstrates her ski technique while racing with the aid of ski outriggers used by disabled skiers. Chyzyk is coached at Whistler Mountain, British Columbia, by Dave Murray, one of the Crazy Canucks. *Simon Hoyle, Courtesy the Association for Disabled Skiing.*

Some skiers lose their leg to the same type of cancer that Terry Fox and Steve Fonyo had. Both Phil Chew and Lynda Chyzyk recovered from their surgery to become Canada's top amputee racers and both will be gunning for victory on their "home hill" in Calgary. Phil Chew trains year round at Whistler, British Columbia, and Lynda Chyzyk cleaned up at the Canadian championships last year.

If Sweden's Ola Rylander's grandfather were still alive, he would have been proud to see his grandson ski. As a young man, he himself had competed in the 1932 Olympic Winter Games at Lake Placid, New York, as a ski jumper. When his grandson was born he had hopes of training and coaching him as a ski jumper. But Ola Rylander was born with a withered leg that wouldn't grow, and when he was twelve years old, the leg was amputated.

Rylander started to ski on one ski, and it wasn't long before Swedish skiing ace Ingemar Stenmark noticed his talent and invited him to train with the Swedish National Ski Team. Stenmark taught Ola Rylander how to ski without outriggers (ski crutches) and today Rylander is one of the few amputee skiers in the world to ski with regular ski poles. Unfortunately, Rylander retired from active competition in 1986, and will not be competing in the 1988 Olympic Winter Games. However, it is hoped that he can forerun the giant slalom course for the Olympic Exhibition. Ola Rylander also holds the distinction of being the fastest man in the world on one ski. *The Guinness Book of World Records* verifies that official record—128 kilometres per hour.

Profiles in courage will be on display in the Disabled Skiing Exhibition at Canada Olympic Park at the 1988 Olympic Winter Games in Calgary, Alberta.

The fastest man in the world on one ski, Ola Rylander of Sweden. *Simon Hoyle, Courtesy the Canadian Association for Disabled Skiing*

# Medalists of the Olympic Winter Games

| Year | Gold Medalists | Silver Medalists | Bronze Medalists |
|------|----------------|------------------|------------------|

# ALPINE SKIING

### Men's Downhill

| Year | Gold Medalists | Silver Medalists | Bronze Medalists |
|------|----------------|------------------|------------------|
| 1948 | Henri Oreiller (FRA) | Franz Gabl (AUT) | Karl Molitor (SUI) |
| | | | Ralph Olinger (SUI) |
| 1952 | Zena Colò (ITA) | Othmar Schneider (AUT) | Christian Pravda (AUT) |
| 1956 | Anton Sailer (AUT) | Raymond Fellay (SUI) | Anderl Molterer (AUT) |
| 1960 | Jean Vuarnet (FRA) | Hans-Peter Lanig (GER) | Guy Périllat (FRA) |
| 1964 | Egon Zimmermann II (AUT) | Léo Lacroix (FRA) | Wolfgang Bartels (GER) |
| 1968 | Jean-Claude Killy (FRA) | Guy Périllat (FRA) | Jean-Daniel Dätwyler (SUI) |
| 1972 | Bernhard Russi (SUI) | Roland Collombin (SUI) | Heini Messner (AUT) |
| 1976 | Franz Klammer (AUT) | Bernhard Russi (SUI) | Herbert Plank (ITA) |
| 1980 | Leonhard Stock (AUT) | Peter Wirnsberger (AUT) | Stephen Podborski (CAN) |
| 1984 | William Johnson (USA) | Peter Mueller (SUI) | Anton Steiner (AUT) |

### Men's Giant Slalom

| Year | Gold Medalists | Silver Medalists | Bronze Medalists |
|------|----------------|------------------|------------------|
| 1952 | Stein Eriksen (NOR) | Christian Pravda (AUT) | Toni Spiss (AUT) |
| 1956 | Anton Sailer (AUT) | Anderl Molterer (AUT) | Walter Shuster (AUT) |
| 1960 | Roger Staub (SUI) | Josef Stiegler (AUT) | Ernst Hinterseer (AUT) |
| 1964 | François Bonlieu (FRA) | Karl Schranz (AUT) | Josef Stiegler (AUT) |
| 1968 | Jean-Claude Killy (FRA) | Willy Favre (SUI) | Heini Messner (AUT) |
| 1972 | Gustavo Thoeni (ITA) | Edmund Bruggmann (SUI) | Werner Mattle (SUI) |
| 1976 | Heini Hemmi (SUI) | Ernst Good (SUI) | Ingemar Stenmark (SWE) |
| 1980 | Ingemar Stenmark (SWE) | Andreas Wenzel (LIE) | Hans Enn (AUT) |
| 1984 | Max Julen (SUI) | Jure Franko (YUG) | Andreas Wenzel (LIE) |

### Men's Slalom

| Year | Gold Medalists | Silver Medalists | Bronze Medalists |
|------|----------------|------------------|------------------|
| 1948 | Edi Reinalter (SUI) | James Couttet (FRA) | Henri Oreiller (FRA) |
| 1952 | Othmar Schneider (AUT) | Stein Eriksen (NOR) | Guttorm Berge (NOR) |
| 1956 | Anton Sailer (AUT) | Chiharu Igaya (JPN) | Stig Sollander (SWE) |
| 1960 | Ernst Hinterseer (AUT) | Hias Leitner (AUT) | Charles Bozon (FRA) |
| 1964 | Josef Stiegler (AUT) | Bill Kidd (USA) | James Heuga (USA) |
| 1968 | Jean-Claude Killy (FRA) | Herbert Huber (AUT) | Alfred Matt (AUT) |
| 1972 | Francisco Fernández-Ochoa (ESP) | Gustavo Thoeni (ITA) | Roland Thoeni (ITA) |
| 1976 | Piero Gros (ITA) | Gustavo Thoeni (ITA) | Willy Frommelt (LIE) |
| 1980 | Ingemar Stenmark (SWE) | Phillip Mahre (USA) | Jacques Luethy (SUI) |
| 1984 | Phillip Mahre (USA) | Steven Mahre (USA) | Didier Bouvet (FRA) |

### Women's Downhill

| Year | Gold Medalists | Silver Medalists | Bronze Medalists |
|------|----------------|------------------|------------------|
| 1948 | Hedy Schlunegger (SUI) | Trude Beiser (AUT) | Resi Hammerer (AUT) |
| 1952 | Trude Jochum-Beiser (AUT) | Annemarie Buchner (GER) | Giuliana Minuzzo (ITA) |
| 1956 | Madeleine Berthod (SUI) | Frieda Dänzer (SUI) | Lucile Wheeler (CAN) |
| 1960 | Heidi Biebl (GER) | Penny Pitou (USA) | Traudl Hecher (USA) |
| 1964 | Christl Haas (AUT) | Edith Zimmermann (AUT) | Traudl Hecher (AUT) |
| 1968 | Olga Pall (AUT) | Isabelle Mir (FRA) | Christl Haas (AUT) |
| 1972 | Marie-Theres Nadig (SUI) | Annemarie Proell (AUT) | Susan Corrock (USA) |
| 1976 | Rosi Mittermaier (GER) | Brigitte Totschnig (AUT) | Cindy Nelson (USA) |
| 1980 | Annemarie Moser-Proell (AUT) | Hanni Wenzel (LIE) | Marie-Theres Nadig (SUI) |
| 1984 | Michela Figini (SUI) | Maria Walliser (SUI) | Olga Charvatova (TCH) |

### Women's Giant Slalom

| Year | Gold Medalists | Silver Medalists | Bronze Medalists |
|------|----------------|------------------|------------------|
| 1952 | Andrea Mead Lawrence (USA) | Dagmar Rom (AUT) | Annemarie Buchner (GER) |
| 1956 | Ossi Reichert (GER) | Josefine Frandl (AUT) | Dorothea Hochleitner (AUT) |
| 1960 | Yvonne Rüegg (SUI) | Penny Pitou (USA) | Giuliana Chenal-Minuzzo (ITA) |
| 1964 | Marielle Goitschel (FRA) | Christine Goitschel (FRA) | Jean Saubert (USA) |
| 1968 | Nancy Greene (CAN) | Annie Famose (FRA) | Fernande Bochatay (SUI) |
| 1972 | Marie-Theres Nadig (SUI) | Annemarie Proell (AUT) | Wiltrud Drexel (AUT) |
| 1976 | Kathy Kreiner (CAN) | Rosi Mittermaier (GER) | Danièle Debernard (FRA) |
| 1980 | Hanni Wenzel (LIE) | Irene Epple (GER) | Perrine Pelen (FRA) |
| 1984 | Debbie Armstrong (USA) | Christin Cooper (USA) | Perrine Pelen (FRA) |

### Women's Slalom

| Year | Gold Medalists | Silver Medalists | Bronze Medalists |
|------|----------------|------------------|------------------|
| 1948 | Gretchen Fraser (USA) | Antoinette Meyer (SUI) | Erika Mahringer (AUT) |
| 1952 | Andrea Mead Lawrence (USA) | Ossi Reichert (GER) | Annemarie Buchner (GER) |

| 1956 | Renée Colliard (SUI) | Regina Schopf (AUT) | Yevgeniya Sidorowa (URS) |
|------|----------------------|---------------------|--------------------------|
| 1960 | Anne Heggtveit (CAN) | Betsy Snite (USA) | Barbi Henneberger (GER) |
| 1964 | Christine Goitschel (FRA) | Marielle Goitschel (FRA) | Jean Saubert (USA) |
| 1968 | Marielle Goitschel (FRA) | Nancy Greene (CAN) | Annie Famose (FRA) |
| 1972 | Barbara Cochran (USA) | Danièle Debernard (FRA) | Florence Steurer (FRA) |
| 1976 | Rosi Mittermaier (GER) | Claudia Giordani (ITA) | Hanni Wenzel (LIE) |
| 1980 | Hanni Wenzel (LIE) | Christa Kinshofer (GER) | Erika Hess (SUI) |
| 1984 | Paoletta Magoni (ITA) | Perrine Pelen (FRA) | Ursula Konzett (LIE) |

| Year | Gold Medalists | Silver Medalists | Bronze Medalists |
|------|----------------|------------------|------------------|

# BIATHLON

## 10 Kilometre Individual

| 1980 | Frank Ullrich (GDR) | Vladimir Alikin (URS) | Anatoli Aljabiev (URS) |
|------|---------------------|-----------------------|------------------------|
| 1984 | Eirik Kvalfoss (NOR) | Peter Angerer (GER) | Jacob Matthias (GDR) |

## 20 Kilometre Individual

| 1960 | Klas Lestander (SWE) | Antti Tyrväinen (FIN) | Aleksandr Privalov (URS) |
|------|----------------------|-----------------------|--------------------------|
| 1964 | Vladimir Melanin (URS) | Aleksandr Privalov (URS) | Olav Jordet (NOR) |
| 1968 | Magnar Solberg (NOR) | Alexander Tikhonov (URS) | Vladimir Gundartsev (URS) |
| 1972 | Magnar Solberg (NOR) | Hans-Jörg Knauthe (GDR) | Lars-Göran Arwidson (SWE) |
| 1976 | Nikolai Kruglov (URS) | Heikki Ikola (FIN) | Aleksandr Elizarov (URS) |
| 1980 | Anatoli Aljabiev (URS) | Frank Ullrich (GDR) | Eberhard Rosch (GDR) |
| 1984 | Peter Angerer (GER) | Frank Peter Roetsch (GDR) | Eirik Kvalfoss (NOR) |

## Relay

| 1968 | URS (Alexander Tikhonov, Nikolai Pussanov, Viktor Mamatov, Vladimir Gundartsev) | NOR (Ola Waerhaug, Olav Jordet, Magnar Solberg, Jon Istad) | SWE (Lars-Göran Arwidson, Tore Eriksson, Olle Petrusson, Holmfrid Olsson) |
|------|---------------------------------------------------------------------------------|-----------------------------------------------------------|---------------------------------------------------------------------------|
| 1972 | URS (Alexander Tikhonov, Rinnat Safin, Ivan Bjakov, Viktor Mamatov) | FIN (Esko Saira, Juhani Suutarinen, Heikki Ikola, Mauri Röppänen) | GDR (Hans-Jörg Knauthe, Joachim Meischner, Deiter Speer, Horst Koschka) |
| 1976 | URS (Aleksandr Elizarov, Ivan Bjakov, Nikolai Kruglov, Alexander Tikhonov) | FIN (Henrik Flöjt, Esko Saira, Juhani Suutarinen, Heikki Ikola) | GDR (Karl-Heinz Menz, Frank Ullrich, Manfred Beer, Manfred Geyer) |
| 1980 | URS (Vladimir Alikin, Alexander Tikhonov, Vladimir Barnaschov, Anatoli Aljabiev) | GDR (Mathias Jung, Klaus Siebert, Frank Ullrich, Eberhard Rosch) | GER (Franz Bernreiter, Hansi Estner, Peter Angerer, Gerd Winkler) |
| 1984 | URS (Dmitry Vassiliev, Youry Kachkarov, Alguimantas Shalna, Serguey Bouliguin) | NOR (Odd Lirhus, Eirik Kvalfoss, Rolf Storsveen, Kjel Soebak) | GER (Ernst Reiter, Walter Pichler, Peter Angerer, Fritz Fischer) |

| Year | Gold Medalists | Silver Medalists | Bronze Medalists |
|------|----------------|------------------|------------------|

# BOBSLEIGH

## Two-Man

| Year | Gold Medalists | Silver Medalists | Bronze Medalists |
|------|----------------|------------------|------------------|
| 1932 | USA (Hubert Stevens, Curtis Stevens) | SUI (Reto Capadrutt, Oscar Geier) | USA (John R. Heaton, Robert Minton) |
| 1936 | USA (Ivan Brown, Alan Washbond) | SUI (Fritz Feierabend, Joseph Beerli) | USA (Gilbert Colgate, Richard Lawrence) |
| 1948 | SUI (Felix Endrich, Friedrich Waller) | SUI (Fritz Feierabend, Paul Eberhard) | USA (Fred Fortune, Schuyler Carron) |
| 1952 | GER (Andreas Ostler, Lorenz Nieberl) | USA (Stanley Benham, Patrick Martin) | SUI (Fritz Feierabend, Stephan Waser) |
| 1956 | ITA (Lamberto Dalla Costa, Giacomo Conti) | ITA (Eugenio Monti, Renzo Alverà) | SUI (Max Angst, Harry Warburton) |
| 1960 | Not Held | | |
| 1964 | GBR (Anthony Nash, Robin Dixon) | ITA (Sergio Zardini, Romano Bonagura) | ITA (Eugenio Monti, Sergio Siorpaes) |
| 1968 | ITA (Eugenio Monti, Luciano De Paolis) | GER (Horst Floth, Pepi Bader) | RUM (Ion Panturu, Nicolae Neagoe) |
| 1972 | GER (Wolfgang Zimmerer, Peter Utzschneider) | GER (Horst Floth, Pepi Bader) | SUI (Jean Wicki, Edy Hubacher) |
| 1976 | GDR (Meinhard Nehmer, Bernhard Germeshausen) | GER (Wolfgang Zimmerer, Manfred Schumann) | SUI (Erich Schaerer, Josef Benz) |
| 1980 | SUI (Erich Schaerer, Josef Benz) | GDR (Bernhard Germeshausen, Hans Jurgen Gerhardt) | GDR (Meinhard Nehmer, Bosdan Musiol) |
| 1984 | GDR (Wolfgang Hoppe, Dietmar Schauerhammer) | GDR (Bernhard Lehmann, Bosdan Musiol | URS (Zintis Ekmanis, Vladimir Aleksandrov) |

## Four-Man

| Year | Gold Medalists | Silver Medalists | Bronze Medalists |
|------|----------------|------------------|------------------|
| 1924 | SUI (Eduard Scherrer, Alfred Neveu, Alfred Schläppi, Henrich Schläppi) | GBR (Ralph H. Broome, T.A. Arnold, H.A.W. Richardson, Rodney E. Soher) | BEL (Charles Mulder, René Mortiaux, Paul van den Broeck, Victor Verschueren, Henri Willems) |
| 1928 | USA (William Fiske, Nion Tocker, Charles Mason, Clifford Gray, Richard Parke) | USA (Jennison Heaton, David Granger, Lyman Hine, Thomas Doe, Jay O'Brien) | GER (Hanns Kilian, Valentin Krempl, Hans Hess, Sebastian Huber, Hans Nägle) |
| 1932 | USA (William Fiske, Edward Eagan, Clifford Gray, Jay O'Brien) | USA (Henry Homburger, Percy Bryant, Paul Stevens, Edmund Horton) | GER (Hanns Kilian, Max Ludwig, Hans Mehlhorn, Sebastian Huber) |
| 1936 | SUI (Pierre Musy, Arnold Gartmann, Charles Bouvier, Joseph Beerli) | SUI (Reto Capadrutt, Hans Aichele, Fritz Feierabend, Hans Bütikofer) | GBR (Frederick McEvoy, James Cardno, Guy Dugdale, Charles Green) |
| 1948 | USA (Francis Tyler, Patrick Martin, Edward Rimkus, William D'Amico) | BEL (Max Houben, Freddy Mansveld, Louis-Georges Niels, Jacques Mouvet) | USA (James Bickford, Thomas Hicks, Donald Dupree, William Dupree) |
| 1952 | GER (Andreas Ostler, Friedrich Kuhn, Lorenz Nieberl, Franz Kemser) | USA (Stanley Benham, Patrick Martin, Howard Crossett, James Atkinson) | SUI (Fritz Feierabend, Albert Madörin, André Filippini, Stephan Waser |
| 1956 | SUI (Franz Kapus, Gottfried Diener, Robert Alt, Heinrich Angst) | ITA (Eugenio Monti, Ulrico Girardi, Renzo Alverà, Renato Mocellini) | USA (Arthur Tyler, William Dodge, Charles Butler, James Lamy) |
| 1960 | Not Held | | |
| 1964 | CAN (Victor Emery, Peter Kirby, Douglas Anakin, John Emery) | AUT (Erwin Thaler, Adolf Koxeder, Josef Nairz, Reinhold Durnthaler) | ITA (Eugenio Monti, Sergio Siorpaes, Benito Rigoni, Gildo Siorpaes) |
| 1968 | ITA (Eugenio Monti, Luciano De Paolis, Roberto Zandonella, Mario Armano) | AUT (Erwin Thaler, Reinhold Durnthaler, Herbert Gruber, Josef Eder) | SUI (Jean Wicki, Hans Candrian, Willi Hofmann, Walter Graf) |
| 1972 | SUI (Jean Wicki, Hans Leutenegger, Werner Camichel, Edy Hubacher) | ITA (Nevio De Zordo, Adriano Frassinelli, Corroda Dal Fabbro, Giani Bonichon) | GER (Wolfgang Zimmerer, Stefan Gaisreiter, Walter Steinbauer, Peter Utzschneider) |
| 1976 | GDR (Meinhard Nehmer, Jochen Babok, Bernhard Germeshausen, Bernhard Lehmann) | SUI (Erich Schaerer, Ulrich Baechli, Rudolf Marti, Josef Benz) | GER (Wolfgang Zimmerer, Peter Utzschneider, Bodo Bittner, Manfred Schumann) |
| 1980 | GDR (Meinhard Nehmer, Bosdan Musiol, Bernhard Germeshausen, H.J. Gerhardt) | SUI (Erich Schaerer, Ulrich Baechli, Rudolf Marti, Josef Benz) | GDR (Horst Schoenau, Roland Wetzig, Detlef Richter, Andreas Kirchner) |
| 1984 | GDR (Wolfgang Hoppe, Roland Wetzig, Dietmar Schauerhammer, Andreas Kirchner) | GDR (Bernhard Lehmann, Bogdan Musiol, Ingo Voge, Eberhard Weise) | SUI (Silvio Giobellina, Hein Stettler, Urs Salzmann, Rico Freiermuth) |

| Year | Gold Medalists | Silver Medalists | Bronze Medalists |
|------|----------------|------------------|------------------|

# FIGURE SKATING

## Pairs

| Year | Gold Medalists | Silver Medalists | Bronze Medalists |
|------|----------------|------------------|------------------|
| 1908 | GER (Anna Hübler, Heinrich Burger) | GBR (Phyllis Johnson, James Johnson) | GBR (Madge Syers, Edgar Syers) |
| 1920 | FIN (Ludowika Jakobsson-Eilers, Walter Jakobsson-Eilers) | NOR (Alexia Bryn, Yngvar Bryn) | GBR (Phyllis Johnson, Basil Williams) |
| 1924 | AUT (Helene Engelmann, Alfred Berger) | FIN (Ludowika Jakobsson-Eilers, Walter Jakobsson-Eilers) | FRA (Andrée Joly, Pierre Brunet) |
| 1928 | FRA (Andrée Joly, Pierre Brunet) | AUT (Lilly Scholz, Otto Kaiser) | AUT (Melitta Brunner, Ludwig Wrede) |
| 1932 | FRA (Andrée Brunet, Pierre Brunet) | USA (Beatrix Loughran, Sherwin Badger) | HUN (Emilia Rotter, László Szollás) |
| 1936 | GER (Maxie Herber, Ernst Baier) | AUT (Ilse Pausin, Erik Pausin) | HUN (Emilia Rotter, László Szollás) |
| 1948 | BEL (Micheline Lannoy, Pierre Baugniet) | HUN (Andrea Kékessy, Ede Király) | CAN (Suzanne Morrow, Wallace Diestelmeyer) |
| 1952 | GER (Ria Falk, Paul Falk) | USA (Karol Kennedy, Michael Kennedy) | HUN (Marianna Nagy, László Nagy) |
| 1956 | AUT (Elisabeth Schwarz, Kurt Oppelt) | CAN (Frances Dafoe, Norris Bowden) | HUN (Marianna Nagy, László Nagy) |
| 1960 | CAN (Barbara Wagner, Robert Paul) | GER (Marika Kilius, Hans-Jürgen Bäumler) | USA (Nancy Ludington, Ronald Ludington) |
| 1964 | URS (Ludmilla Beloussova, Oleg Protopopov) | GER (Marika Kilius, Hans-Jürgen Bäumler) | CAN (Debbi Wilkes, Guy Revell) |
| 1968 | URS (Ludmilla Beloussova, Oleg Protopopov) | URS (Tatjana Schuk, Aleksandr Gorelik) | GER (Margot Glockshuber, Wolfgang Danne) |
| 1972 | URS (Irina Rodnina, Aleksei Ulanov) | URS (Ludmilla Smirnova, Andrei Suraikin) | GDR (Manuela Gross, Uwe Kagelmann) |
| 1976 | URS (Irina Rodnina, Aleksandr Zaitsev) | GDR (Romy Kermer, Rolf Österreich) | GDR (Manuela Gross, Uwe Kagelmann) |
| 1980 | URS (Irina Rodnina, Aleksandr Zaitsev) | URS (Marina Cherkosova, Sergei Shakrai) | GDR (Manuela Mager, Uwe Bewersdorff) |
| 1984 | URS (Elena Valova, Oleg Vassiliev) | USA (Kitty Carruthers, Peter Carruthers) | URS (Larissa Selezneva, Oleg Makarov) |

## Men's Singles

| Year | Gold Medalists | Silver Medalists | Bronze Medalists |
|------|----------------|------------------|------------------|
| 1908 | Ulrich Salchow (SWE) | Richard Johansson (SWE) | Per Thorén (SWE) |
| 1920 | Gillis Grafström (SWE) | Andreas Krogh (NOR) | Martin Strixrud (NOR) |
| 1924 | Gillis Granström (SWE) | Willy Böckl (AUT) | Georges Gautschi (SUI) |
| 1928 | Gillis Grafström (SWE) | Willy Böckl (AUT) | Robert van Zeebroeck (BEL) |
| 1932 | Karl Schaefer (AUT) | Gillis Grafström (SWE) | Montgomery Wilson (CAN) |
| 1936 | Karl Schaefer (AUT) | Ernst Baier (GER) | Felix Kaspar (AUT) |
| 1948 | Richard Button (USA) | Hans Gerschwiler (SUI) | Edi Rada (AUT) |
| 1952 | Richard Button (USA) | Helmut Seibt (AUT) | James Grogan (USA) |
| 1956 | Hayes Alan Jenkins (USA) | Ronald Robertson (USA) | David Jenkins (USA) |
| 1960 | David Jenkins (USA) | Karol Divin (TCH) | Donald Jackson (CAN) |
| 1964 | Manfred Schnelldorfer (GER) | Alain Calmat (FRA) | Scott Allen (USA) |
| 1968 | Wolfgang Schwarz (AUT) | Timothy Wood (USA) | Patrick Péra (FRA) |
| 1972 | Ondrej Nepela (TCH) | Sergei Chetveroukhin (URS) | Patrick Péra (FRA) |
| 1976 | John Curry (GDR) | Vladimir Kovalev (URS) | Toller Cranston (CAN) |
| 1980 | Robin Cousin (GBR) | Jan Hoffmann (GDR) | Charles Tickner (USA) |
| 1984 | Scott Hamiton (USA) | Brian Orser (CAN) | Jozef Sabovtchik (TCH) |

## Women's Singles

| Year | Gold Medalists | Silver Medalists | Bronze Medalists |
|------|----------------|------------------|------------------|
| 1908* | Madge Syers (GBR) | Elsa Rendschmidt (GER) | Dorothy Greenhough-Smith (GBR) |
| 1920* | Magda Julin-Mauroy (SWE) | Svea Norén (SWE) | Theresa Weld (USA) |
| 1924 | Herma Plank-Szabó (AUT) | Beatrix Loughran (USA) | Ethel Muckelt (GBR) |
| 1928 | Sonja Henie (NOR) | Fritzi Burger (AUT) | Beatrix Loughran (USA) |
| 1932 | Sonja Henie (NOR) | Fritzi Burger (AUT) | Maribel Vinson (USA) |
| 1936 | Sonja Henie (NOR) | Cecilia Colledge (GBR) | Vivi-Anne Hultén (SWE) |
| 1948 | Barbara Ann Scott (CAN) | Eva Pawlik (AUT) | Jeanette Altwegg (GBR) |
| 1952 | Jeanette Altwegg (GBR) | Tenley Albright (USA) | Jacqueline du Bief (FRA) |
| 1956 | Tenley Albright (USA) | Carol Heiss (USA) | Ingrid Wendl (AUT) |
| 1960 | Carol Heiss (USA) | Sjoukje Dijkstra (HOL) | Barbara Roles (USA) |
| 1964 | Sjoukje Dijkstra (HOL) | Regine Heitzer (AUT) | Petra Burka (CAN) |
| 1968 | Peggy Fleming (USA) | Gabriele Seyfert (GDR) | Hana Másková (TCH) |
| 1972 | Beatrix Schuba (AUT) | Karen Magnussen (CAN) | Janet Lynn (USA) |
| 1976 | Dorothy Hamill (USA) | Dianne de Leeuw (HOL) | Christine Errath (GDR) |
| 1980 | Anett Poetzsch (GDR) | Linda Fratianne (USA) | Dagmar Lurz (GER) |
| 1984 | Katarina Witt (GDR) | Rosalyn Sumners (USA) | Kira Ivanova (URS) |

*1908 & 1920 are Olympic Summer Games records

## Ice Dancing

| | | | |
|---|---|---|---|
| 1976 | URS (Ludmila Pakhomova, Aleksandr Gorshkov) | URS (Irina Moiseeva, Andrey Minenkov) | USA (Colleen O'Connor, James G. Millns) |
| 1980 | URS (Natalia Linichuk, Gennadi Karponosov) | HUN (Krisztina Regoczy, Andras Sallay) | URS (Irina Moiseeva, Andrey Minenkov) |
| 1984 | GBR (Jayne Torvill, Christopher Dean) | URS (Natalya Bestemyanova, Andrey Boukin) | URS (Marina Klimova, Serguey Ponomarenko) |

| Year | Gold Medalists | Silver Medalists | Bronze Medalists |
|---|---|---|---|

# ICE HOCKEY

| Year | Gold Medalists | Silver Medalists | Bronze Medalists |
|---|---|---|---|
| 1920 | CAN | USA | TCH |
| 1924 | CAN | USA | GBR |
| 1928 | CAN | SWE | SUI |
| 1932 | CAN | USA | GER |
| 1936 | GBR | CAN | USA |
| 1948 | CAN | TCH | SUI |
| 1952 | CAN | USA | SWE |
| 1956 | URS | USA | CAN |
| 1960 | USA | CAN | URS |
| 1964 | URS | SWE | TCH |
| 1968 | URS | TCH | CAN |
| 1972 | URS | USA | TCH |
| 1976 | URS | TCH | GER |
| 1980 | USA | URS | SWE |
| 1984 | URS | TCH | SWE |

| Year | Gold Medalists | Silver Medalists | Bronze Medalists |
|---|---|---|---|

# LUGE

### Men's Singles

| Year | Gold Medalists | Silver Medalists | Bronze Medalists |
|---|---|---|---|
| 1964 | Thomas Kohler (GER) | Klaus Bonsack (GER) | Hans Plenk (GER) |
| 1968 | Manfred Schmid (AUT) | Thomas Koehler (GER) | Klaus Bonsack (GDR) |
| 1972 | Wolfgang Scheidl (GDR) | Harald Ehrig (GDR) | Wolfram Fiedler (GDR) |
| 1976 | Detlef Guenther (GDR) | Josef Fendt (GER) | Hans Rinn (GDR) |
| 1980 | Bernhard Glass (GDR) | Paul Hildgartner (ITA) | Anton Winkler(GER) |
| 1984 | Paul Hildgartner (ITA) | Serguey Danilin (URS) | Valery Doudin (URS) |

### Men's Doubles

| Year | Gold Medalists | Silver Medalists | Bronze Medalists |
|---|---|---|---|
| 1964 | AUT (Josef Feistmantl, Manfred Stengl) | AUT (Reinhold Senn, Helmut Thaler) | ITA (Walter Aussendorfer, Sigisfredo Mair) |
| 1968 | GDR (Klaus Bonsack, Thomas Koehler) | AUT (Manfred Schmid, Ewald Walch) | GER (Wolfgang Winkler, Fritz Nachmann) |
| 1972 | ITA (Paul Hildgartner, Walter Plaikner) GDR (Horst Hörnlein, Reinhard Bredow) (tie) | no medal | GDR (Klaus Bonsack, Wolfram Fiedler) |
| 1976 | GDR (Hans Rinn, Norbert Hahn) | GER (Hans Brandner, Balthasar Schwarm) | AUT (Rudolf Schmid, Franz Schachner) |
| 1980 | GDR (Hans Rinn, Norbert Hahn) | ITA (Peter Gschnitzer, Karl Brunner) | AUT (Georg Fluckinger, Karl Schrott) |
| 1984 | GER (Hans Stangassinger, Franz Wembacher) | URS (Evgueny Beloossov, Alexandre Belyakov) | GDR (Joerg Hoffman, Jochen Pietzsch) |

### Women's Singles

| Year | Gold Medalists | Silver Medalists | Bronze Medalists |
|---|---|---|---|
| 1964 | Ortrun Enderlein (GER) | Ilse Geisler (GER) | Helene Thurner (AUT) |
| 1968 | Erica Lechner (ITA) | Christa Schmuck (GER) | Angelika Dünhaupt (GER) |
| 1972 | Anna-Maria Müller (GDR) | Ute Rührold (GDR) | Margit Schumann (GDR) |
| 1976 | Margit Schumann (GDR) | Ure Rührold (GDR) | Elisabeth Demleitner (GER) |
| 1980 | Vera Zozulia (URS) | Melitta Sollmann (GDR) | Ingrida Amantova (URS) |
| 1984 | Steffi Martin (GDR) | Bettino Schmidt (GDR) | Ute Weiss (GDR) |

| Year | Gold Medalists | Silver Medalists | Bronze Medalists |
|------|----------------|------------------|------------------|

# NORDIC SKIING

### Men's 15 Kilometre Cross-Country

| Year | Gold Medalists | Silver Medalists | Bronze Medalists |
|------|----------------|------------------|------------------|
| 1924 | Thorleif Haug (NOR) | Johan Gröttumsbraaten (NOR) | Tapani Niku (FIN) |
| 1928 | Johan Gröttumsbraaten (NOR) | Ole Hegge (NOR) | Reidar Odegaard (NOR) |
| 1932 | Sven Utterström (SWE) | Axel T. Wikström (SWE) | Veli Saarinen (FIN) |
| 1936 | Erik-August Larsson (SWE) | Oddbjörn Hagen (NOR) | Pekka Niema (FIN) |
| 1948 | Martin Lundström (SWE) | Nils Östensson (SWE) | Gunnar Eriksson (SWE) |
| 1952 | Hallgeir Brenden (NOR) | Tapio Mäkelä (FIN) | Paavo Lonkila (FIN) |
| 1956 | Hallgeir Brenden (NOR) | Sixten Jernberg (SWE) | Pavel Koltschin (URS) |
| 1960 | Haakon Brusveen (NOR) | Sixten Jernberg (SWE) | Veikko Hakulinen (FIN) |
| 1964 | Eero Mäntyranta (FIN) | Harald Grönningen (NOR) | Sixten Jernberg (SWE) |
| 1968 | Harald Grönningen (NOR) | Eero Mäntyrana (FIN) | Gunnar Larsson (SWE) |
| 1972 | Sven-Ake Lundbäck (SWE) | Fjodor Simaschew (URS) | Ivar Formo (NOR) |
| 1976 | Nikolai Bajukov (URS) | Evgeni Beliaev (URS) | Arto Koivisto (FIN) |
| 1980 | Thomas Wassberg (SWE) | Juha Mieto (FIN) | Ove Aunli (NOR) |
| 1984 | Gunde Swan (SWE) | Aki Kirvesniemi (FIN) | Harri Kirvesniemi (FIN) |

### Men's 30 Kilometre Cross-Country

| Year | Gold Medalists | Silver Medalists | Bronze Medalists |
|------|----------------|------------------|------------------|
| 1956 | Veikko Hakulinen (FIN) | Sixten Jernberg (SWE) | Pavel Koltschin (URS) |
| 1960 | Sixten Jernberg (SWE) | Rolf Rämgard (SWE) | Nikolai Anikin (URS) |
| 1964 | Eero Mäntyranta (FIN) | Harald Grönningen (NOR) | Igor Worontschichin (URS) |
| 1968 | Franco Nones (ITA) | Odd Martinsen (NOR) | Eero Mäntyranta (FIN) |
| 1972 | Vyacheslav Vedenin (URS) | Paal Tyldum (NOR) | Johs Harviken (NOR) |
| 1976 | Sergei Saveliev (URS) | William Koch (USA) | Ivan Garanin (URS) |
| 1980 | Nikolai Zimyatov (URS) | Vasili Rochev (URS) | Ivan Lebanov (BUL) |
| 1984 | Nikolai Zimyatov (URS) | Alexandre Zavialov (URS) | Gunde Swan (SWE) |

### Men's 50 Kilometre Cross-Country

| Year | Gold Medalists | Silver Medalists | Bronze Medalists |
|------|----------------|------------------|------------------|
| 1924 | Thorleif Haug (NOR) | Thoralf Strömstad (NOR) | Johan Gröttumsbraaten (NOR) |
| 1928 | Per Erik Hedlunk (SWE) | Gustaf Jonsson (SWE) | Volger Andersson (SWE) |
| 1932 | Veli Saarinen (FIN) | Väinö Liikkanen (FIN) | Arne Kustadstuen (NOR) |
| 1936 | Elis Viklund (SWE) | Axel Wikström (SWE) | Nils-Joel Englund (SWE) |
| 1948 | Nils Karlsson (SWE) | Harald Eriksson (SWE) | Benjamin Vanninen (FIN) |
| 1952 | Veikko Hakulinen (FIN) | Eero Kolehmainen (FIN) | Magnar Estenstad (NOR) |
| 1956 | Sixten Jernberg (SWE) | Veikko Hakulinen (FIN) | Fjodor Terentjev (URS) |
| 1960 | Kalevi Hämäläinen (FIN) | Veikko Hakulinen (FIN) | Rolf Rämgard (SWE) |
| 1964 | Sixten Jernberg (SWE) | Assar Rönnlund (SWE) | Arto Tiainen (FIN) |
| 1968 | Ole Ellefsaeter (NOR) | Vyacheslav Vedenin (URS) | Josef Haas (SUI) |
| 1972 | Paal Tyldum (NOR) | Magne Myrmo (NOR) | Vyacheslav Vedenin (URS) |
| 1976 | Ivar Formo (NOR) | Gert-Dietmar Klause (GDR) | Benny Soedergren (SWE) |
| 1980 | Nikolai Zimyatov (URS) | Juha Mieto (FIN) | Aleksandr Zavjalov (URS) |
| 1984 | Thomas Wassberg (SWE) | Gunde Swan (SWE) | Aki Karvonen (FIN) |

### Men's Combined

| Year | Gold Medalists | Silver Medalists | Bronze Medalists |
|------|----------------|------------------|------------------|
| 1924 | Thorleif Haug (NOR) | Thoralf Strömstad (NOR) | Johan Gröttumsbraaten (NOR) |
| 1928 | Johan Gröttumsbraaten (NOR) | Hans Vinjarengen (NOR) | John Snersrud (NOR) |
| 1932 | Johan Gröttumsbraaten (NOR) | Ole Stenen (NOR) | Hans Vinjarengen (NOR) |
| 1936 | Oddbjörn Hagen (NOR) | Olaf Hoffsbakken (NOR) | Sverre Brodahl (NOR) |
| 1948 | Heikki Hasu (FIN) | Martti Huhtala (FIN) | Sven Israelsson (SWE) |
| 1952 | Simon Slättvik (NOR) | Heikki Hasu (FIN) | Sverre Stenersen (NOR) |
| 1956 | Sverre Stenersen (NOR) | Bengt Eriksson (SWE) | Franciszek Gron-Gasienica (POL) |
| 1960 | Georg Thoma (GER) | Tormod Knutsen (NOR) | Nikolai Gusakov (URS) |
| 1964 | Tormod Knutsen (NOR) | Nikolai Kiselev (URS) | Georg Thoma (GER) |
| 1968 | Franz Keller (GER) | Alois Kälin (SUI) | Andreas Kunz (GDR) |
| 1972 | Ulrich Wehling (GDR) | Rauno Miettinen (FIN) | Karl-Heinz Luck (GDR) |
| 1976 | Ulrich Wehling (GDR) | Urban Hettich (GER) | Konrad Winkler (GDR) |
| 1980 | Ulrich Wehling (GDR) | Jouko Karjalainen (FIN) | Konrad Winkler (GDR) |
| 1984 | Tom Sandberg (NOR) | Jouko Karjalainen (FIN) | Jukka Ylipulli (FIN) |

### Men's 4 x 10 Kilometre Cross-Country Relay

| Year | Gold Medalists | Silver Medalists | Bronze Medalists |
|------|----------------|------------------|------------------|
| 1936 | FIN (Sulo Nurmela, Klaes Karppinen, Matti Lähde, Kalle Jalkanen) | NOR (Oddbjörn Hagen, Olaf Hoffsbakken, Sverre Brodahl, Bjarne Iversen) | SWE (John Berger, Erik A. Larsson, Artur Häggblad, Martin Matsbo) |

| 1948 | SWE (Nils Östensson, Nils Täpp, Gunnar Eriksson, Martin Lundström) | FIN (Lauri Silvennoinen, Teuvo Laukkanen, Sauli Rytky, August Kiruru) | NOR (Erling Evensen, Olav Ökern, Reidar Nyborg, Olav Hagen) |
|---|---|---|---|
| 1952 | FIN (Heikki Hasu, Paavo Lonkila, Urpo Korhonen, Tapio Mäkelä) | NOR (Magnar Estenstad, Mikal Kirkholt, Martin Stokken, Hallgeir Brenden) | SWE (Nils Täpp, Sigurd Andersson, Enar Josefsson, Martin Lundström) |
| 1956 | URS (Fyedor Terentjev, Pavel Koltschin, Nikolai Anikin, Vladimir Kusin) | FIN (August Kiuru, Jorma Kortalainen, Arvo Viitanen, Veikko Hakulinen) | SWE (Lennart Larsson, Gunnar Samuelsson, Per-Erik Larsson, Sixten Jernberg) |
| 1960 | FIN (Toimi Alatalo, Eero Mäntyranta, Väinö Huhtala, Veikko Hakulinen) | NOR (Harald Grönningen, Hallgeir Brenden, Einar Östby, Haakon Brusveen) | URS (Anatoli Scheljuchin, Gennadi Waganow, Aleksei Kusnjetsow, Nikolai Anikin) |
| 1964 | SWE (Karl-Ake Asph, Sixten Jernberg, Janne Stefansson, Assar Rönnlund) | FIN (Väinö Huhtala, Arto Tiainen, Kalevi Laurila, Eero Mäntyranta) | URS (Ivan Utrobin, Gennadi Waganow, Igor Worontschichin, Pavel Koltschin) |
| 1968 | NOR (Odd Martinsen, Paal Tyldum, Harald Grönningen, Ole Ellefsaeter) | SWE (Jan Halvarsson, Bjarne Andersson, Gunnar Larsson, Assar Rönnlund) | FIN (Kalevi Oikarainen, Hannu Taipale, Kalevi Laurila, Eero Mäntyranta) |
| 1972 | URS (Vladimir Woronkov, Juri Skobov, Fedor Simaschov, Vyacheslav Vedenin) | NOR (Oddvar Braa, Paal Tyldum, Ivar Formo, Johs Harviken) | SUI (Alfred Kälin, Albert Giger, Alois Kälin, Eduard Hauser) |
| 1976 | FIN (Matti Pitkänen, Juha Mieto, Pertti Teurajärvi, Arto Koivisto) | NOR (Paal Tyldum, Einar Sagstuen, Ivar Formo, Odd Martinsen) | URS (Evgeni Beliaev, Nikolai Baschukov, Sergei Saveliev, Ivan Garanin) |
| 1980 | URS (Vasili Rochev, Nikolai Bazhukov, Evgeni Beliaev, Nikolai Zimyatov) | NOR (L.E. Eriksen, P.K. Aaland, O. Aunli, O. Braa) | FIN (H. Kirvesniemi, Pertti Teurajärvi, Matti Pitkanen, Juha Mieto) |
| 1984 | SWE (Thomas Wassberg, Benny Tord Kohlberg, Jan Bo Otto Ottosson, Gunde Swan) | URS (Alexandre Batuk, Alexandre Zavialov, Viadimir Nikitin, Nikolay Zimiatov) | FIN (Kari Ristanen, Juha Mieto, Harri Kirvesniemi, Aki Karvonen) |

## Women's 5 Kilometre Cross-Country

| 1964 | Claudia Boyarskikh (URS) | Mirja Lehtonen (FIN) | Alevtina Koltschina (URS) |
|---|---|---|---|
| 1968 | Toini Gustafsson (SWE) | Galina Kulakova (URS) | Alevtina Koltschina (URS) |
| 1972 | Galina Kulakova (URS) | Marjatta Kajosmaa (FIN) | Helena Sikolová (TCH) |
| 1976 | Helena Takalo (FIN) | Raisa Smetanina (URS) | Nina Baldicheva (URS) |
| 1980 | Raisa Smetanina (URS) | Hilkka Riihivuori (FIN) | Kveta Jeriova (TCH) |
| 1984 | Liisa Haemaelainen (FIN) | Berit Aunli (NOR) | Kveta Jeriova (TCH) |

## Women's 10 Kilometre Cross-Country

| 1952 | Lydia Wideman (FIN) | Mirja Hietamies (FIN) | Siiri Rantanen (FIN) |
|---|---|---|---|
| 1956 | Ljubovj Kozyreva (URS) | Radya Jeroschina (URS) | Sonja Edström (SWE) |
| 1960 | Maria Gusakova (URS) | Ljubovj Kozyreva (URS) | Radya Jeroschina (URS) |
| 1964 | Claudia Boyarskikh (URS) | Eudokia Mekschilo (URS) | Maria Gusakova (URS) |
| 1968 | Toini Gustafsson (SWE) | Berit Mördre (NOR) | Inger Aufles (NOR) |
| 1972 | Galina Kulakova (URS) | Alevtina Olunina (URS) | Marjatta Kajosmaa (FIN) |
| 1976 | Raisa Smetanina (URS) | Helena Takalo (FIN) | Galina Kulakova (URS) |
| 1980 | Barbara Petzold (GDR) | Hilkka Riihivuori (FIN) | Helena Takalo (FIN) |
| 1984 | Liisa Haemaelainen (FIN) | Raisa Smetanina (URS) | Brit Pettersen (NOR) |

## Women's 4 x 5 Kilometre Cross-Country Relay
## (1956 - 1972 15 Kilometre)

| 1956 | FIN (Sirkka Polkunen, Mirja Hietamies, Siiri Rantanen) | URS (Ljubovj Kozyreva, Alevtina Koltschina, Radya Jeroschina) | SWE (Irma Johansson, Anna-Lisa Eriksson, Sonja Edström) |
|---|---|---|---|
| 1960 | SWE (Irma Johansson, Britt Strandberg, Sonja Ruthström-Edström) | URS (Radya Jeroschina, Maria Gusakova, Ljubovj Baranova-Kozyreva) | FIN (Siiri Rantanen, Eeva Ruoppa, Toini Pöysti) |
| 1964 | URS (Alevtina Koltschina, Eudokia Mekschilo, Claudia Boyarskikh) | SWE (Barbo Martinsson, Britt Strandberg, Toini Gustafsson) | FIN (Senja Pusula, Toini Pöysti, Mirja Lehtonen) |
| 1968 | NOR (Inger Aufles, Babben Enger Damon, Berit Mördre) | SWE (Britt Strandberg, Toini Gustafsson, Barbro Martinsson) | URS (Alevtina Koltschina, Rita Atschkina, Galina Kulakova) |
| 1972 | URS (Ljubov Muchatscheva, Alevtina Olunina, Galina Kulakova) | FIN (Helena Takalo, Hilkka Kuntola, Marjatta Kajosmaa) | NOR (Inger Aufles, Aslaug Dahl, Berit Lammedal-Mördre) |
| 1976 | URS (Nina Baldycheva, Sinaida Amossowa, Raisa Smetanina, Galina Kulakova) | FIN (Liisa Suihkonen, Marjatta Kajosmaa, Hilkka Kuntola, Helena Takalo) | GDR (Monika Debertshäuser, Sigrun Krause, Barbara Petzold, Veronika Schmidt) |
| 1980 | GDR (Marlies Rostock, Carola Anding, Veronika Hesse, Barbara Petzold) | URS (Nina Baldycheva, Nina Rocheva, Galina Kulakova, Raisa Smetanina) | NOR (Brit Pettersen, Anette Boe, Marit Myrmael, Berit Aunli) |
| 1984 | NOR (Inger Helene Nybraaten, Ann Jahren, Brit Pettersen, Aunli Berit) | TCH (Dagmar Schvubova, Blanka Paulu, Gabriela Svobodova, Kvetoslava Jeriova) | FIN (Pirkko Maatta, Eija Hyytiainen, Marjo Matikainen, Marja-Liisa Haemaelainen) |

| Year | Gold Medalists | Silver Medalists | Bronze Medalists |
|------|----------------|------------------|------------------|

## SKI JUMPING

### Men's Ski Jumping (70 Metre)

| Year | Gold Medalists | Silver Medalists | Bronze Medalists |
|------|----------------|------------------|------------------|
| 1924 | Jacob Tullin Thams (NOR) | Narve Bonna (NOR) | Thorleif Haug (NOR) |
| 1928 | Alfred Andersen (NOR) | Sigmund Ruud (NOR) | Rudolf Burkert (TCH) |
| 1932 | Birger Ruud (NOR) | Hans Beck (NOR) | Kaare Wahlberg (NOR) |
| 1936 | Birger Ruud (NOR) | Sven Eriksson (SWE) | Reidar Andersen (NOR) |
| 1948 | Petter Hugsted (NOR) | Birger Ruud (NOR) | Thorleif Schjelderup (NOR) |
| 1952 | Arnfinn Bergmann (NOR) | Torbjörn Falkanger (NOR) | Karl Holmström (SWE) |
| 1956 | Antti Hyvärinen (FIN) | Aulis Kallakorpi (FIN) | Harry Glass (GER) |
| 1960 | Helmut Recknagel (GER) | Niilo Halonen (FIN) | Otto Leodolter (AUT) |
| 1964 | Veikko Kankkonen (FIN) | Toralf Engan (NOR) | Torgeir Brandtzaeg (NOR) |
| 1968 | Jiri Raska (TCH) | Reinhold Bachler (AUT) | Baldur Preiml (AUT) |
| 1972 | Yukio Kasaya (JPN) | Akitsugu Konno (JPN) | Seiji Aochi (JPN) |
| 1976 | Hans-Georg Aschenbach (GDR) | Jochen Danneberg (GDR) | Karl Schnabl (AUT) |
| 1980 | Anton Innauer (AUT) | Hirokazu Yagi (JPN) | no medal |
| 1984 | Jens Weissflog (GDR) | Manfred Dechert (GDR) | |
|      | Matti Nykaenen (FIN) | Jari Puikkonen (FIN) | |

### Men's Ski Jumping (90 Metre)

| Year | Gold Medalists | Silver Medalists | Bronze Medalists |
|------|----------------|------------------|------------------|
| 1964 | Toralf Engan (NOR) | Veikko Kankkonen (FIN) | Torgeir Brandtzaeg (NOR) |
| 1968 | Vladimir Beloussov (URS) | Jiri Raska (TCH) | Lars Grini (NOR) |
| 1972 | Wojciech Fortuna (POL) | Walter Steiner (SUI) | Rainer Schmidt (GDR) |
| 1976 | Karl Schnabl (AUT) | Anton Innauer (AUT) | Henry Glass (GDR) |
| 1980 | Jouko Tormanen (FIN) | Hubert Neuper (AUT) | Jari Puikkonen (FIN) |
| 1984 | Matti Nykaenen (FIN) | Jens Weissflog (GDR) | Pavel Ploc (TCH) |

| Year | Gold Medalists | Silver Medalists | Bronze Medalists |
|------|----------------|------------------|------------------|

## SPEED SKATING

### Men's 500 Metres

| Year | Gold Medalists | Silver Medalists | Bronze Medalists |
|------|----------------|------------------|------------------|
| 1924 | Charles Jewtraw (USA) | Oskar Olsen (NOR) | Roald Larsen (NOR) Clas Thunberg (FIN) (tie) |
| 1928 | Clas Thunberg (FIN) Bernt Evensen (NOR) (tie) | no medal | Johnny Farrell (USA) Roald Larsen (NOR) Jaakko Friman (FIN) (tie) |
| 1932 | John A. Shea (USA) | Bernt Evensen (NOR) | Alexander Hurd (CAN) |
| 1936 | Ivar Ballangrud (NOR) | Georg Krog (NOR) | Leo Freisinger (USA) |
| 1948 | Finn Helgesen (NOR) | Ken Bartholomew (USA) tie Thomas Byberg (NOR) Robert Fitzgerald (USA) (tie) | no medal |
| 1952 | Kenneth Henry (USA) | Donald McDermott (USA) | Arne Johansen (NOR) Gordon Audley (CAN) (tie) |
| 1956 | Yevgeni Grishin (URS) | Rafael Gratsch (URS) | Alv Gjestvang (NOR) |
| 1960 | Yevgeni Grishin (URS) | William Disney (USA) | Rafael Gratsch (URS) |
| 1964 | Richard McDermott (USA) | Yevgeni Grishin (URS) Vladimir Orlov (URS) Alv Gjestvang (NOR) (tie) | no medal |
| 1968 | Erhard Keller (GER) | Magne Thomassen (NOR) Richard McDermott (USA) (tie) | no medal |
| 1972 | Erhard Keller (GER) | Hasse Börjes (SWE) | Valery Muratov (URS) |
| 1976 | Yevgeni Kulikov (URS) | Valery Muratov (URS) | Daniel Immerfall (USA) |
| 1980 | Eric Heiden (USA) | Yevgeni Kulikov (URS) | Lieuwe De Boer (HOL) |
| 1984 | Serguey Fokitchev (URS) | Yoshihiro Kitazawa (JPN) | Gaetan Boucher (CAN) |

### Men's 1,000 Metres

| Year | Gold Medalists | Silver Medalists | Bronze Medalists |
|------|----------------|------------------|------------------|
| 1976 | Peter Mueller (USA) | Jörn Didriksen (NOR) | Valery Muratov (URS) |
| 1980 | Eric Heiden (USA) | Gaetan Boucher (CAN) | Froede Roenning (NOR) Vladimir Lobanov (URS) (tie) |
| 1984 | Gaetan Boucher (CAN) | Serguey Khlebnikov (URS) | Arne Kai Engelstad (NOR) |

## Men's 1,500 Metres

| 1924 | Clas Thunberg (FIN) | Roald Larsen (NOR) | Sigurd Moen (NOR) |
|------|---------------------|--------------------|--------------------|
| 1928 | Clas Thunberg (FIN) | Bernt Evensen (NOR) | Ivar Ballangrud (NOR) |
| 1932 | John A. Shea (USA) | Alexander Hurd (CAN) | William F. Logan (CAN) |
| 1936 | Charles Mathiesen (NOR) | Ivar Ballangrud (NOR) | Birger Wasenius (FIN) |
| 1948 | Sverre Farstad (NOR) | Ake Seyffarth (SWE) | Odd Lundberg (NOR) |
| 1952 | Hjalmar Andersen (NOR) | Willem van der Voort (HOL) | Roald Aas (NOR) |
| 1956 | Yevgeni Grischin (URS) Yuri Mikhailov (URS) (tie) | no medal | Toivo Salonen (FIN) |
| 1960 | Yevgeni Grischin (URS) Roald Aas (NOR) (tie) | no medal | Boris Stenin (URS) |
| 1964 | Ants Antson (URS) | Cornelis Verkerk (HOL) | Villy Haugen (NOR) |
| 1968 | Cornelis Verkerk (HOL) | Ard Schenk (HOL) | Ivar Eriksen (NOR) |
| 1972 | Ard Schenk (HOL) | Roar Grönvold (NOR) | Göran Claeson (SWE) |
| 1976 | Jan Egil Storholt (NOR) | Yuri Kondakov (URS) | Hans van Helden (HOL) |
| 1980 | Eric Heiden (USA) | Kai Arne Stenshjemmet (NOR) | Terje Andersen (NOR) |
| 1984 | Gaetan Boucher (CAN) | Serguey Khlebnikov (URS) | Oleg Bogiev (URS) |

## Men's 5,000 Metres

| 1924 | Clas Thunberg (FIN) | Julius Skutnabb (FIN) | Roald Larsen (NOR) |
|------|---------------------|-----------------------|--------------------|
| 1928 | Ivar Ballangrud (NOR) | Julius Skutnabb (FIN) | Bernt Evensen (NOR) |
| 1932 | Irving Jaffee (USA) | Edward S. Murphy (USA) | William F. Logan (CAN) |
| 1936 | Ivar Ballangrud (NOR) | Birger Wasenius (FIN) | Antero Ojala (FIN) |
| 1948 | Reidar Liaklev (NOR) | Odd Lundberg (NOR) | Göthe Hedlund (SWE) |
| 1952 | Hjalmar Andersen (NOR) | Kees Broekman (HOL) | Sverre Haugli (NOR) |
| 1956 | Boris Shilkov (URS) | Sigvard Ericsson (SWE) | Oleg Gontscharenko (URS) |
| 1960 | Viktor Kosichkin (URS) | Knut Johannesen (NOR) | Jan Pesman (HOL) |
| 1964 | Knut Johannesen (NOR) | Per Ivar Moe (NOR) | Fred Anton Maier (NOR) |
| 1968 | Fred Anton Maier (NOR) | Cornelis Verkerk (HOL) | Petrus Nottet (HOL) |
| 1972 | Ard Schenk (HOL) | Roar Grönvold (NOR) | Sten Stensen (NOR) |
| 1976 | Sten Stensen (NOR) | Piet Kleine (HOL) | Hans van Helden (HOL) |
| 1980 | Eric Heiden (USA) | Kai Arne Stenshjemmet (NOR) | Tom Erik Oxholm (NOR) |
| 1984 | Tomas Gustafson (SWE) | Igor Malkov (URS) | Rene Schoefisch (GDR) |

## Men's 10,000 Metres

| 1924 | Julius Skutnabb (FIN) | Clas Thunberg (FIN) | Roald Larsen (NOR) |
|------|-----------------------|---------------------|--------------------|
| 1932 | Irving Jaffee (USA) | Ivar Ballangrud (NOR) | Frank Stack (CAN) |
| 1936 | Ivar Ballangrud (NOR) | Birger Vasenius (FIN) | Max Stiepl (AUT) |
| 1948 | Ake Seyffarth (SWE) | Lauri Parkkinen (FIN) | Pentti Lammio (FIN) |
| 1952 | Hjalmar Andersen (NOR) | Kees Broekman (HOL) | Carl-Erik Asplund (SWE) |
| 1956 | Sigvard Ericsson (SWE) | Knut Johannesen (NOR) | Oleg Gontscharenko (URS) |
| 1960 | Knut Johannesen (NOR) | Viktor Kosichkin (URS) | Kjell Bäckman (SWE) |
| 1964 | Jonny Nilsson (SWE) | Fred Anton Maier (NOR) | Knut Johannesen (NOR) |
| 1968 | Jonny Hoeglin (SWE) | Fred Anton Maier (NOR) | Örjan Sandler (SWE) |
| 1972 | Ard Schenk (HOL) | Cornelis Verkerk (HOL) | Sten Stensen (NOR) |
| 1976 | Piet Kleine (HOL) | Sten Stensen (NOR) | Hans van Helden (HOL) |
| 1980 | Eric Heiden (USA) | Piet Kleine (HOL) | Tom Erik Oxholm (NOR) |
| 1984 | Igor Malkov (URS) | Tomas Gustafson (SWE) | Rene Schoefisch (GDR) |

## Women's 500 Metres

| 1960 | Helga Haase (GER) | Natalia Dontschenko (URS) | Jeanne Ashworth (USA) |
|------|-------------------|----------------------------|------------------------|
| 1964 | Lidia Skoblikova (URS) | Irina Jegorowa (URS) | Tatyana Sidorova (URS) |
| 1968 | Ludmila Titova (URS) | Mary Meyers (USA) Dianne Holum (USA) Jennifer Fish (USA) (tie) | no medal |
| 1972 | Anne Henning (USA) | Vera Krasnova (URS) | Ludmila Titova (URS) |
| 1976 | Sheila Young (USA) | Cathy Priestner (CAN) | Tatiana Averina (URS) |
| 1980 | Karin Enke (GDR) | Leah Poulos Mueller (USA) | Natalia Petruseva (URS) |
| 1984 | Christa Rothenburger (GDR) | Karin Enke (GDR) | Natalya Chive (URS) |

## Women's 1,000 Metres

| 1960 | Klara Guseva (URS) | Helga Haase (GER) | Tamara Rylova (URS) |
|------|--------------------|-------------------|---------------------|
| 1964 | Lidia Skoblikova (URS) | Irina Jegorowa (URS) | Kaija Mustonen (FIN) |
| 1968 | Carolina Geijssen (HOL) | Ludmila Titova (URS) | Dianne Holum (USA) |
| 1972 | Monika Pflug (GER) | Atje Keulen-Deelstra (HOL) | Anne Henning (USA) |
| 1976 | Tatiana Averina (URS) | Leah Poulos (USA) | Sheila Young (USA) |
| 1980 | Natalia Petruseva (URS) | Leah Poulos Mueller (USA) | Silvia Albrecht (GDR) |

| 1984 | Karin Enke (GDR) | Andrea Schoene (GDR) | Natalia Petruseva (URS) |

### Women's 1,500 Metres

| 1960 | Lidia Skoblikova (URS) | Elwira Seroczynska (POL) | Helena Pilejczyk (POL) |
| 1964 | Lidia Skoblikova (URS) | Kaija Mustonen (FIN) | Berta Kolokolzewa (URS) |
| 1968 | Kaija Mustonen (FIN) | Carolina Geijssen (HOL) | Christina Kaiser (HOL) |
| 1972 | Dianne Holum (USA) | Christina Baas-Kaiser (HOL) | Atje Keulen-Deelstra (HOL) |
| 1976 | Galina Stepanskaya (URS) | Sheila Young (USA) | Tatiana Averina (URS) |
| 1980 | Annie Borckink (HOL) | Ria Visser (HOL) | Sabine Becker (GDR) |
| 1984 | Karin Enke (GDR) | Andrea Schoene (GDR) | Natalia Petruseva (URS) |

### Women's 3,000 Metres

| 1960 | Lidia Skoblikova (URS) | Valentina Stenina (URS) | Eevi Huttunen (FIN) |
| 1964 | Lidia Skoblikova (URS) | Valentina Stenina (URS) | Pil Hwa Han (PAK) |
| 1968 | Johanna Schut (HOL) | Kaija Mustonen (FIN) | Christina Kaiser (HOL) |
| 1972 | Christina Baas-Kaiser (HOL) | Dianne Holum (USA) | Atje Keulen-Deelstra (HOL) |
| 1976 | Tatiana Averina (URS) | Andrea Mitscherlich (GDR) | Lisbeth Korsmo (NOR) |
| 1980 | Bjoerg Eva Jensen (NOR) | Sabine Becker (GDR) | Beth Heiden (USA) |
| 1984 | Andrea Schoene (GDR) | Karin Enke (GDR) | Gabie Schoenbrunn (GDR) |

| Year | Gold Medalists | Silver Medalists | Bronze Medalists |
| --- | --- | --- | --- |

# DISCONTINUED EVENTS

### * Cresta Run

| 1928 | Jennison Heaton (USA) | John Heaton (USA) | David Northesk (GBR) |
| 1932 | Not held | | |
| 1936 | Not held | | |
| 1948 | Nino Bibbia (ITA) | John Heaton (USA) | John Crammond (GBR) |

### Speedskating — Four Races Combined Event

| 1924 | Clas Thunberg (FIN) | Roald Larsen (NOR) | Julius Skutnabb (FIN) |

### Alpine Skiing — Men's Alpine Combined

| 1924 | Not held | | |
| 1928 | Not held | | |
| 1936 | Franz Pfnur (GER) | Gustay Lantschner (GER) | Emile Allais (FRA) |
| 1948 | Henri Oreiller (FRA) | Karl Molitor (SWI) | James Couttet (FRA) |

### Women's Alpine Combined

| 1924 | Not held | | |
| 1928 | Not held | | |
| 1936 | Christl Cranz (GER) | Kathe Grasegger (GER) | Laila Schou Nilsen (NOR) |
| 1948 | Trude Beiser (AUT) | Gretchen Fraser (USA) | Erika Mahringer (AUT) |

* The athlete rides the Cresta Run on a heavy sled called the skeleton. The position on the sled is head first, prone. The event has been held only twice in the Olympics, both times when the Games were in St. Moritz, Switzerland, in 1928 and 1948.

# Bibliography

Athans, Greg. *Ski Free*. Toronto/Vancouver: Clarke, Irwin, 1978.

Burka, Ellen. *Figure Skating*. Don Mills, Ont.: Collier Macmillan, 1974.

*Canadian Olympic Association, Quadrennial Report 1980-84*. Montreal: Canadian Olympic Association, 1985.

Churchill, James, Jr. *The Olympic Story 1980*. Connecticut: Grolier, 1980.

Doucette, Sylvia, and Irene Schachtler. *Canadians At the Winter Olympic Games, 1924-1980*. Montreal: Canadian Olympic Association, 1982.

Emery, David, *Who's Who in International Winter Sports*. London: Sphere Books, 1983.

Ferguson, Bob. *Who's Who in Canadian Sport*. Toronto: Summerhill Press, 1985.

Foran, Max, and Heather MacEwan Foran. *Calgary: Canada's Frontier Metropolis; an Illustrated History*. Burlington, Ont.: Windsor Publications, 1982.

Gibbs, Roger. *The Cresta Run — 1885-1985*, Henry Melland, London, England.

Greene, Nancy. *Nancy Greene: An Autobiography* with Jack Batten. Don Mills: General, 1968.

Gross, George. *Donald Jackson, King of the Blades*. Toronto: Queen City, 1977.

Gzowski, Peter. *The Game of Our Lives*. Toronto: McClelland & Stewart, 1981.

Hocum, Dianne, *The Complete Handbook of Speed Skating*. Hillside, N.J.: Enslow, 1984.

Hunter, Jim, and Marshall Shelley. *Man Against the Mountain*. Elgin, Ill.: D.C. Cook, 1978.

Hurdis, John. *Speedskating in Canada, 1854-1981: A Chronological History*. Toronto: John Hurdis, 1980.

Isatitsch, Bert. *100 Jahre Rodelsport (1882-1983)*. Rottenhamm, Austria: Eigenverlag, 1983.

Jelinek, Jr., Henry, and Ann Pinchot. *On Thin Ice*. Markham: Paperjacks, 1978.

*Lake Placid 1980*. Salt Lake City, Utah: Sport and Culture USA, 1980.

McDonald, David, and Lauren Drewery. *For the Record: Canada's Greatest Women Athletes*. Toronto: Mesa, 1981.

Mellor, Bob, and Maureen O'Bryan. *Skiing (Olympic Library, Unit 1, Volume 2)*. Colban, 1976.

Murray, Shaw. "Ski Jumping" in *The Canadian Encyclopedia*. Edmonton: Hurtig, 1985. Vol. III, p. 1702.

Oglanby, Elva. *Toller*. Agincourt, Ont.: Gage, 1975.

*Olympic Charter 1982-1984*. Lausanne: Comité International Olympique, 1982-84.

*Olympic Games: 80 Years of People, Events and Records*. Ed. by Lord Killanin and John Rodda. Don Mills, Ont.: Collier Macmillan, 1976.

Ondaatje, Christopher, and Gordon Currie. *Olympic Victory,* Toronto, Ont.: Pagurian Press, 1967.

Pettersen, Bjorger. *Test Program Progress Report 1970-71.* Inuvik, N.W.T., 1971.

Rees, David. *Cross Country Skiing: Touring and Competition.* 3rd Ed. Toronto: Copp Clark Pitman, 1981.

Riger, Robert. *The Athlete.* New York: Simon and Schuster, 1980.

Ritchie, David. *Ski The Canadian Way.* David Ritchie and members of the Canadian Ski Team. Scarborough: Prentice-Hall, 1979.

Roxborough, Henry Hall. *Canada at the Olympics.* Toronto: Ryerson Press, 1963.

Wise, Sidney Francis, and Douglas Fisher. *Canada's Sporting Heros.* Don Mills: General, 1974.

Wormington, Sam. *The Ski Race.* Sandpoint: Selkirk Press, 1980.

Young, David. *The Golden Age of Canadian Figure Skating.* Toronto: Summerhill Press, 1984.